Studying
the Media

Praise for the previous editions of *Studying the Media*

'*Easily the best available book on the market for A level media studies.*' **Dr Len Masterman, University of Liverpool, and Visiting Professor, University of Central England, UK**

'*A sexy book which is very user friendly.*' **S. Kochberg, University of Portsmouth, UK**

'*…a first-class book which we've used with first year students for the past two years…*' **David Browne, University of Ripon and York St John, UK**

'*…an excellent publication – by far the most useful and comprehensive of all the general introductions which I have encountered.*' **Jerry Slater, Colchester Institute, UK**

'*…an excellent, up-to-date and well-written text…highly accessible and student friendly.*' **University of Glamorgan, UK**

'*Brilliant, necessary and so well done! The book is a breath of fresh air and reason.*' **Melanie Dante, Journalism student**

Studying the Media
An Introduction

Third Edition

Tim O'Sullivan
Brian Dutton
Philip Rayner

Hodder Arnold

A MEMBER OF THE HODDER HEADLINE GROUP

First published in Great Britain in 1994
Second edition published in 1998
Third edition published in 2003 by
Hodder Arnold, a member of the Hodder Headline Group
338 Euston Road, London NW1 3BH

http://www.hoddereducation.co.uk

Distributed in the United States of America by
Oxford University Press, Inc,
198 Madison Avenue, New York, NY 10016

British Library Cataloguing in Publication Data
A catalogue entry for this book is available from the British Library

Library of Congress Cataloging-in-Publication Data
A catalog record for this book is available from the Library of Congress

ISBN-10: 0 340 807652

ISBN-13: 978 0 340 80765 1

4 5 6 7 8

Typeset in garamond by HL Studios, Long Hanborough, Oxford
Printed and bound in Great Britain by Scotprint

CONTENTS

ACKNOWLEDGEMENTS   *vii*

PREFACE   *ix*

1. The media and modern culture   *1*

2. Media forms, images and analysis   *25*

3. Genre, stars and celebrities   *52*

4. Representations and realism   *69*

5. Audiences   *112*

6. Media institutions and production   *140*

7. Histories   *190*

8. Changing media worlds   *221*

9. Media practice   *241*

10. Media investigation and research   *263*

GLOSSARY   *285*

BIBLIOGRAPHY   *293*

INDEX   *307*

ACKNOWLEDGEMENTS:

We would like to thank the many people who have directly and indirectly helped with the development and production of this book. The processes involved in producing this third edition, like the first two, would have made an interesting case study and many of these processes began 'at home'. As a result, our thanks go first to the everyday support from our families and partners.

In addition, we also wish to acknowledge:

Colleagues, students and friends, past and present, inside and outside the institutions we work in.

Alexia Chan, Lesley Riddle, Hannah McEwen, Tessa Heath and the team at Hodder Arnold, who managed the project with enthusiasm and considerable patience.

Colleagues and friends who we have worked with over the years at the Welsh Joint Education Committee and The Northern Examinations and Assessment Board, now the Assessment and Qualifications Alliance (AQA).

The British Film Institute and their continuing work in the field of Media Education.

Victoria Knight, Lydia Rose and Hannah Walker for research and editorial assistance.

Jarrod Cripps, Paul Hickinbotham, Barbara Hind, John Muncie and Franco Bianchini for photographic work.

The *Newbury Weekly News*.

The School of Media and Cultural Production and the British Cinema and Television Research Group, De Montfort University, Leicester. The Midlands Television Research Group. MeCCSA – the Media, Communications and Cultural Studies Association **http:\\www.meccsa.org.uk**

HL Studios Ltd

The authors and publishers would also like to acknowledge the following for permission to use copyright material in this book:

www.adbusters.com for figure 2.15; ACE for figure 4.16; the Advertising Association for figure 6.4; ABC data/National Readership Surveys Ltd for figure 6.5; Arnold for figure 8.10; BBC Picture Archive for figure 7.12; Victoria Beckham.mu for figure 3.10; Bloomsbury publishing plc for figure 2.5; Bloomsbury publishing plc/©Thomas Taylor for figure 2.6; Bodleian Library for figures 7.2, 7.3, and 7.4; British Phonographic Industries for figures 6.13 and 6.14; *Broadcast* for figure 5.11; the Broadcasting Standards Commission for figures 4.14a, 10.5, 10.6 and 10.7; CAA/Caviar (Cinema and Video Industry Audience Research) for figure 5.7; the Central Office of Information for figure 5.4; Cinema Advertising Association for figure 10.2; Creature Labs for figure 2.16; Comedia for figure 6.6; Commission for Racial Equality for figures 10.3 and 10.4; Corbis for figure 4.2; Coty for figure 4.19; Jarrod Cripps for figures 1.3, 8.3, 8.12, 8.13 and 9.4; Cyberia Internet Cafe for figure 8.9; Discovery Channel for figure 1.1 (top); E.P. Dutton & Co for figures 7.6, 7.7, 7.8 and 7.9; Emap Consumer Media for figure 4.17; Express Newspapers for figure 4.34; Simon Frith/Pantheon Books for figure 6.18; garagenation.com for figure 6.21; D. Gauntlett & A Hill TV Living (Routledge) for figure 5.12; Ronald Grant Archive for figure 4.1 and 6.11; The *Guardian* for figures 2.10, 4.31, 5.2, 5.3, 5.8, 6.7, 6.9, 6.15 and 7.13, The *Guardian*/©John Arlige for figure 4.14; The *Guardian*/©Mike Bygrave for figure 4.37; Brian Harris for figure 2.8; Heinemann for figure 10.8; Hello for figure 3.9; Paul Hickinbotham for figures 6.16, 8.1, 8.2, 8.5 and 8.14; ©Barbara Hind for figure 8.15; Thomas Hoepker/Magnum Photos for figure 1.1 (left); Houghton for figures 2.2 and 2.3; Hovis, CDP/Travis Sully for figure 4.3; Hulton Getty Pictures Collection Ltd for figure 7.11; Hutchinson for figure 5.5; The *Independent* for figures 2.9a, and 2.9b; The *Independent on Sunday*/Robert Fisk for figure 4.43; IPC Magazines for figure 4.27; ITC The Publisher's View 2001 for figure 5.10a; The Kobal Collection for figures 1.1a, 2.17, 3.1, 3.2, 3.3, 3.4. 3.5, 3.6. 3.7a and 3.7b; 4.5, 4.6, 4.11, 4.12, 4.21, 4.22, 4.23, 4.24, 4.25, 4.28, 4.32, 4.33, 4.40, 4.41 and 6.19; the Lifestyle Pocket Book 2001 for figure 8.11; Longman for figure 1.5; *Daily Mail* for figure 4.36; Marketing Pocket Book for figure 1.4; Macmillan for figure 9.2; Megastar for figure 4.13; Men's Health for figure 4.15; michaeldouglas.com for figure 3.8; Stuart Millar & Janine Gibson, ©Guardian for figure 4.29; the Mirror Group for figures 2.11, 4.7, 4.8, 4.9, 4.10 and 6.3; News International Newspapers Limited for figure 4.35; Taylor Nelson Sofres 'Audio Visual Trak Survey' for figure 6.17; *Newbury Weekly News* for figure 6.23; *Observer Magazine*/Panos Pictures for figure 4.39; the Observer Newspaper for figure 5.1; Ogilvy & Mather/Roy Mehta (photo) and Vicki Maguire (text) for figure 2.18; Tim O'Sullivan for figures 1.2, 7.5, 8.4, 8.6, 8.16, 9.1; Tim O'Sullivan/Internet Bookshop for figure 8.8; *Over Land and Sea* for figure 6.10; PA photos for figure 2.4; Philips for figure 2.1; the *Telegraph* for figure 2.7; ©Jill Posener for figure 5.6; the Press Complaints Commission for figure 6.8; Policy Studies Institute for figure 10.1; the *Radio Times* for figures 4.4, 4.30 and 7.10 ; Rainey Kelly Campbell Roalfe for figure 4.18; Reckitt Benckiser for figure 2.19; Redferns Music Picture Library/Nicky J. Sims for figure 6.20; Red Flannel Films for figure 6.12; David Rowan ©Guardian for figure 6.1; The *Sun* for figure 6.2; Samsung for figure 2.14; TBWA Ltd for figure 4.20; Susan Thompson for figure 5.10; Triumph International for figure 2.12; The *Times* for figure 7.1; Vodafone Group Services for figure 2.13; The *Voice* for figure 4.42; Wendy Wallace for figure 4.38; www.xenafanfiction.com for figure 5.9 and Yves Saint Laurent for figure 4.26

PREFACE

In the last twenty years, Media Studies has become a well-known and established subject in many schools, colleges and universities. This development has been rapid, and, if sometimes depicted as against the grain of educational policy and press opinion in the period, the subject has proved to be worthwhile and popular for many students, teachers and graduates. This growth and popularity has also provoked controversy. On the one hand, some critics have condemned Media Studies as symptomatic of the 'dumbing down' of modern times, a threat to their longer-established disciplines, traditions and values. On the other, some commentators have argued that it offers little in the way of a 'real' training for work in the media industries. This view is part of a common misconception which fails to understand that Media Studies has been primarily motivated by academic enquiry and analysis.[1]

You will not find it surprising that this book rejects these views, instead arguing for the centrality of the systematic study of the media and their vital presence in modern life and our circumstances. Media Studies is a diverse field of enquiry with a particular hybrid history but this book is based on the view that the field is united by a number of key preoccupations and fundamental concerns. These form the basic 'stepping stones' in the chapters ahead, and in the links between them.

This third edition of the book is the product of our combined experience of learning, examining and teaching about the media in a variety of different contexts and syllabuses – on GCSE, A-level, AS/A2, BTEC, GNVQ, undergraduate and postgraduate courses – over the last twenty five years. These varied experiences, in secondary, further and higher educational settings, continue to provide the main impetus for this third edition and the project as a whole. We hope it will maintain its wide application and prove generally useful for the range of post-16 courses in Media Studies, as well as providing helpful introductory reading for undergraduate courses.

You will find that the book is addressed directly to 'you', the media student, and that it aims to provide an *accessible and stimulating introduction* to the systematic study of the media. The book covers key areas of study relevant to AS and A2-level students but will also be useful in a number of other courses of study and investigation. It provides a *foundation framework* to build upon, and the range of activities and suggestions for further reading and research is an important component of each chapter. These have been fully updated for the third edition, including online resources.

From the beginning of the twenty-first century, Media Studies continues to be a broad-ranging, dynamic and fast-moving field of enquiry. It has to be – to keep up with the shifts in modern media and their consequences for cultural life. We have had to be selective, and while we have tried to use relevant and current examples wherever possible, it is in the nature of the subject that some of these will become dated fairly quickly. You must update and add to the examples in your own work.

There is no *one* right way to use or read this book, although we have re-organised this third edition according to feedback from readers and users of the first two and in the light of changes in the specification of relevant syllabuses. As a result, this edition follows a slightly different sequence from the first and second. This sequence may and should be varied, however, according to your own specific interests and focus; each chapter continues to provide a relatively self-contained discussion and analysis, but there are a number of key themes that recur throughout the book as a whole.

The first chapter begins by examining the presence of the media in our everyday lives – 'at home', in 'our' private spaces. The conditions of *media saturation* are outlined and discussed, and these provide a central theme and thread that is revisited throughout later sections. Chapter 2 begins to explore the *images and forms of media output* and develops an analytical framework for studying media texts in detail. This emphasis is, in turn, extended in Chapter 3, which examines related issues concerning media genres and the public sphere of media personalities, stars and celebrities. Questions surrounding debates over forms of *media representation and realism* form the focus for Chapter 4. Chapter 5 is devoted to the study of *media audiences*, and the relationships between audiences and media output. Chapter 6 discusses some of the central characteristics of media institutions in the current period. Using case studies, it focuses on some of the major determinants of media industries and organisations in the current phase. Chapter 7 focuses on *media histories*, looking back at the growth and development of key media institutions and audiences from the nineteenth century to the present day. Chapter 8 addresses issues surrounding change in the current period, in particular examining key developments in *new media technologies* and the emergence of global or *worldwide media networks*. Chapter 9 looks at forms of *media practice* and stresses the value and importance of practical production work and professional contacts within the context of media studies as a whole. Finally, the concluding Chapter 10 offers a guide to *researching and investigating the media*. A glossary and full bibliography are provided at the end of the book.

Media studies in particular and media education more generally have now reached an important and critical stage of development. This book seeks to introduce some of the most important areas of study and the principal analytical approaches and questions that currently constitute the subject area. In the twenty-first century – more than ever before – the significance of the systematic study of the media will not go away, although the form and focus may have to change to keep up with transformations within and across the media themselves. If this book enables you to ask the right kinds of questions about the media and to keep pace with their relationships within modern social and cultural life, then it will have worked. The real test of the book, however, lies in its use and application. We welcome any responses to, or comments about, the book, or any suggestions you might have for subsequent editions. Please write to us via the publishers: **http:\\www.arnoldpublishers.com**

Tim O'Sullivan, Brian Dutton, Philip Rayner, October 2002

[1] For related discussion of these criticisms and the issues they raise see:

Barker, M. and Petley, J. 2000: 'On the problems of being a 'Trendy Travesty', Chapter 12, *Ill Effects: The Media/Violence Debate*. ROUTLEDGE.

Bazalgette, C. 1998: 'Still only 1898', *Media Education Journal*, Issue 24, Summer.

Geraghty, C. 2002: 'Doing Media Studies: Reflections on an Unruly Discipline', in *Art, Design and Communication in Higher Education*, Volume 1, Number 1, pp. 25–36. INTELLECT PRESS.

Masterman, L. 1997: 'A Rationale for Media Education' in Kubey, R. (ed). *Media Literacy in the Information Age: Current Perspectives*, pp. 15–69. TRANSACTION PUBLISHERS.

O'Sullivan, T. 1997: 'What Lies between Mechatronics and Medicine? The Critical Mass of Media Studies' in *Soundings*, Issue 5, Spring, pp. 211–21.

CHAPTER ONE

The Media and Modern Culture

Introduction: Why Study the Media?

We cannot escape the media. They are involved in every aspect of our everyday lives.
Roger Silverstone (1999), p.ix

It was only in the 1920s – according to the Oxford English Dictionary – that people began to speak of 'the media', and a generation later, in the 1950s, of a 'communication revolution', but a concern with the means of communication is very much older than that.
Asa Briggs and Peter Burke (2002), p. 1

For those thousands in the south tower, the second plane meant the end of everything. For us, its glint was the worldflash of a coming future. Terrorism is political communication by other means. …"What has happened today was not credible" (The wooden words of Tom Clancy, the author of The Sum of All Fears*)… The plan was to capture four airliners – in the space of half an hour. All four would be bound for the west coast, to ensure maximum fuel load. The first would crash into the north tower just as the working day hit full stride.* **Then a pause of 15 minutes, to give the world time to gather round its TV sets. With that attention secured**, *the second plane would crash into the south tower, and in that instant America's youth would turn into age.*

'The First Circle of Hell', Martin Amis, The Guardian, (18.9.2001) G2, pp. 2–4. [Our emphasis.]

FIGURE 1.1
'Terrorism has changed the way we view the world'
Source: Discovery Channel and Image across river of twin tower smoke (*Observer*)
Source: © Thomas Hoepker/Magnum Photos

1

It is important to begin this book by questioning the presence and power of the media in modern public and private life. Living in modern societies means inhabiting cultures and worlds that have been described as *media saturated*. This central fact of modern life and environment provides both a major *reason for* media studies and at the same time an important *way into* the subject. Why study the media? This chapter begins to provide answers to this question by developing a number of key issues at stake in the idea of *media saturation* – time, money and meanings. Subsequent chapters draw upon a range of distinctive arguments, debates and evidence addressing this theme and provide answers to the question, and a vital part of their work is contained in suggestions for developing your own relevant reading, projects and activities.

Activity 1.1

At this initial stage of your course, how would you argue the case for Media Studies? Why is it important? Why should we study the media? List 5 key points.

September 30, 1659. I, poor miserable Robinson Crusoe, being shipwrecked, during a dreadful storm in the offing, came on shore on this dismal unfortunate island, which I called the Island of Despair, all the rest of the ship's company being drowned, and myself almost dead.

Daniel Defoe, Robinson Crusoe, first published 1719. Penguin (1985), p. 87

Imagine living in a world *without* mass media and mass communication – is it conceivable? Living *without* television, radio, cinema, newspapers, magazines, books, videos, CDs, DVDs, mobile phones, Internet and so on. What would such a world be like? How would your everyday life change? What would you miss? Also: Is there anything in this world not touched upon or that remains 'untouched' by modern media?

It is useful to start your study of the mass media by systematically considering **your own, personal patterns of media involvement** and use. Throughout this chapter you will also encounter a range of ideas and evidence that may help you to start to identify the distinctive aspects of your own personal forms of media involvement, access and preference. You will also find it useful to compare these with some of the more general, social patterns of media involvement and use, that characterise current trends.

FIGURE 1.1a
Tom Hanks in Cast Away (2000)
Source: The Kobal Collection

Two-thirds of UK children and teenagers have a television in their bedroom. Over half of UK homes with children have at least one personal computer, with Internet access growing rapidly. Overall, 6–17 year olds are spending some five hours per day with the media.

Livingstone (2002), p. 77

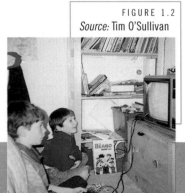

FIGURE 1.2
Source: Tim O'Sullivan

FIGURE 1.3
Source: Jarrod Cripps

Activity 1.2

Note down the details of your media involvement in the last 24 hours.

What are your earliest memories of television and other different media?

List your most powerful memories of media coverage – images that shocked or excited you.

Where do the media take us? Monitor where television takes you in an evening's viewing.

A more developed project entails keeping a diary for one week, noting your daily involvements with different media. Analyse the patterns and habits which emerge as a result. When do you tend to use different media and for what kinds of purpose? How do you use different media?

Tunstall (1983) makes a distinction between primary, secondary and tertiary forms of media consumption. *Primary* involvement occurs when the television programme, magazine, newspaper or radio broadcast is the exclusive and focused activity. *Secondary* types of involvement are those forms of media consumption and use which accompany other activities; for instance, listening to the radio or music while doing other forms of work at home. The *tertiary* category of use is in one sense the weakest and least intensive relationship, where, for example, the TV or radio set is on in the background, or in another room in the household. As Tunstall notes:

> *Tertiary could literally mean that one listens to the sound through the wall, while awaiting the next item; or tertiary might refer to glancing back and forth at a newspaper, opened at the TV schedule or the sports fixtures ... one might be glancing at the television with its sound turned down, listening to radio news-on-the-hour, while inspecting the schedules in the newspaper.*
>
> *Tunstall (1983), p.135*

Using these distinctions, you should be able to arrive at a rough estimate of the number of hours in the week you spend in differing forms of media involvement and consumption. You may also want to consider use of video, visits to the cinema and other 'out-of-home' forms of media consumption. How does the CD player, the personal computer or the mobile phone fit into this picture?

The results of diary research (as in Activity 1.2) generally provide evidence at the personal or biographical level for our extensive, patterned and everyday involvement with the mass media. In many ways we accept as natural our reliance upon regular contact with the media for information, news, opinion, entertainment, ideas and other kinds of mediated experience. These are deeply bound up with our attempts to maintain a coherent sense of 'who' and 'where' we think we are – our ongoing, 'sense of identity' and, as David Morley (2000) has noted recently, our ideas of 'home'. The American writer, Michael Real (1996), has drawn attention to the significance of what he calls our *ritual interaction* with modern media. By this he means that forms of media consumption and contact – reading, watching, listening, logging on and so on – are important ways of participating creatively in modern culture. This participation expresses aspects of collective identity and binds individuals into their society and culture as a whole. We begin by noting, then, that the nature of cultural experience in modern societies has been profoundly affected by the development of systems of mass communication. Indeed, many writers have argued that what we understand as modern life and 'modern times' would be impossible without those specialised institutions which until recently have been generically referred to as the *mass media*. Their products: books, magazines, adverts, newspapers, radio and television programmes, films and videos, computer networks or games, records, tapes, DVDs, CDs and websites occupy a central role in our lives, providing continuous and rapidly expanding flows of information and leisure.

In order to participate in this mediated culture, we spend time with and on them. We also spend money investing in them and we employ them to understand, make contact with and develop a sense of 'our' world.

Media Saturation

All the Time in the World?

One of the first ways in which we can start to get a grip on the notion of 'media saturation' is to consider the amounts of time that we spend in media-related activities, largely in forms and practices of media consumption – reading, watching, surfing or listening. At a general level, these activities account for considerable proportions of our non-sleep, discretionary or 'free' time. If we start by taking that most domestic of media, television, recent measures of TV viewing in the UK indicate that British television sets are switched on for an average of 5.2 hours per day and that over one-fifth of the population watch television for 36 hours or more per week. These figures do not include time spent in timeshifting, watching material recorded off-air by VCR, watching pre-recorded videos or DVDs or watching subscriber cable, satellite or digital services. The figures do point to some significant differences in patterns of viewing. We do not all watch the average amount. Our age, our gender and social class are factors which all appear to have important implications for our amounts and types of viewing. As a result, we don't all choose to watch the same programmes. Summaries of the types of television programmes watched indicate that the average diet of TV for those in the 16–24 age range, for instance, is made up of about 30 per cent drama, 20 per cent light entertainment, 20 per cent films, 10 per cent documentaries and features, 10 per cent sport, 5 per cent news, and 5 per cent children's programmes. Television provides a background for almost every activity in the home and one in two people say that they would be lonely without TV. Asked what they do regularly while watching television, over 40 per cent eat their main meal, 40 per cent do the housework, 30 per cent make telephone calls and 20 per cent cook or read.

In spite of these measures, longer-term monitoring points to a decrease in average amounts of time spent watching conventional, terrestrial broadcast TV. This average long-term decrease has been the source of considerable concern in recent years on the part of the BBC and ITV television companies who have had to recognise that video, DVD, cable, satellite and digital services have started to make significant inroads into what was previously their exclusive territory (see Chapter 7, p. 212 for further discussion). However, for our purposes here, we should note that it is 'normal' to spend between three and five hours per day in the company of a television set which is switched on. To put this another way, this is the equivalent of spending an average of around one full day per week continuously in the presence of TV. Commenting on the patterns of time spent with television in Britain and America as long ago as the 1980s, one study suggested:

> *If in such countries a typical viewer's total viewing during the year were laid end to end, it would fill two months, the whole of January and February say, for 24 hours each day! Although that may be hard to accept, it may be harder still to think of our imaginary television viewer having the set totally switched off throughout the other ten months of the year.*
>
> Barwise and Ehrenberg (1988), p. 20

From a slightly different point of view, the White Dot Society, an anti-television campaign group, calculate that television viewing will account for half of the time not spent working or sleeping, ten years out of the average life! (Burke, D. and Lotus, J. 1998 or see **http://www.whitedot.org**).

Clearly, not all media demand and get the same kinds of time and attention as the changing face of television and related computer screens but they each make their distinctive contributions to the 'media-mix' of modern times. Listening to radio, for example, is estimated on average in 2002 to account for about 22 additional hours per week, across an expanding range, if not always diversity, of radio stations and their services. Radio is the most popular broadcasting medium in the UK until 4pm each day, and some recent research has suggested that radio listening exceeds television viewing for some groups. These figures have been hotly contested as different methods of measurement produce contrasting versions of radio listening. Behind these averages, however, radio listening, like television viewing, varies by age and other social or lifestyle differences. For media relationships which take us out of the home, average weekly attendances at cinemas in the UK have increased steadily since the mid 1980s, although this growth needs to be understood against a historical slump in attendances which commenced in the 1950s, reaching an all-time low of 54 million admissions in 1984. In recent years, the recovery of British cinema-going has been quite dramatic, with annual admissions more than doubling within ten years. We now make an average of two visits per year to the cinema, although there are significant variations, especially according to age – about 10 per cent of the population visit the cinema twice a month, and we do not all choose to watch the same films (see Chapter 5, p. 127).

In general, it is worth noting that much of the data discussed here (which we hope you will add to through your own research), are based on *averages*, large-scale estimates of media consumption and use which, on closer scrutiny, may vary considerably in the context of different lifestyles and their associated dimensions of age, gender, ethnicity, class, affluence and other significant historical factors (see Livingstone, 2002). In addition, some of the key assumptions concerning the ability of this kind of data to 'measure' accurately what counts as average 'television viewing' or 'radio listening' have quite rightly been called into question in recent years. The set may be on, for instance, but whether and how people listen and view varies considerably (this is a theme that is developed in more detail in Chapter 5). In spite of these important reservations, however, it remains the case that we continue to spend large and perhaps increasing proportions of our time in a range of media-related activities – participating in mediated experience. In order to capture and gain access to this time and attention, advertisers spend very large amounts of money and this both 'fuels' and influences many sectors of media production. In the current period, for example, over £10 billion is spent per year on advertising in the UK, with an interesting spread of expenditure across the different media and advertising sectors (see Figure 6.4, p.146). Commercial television claims over 30 per cent of the total with about 60 per cent going to local newspapers, national papers and magazines. Direct mail and 'outdoor' (hoardings, buses, buildings, etc) takes most of the remainder, with commercial radio taking about 3 per cent and cinema about 1 per cent of the total.

Hardware and Commodities

In order to participate in these activities, we need access to certain media technologies or commodities (see Figure 1.4). You cannot watch TV if you do not have one available to you. You cannot surf the Internet without access to a networked computer, you cannot rent, buy and view videos or DVDs if you do not have access to playback facilities, cannot read certain magazines if you cannot afford them, and so on.

So, another way of indexing the 'media saturation' of contemporary cultures, is by examining available evidence 'mapping' either the diffusion or the developing 'penetration' of media hardware and commodities – the circulation of particular media products. Of all households in Britain, now in the early years of the twenty-first century, 98 per cent have at least one colour television and more than 70 per cent of these are now 'multi-set' homes, with a number of televisions distributed about the house, in different locations; the main living room, in bedrooms or in the kitchen. Statistically and culturally, it is deviant to live without at least one TV. More than 80 per cent of households in Britain now have at least one video cassette recorder and about a quarter of these are used regularly each week to replay at least one rented video film. DVDs have recently started to make inroads into the older video format. Radios are very widely available in the UK. It is calculated that each house has between five and seven receivers and that there are more than one and a half radio sets per head of population, for use in the home, at work and in the car. The 1990s saw important changes in patterns of musical consumption and technical format. Compact discs currently account for over 85 per cent of sales with cassettes and vinyl now in steep decline (see Figures 6.13, p. 165 and 6.14, p. 166 for related discussion). Personal stereos, home computers and mobile phones have also played their part in transforming the present media environment. Around 45 per cent of British homes are now estimated to be online. (For a discussion of children's media equipment see Figure 5.10a, p. 133.)

FIGURE 1.4
Source: Marketing Pocket Book

PENETRATION OF SELECTED LEISURE EQUIPMENT 2001:

% of adults owning:

Radio/Cassette/CD	15.8
Radio/Cassette	8.2
Personal Cassette or Radio/Cassette	18.2
Personal CD	17.6
Pocket sized TV	2.4
Car Radio	9.8
Car Radio/Cassette	46.7
Car CD/Cassette	7.0
Car CD	5.9
Personal Computer	51.6
Electric Calculator	40.8
Personal Electronic Organiser	13.2
DVD Player	11.6
Laser Disc Player	1.3
Recordable CD Player	7.1
Sky Digital Subscription	21.4
Video Camera/Camcorder	19.7
Digital Camera	4.5

Activity 1.3

Since the early 1980s, the personal stereo (or the Walkman to give it its Sony tradename) has had a significant impact on the ways in which music and other audio material are consumed. Do you have or have you used a Walkman? How have they changed or developed the standard cassette player, radio or CD player? And how are they being developed in the current phase with new disc formats, etc? Carry out some informal interviews with people who regularly use (or perhaps don't use) a Walkman to ascertain how they use them and what they think of them. Discuss the results of these interviews. What do they tell us about the historical development and use of the personal stereo? For detailed development of this activity you will find it useful to consult: Du Gay *et al, Doing Cultural Studies: The Story of the Sony Walkman*, 1997, Open University/Sage and Bull, M., *Sounding out the City: Personal Stereos and the Management of Everyday Life*, 2000, Berg.

What about the circulation of newspapers and magazines? In 2000, the most widely read daily national newspaper in Great Britain was *The Sun*, which was read regularly by about one in four men and about one in six women (see Figure 6.5, p. 147). The net total readership and sales of newspapers has declined from the 1950s onwards, as have magazine circulations, although the period from the late 1980s onwards has seen some important developments at the level of production technologies and shifts in patterns of marketing, advertising and readership. However, in 2002 over 60 per cent of men and over 50 per cent of women regularly read a national daily or Sunday paper. Nearly half of all women regularly read a women's weekly magazine and over half of men read a general monthly magazine. The *Sky TV Guide, Readers Digest* and *Take a Break* achieve the highest circulation of all UK magazines, closely followed by a number of newer titles, *FHM* or *GQ* or older established titles like *Woman's Own* or *The Radio Times* competing in the weekly television schedules' market.

This kind of analysis, concerned with either the time we spend with different media or the 'reach', frequency or diffusion of certain forms of media activity, offers important, if not altogether unproblematic, measures of the 'media saturation' of modern cultures. The data indicate that some forms of media consumption are indeed very widespread activities and they accord well with a predominant way of thinking about the *mass* media in terms of *numbers* – usually large statistical profiles or percentages of readership, attendance, sales or ratings. These kinds of numerical expression are important, but they are always open to a range of interpretations and can be misleading (see Chapter 10). They are frequently used as historical evidence, to point to the growth, for example, of new media forms from the development of popular print media in the nineteenth century, through to current shifts in broadcasting and other emergent computer based electronic media networks. Here, the data are often rather uncritically held to map or transparently measure the declines or shifts in the 'popularity' of certain cultural forms and practices or the 'inevitability' of new technologies. These issues deserve further discussion and they are developed in subsequent sections of the book (see especially Chapters 7 and 8).

For now, a key general point to note is that our own personal, private patterns of media consumption and use are parts of wider social and cultural relationships and structures. Our individual media relations and choices are parts of a 'bigger picture', part of the wider structure of the social world we are born into and inhabit. This suggests that the mass media are amongst the most central of the social institutions which *constitute* modern life (see Chapter 6). In order to develop further the theme of 'media saturation', we need to move on from asking questions about the basic scale and scope of media activities, to consider in more detail what is at stake in the time, money, contact and attention we regularly and routinely give to the media.

Situation and Mediation

We all inhabit particular situations. These are defined not only in the geographical sense of specific place – a territory and location – but also in terms of the patterns of culture, the 'dialects' and the social relationships which distinguish these contexts and spaces (see Morley, D. 2000, Livingstone, S. 2002). Our identities are fundamentally linked with this idea of personal place, culture and biography. Much of this sense of identity and belonging is rooted in and derived from the immediate, familiar surroundings of place and from networks of regular, face-to-face contacts with family or friends in home, school, college, workplace, locality and so on. Through these networks of direct interpersonal communication we both participate in and are a part of a *situated culture*. We hear and pass on news of recent events in the neighbourhood, likewise rumours, gossip, stories or jokes. We attend and participate in local events, entertainments, family ceremonies or other rituals. These cultures of situation are primarily *oral*, that is, communicated by word-of-mouth relationships, and although they have important historical and generational dimensions, they tend to be limited and defined in relation to a particular place, often within the private sphere of the household. In certain ways they embody elements of pre-industrial cultures, based on relatively small-scale forms of social interaction and groupings and derived from the immediate, face-to-face environment and its daily experience and routines.

We know these cultures and their situations to be distinctive, but they are also bound by a number of limiting factors. Of these, perhaps the most obvious is physical space. Like Robinson Crusoe or Chuck Noland, the character played by Tom Hanks in *Cast Away*, we do not know about events and issues occurring beyond the immediate horizons of the known situation or locality – that is, we do not know in the direct, experiential or first-hand sense. Since the mid-nineteenth century, however, we have increasingly learned to live not only in our situated culture, but also in a *culture of mediation*, whereby specialised social agencies – the press, film and cinema, radio and television broadcasting – developed to supply and cultivate larger-scale forms of public communication, mediating news and other forms of culture into the situation. 'Our' immediate private worlds co-exist with the mediated 'world out there'. Television is identified by the majority of the UK population as their principal source of world news, regarded as the most trustworthy and credible source. For local news, however, local newspapers feature first, followed by television and radio.

The contrast between social formations *without* mass media and those *with* mass media systems has been explored in a number of significant ways. Writing in the 1960s, Marshall McLuhan, for example, pointed to the ways in which modern media have 'shrunk' the world – by regularly 'transporting' or 'networking' us around the globe – effortlessly, as we don't have to move from the room. At that time he prophesied the potential for modern media technologies and communication networks to establish what he called 'the global village', to connect the myriad situated cultures into one, idealised, face-to-face planet-wide unity (for development of this idea, see discussion of globalisation in Chapter 8). Another important way in which this distinction has been employed is in the definition of *mass communication*, which is held to be distinctively different from the direct and face-to-face forms and relations characteristic of interpersonal communication and immediate situation.

Activity 1.4

As a group, draw up two lists. On the first, list as many forms of *communication* as you can think of. On the second, list only forms of *mass communication* and *mass media*. When you have drawn up the lists, note down the key differences between them and the general features that distinguish them.

On the first list, you may expect to find all sorts of entries: speaking, writing, hieroglyphics, tom-toms, smoke signals, Morse Code, music, art, theatre, gesture, mime, facial expression, body language, semaphore, walkie-talkies, CB radio, teaching, sermons, railways, roads, telephones, telex, satellite, letters, nudging, winking, the Post Office, war, photocopies, snapshots, architecture, clothes, hairstyles, handshakes, etc.

The second list is likely to be much shorter, and no matter what else appears in it, you are likely to find that only a very few candidates get unanimous agreement about their status as mass media. These are: television, radio, cinema, newspapers. In addition, people may mention publishing, popular music, advertising, theatre, music, video, telephones, speech, photography, computers, magazines, the music industry, the Internet, teletext...

Some important differences might be that those on your second list all:
- reach large numbers of people;
- employ high technology;
- are modern;
- involve large-scale commercial corporations and finance;
- are state-controlled or -regulated;
- are centrally produced but privately consumed;
- are co-operative, not individual forms of communication;
- are popular (widespread and/or well liked).

In fact, once such a set of characteristics has been found, it is quite easy to think of things that fulfil these criteria but are *not* mass media as commonly understood – religion and education being clear examples.

Further, there are things like music, photography, pictures, drama, advertising, speech and printing that appear in more than one of the mass media. Are these *forms* of communication, or *media* in their own right?

Working with lists generated in this way does serve one useful purpose, beyond showing that there's no *single* definition of the media.

That is, despite their plurality and the differences between them, the media are nevertheless *socially recognised*; everyone agrees that they include TV, radio, cinema, newspapers. After discussion, most will agree that music and publishing (magazines and books) should be included, as well as advertising. Usually, people will express their recognition of mass media most easily by reference to a *technological apparatus*, which explains why TV, radio, cinema and the press recur. But people are less used to thinking of the media as *social and commercial institutions* – although they can recognise one when they see it in the shape of the advertising and music industries, or popular magazines, films, computer games and books.

Adapted from: Hartley, Goulden and O'Sullivan (1985), Volume 1, p.12

Identifying the 'Mass Media'

In general terms, communication has often been understood, rather mechanistically, as the successful transmission and reception of meaningful 'messages', from a 'sender' to a 'receiver'. These are often expressed in language and speech but are also conveyed and mediated by means of other symbolic systems in accordance with shared codes, signs and symbols (see Chapter 2). A great deal of communication in everyday life takes place in the situated context of direct face-to-face interaction, between people who are physically together, involved in dialogue or conversation, more or less continuously reacting and responding to each other. In the case of mass communication, the nature of the communicative relationship appears to be quite different and conventionally four main differences are identified (see Thompson, 1995, and McQuail, 2000, for further discussion).

First of all, when we are engaged with mass media, there is an *institutional break* or *gap* between the participants in the communicative relationship. In crude terms, the 'senders' of mass-mediated messages do not have the same tangible or direct forms of feedback or dialogue with the 'receivers' – the audiences. This is not to say that people do not regularly shout at their television screens or radios, argue about a film they have just seen or disagree with the editor of their magazine or newspaper. It is, however, to say that such responses are rarely heard or received in such direct and unmediated ways by the 'senders'. It is in the nature of the relationship that they cannot be. Admittedly, there are specialised systems for feedback and interactivity – viewers' or readers' letters, faxes, e-mails or phone calls, and the interactivity of digital television for example – but these systems differ in a number of ways from those which characterise face-to-face interaction.

Partly because of this, mass-mediated culture has tended to be 'one-way', directed either at unknown 'people out there', in general, or at specified 'target' or 'niche' groups. Not only are there issues here concerning the people who receive mass-mediated information and the position that this relationship places them in, but also this situation raises problems for those who 'send' or produce the programmes, films, newspapers and so on. *Who* are they talking to? Or rather, who do they *think* they are talking to? To overcome this problem of not knowing who their actual audiences or readers might be, media producers often have to work to imaginary, generalised constructs or stereotypes. The 'general public', the 'person (historically, usually a man) in the street', 'young people', the 'busy housewife' or the 'active career woman', are some conventional examples (the concept stereotype is discussed in more detail in Chapter 4). These constructs allow media producers to select and 'shape' their products with the aim of establishing credible and engaging forms of communication and discourse with large numbers of people whom they cannot see or know and whose situation they may not share.

Part of this situation is the result of a related but second distinction. Most commonly, mass media or mass communications are defined in terms of *specialised technologies*, and indeed the technical means of exchange of direct, interpersonal forms of interaction and those characteristic of mass-mediated culture differ considerably. How for instance does the telephone, the radio or the television intervene in communication between people? As noted above, media technologies have traditionally tended to reinforce a one-way system of communication *from* media producers *to* media audiences, giving rise to an 'unbalanced' relationship between participants. There is a long tradition of attempts to change or challenge this 'one-sidedness' and some of the assumptions that have often accompanied it. Some of these initiatives have often been classed together as 'alternative media' (see Chapter 6 for further discussion). Recent assessments have argued that in the twenty-first century, the development of the

Internet, world-wide web and other computer networks has fundamentally challenged this traditional model of how the media *have* worked, and therefore how their study should proceed. (See Gauntlett, 2000 and discussion in Chapter 8).

There are related, interesting issues worth considering here, however. These concern the ways in which mass communications are made available in material, reproducible and physical forms. Unlike the transient, ephemeral nature of much face-to-face interaction – here, then gone, as with conversations, gestures, and so on – mass communications have tended to be inscribed or stored in physical and reproducible forms or texts: the book, the film, the video, the disc, the tape, the newspaper, the comic, the computer file, and so on. These material forms of communication have had consequences for the nature of the message itself, giving, for example, a permanency or reproducibility which is not conventionally found in everyday, direct, interpersonal interaction. This technical ability to record, distribute and reproduce messages and many varied forms of cultural information results in a *historical permanence* – a *record*. A good example here is to be found in the history of photography and film, where various writers have noted the impact that the technical ability to capture, hold and socially distribute visual records has had on the modern sense of 'history' (see Chapter 7). In this context, it has been argued that our sense of the 'modern world' is very much bound up with the period that first saw the emergence of film and photographic records (Chanan, 1995). Subsequently this has encompassed the historical 'immediacy' of forms of broadcasting coverage (see Zelizer and Allan, 2002). In the age of the Internet, recent controversies concerning the ownership and distribution rights relating to images and music have provided a telling case in point (see Chapter 6, p168 for further discussion).

A third distinctive feature of mass media and mass communication is derived from this characteristic of technical reproducibility. Media messages differ from interpersonal forms of communication in that their potential *scale and availability* are greatly extended 'outwards', across space, time, population and public culture. This means, for example, that events taking place in specific national, regional or local locations can receive 'world-wide' distribution and, with the intervention of satellite and digital technologies, 'live' or simultaneous forms of global coverage and mediation. Audiences for major sporting spectaculars, such as the Olympic Games or other international 'mega' events – environmental disasters or political or terrorist crises, for example the events in New York on 11 September 2001 – are frequently calculated in billions.

Having noted, however, that mass communications are potentially available across time, space, population and geography, this does not mean that they are available in an unrestricted fashion – 'open to all'. On the contrary, access to this potential tends to be regulated in a number of important and decisive ways, notably by the operation of commercial markets, and state, political and legal forms of control, which may differ significantly from one national or cultural context to another.

The fourth and final factor that is used to distinguish mass communication from interpersonal forms of direct, face-to-face interaction relates to this last point. In general, modern media deal in particular forms of modern *commodity*. Despite the tendency to talk in terms of media 'messages' or 'flows' of information, we need to bear in mind that mass communications are distributed as products and services, commodities which are developed and sold according to the dynamics of supply and demand of commercial markets (see Chapter 6). Profitability continues to be a decisive and driving factor in shaping the available forms of mass communication. Indeed, at a basic level, modern media have to operate as specialised, industrialised agencies involved in highly competitive markets. As such they are dependent upon the commercial supply and cultivation of demands for diverse forms of information, communication and entertainment commodities.

While an index of media saturation is gained, as we have suggested, by examining the patterns of time, involvement and attention routinely accorded to varying forms of media, this introductory section really only begins to prompt starting points for further analysis. As the presence of successive media, from newspapers to film to radio, TV and the web has become accepted as everyday 'facts of life' and social existence, so, it is argued, we have become socially and culturally more dependent upon them. Limited, to an extent, by the particular confines of our respective situations, we have learned to rely on different media, in particular, for news and information about the wider public sphere and global social processes and events. At a time when digital media networks, technologies and forms appear to offer a realignment of the traditional balance between the private, domestic, mobile and public dimensions of mediated culture and communication, a number of key debates continue to lie at the heart of Media Studies.

The Power of the Media

It has now become somewhat of a cliché to suggest that the media collectively act to provide audiences with their 'windows on the world' and with 'definitions of social reality'. Implicit in this kind of claim is the idea that the media act as powerful agencies capable of shaping and directing public and private understandings of the world and awareness of its social, economic, moral, cultural, technological and political affairs. In this manner, the media have been termed 'agenda setters' and 'consciousness industries', involved in the manufacture and management of the public sphere, of cultural consensus and consent. That is, in providing images, interpretations and explanations of events occurring in the wider world, the modern media do not simply and neutrally provide information about that world but actively encourage us to see and understand it in particular ways and in certain terms. Rather than faithfully 'reflecting' or 'mirroring' the external world and its 'reality', our daily media consumption has come to play an increasingly central role in constructing and interpreting the nature of that world according to certain values, ideological frameworks and cultural principles. For those engaged in the systematic study of the media, this recognition has resulted in a general and sustained focus upon questions of *media representation* – how and in what terms do the media *re-present* aspects of local and global society and social process to their audiences? This theme is explored in more detail in Chapter 4.

Questions of media saturation encompass some major issues, bound up with arguments about the social or political consequences of our participation in and dependence upon mediated culture (see, for useful discussion, Tolson, 1996). These are key questions which concern not only the nature of the images and versions of the world which are now as familiar and 'natural' as water, gas or electricity. They also focus on the ways in which such images and accounts are produced, under what kinds of conditions and in response to what kinds of social, commercial and political forces. In recent years, for instance, much has been made of the activities of 'spin-doctors' and their ability to put a particular 'spin' on news stories (see related discussion in Chapter 4 concerning 'media management'). How are the relations between the controls over the mediation of information and entertainment to people and the dispositions of political power more generally configured? We also need to be aware of the diverse ways in which different everyday cultures may respond to, interact with and refract media saturation. (This theme is developed in Chapter 5, dealing with media audiences.)

Many have argued that the case for this type of investigation has in fact become more urgent in recent times, given the growth in the management and 'spinning' of information and publicity, the development of new media networks and the increasing presence of the media in both private and public spheres. We now inhabit an *information* and *consumer* society, where the manufacture and dissemination of information and image has become an essential facet of modern democratic and commercial processes. The media and cultural industries now encompass multinational corporations, government agencies and departments, political parties, advertisers, public relations firms and many other forms of corporate, private and public organisation. These are locked into increasingly sophisticated networks of information gathering, management, manipulation and distribution. In the specific sphere of institutionalised politics, for example, elections have virtually ceased to have a social significance for the general public, outside of their construction and mediation as 'media events' (see Negrine, 1994, Seymour-Ure, 1991, Franklin, 1994, McNair, 1999, 2000). In the sphere of music production and the music industry, the synthetic manufacture of image and performance has also given rise to some related arguments in recent times.

Given these and related developments in the levels, networks and dynamics of media saturation in the modern period, it is not surprising that the media have attracted considerable public debate and criticism. It is useful at this stage to briefly consider some of the dominant concerns and themes that have accompanied the growth of media saturation.

Mediation and Social Concern

As the media have developed as part of modern societies, so have a number of competing claims about their social consequence and impact. In historical terms, the various media have often operated both to condense and to relay anxieties and fears about the nature of change in a rapidly changing world. As such they themselves have often been singled out as if they were the sole cause of particular tendencies in society and culture. This debate is taken up in later chapters, especially Chapter 5. For now, however, it is worth noting some of the predominant concerns that have regularly and recurrently shaped public and private ideas and thinking about the media. These have often formed the basis for advocating increased media regulation or control. Many of the concerns of the current period, dealing, for instance, with the 'invasion' of privacy by the popular tabloid press, the anti-social effects of films, video 'nasties' or computer games, the 'dumbing down' of contemporary culture, or controversial websites and chatrooms, have a lengthy heritage, stretching back to the nineteenth century. Three general themes have recurred, all focusing upon 'effects' that the media are claimed to have had on people, culture and society.

The first of these concerns the political or persuasive powers of the mass media, particularly in terms of their supposed abilities to manipulate whole populations' attitudes. George Orwell's novel *Nineteen Eighty-four*, first published in 1949, represents an interesting example of a 'dystopian' vision of a society where control over the masses is in part exerted through the incessant surveillance and propaganda of the 'telescreens'. Film versions of the novel were released in 1955 and 1984. In the context of the rise of fascism and dictatorships in a number of European states in the 1930s, and the widespread use of propaganda techniques to manipulate the hearts and minds of whole populations prior to and during the Second World War, the twentieth century media appeared to have enormous and frightening political potential. The theme of mass persuasion was also foregrounded in consideration of the rise of advertising in the 1930s and in the period following the war. The theme of the 'mind-bending', omnipotent powers of the media is one that still has considerable common currency. (See discussion of mass manipulation theory in Chapter 5).

A second recurrent theme can be traced back to the middle of the nineteenth century. This was rooted in a concern for conserving certain traditions, especially in aesthetic and cultural terms, and articulated a general opposition to the 'new' popular media and what was seen as their damaging impact upon long-established cultural values and practices. The popular press and publishing, followed by cinema and, later, radio and television, have all been accused of degrading or debasing cultural traditions and standards, eroding the authentic and replacing it with the 'trivial', 'vulgar' and 'dumbed down' substitutes of the modern age. Once again, this theme continues to exercise considerable influence in debates about the position and place of the media in the current period. A good example here is the series of debates that has emerged in the context of the future of public service broadcasting in Britain in recent years. In an age of shrinking budgets and competition from satellite, video, cable and digital services, the question of what should be at the core of public service provision in the new broadcast and multi-media markets has emerged as a key issue. A significant part of this debate has involved contending definitions of 'quality' and cultural value in broadcast output (see the case study in Chapter 7 for further discussion).

The final theme has perhaps been the most influential. It concerns arguments and assumptions about the direct impacts or 'effects' of the mass media on social behaviour – in fact, usually anti-social behaviour – and the moral contours of society. The most debated area in this context has been the issue of violence and delinquency, where the media have regularly been held to 'cause' outbreaks of violent or aggressive activity. These incidents have usually been part of wider and regular cycles of social concern, often referred to as 'moral panics' (see Thompson, 2000), and they continue to make their presence felt in the current era. (See Chapter 5 for examples and further discussion).

Culture and Mass Communication

The discussion so far has introduced a series of themes and issues concerning the presence and the defining characteristics of mass communication in modern social life. We have also noted that the media have been a particularly powerful focus and target for a number of debates about the nature of modernity. In order to develop these issues further, it is important to consider briefly some general questions about the nature of the interrelations between culture and mass communication.

Culture, as we have employed the term, first and foremost concerns the ways in which we understand and relate to social situations. We are socialised into a particular set of cultural orientations, rituals and ways of making sense of the world, and these encompass two particular dimensions. First of all, culture in the general sense refers to the beliefs, values or other frames of reference through which we learn to make sense of and respond to our experiences on a daily and ongoing basis. Secondly, definitions of culture usually refer to the various means by which people communicate or articulate a sense of self and situation. As a result:

> cultures are not primarily collections of objects, but stocks of shared understandings and responses accumulated in the course of confronting a common set of social conditions. They provide a pool of available meanings and modes of expression which people can draw upon to describe and respond to their own particular experiences. Far from being separated from everyday life, therefore, involvement in culture is an integral part of people's continuing attempt to make sense of their situation and to find ways of coming to terms with it, or else of changing it.
>
> *Murdock (1974), p. 90*

In the first decade of the twenty-first century, what we understand as the media are centrally involved and implicated in the production and direction of modern culture. Most modern, technologically advanced societies now encompass a great diversity and globally derived plurality of cultures which correspond to the major and varied social groupings of class, gender, ethnicity, generation, and so on. Since the mid-nineteenth century, the growth of the media has undoubtedly assisted in processes whereby certain forms of cultural differentiation have taken place – various media have responded to the particular needs or values of particular cultural groups – particularly when they have represented commercially viable forms of investment and profitability. However, at the same time, the media have also been involved in the consolidation of forms of centralised, non-specific, 'public' or national cultures that have unified sectional interests and constituted forms of democratic exchange and participation. The health and precise condition of the public sphere, when viewed under modern global and technical circumstances, continues to be hotly debated, as it has been since the seventeenth century (see Webster, 1995, Garnham, 2000 and Mackay *et al*, 2001, for further discussion). In part, one's view of this dilemma is dependent upon whichever perspective or model of mass communication and its dynamics one adopts.

Traditional, early twentieth century perspectives on 'mass' communication tended to emphasise a singular, mechanistic, process model. In these terms, 'messages' are sent to 'the mass'. At its crudest, this assumes a central, unitary 'sender', technically capable of transmitting a message to a large-scale 'mass' population, who react, as to a common stimulus, with virtually identical responses. The shortcomings of this notion are many, and we will suggest throughout this book that you consider viewing mediated communication as part of a set of cultural 'circuits', composed of relations between forms of *media production, media texts* and *media reception*. In particular, it is important to avoid the tendency to cut the media off from their social, commercial and historical contexts. There are significant social and cultural conditions which surround both the composition of the screen, the page, the programme, the website and so on, and their reception by diverse audiences, their readers, listeners and viewers.

The 'map' of cultural circulation in Figure 1.5 provides a useful summary of the major relationships and moments at stake in the study of the media. It suggests a cycle of production, circulation and reception of cultural products. It can be applied in the analysis of virtually any form of media and it directs our attention towards an encompassing mode of enquiry. The circuit links moments and conditions of media production to the texts and forms so produced, to the readings or forms of reception they may activate, which relate in turn to lived or situated cultures and wider social relations, which are both directly and indirectly implicated in the circuit.

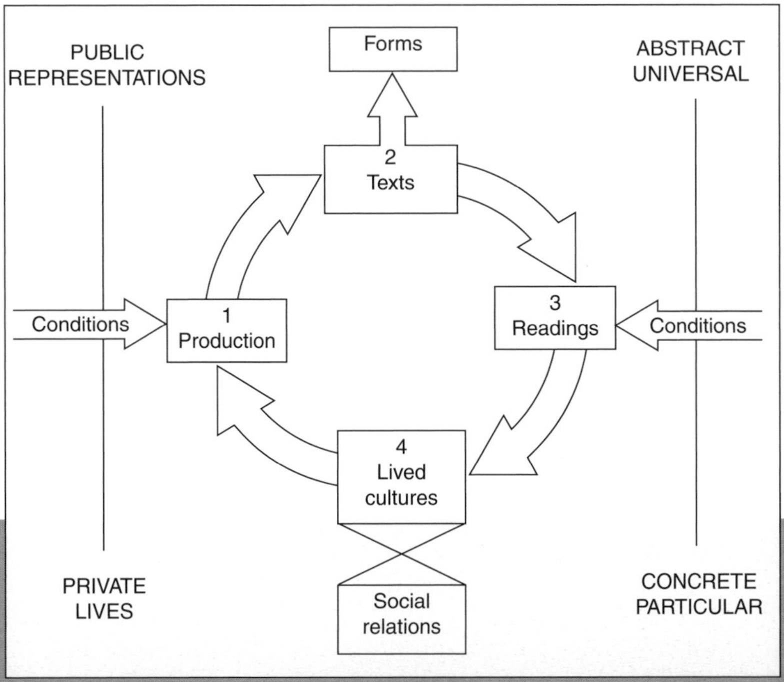

FIGURE 1.5
Cultural circulation
Source: Johnson, R. in Punter, D. (ed.) *Introduction to Contemporary Cultural Studies*, p. 284, Longman, 1986

15

Activity 1.5

The framework outlined in Figure 1.5 will be examined in more detail in the chapters that follow. As a way of opening up some of the issues initially, you will find it useful to note down and discuss one or two examples of contemporary media texts or output that you are familiar with. Work round the circuit noting some of the conditions or questions which may shape or have consequences for your chosen cases. What do you know about the circumstances surrounding production? How is your chosen example produced? How does that production process have consequences for the form of the text? How do audiences and users make sense of the output, under what conditions and with what particular or general results? You will find it useful to develop this work by reading the introduction to du Gay *et al, Doing Cultural Studies: The Story of the Sony Walkman*, 1997, Open University/Sage.

From Popular Culture to Postmodernism

For some writers, the study of the media can be dismissed as a valid area of enquiry, precisely because it embraces the study of *popular* culture. Often implicit in this view is the idea that popular culture is something we all 'live' and know about already and that it is something rather simplistic or of little worth. It is impossible to study the modern media without encountering a series of debates about popular culture and its quality, direction and values. The continued growth in media industries has been accompanied by rapid expansion in many multiplying forms of cultural output and networks – films, music, magazines, adverts, news, sports, fashions and so on. These, in turn, continue to stimulate related 'cross-overs', 'synergies' or 'spin-offs', in the form of stars, celebrities or merchandising campaigns, for instance. There is little doubt that these developments have massively expanded the notion of what is popular at any one point in time. But the idea of popular culture continues to spark several debates that go well beyond the purely numerical frequency or prevalence of current products or practices, trends or fashions.

What does it mean to call something 'popular'? The term combines some contradictory ideas and meanings. In historical perspective, Raymond Williams (1976) noted that to call something 'popular' was a negative description until the nineteenth century, a bad thing. More positive connotations – the idea that 'popular' could be good – developed from that time onwards. In the modern media age, if something is popular and part of popular culture, it is understood first of all to be *widespread*, to be liked by or at least encountered by many people. A prerequisite for this in the modern period has been the development of mass production and distribution systems, industries and technologies devoted to the mass mediation of culture. So, in addition to the idea of 'liked by many', the notion of popular culture also often carries the implication of *mass-produced* culture. Associated with this theme are ideas that popular culture is 'machine-made' for the 'mass' of people and not the discerning elite, not based for example on traditions and regarded as trashy, contrived, ephemeral and exploitative.

In this context of values and tastes, discussions of popular media culture invariably clash with another set of definitions, especially those that have attempted to distinguish between 'high' and 'low' culture. These often pose fundamental questions of cultural value and worth. Accepted definitions of cultural value or excellence have traditionally been associated with dominant or powerful groups and classes in society. Such definitions have often made distinctions between 'high' culture – the educated appreciation of works which are often classical in origin in terms of music, art, theatre, ballet, opera, literature – and 'low' or popular culture. Whilst 'high' culture tends to be equated with the educated discernment, taste and distance of an intellectually refined elite, seeking to universalise its values, 'low' culture is all that is not approved or classified in these terms. It is therefore perceived as 'popular', vulgar, common and sometimes, as for instance in the case of some computer games or websites, dangerous. Modern media and popular culture in general have often been denigrated from this standpoint, although to confuse matters somewhat, modern media have also played a significant role in 'popularising' aspects of 'high' or elite culture, as for instance in the case of Classic FM (see Lewis, 1990). Although the term 'dumbing down' originated in Hollywood in the 1930s, it has returned to refer to these perceived tendencies in cultural values and quality from the early 1990s onwards.

Activity 1.6

Draw up two lists of examples of cultural works or activities that you would label as 'high' culture and 'popular' culture respectively. Try to select a range of examples from different media and cultural forms. What general characteristics divide your examples? Is this division still important or significant today, in the early twenty-first century? Summarise some of your general views on popular culture, using your examples.

There is a final twist in the debate over popular culture and it brings into play another inflection in the term 'popular'. This emphasises the idea that popular culture is 'of the people', a kind of modern equivalent of folk culture and the carnival. This view stresses the idea that popular culture is the modern site or arena, where all sorts of ideas, images, styles and values can be expressed, articulated and compete for allegiance; where resistance and challenge as well as forms of conformity can be symbolically advanced, and where dominant or powerful values can be subverted or countered. Popular, satirical films or television comedies or alternative websites would be examples here. The extent to which involvement in the consumption of forms of popular media culture can be seen as predictably conformist in its outcome and impact, as opposed to unpredictable and resistant, has formed a key area for debate in recent studies of media audiences (see Chapter 5 for related discussion).

If the study of the media has always involved controversial questions of popular culture, late twentieth century debates began to focus on claims that modern culture has entered a postmodern phase. For many cultural critics and writers, recent developments in society and culture – linked to the growth and saturation of modern media – have led them to suggest that we are currently living in *postmodern times*, experiencing the *postmodern condition*. This idea has been used to describe a number of features of contemporary media culture, including, for instance, the styles of adverts and music videos including those shown on MTV, magazine design (from *The Face*, to '*new lad*' mags), films, for instance *Blade Runner*, and the work of David Lynch (notably *Blue Velvet* and *Twin Peaks*), and the films of Quentin Tarantino (*Pulp Fiction*, for example). There have been a number of approaches to defining postmodernism drawn from architecture, history, literature and a range of other disciplines and traditions. As Michael Real has suggested:

> *When we use postmodernism as a vehicle for exploring media culture, we note certain characteristics of the specific media experience – a sense of irony, bald commercialism, a playful ambiguity, a nostalgic blend of past and present, disparate art styles, a lack of absolutes, and more...*
> Real (1996), p. 238

Postmodernism continues to be used in the attempt to refer to a number of developments in contemporary media cultures which relate to central themes in this chapter and the rest of the book. First, these include the idea that popular culture and media images saturate, as never before, our sense of reality and identity and that, as a result, there is no longer an actual 'world' or reality outside of popular culture, the popular media and their fragmenting, increasingly *intertextual* and *interactive* worlds. The widespread success of the 'Big Brother' series format provides an interesting case for discussion in this context. What were we watching, a performance or 'real lives'? How did the 'series' success involve not only television but other media? Communication networks and technologies provide global access to a culture of mass digital reproduction. Images, copies, and virtual simulations exist without any longer being tied to an authentic original. As a result, popular culture has eclipsed and 'dumbed down' the old hierarchies and values of art and high culture. The simulated, contrived world of celebrities has replaced the real world of experience and history. Under current conditions it is argued that how and what we consume, 'our style and looks', in the mediated world, have become more important than what we do and produce.

Second, postmodernism refers to the prevalence of certain styles, particularly styles of pastiche or collage in art, advertising and architecture, for instance. Style is the message emphasised at the expense of content or substance. Media styles now select, mix together and juxtapose elements borrowed from past styles and influences into new, intertextual ensembles and cultural products. The term **bricolage** – a kind of 'borrowing', re-using and mixing of signs and symbols – has been employed to describe this aspect of postmodern culture.

Third, time and space, history and place, once secure and dominant anchors of identity, have become confused and unstable entities or spaces. National cultures and their media networks have lost ground, eroded by the forces of global communication networks and their endless, dislocating flows of imagery and information, their 'news from nowhere'. In postmodern times, one of the key tensions is that which emerges in the tugs between the local situation and the proliferating global culture of networks and images. The private and the public are redefined on a world and virtual stage.

Fourth and finally, postmodern perspectives refuse claims to absolute truth, whether scientific, historical, artistic or political. In the same way that notions of historical time and progress are seen as obsolete ideologies, and the securities of a sense of place and environment are becoming difficult to sustain, so all-embracing claims to knowledge and large-scale theory are increasingly open to scepticism, question and doubt.

Summary: Public, Private and Popular

In concluding and reviewing this chapter, we recommend that you consider some of the ways in which the historical development of the media in your own lifetime have been instrumental in the distinctive textures and transformations that we understand as modern social and cultural life. Three key aspects of their presence and operation have recurred in the discussion so far.

First, the media have developed and extended large-scale systems of *public* communication, linked to what has been called the *public sphere,* political and corporate forms of power. At this level, newspapers and print media from the 1850s, followed by photography in the 1880s, cinema in the 1900s, radio in the 1920s, television in the 1950s and the Internet in the 1990s, all represent important developments in, and extensions to, public culture. Key themes here continue to concern questions of power, ideology, access, representation and mediation.

At the same time, these developments have also had important implications for the *private* sphere and everyday life 'at home'. Radio and television, for example, have accompanied what one writer has called 'the withdrawal into inner space' (Donzelot, 1980), whereby leisure activities have become progressively concentrated in 'the home', the domestic sphere. While important changes might be said to be taking place inside households in the current phase, the private sphere is still 'connected' to the outside world in important and decisive ways via the media and their networks (see Livingstone, 2002).

Finally, the media and mass communications have interacted with pre-existing cultures, forms and values in a number of significant ways. Of these, perhaps the most central has been in the development of *popular* culture, that 'site of struggle and contest' which, as this discussion has noted, contains a number of contradictory ideas: from 'liked by many' to 'not elite or high culture'; from that of 'the common people' to 'mass-produced' culture, in postmodern times.

These three themes – public, private and popular – will be explored in the chapters that follow. In the next chapter we turn to consideration of the forms and texts which make up media output. Before you begin the next chapter, however, you may find it useful at this point to return to and review your notes from Activity 1.1.

Further Reading

Barnard, S. 2000: Studying Radio. ARNOLD.

Bignall, J. 2002: Media Semiotics: An Introduction. MANCHESTER UNIVERSITY PRESS.

Branston, G. and Stafford, R. 1999: The Media Student's Book. ROUTLEDGE.

Burton, G. 2002: More Than Meets the Eye: An Introduction to Media Studies. ARNOLD.

Corner, J. 1998: Studying Media: Problems of Theory and Method. EDINBURGH UNIVERSITY PRESS.

Curran, J. and Seaton, J. 1997: Power without Responsibility. ROUTLEDGE.

Curran, J. 2002: Media and Power. ROUTLEDGE.

Danesi, M. 2002: Understanding Media Semiotics. ARNOLD.

Dutton, B. 1995, 2002: *Media Studies:* An Introduction. LONGMAN.

Dutton, B. 1997: The Media. LONGMAN.

Eldridge, J., Kitzinger, J. and Williams, K. 1997: The Mass Media and Power in Modern Britain. OXFORD UNIVERSITY PRESS.

Fleming, D. (ed). 2000: Formations: A 21st Century Media Studies Textbook. MANCHESTER UNIVERSITY PRESS.

Garnham, N. 2000: Emancipation, the Media and Modernity: Arguments about the Media and Social Theory. OXFORD UNIVERSITY PRESS.

Gauntlett, D. (ed). 2000: web.studies: rewiring media studies for the digital age. ARNOLD.

Gauntlett, D. and Hill, A. 1999: TV Living: Television, Culture and Everyday Life. ROUTLEDGE.

Gripsrud, J. 2002: Understanding Media Culture. ARNOLD.

Livingstone, S. 2002: Young People and New Media. SAGE.

Lull, J. 2000: Media, Communication, Culture. POLITY.

Mackay, H. and O'Sullivan, T. (eds). 1999: The Media Reader: Continuity and Transformation. OPEN UNIVERSITY/SAGE.

Mackay, H. with Maples, W., and Reynolds, P. 2001: Investigating the Information Society. OPEN UNIVERSITY.

McGuigan, J. 1992: Cultural Populism. ROUTLEDGE.

McGuigan, J. 1999: Modernity and Postmodern Culture. OPEN UNIVERSITY PRESS.

McQuail, D. 2000: Mass Communication Theory: An Introduction. SAGE.

Morley, D. 2000: Home Territories: Media, Mobility and Identity. ROUTLEDGE.

Negrine, R. 1994: Politics and the Mass Media in Britain. ROUTLEDGE.

Nelmes, J. (ed). 1999: An Introduction to Film Studies. ROUTLEDGE.

O'Sullivan, T., Hartley, J., Saunders, D., Montgomery, M. and Fiske, J. 1994: Key Concepts in Communication and Cultural Studies. ROUTLEDGE.

O'Sullivan, T. and Jewkes, Y. (eds). 1997: The Media Studies Reader. ARNOLD.

Price, S. 1998: Media Studies. LONGMAN.

Rayner, P., Wall, P. and Kruger, S. 2001: Media Studies: The Essential Introduction. ROUTLEDGE

Real, M.R. 1996: Exploring Media Culture: A Guide. SAGE.

Silverstone, R. 1999: Why Study the Media? SAGE.

Stevenson, N. 2002: Understanding Media Cultures: Social Theory and Mass Communication. SAGE.

Stokes, J. and Reading, A. (eds). 1999: The Media in Britain: Current Debates and Developments. MACMILLAN.

Svennevig, M. 1998: Television Across the Years: The British Public's View. ITC/UNIVERSITY OF LUTON PRESS.

Thompson, J.B. 1995: The Media and Modernity. POLITY PRESS.

Tolson, A. 1996: Mediations: Text and Discourse in Media Studies. ARNOLD.

Trowler, P. 1996: Investigating the Media. HARPERCOLLINS.

Turner, G. 2002: British Cultural Studies: An Introduction. ROUTLEDGE.

Van Zoonen, L. 1994: Feminist Media Studies. SAGE.

Watson, J. and Hill, A. 1999: A Dictionary of Communication and Media Studies. ARNOLD.

Webster, F. 1995: Theories of the Information Society. ROUTLEDGE.

Zelizer, B. and Allan, S. (eds). 2002: Journalism after September 11. ROUTLEDGE

Useful Additional References and Sources

British Rate & Data (BRAD). A range of reference publications (including electronic databases) which are produced annually and bi-monthly and concern all forms of media. Used especially by media planners and advertisers.

Broadcast. The leading weekly news journal on the TV and radio industries in Britain.

Campaign. The leading weekly news magazine for the advertising industry.

Cultural Trends. Annual publication from the Policy Studies Institute which regularly surveys trends in video, cinema, broadcasting and other relevant areas.

The Guardian Media Guide. Edited by Steve Peak and Paul Fisher, published by Fourth Estate for the *Guardian,* this is an annual reference book covering many useful details and addresses concerning the media in Britain.

Social Trends. Annual publication of the Government Statistical Service which details shifts and patterns in demographics. It has useful sections on home, leisure and social and cultural activities.

Press Gazette. The leading weekly paper for all journalists in newspapers, magazines, television and radio.

Sight & Sound. The monthly magazine published by the British Film Institute, devoted to reviews of films and critical discussions of film and television culture.

A number of other academic journals are also useful sources. These include:

Media Culture & Society, Convergence, Screen, European Journal of Communication, Media Education Journal.

MEDIA STUDIES WEBSITES

There are now so many websites that relate to media issues that it is quite difficult to separate the authoritative and useful from the weird and wacky. Below are a selection of some websites that may be useful to you in supporting and developing your studies. In general, we recommend that you treat websites with a degree of caution. Clarify who the people or organisations are who have constructed the sites and bear this in mind when you view them. (See relevant discussion in Chapter 10).

CRITICAL DISCUSSION and LEARNING RESOURCES

http://culturemachine.tees.ac.uk (e-journal researching culture and theory)

http://laurel.conncoll.edu/politicsandculture/arts.cfm?id=33 (e-journal focusing on culture and politics)

http://carmen.artsci.washington.edu/panop/home.htm (American e-journal focusing on cultural theory)

http://www.arasite.org

http://www.arasite.org/nsamps2.htm (Sites organised by an English College lecturer, contains teaching materials/handouts on many topics)

http://www.newmediastudies.com (Contains links to articles and sites which are concerned with the study of digital culture)

http://www.cddc.vt.edu (Contains links to other e-journals, conference details and organisations and is the Centre for Digital Discourse and Culture website)

http://www2.cddc.vt.edu/illuminations/ (Illuminations: The Critical Theory Website maintained by the Centre for Digital Discourse and Culture)

http://www.writing.berkeley.edu/chorus/index.html (An international resource exploring and supporting the use of new media in the arts and humanities)

http://hypertext.rmit.edu.au/index2.html (This site contains useful definitions of key theories as well as excellent links to other resources)

www.eserver.org/theory/ (US cultural studies/cultural theory site)

http://www.pmc@jefferson.village.virginia.edu (A site specialising in Postmodern Culture)

http://www.luton.ac.uk/Convergence (The site of *Convergence: The Journal of Research into New Media Technologies*)

www.popcultures.com/ (US cultural theory site)

http://www.ctheory.com (Online journal)

http://www.theory.org.uk/ct-id.htm

www.aber.ac.uk/media/index.html

http://mediaed.org.uk/home.htm (UK Media education site mainly addressing needs of secondary/FE/6th Form schools and Colleges)

www.cultsock.ndirect.co.uk/MUHome/cshtml/ (Another UK site aimed mainly at teachers of A level)

www.filmunlimited.co.uk

www.mrqe.com (Movie review query engine)

www.filmref.com

http://analysis.bournemouth.ac.uk/rrdb/ (Radio Research Database)

www.nottingham.ac.uk/film (Institute of Film Studies)

www.mediaknowall.com

www.only.at/mediastudies (Both of these are primarily for A level students)

http://www.adflip.com/

http://www.bufvc.ac.uk/aboutus/index.html (British Universities Film and Video Council)

http://www.theory.org.uk/ct-id.htm

http://www.filmeducation.org/

http://carmen.artsci.washington.edu/panop/home.htm

www.bfi.org.uk (British Film Institute)

www.homeoffice.gov.uk (Some reference to media research can be found on this site)

www.meccsa.org.uk

www.mediaedwales.org.uk (Media Education Wales)

www.archivefilms.com (Film and Photographic Archives)

www.nmpft.org.uk (National Museum of Film, Photography and Television)

www.englishandmedia.co.uk (English and Media Centre)

MEDIA INSTITUTIONS AND INDUSTRY SITES:

Nearly all media institutions have their own websites, below is just a selection. However, you need to remember that what is on the website is often influenced by what they want to promote and so, again, should be treated with some degree of caution.

http://www.zen.co.uk/home/page/wrx/alltnews.htm (British media online with links to almost everything)

www.cpbf.demon.co.uk (Campaign for Press and Broadcasting Freedom)

www.bbc.co.uk

www.telegraph.co.uk

www.dailyexpress.co.uk

www.ft.com

www.guardian.co.uk

www.independent.co.uk

www.itc.co.uk

www.itn.co.uk

www.carlton.co.uk

www.granadatv.co.uk

www.htv.co.uk

www.Channel4.co.uk

www.channel5.co.uk

www.sky.co.uk

www.the-times.co.uk

www.disneychannel.co.uk

www.s4c.co.uk

www.itv.co.uk

www.reuters.com

www.cnn.com

www.empireonline.co.uk

www.radioauthority.org.uk

www.adassoc.org.uk

www.newsint.co.uk

www.mediachannel.org

www.tssphoto.com/ (A UK Stock Photo Agency)

www.thebookseller.com

www.discover.co.uk/NET/NEWS/news

www.sony.com

www.benetton.co.uk

http://www.nua.ie/surveys/how_many_online/index.html (Useful for monitoring internet usage)

http://home.eunet.no/~trondhu/links/journalist_tools.html

www.mediazoo.co.uk

www.mad.co.uk

www.mediachannel.org

www.mediauk.com

www.discover.co.uk/NET/NEWS/news.html

http://www.commedia.org.uk (The Community Media Association)

www.theherald.co.uk (Scottish news)

www.mediavillage.co.uk

www.bpi.co.uk (British Phonographic industry)

www.nab.org (National Association of Broadcasters)

www.unm.com (United News and Media)

www.oneworld.org (Commonwealth Broadcasting Association)

www.uktvadverts.com

http://jiab.jicreg.co.uk/index.cfm (Readership figures for regional press)

www.barb.co.uk (Television viewing figures)

www.rajar.co.uk (Radio listening figures)

http://uk.imdb.com/ (Internet movie database)

www.rab.co.uk (Radio Advertising Bureau)

www.theradiomagazine.co.uk (Radio industry news)

www.abc.org.uk (Audit Bureau of Circulations)

www.bsc.org.uk (Broadcasting Standards Commission)

www.pcc.org.uk (Press Complaints Commission)

www.bbfc.co.uk (British Board of Film Classification)

www.alternet.org (American independent media organisation)

www.thestandard.com (All about the internet)

www.asa.co.uk (Advertising standards)

http://indigo.ie/~nujdub/append-a.htm (NUJ guidelines)

AND SOME ALTERNATIVES:

www.melonfarmers.co.uk (Gives an insight into what the censors don't allow us to see)

http://www.adflip.com/ (American vintage advertisements)

http://adbusters.org/home/index.html (Site of anti-capitalism and 'turn-off tv' campaigns.

www.whitedot.org (Anti-television Campaign site.)

www.theonion.com (News satire/spoof news)

www.freepress.org.uk

www.tvgohome.com (Satirical TV schedules)

CHAPTER TWO
Media Forms, Images and Analysis

The idea that we live in a *media saturated society* was highlighted in the first chapter. In our everyday lives, we come into contact with a wide variety of media and their forms of output. These may include the radio that wakes us up in the morning and the same radio that switches itself off at night after sending us off to sleep. In between we may have read a daily newspaper and watched television either at breakfast or during the evening 'peak' schedule. We could have glanced through a magazine or watched a film, either in the cinema or by renting a video or DVD. We might also have listened to some music either being played on the radio by a DJ, on our own hi-fi system or downloaded from the Internet and played on a personal MP3 player. At some point during the day, either at home, work or college, we may well have accessed websites or used email. Throughout much of this daily consumption we will have encountered advertising – on radio, on television, in magazines or newspapers, on websites, advertising billboards or through our mobile phones.

As members of modern, increasingly global and network cultures we feel comfortable with this diversity of media texts, largely taking them for granted and assuming that their meanings are more or less obvious and 'natural'. However, the 'meanings' of all these media texts, like languages themselves, are social constructs that we 'learn' to read and make sense of according to particular social and cultural codes and conventions.

This chapter starts to explore the relationship between the forms that different media texts take and how we, as audiences, 'construct' the meanings of media texts. In particular there will be explanations of the encoding and decoding process of media texts, semiotics, discourse analysis and narrative codes.

We understand the meaning of media texts because we have learned to 'read' them in the same way that we learned to read the words and sequences of letters which make up particular sentences or the keyboard on a computer, control buttons on our hi-fi equipment or mobile phone. Those words and sequences will vary according to context: in France, for instance, they will use different words, and in Germany, where the verb appears at the end of the sentence, the sequence of words is different to Britain and France. Part of the context that influences the words and their sequence can also include technological situations. For instance the widespread use of computers has, it could be argued, introduced us to a new type of language. Other recent technological innovations have also required us to learn new languages.

Stop, Play, Rewind, Record, Text

We increasingly use a range of technical equipment to access and in some cases produce and send media texts; televisions and DVD or video recorders, the Internet, MP3 players or hi-fi systems that use mini-discs, CDs or audio cassettes. All of these pieces of equipment have controls to enable us to use them (Figure 2.1). Some of the individual controls may say what their function is, for example 'Stop', 'Play', 'Rewind', 'Record', 'Text', etc. However, increasingly these controls will have only symbols. This means that the companies that make and sell the equipment do not need to have different models and production lines for different countries. They rely on us all, in whatever country or part of the world, to understand the various symbols for 'Stop', 'Play', 'Rewind', 'Record', 'Text', etc. This means that the same machine can be sold and understood around the world. In effect, as consumers we have learned a new language, how to 'read' a simple sign system like the control buttons. We have also learnt to 'read' the sequence of buttons that tell us how to set the timer to record a programme or to duplicate a track.

FIGURE 2.1
Remote Control
Source: Philips

Just as words have to be put into an order that we can recognise and interpret, so media texts work by being put together, or constructed, in particular ways that allow for recognition and interpretation. This process of putting together media texts, assembling them into more or less coherent and meaningful messages, has been referred to as *encoding*.

We live in a world of signs, and communication is possible only by means of signs and sign systems, whether they are letters on a page, sounds or visual images. We can understand visual images because we learn to read them – to *decode* them – in the same way as we do the codes of language: by learning the rules and conventions which govern how the components go together to make up recognisable units of meaning. For instance, we recognise the theme tune of BBC News programmes as somehow being different to other theme tunes, say the popular TV soap opera *EastEnders*. Different in that the news theme signifies something 'serious'; the images of the title sequence that accompanies the theme tune reinforce this notion of 'serious' topicality, referring to the up-to-the-minute world of public events and affairs.

Another type of new language that is also the result of new technology is the text messaging that is sent via mobile phones. There are over 40 million text messages sent by mobile phones everyday in the UK. These messages are predominantly sent and received by young people who have been very quick at learning both the technical skills required to 'text' and the language involved. Because a standard SMS (short message service) text message is limited to a maximum of 160 characters, a new type of language has developed that consists of abbreviations such as ABT, EOD, GR8, etc. In the run up to the 2001 General Election, the Labour Party sent the following text messages to young voters:

CLDNT GVE A XXXX 4 LST ORDRS   VTE LBR ON THRSDY 4 XTRA TIME

The Labour Party was trying to target a particular group of people by encoding messages to them in a particular manner that they thought young people would understand and be able to decode. They chose a particular medium to send these messages, one that their research suggested was used predominately

FIGURE 2.2 AND 2.3
Raj Family Photograph
and Wedding Photograph
Source: Houghton

by young people. To be able to decode these messages the receiver had to have access to a particular type of technology, a mobile phone, as well as be familiar with the system of text messaging. They had to be familiar with the set of signs, the particular type of language. Those that received these text messages would need to understand terms such as XXXX. The 'meaning' of these texts, like language itself, and the use of mobile phones for text messaging, is a social construct that has been 'learned' and is made sense of according to particular social and cultural codes and conventions.

Semiotics

To better understand how these codes work we have to examine sign systems and their conventions or rules. The study of signs and sign systems and their role in the construction and organisation of meaning is called *semiotics*, and it has become influential as one of the main methods for analysing media texts and output (see also relevant discussion in Chapter 10.)

Semiotics has become an important part of media and cultural studies, due partly to the work of French writer Roland Barthes, who based his studies of culture on linguistic models developed by earlier writers such as C.S. Pierce and Ferdinand de Saussure. Barthes, however, applied these models to the more general study of cultural and visual signs and their meanings. For example, he suggested that we are likely to 'read' photographs like the two in Figures 2.2 and 2.3 by interpreting the various elements and 'clues' within them, rather than by simply reading a fixed and unitary message. A photograph, Barthes claimed, involves a mechanical process where the image – that which is *denoted* – is transferred on to photographic paper, but there is also an expressive, human and cultural process that involves the selection and interpretation of such elements as camera angles, framing, lighting techniques and focus. These extra *connotations* provide different meanings depending upon the culture, especially the *situated culture* (see Chapter 1, p. 8) of both the photographer (the encoder) and the viewer (the decoder) of the photograph. How we read Figure 2.2 may be influenced by our knowledge and our particular view of the image of the group that is portrayed in the photograph. One person may see this as a remembrance of the glorious days of the British Raj; others may view it as an image standing for the elitist and exploitative British imperial past.

According to this view, media texts always have a number of potential meanings and readings; that is, they are *polysemic* – potentially open to many interpretations. An *open* text, for instance, can have many different meanings depending upon time and place, as well as the class, gender, lifestyle, values and experience of the 'reader'. *Closed* texts, by contrast, strongly encourage and prefer a particular meaning, allowing little space for the reader to produce different ranges of meaning.

Each media text is 'read' and interpreted individually, either alone, for instance in the case of reading a newspaper, magazine, DVD or computer screen, or in social situations with family or friends watching a television programme or cinema film. But however private and individualised our media consumption may seem to be, we always draw upon shared codes and conventions to make sense of media output. Often, we make sense of media images and texts by means of what is known as the 'preferred' or 'dominant' reading. In order to understand this idea, which is also taken up in later chapters, we need to consider the relationships between the *encoding* and *decoding* of media texts.

Encoding and Decoding

Individual interpretations of the meaning of media texts are dependent upon a variety of factors all closely linked to the individual viewer and their identity: these include age, gender, social class and ethnic background. Audiences learn to make sense and organise the possible multiple meanings by using a 'grammar' or system of codes and signs similar to those which govern written or spoken language but which also combine with visual and audio dimensions.

To analyse the meanings of media texts we not only have to consider how and under what particular conditions audiences 'read' the particular signs and codes but also to consider both the forms and the contexts in which particular texts have been produced. These forms are the result of organised production systems of *encoding*, the production of the programme, film, web page, etc, by the author or production team and then the processes of *decoding*, whereby they are received and read by audiences. In the nineteenth century naval communication was made possible by semaphore, using combinations of flags that represented or stood for different letters of the alphabet. One sailor would *encode* a message into a series of flag sequences, with each combination representing a particular letter or phrase. This would then be used to 'signal' to another sailor, on land or on another ship, who would 'read' or *decode* this combination of flags by spelling out the letters that made up the message. Only sailors who were trained could understand the 'code' of the flags and this particular form of communication developed in response to the specific requirements and context of the navy at that time.

Some things have changed a great deal since the nineteenth century, and semaphore today would seem to be a very slow and old-fashioned means of communication. In modern times we are more familiar with faster, moving images but nonetheless the model of encoding and decoding remains useful in analysing forms of media and communication. Whether it is naval semaphore, a web page, a CCTV image, a television show or a tabloid newspaper, conditions and practices of production, the *encoding*, will have implications for the *decoding* processes which may often be diverse. We therefore need to highlight the key stages of communicating meaning, the way meanings are encoded or packaged by producers or 'senders' and decoded or unpacked by audiences or 'receivers'. The possible steps and relations in this encoding and decoding process become apparent when the meanings of any media text are analysed. (There is further discussion of the encoding–decoding model in Chapter 5.)

Codes

Codes are systems of signs and McMahon and Quinn (1988) provide a useful framework for beginning to understand and classify codes with reference to their analysis of newspapers and magazines. They identify three types of code: *technical, symbolic* and *written*. For most written or printed texts these categories include the following elements:

Technical:	Symbolic:	Written:
Camera angle	Objects	Headlines
Lens choice	Setting	Captions
Framing	Body language	Speech bubbles
Shutter speed	Clothing	Style
Depth of field	Colour	
Lighting and exposure		
Juxtaposition		

When we *decode* the pages of a magazine, newspaper or this book, for instance, we routinely and invisibly draw on these codes to make sense of the particular article or image that catches our attention. The codes both regulate and allow us to make meaningful sense, or arrive at some interpretation of the pages. Some of these issues can be highlighted by considering photographs which are strongly bound up with our own sense of personal and biographical identity. We are all familiar with the idea of the family photograph album whose contents can cover several generations of a family but will tend to highlight the positive, the great occasions: marriages, holidays, births, anniversaries. Like soap operas, family photograph albums often appear to represent life with 'the boring [or unhappy?] bits left out'. Both Kuhn (1995) and Sontag (1977) focus on the family photograph album as a good illustration of the selective stories families tell about themselves and how their history is a particular form of social and narrative construct.

In 'reading' photographs, like the ones contained in family albums, we make use of and draw upon a series of codes embodied in the photographs and the times that they were taken. These codes include the technical codes involved in taking the photographs in the first place – black and white or colour, for instance, as well as the codes of dress, colour and posture involved and how these combine to symbolise the occasion depicted.

We quickly learn to 'read' these texts and come to some understanding of their meaning; for instance, because the photograph in Figure 2.2 is black and white we may understand that it is 'old'. The clothes that the people in the photograph are wearing reinforce this interpretation. Looking more closely we identify some 'clues' about both the uniform and postures of the black servants as well as some of the furniture and general setting. We see that some of the people are sitting and others standing. So we start to piece together an idea about the relationship between the people in the photograph and perhaps develop some notion of the occasion. However, it is likely that only those in the family, or their descendants, will know the exact details of who the people are and where and when the photograph was taken.

Activity 2.1

Look through a family photograph album or a recent set of holiday snaps. How do you make sense of the photographs that it contains? Make a list of all the code systems which you can identify and which you make use of in decoding the images.

How is the family portrayed? What stories do the photographs tell? How do they relate to our own personal experiences of the family and to general ideals about family life?

Because the photograph in Figure 2.3 is in colour and the clothes the people are wearing are clearly signifying a particular, and familiar, social convention, we can 'read' its meaning more easily – a more modern family's wedding with bride, groom, bridesmaid, page-boy and other members of the family. Although the photograph in Figure 2.2 probably took longer to take and was more of a technical novelty, the poses of the people look more natural or casual with some of the people appearing to be ignoring the camera and looking elsewhere. This makes it less clear as to whether the camera is recording an everyday event or a special occasion. In Figure 2.3 everyone is standing in a formal line looking into the camera and because we recognise the occasion we understand that this is one of the 'formal' wedding photographs that will form part of the 'official' record, or *narrative* (see p. 44) of the event.

As visual and linguistic codes are socially and culturally defined, they change over time, reflecting shifts in, for example, social attitudes or opinions, the 'currency' or value of certain images, and the changing position of intended audiences. Examples of how images can change their meaning could include any image that contained the New York 'twin towers' of the World Trade Centre and the connotations of those images before and after 11 September 2001 or how words like 'gay' and 'wicked' have changed their meaning over time.

FIGURE 2.4
CCTV Image, attempted robbery at the Millennium Dome
Source: PA Photos

A recent photographic *genre* (see Chapter 3) that we have become increasingly familiar with is the close-circuit television image (CCTV) (Figure 2.4). This type of photographic image is a recent innovation made possible by technological developments such as auto-focus, the 'shrinking' of camera lenses and the digital recording of images. The widespread use of this technology reflects the way in which social attitudes have changed. CCTV may, for some people, have connotations of George Orwell's Big Brother, the state 'spying' on its citizens, but for many people CCTV is now something reassuring, a sign of security. Perhaps one of the most infamous of these images is associated with the murder of James Bulger in 1993. It has become an 'iconic' image that seems to sum up much of the horror that people felt at the crime. Similar images had become well-known as the result of other criminal investigations such as the pictures of David Copeland, the 'nail bomber' in Brixton, Jill Dando shopping just prior to being shot, or tracing the route taken by Damilola Taylor on his way home from school the day he was murdered (see also Figure 4.37). We have become familiar with these types of images and their association with criminal activity. We have also become familiar with similar technology through the use of speed cameras and the footage from police cars that are used in programmes like *Police, Camera, Action*. Although initially the audience for these images may be those who are responsible for our security and tracking down criminals, we as 'ordinary people' are also part of the larger audience that has learned to identify and read the codes that make up CCTV images.

Meanings are established through the particular codes used by CCTV images. If we look at Figure 2.4 we can see some of the written codes, the printed information at the top and bottom of the image giving details of the date, time and place the image was captured. It also indicates the camera number. In terms of technical codes the black and white image reinforces a sense of *realism* (see p. 104) and the camera angle that is looking down, usually on a public area, reinforces the notion that this is a surveillance camera watching the public. The graininess of the image or the fact that it may be a 'strobed' sequence all add to the technical codes that we have come to associate with CCTV cameras although increasingly sophisticated technology is making these effects less and less apparent.

Figures 2.5 and 2.6 show two covers of the same book, *Harry Potter and the Philosopher's Stone*. They were both published in 1997 but they have different covers because one edition is for adults and the other is for children. How do we 'know' which edition is which? What codes do we use in determining which cover belongs to which edition? Why did the publishers feel that they had to have two different covers for the two different sets of readers? Book covers are an important part of the marketing of a book, particularly popular fiction like the *Harry Potter* series that will probably be prominently displayed in book stores.

The image on the edition aimed at adult readers (Figure 2.5) is fairly straightforward with one clear, unambiguous image, that of a steam train coming straight towards the reader. Its preferred meaning, however, is perhaps a little more complicated. Technically it is a simple graphic in black and white, probably a photograph. However, there are no clues as to when and where this photograph was taken. We can make certain assumptions, for instance that it is an American train and probably not a modern one. There is, however, a question about why that particular image of a train has been used. Is it clear what the significance is between this image and the title of the book? What, if any, pre-knowledge do the publishers assume the reader has?

The image on the cover of the children's edition (Figure 2.6) is more garish and complex and offers a greater variety of possible readings; it is more *polysemic*, although the general sense of the image is still to do with steam trains. The ambiguity partly lies in the positioning of the boy in the foreground and his expression. The graphic is more cartoon-like and offers additional information, for example the sign saying '9 3/4' and the modern train in the background. Again it

may not be clear to all readers what the significance is of this image to the title of the book. Again there is some pre-knowledge assumed by the publishers. Would everyone know, for example, that the boy in the foreground with the school scarf and bag is Harry Potter? Some readers who may be familiar with the stories will perhaps make the connection between Harry Potter and the train but many others may not. Does this matter in terms of marketing the book?

There are clearer clues here as to the publisher's assumptions about the identity of its target audience. To younger readers, for example, the cartoon image presents a friendlier connotation of the train in comparison with the rather harsh realism of the adult cover. The use of large amounts

FIGURE 2.5
Harry Potter (Adult)
Source: Bloomsbury Publishing PLC

and FIGURE 2.6
Harry Potter (Children)
Source: Bloomsbury Publishing PLC/
©Thomas Taylor

of bright red for the front of the train and the top of the cover has certain connotations. The colour red is used on both covers but to a lesser extent on the adult cover. What does the colour red in this context signify? Would another colour, such as blue, work equally well? If not, why not? Are there other colours that you think might work better?

All this is in contrast with the rather stark black and white image of a train in the adult's cover. The children's cover also has the figure of the boy in it, perhaps making it more human, more personal, more friendly. He is wearing a particular type of glasses: what connotations do they have? Is his expression important? He seems to be looking puzzled. Do we know why? Do we need to read the book to find out why?

Activity 2.2

1   You could take a book of your own choice and alter its cover to attract a different set of readers. What assumptions are you making about your new readers and how is this reflected in the design that you have chosen?

2   Consider the cover of this book 'Studying the Media'. In what ways does it try to appeal to its readers and their interests? How successfully do you think this cover markets this book? Your library may have copies of the first and second editions and you could look at these covers and see how they have changed over time. You could also look at other media textbooks to see if there are any common styles or images. Design another cover for this book that you think would be more effective. You could then send it to the publishers at www.arnoldpublishers.com so that they might consider using it for the next edition.

FIGURE 2.7
'Locked out: Gerry Adams and Martin McGuinness of Sinn Fein keep watch from outside the gates as the delegations arrive at the Northern Ireland talks yesterday.'
Source: Pacemaker Press International Ltd/Daily Telegraph, 11 June 1996 (original caption)

FIGURE 2.8
'Outside: Sinn Fein leaders Gerry Adams and Martin McGuinness on the wrong side of the wire fence surrounding castle buildings after they were refused entry to yesterday's talks.'
Source: Independent, 11 June 1996 (original caption)/Brian Harris

Figures 2.7 and 2.8 show news photographs of the same event and were taken at the same place at about the same time; however, the different angles and *cropping* – cutting the frame of the picture in different ways – offer different meanings. Figure 2.7 is perhaps more closed in its connotative meanings, illustrating in a graphic and emotional manner the view that Sinn Fein representatives were being 'barred' or 'imprisoned' for their views. The *Daily Telegraph* newspaper was criticised by some Members of Parliament for printing this photograph because they felt that it aided Sinn Fein in its cause and propaganda. Figure 2.8 is more open to a variety of interpretations. Figure 2.7 shows how the cropping of a photograph can 'direct' the viewer towards a particular or *preferred* reading. Cropping is the process by which the 'superfluous' content of a photograph is removed, thereby highlighting only that which the producer considers essential to establish a particular meaning, theme or focus in a defined context.

Anchorage

Often a text is constructed so that the audience is encouraged into understanding one particular 'dominant' meaning – into taking up one particular stance or viewpoint with regard to the issue or event represented. This is often done through a process referred to as *anchorage*, where words are used to direct or 'anchor' the meaning of an image for the reader, encouraging them to a particular reading. As a result, advertising, news and other images are accompanied, for example, by words, voice-overs, slogans or captions.

Figure 2.9 demonstrates how the *anchorage* of an image can change its reading. Figure 2.9a shows coverage of the 1990 Poll Tax riots in the *Independent Magazine*. The photograph on its own could be rather ambiguous, but the headline and caption seem to anchor the connotative meaning of the photograph in a clear and explicit manner, one that might be considered to meet the expectations of many of the readers of the *Independent Magazine*. Yet the letter from the woman in the photograph which was published in a subsequent edition of the magazine (Figure 2.9b) reveals the 'true' meaning of the picture and caption to be substantially different from its original loading.

THE MOB'S BRIEF RULE

A West End shopper argues with a protester who is being taken away by the police. Photograph: Richard Smith, KATZ.

FIGURE 2.9a and 2.9b
The Poll Tax riot, central London, 6 April 1990
Source: Independent Magazine, 7 April 1990

EYE-WITNESS

Sir: In last week's article about the poll-tax riot in Trafalgar Square ("The Mob's Brief Rule", 7 April) there is a large photograph labelled "A West End shopper argues with a protestor". The woman in the photograph is me, and I thought you might like to know the true story behind the picture.

I was on my way to the theatre, with my husband. As we walked down Regent Street at about 6.30 pm, the windows were intact and there was a large, cheerful, noisy group of poll-tax protestors walking up from Piccadilly Circus. We saw ordinary uniformed police walking alongside, on the pavement, keeping a low profile. The atmosphere was changed dramatically in moments when a fast-walking, threatening group of riot squad police appeared.

We walked on to the top of Haymarket, where the atmosphere was more tense and more protestors were streaming up

Haymarket from the Trafalgar Square end. Suddenly, a group of mounted police charged at full gallop into the rear of the group of protestors, scattering them, passers-by and us and creating panic. People screamed and some fell. Next to me and my husband another group of riot squad police appeared, in a most intimidating manner.

The next thing that happened is what horrified me most. Four of the riot squad police grabbed a young girl of 18 or 19 for no reason and forced her in a brutal manner on to the crowd control railings, with her throat across the top of the railings. Her young male companion was frantically trying to reach her and was being held back by one riot squad policeman. In your photograph I was urging the boy to calm down or he might be arrested; he was telling me that the person being held down across the railings was his girlfriend.

My husband remonstrated with the riot squad policeman holding the boy, and I

shouted at the four riot squad men to let the girl go as they were obviously hurting her. To my surprise, they did let her go – it was almost as if they did not know what they were doing.

The riot squad police involved in this incident were *not* wearing any form of identification. Their epaulettes were unbuttoned and flapping loose; I lifted them on two men and neither had any numbers on. There was a sergeant with them, who was numbered, and my husband asked why his men wore no identifying numbers. The sergeant replied that it did not matter as he knew who the men were.

We are a middle-aged, suburban couple who now feel more intimidated by the Metropolitan Police than by a mob. If we feel so angry, how on earth did the young hot-heads at the rally feel?

Mrs R.A. Sare,
Northwood, Middlesex

Activity 2.3

Using a range of photographs taken from different sources, discuss the ways in which the 'meanings' of an event or occasion can be changed by cropping them or by adding different captions or headlines. Then look at some current newspaper photographs to see in what ways they too have been selected, cropped and anchored to create particular meanings. It can be useful to compare the same photographs as they are used across the range of one day's newspapers (like photographs 2.7 and 2.8) to highlight differences.

Design

A newspaper front-page is a complex text made up of several different segments, all contributing to its overall impact and meaning. We tend to focus on headlines and photographs but there are many other sections that can be analysed, for example the newspaper's masthead. John Sutherland, writing in *The Guardian* in 2001, described the connotations behind the newspaper's design. Discussing the way in which the newspaper's title includes two different typefaces (see Figure 2.10), he explains that the aim of italicised *The* is subversive. It is to distinguish the newspaper from other broadsheets that also use

'the' in their title, like *The Times*. He goes on to say that the word *Guardian*, in roman type, refers back to the chiselled inscriptions on classic monuments and is 'hammeringly authoritative'. Italics, Sutherland says, derives from Renaissance Italian calligraphy and can be seen as 'the feathered quill lightly touching paper'.

FIGURE 2.10
The Guardian masthead
28.8.2001
Source:
© Guardian

The article (which can be accessed via Guardian Online at **www.guardian.co.uk/Archive/ Article/0,4273,4241935,00.html**) goes on to discuss the different typefaces and their connotations used in the newspaper's articles. The two main kinds of type used are serif and sans serif (a serif is a line or twist at the tip, or extremity, of the letter – see example below).

A B C D E F G H

Sutherland suggests that a seriffed typeface is used for comment and analysis headlines and that 'subliminally it relaxes the reader, slows down the pace of reading', whereas the 'no-nonsense sans serif is used for news headlines and reporters' by-lines'. To what extent do you think that the readers of *The Guardian* are aware of these connotations?

Newspapers put considerable amounts of thought and money into the way they present themselves. This is partly evidenced by the number of times newspapers change their formats, from broadsheet to tabloid, their typefaces and their different sections and supplements. This may be due to a number of different factors such as changing readership, increased competition, changing production methods and developing risky, new ventures.

Activity 2.4

Using local libraries or searching on the World Wide Web, try to find old copies of newspapers. Compare them with front-pages today. How have they changed? How would you account for these changes? What assumptions are made about their readers? Using John Sutherland's article try to explain why particular newspapers today look the way they do.

The front-page of the newspaper used in Figure 2.11 is a good example of a text that uses a range of different segments to package an attractive and eye-catching front-page. These include the overall scale and dominance of the pictures and their connotations, combined with a dramatic headline. The printing of the headline has been reversed so that it is white print on a black background. There is also the story behind the headline, two 'great British institutions on the ropes'. The photographs are in colour and the gestures of the two people are also quite striking. Think about the two people and the way they are presented on the page, Andy Caddick as a cut-out but the late Queen Mother as a cropped photograph. Look at the way they are both facing inwards towards each other and the expressions on their faces. Consider how the use of colour helps create the page's visual impact: only four colours are used, red, black, white and blue. How and why have these colours been used on this occasion?

Compared to *The Guardian*'s masthead there is little additional information about the newspaper's content. There is the 'Posh exclusive' and a reference at the bottom of the page where to find the main stories. If the story about the Queen Mother is on page 5, to what extent is this then the 'main' story? Why do you think Posh would give an exclusive interview to *The Mirror* and why does it say, in relation to her story, 'I'd drown Geri'?

All these different elements are part of the design deliberately thought out by the newspaper's production team to try to create a front-page that will attract readers and maximise sales. Think about why *The Mirror* would have these two photographs and stories on its front-page, what they suggest about the readers of *The Mirror* and the news values that makes these stories 'newsworthy'? What is the preferred reading of this front-page? How, for instance, does it represent 'Britishness' (see Chapter 5)?

Now, choose at least two newspaper front-pages and use the three categories of codes identified by McMahon and Quinn to analyse how and why each text has been put together as it has. Start by looking at the *technical codes*:

- How is the page laid out – to what effect? In what style?
- What typefaces and fonts have been used? Why?
- What can be said about the size and quality of the photographs?
- Have they been cropped? If so, how and why? How do you know that cropping has taken place?
- How do the photographs relate to the rest of the stories and the front page?
- Why have these particular pictures been selected?

Next focus on the *written* codes:

- How does the size of the headline(s) compare with the rest of the page?
- What are the key words and what do they signify?
- What conventions are being used?
- To what extent does the copy meet the expectations set up by the headline(s)?

- Is any information omitted from the copy?
- How does the headline influence the way the reader might approach the story?
- How do the captions help anchor the meanings?

Then think about the *symbolic* codes:

- What do the masthead and title of the newspaper signify? How do they achieve this?
- Why are particular graphics used and what do they signify?
- What colours are used and what do they signify?
- What symbolic codes are at work in the pictures?

Finally consider the front page as a whole:

- How does the overall layout and style aim to attract readers?
- Is any particular impression or message given out by the overall 'look' of the front page?
- How is this 'look' and style created?

Intertextuality

FIGURE 2.12
Lara Croft/Triumph advert
Source: Triumph International

Although various conventions are discussed separately in this chapter, it is important to understand that they are often integrated and mixed together in the dynamics of everyday media 'flow'. This mixing, chopping-up and cross-referencing, often referred to as *intertextuality*, creates extra layers of association and meaning, so that a text is often partly understood by what preceded it or what will follow it or even perhaps by reference to other media texts. Sometimes this intertextuality can be unintentional or coincidental.

One of the publicity events of the summer of 2001 surrounded the release of the film *Tomb Raider* with Angelina Jolie as Lara Croft. The film, based on the computer game *Tomb Raider* and its central character Lara Croft, described as 'sexy and aggressive' by the game's makers Eidos, has attracted considerable publicity and sales since its release in 1996. 'Lara' has appeared on the cover of *The Face, Newsweek* and *Rolling Stone* magazines. The virtual character of Lara Croft has also been used to advertise various products and brands including Lucozade. The connection between a 'high energy' drink and the character of Lara Croft is an interesting one. They seem to go together partly because we are able to imagine Lara Croft drinking this kind of drink; other drinks such as drinking chocolate or sherry would probably not have the same meaning. The advertisement for Triumph bras (Figure 2.12) seems to be implying a connection with Lara Croft although nowhere on the advertisement does her name or *Tomb Raider* appear. The figure is a computer-generated image and the shape of her face, the style of her hair and her facial expression are all reminiscent of Lara Croft. One of the characteristics of Lara Croft is her figure and the advertisement may be relying on readers to make this connection. There is also a small compass sign indicating North in the advertisement. As this is not part of the Lara Croft *iconography* it is interesting to consider why those who designed the advertisement placed it there.

In fact, the advertisement was part of an advertising campaign created over a year before the film's release to launch a bra in the 'software' range. As a play on this, Triumph decided to create a 'cyberbabe' using state-of-the-art software. This perhaps explains the compass in the advert – it was a theme running throughout the advertisements and does not have any logical link with *Tomb Raider*. However, when the film *Tomb Raider* was released, this particular bra advert did seem to coincide to a certain extent. It is therefore an interesting example of where intertextuality might have occurred although, in this case, unintentionally. It is also an example of how the meaning of texts can change over time: what was seen originally as a 'cyberbabe' image seemingly became a clear reference to Lara Croft.

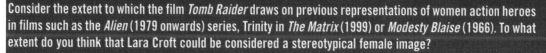

Activity 2.5

Consider the extent to which the film *Tomb Raider* draws on previous representations of women action heroes in films such as the *Alien* (1979 onwards) series, Trinity in *The Matrix* (1999) or *Modesty Blaise* (1966). To what extent do you think that Lara Croft could be considered a stereotypical female image?

This process of 'borrowing' signs and features from different texts, sources and styles, usually in a humorous, ironic or self-conscious manner, and re-using them in different contexts, is called *bricolage* and it has been defined as a particular characteristic of *postmodern* culture (see Chapter 1).

FIGURE 2.13
Source: Vodafone Group Services

Look, for instance, at the Vodafone advert in Figure 2.13, which refers the discerning reader back to a set of earlier, historic images and 'adds' these to 'today's' message. In the 'October 1992' advert, the sombre red and brown colours, the woman in the grey coat, the way she is standing and holding the telephone, the manifesto with its 'declaration of rights' and the form of a 'people's charter' are all signs associated with the codes of revolutionary posters from early communist Russia. These associations are trying to create a sense of revolution, of a 'new dawn breaking'. They can work effectively only if the reader can recognise, and decode, these references. The advertisers therefore have to place the adverts where they think readers will recognise and easily understand these 'quotations', in this case *The Independent* and *The Sunday Times*. A bonus for the advertiser may be that if the reader does decode the references, he or she may then feel 'special' in some way, having 'understood' the story, and that may then be positively associated with the brand identity itself.

It is worth spending some time comparing and contrasting this advert with other adverts for similar products. For instance, how do the Vodafone adverts from 1992 compare with the Samsung adverts for mobile phones taken from 2001 (Figure 2.14)? Are they aimed at similar or different audiences? Has the way in which they represent and promote mobile phones changed? If so, in what ways?

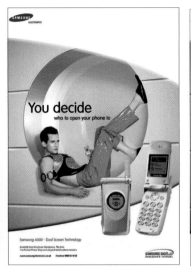

FIGURE 2.14
Samsung mobile phone adverts
Source: Samsung

We can use the three categories of codes identified by McMahon and Quinn to analyse the Samsung WAP phone advertisements.

Start by looking at the *technical* codes:

- The advertisements are good-quality reproductions with the images in varying shades of blue and white. The clarity of the images allows us to see the detail of the man and woman's clothing and the mobile phone.

- The images do not attempt to recreate any sense of 'reality', there are no clues to the context except that it is some kind of 'futuristic' building and setting. It could be somewhere technical, like the man and woman's work place. Their postures, however, suggest that this is not the case. They may be at home although there is no evidence of anything homely. In fact, the situation appears to be a deliberate enigma and the man and woman are placed in some kind of sci-fi fantasy world.
- It is not immediately clear if they are models, who have been photographed inside a real or mocked-up building, or whether the whole image is computer-generated. Even if the man and woman are 'real' there has been a process of manipulation, probably by computer, to digitally enhance the image. The enlarged WAP phones, for example, have presumably been digitally manipulated and added later.
- The enlarged images of the phone allow us to read 'Sara' and 'Mark' on the blue screens and the other features on the green screens.
- Other technical details include the blue shiny walls which reinforce the suggestion of being futuristic as well as having connotations of coolness and depth.

Next consider the *written* codes:

- In this advert the visual image and message dominate the written. There is very little text apart from the slogan 'You decide who to open your phone to', the name of the product itself, the name of the company and some of the places where it is available.
- There appears to be no real attempt to inform us about the product except to say that it offers 'Dual Screen Technology'. Presumably the producers are confident that there is sufficient information in the advertisement for the target audience to understand 'Dual Screen Technology' and what it offers.
- The slogan is written in two different font sizes with 'You Decide' much larger than 'who to open your phone to'. Why is this?
- Is the advert trying to create a sense of coolness and being in control? Does it succeed?

Then focus on the *symbolic* codes:

- The way in which the (young, white, attractive) man and woman are dressed appears cool and fashionable. It is not clear if these are clothes for work or leisure. The clothes are shiny in a way that is associated with the future. He is wearing shoes and has something around his arm, presumably some kind of decoration but it is not clear what it is supposed to signify. She also has something around her arm and is wearing fluffy shoes and a fluffy ball on her head. They are both well groomed and appear to be very 'casual', 'free' and 'cool' and give the impression of being able to do what they want when they want. Presumably neither of them answers the telephone to just anyone.

Finally, when putting all these constituent parts together, consider the overall meaning created by the advertisement:

- There is a sense of the man and woman being in control and at the cutting edge of modern technology. To what extent is this a common theme in advertisements?
- Are we supposed to identify with the man and/or woman? Is there a sense of the advertisement trying to attract men or women who would like to be like this man or woman? Do you find these images desirable as sex role models?
- What is being promised by these adverts? If you buy this product will you become like this man or woman? If, as it is claimed, all media texts have a narrative, what is the story of this advertisement?
- Are there any particular values that are being highlighted in these adverts? Control and freedom? Aloofness? Being 'cutting edge'? Are these values?
- Much of the power of the adverts seems to lie in the apparent coolness and aloofness of the man and woman and his sci-fi, futuristic situation.
- Is this an effective way to try to sell mobile phones? Compare this advert with others for mobile phones.
- Where would you expect to see these advertisements placed?

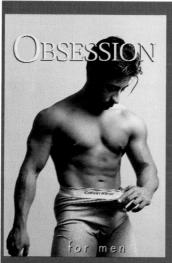

Activity 2.6

Consider Figure 2.15 and carry out a similar analysis. Think about how you decode it and come to some kind of conclusion regarding its meaning. What are its key signs and codes? What prior knowledge does it assume you have? How does it avoid breaking libel laws?

On the rear of the advert is the phrase 'For every doubt there is a product'. What does this mean and how does it add to the meaning of the image?

Who do you think is the target audience for this advert and where would you expect it to appear?

FIGURE 2.15
Adbuster's Obsession
Source: Courtesy www.adbusters.org

Discourse analysis is a means of analysing the relationship between knowledge and power, the contest between modes of address and points of view (there is more detailed discussion on mode of address and point of view in Chapter 5). It therefore focuses on meaning and value systems, suggesting that meaning systems both reflect and carry particular values. Discourses consist of culturally and socially produced sets of ideas and values contained in texts and representations. They contain and articulate abstract and ideological versions of the world. Tolson (1996) suggests that discourse analysis is a synthesis between two key concerns in any study of the media: Semiotics and Ideology. Semiotics has provided a way of analysing meanings in texts whereas ideology provides a way of understanding the relationships between these meanings and our social and political structures (see Chapter 4 for related discussion).

This method of analysing media texts has been developed from the work of the French intellectual Michel Foucault. His early writings looked at the ways in which language, both spoken and written, represent certain meanings that reflect and reproduce social and political power. Foucault claimed that power and knowledge are interdependent: power entails command over discourse and command over discourse entails power.

Discourses organise possible statements about a given area, for instance the family or war or education and they structure the manner in which a particular event, topic, object, or process is talked about or reported. They establish the boundaries of what is acceptable (included) and what is not acceptable (excluded).

Discourse analysis is useful in studying the media because it provides the means by which films, television programmes and all other media output can be understood. The text will reproduce, use, serve and relate to discourses that exist outside of the text itself. Discourse analysis is therefore the study of the discursive aspects of any given media or communicative text. Questions we might ask regarding discourse and media texts include:

- **What discourses does the text use or draw on?**
- **What 'truth-claims' does the text make and how?**
- **How might these reflect wider power relations?**
- **Whose interests are being served?**

These ideas have been used in particular to identify the specific discourses that surround news bulletins that place 'us', the audience and society, together in one position while 'they', the criminal, the dangerous, outsiders, are placed in opposition to us. All discourses are framed within narratives of one form or another. In news the story is what happened, the discourse is how the story is told and the connotations or meanings embedded within its preferred readings.

Part of the discourse of television or radio news bulletins is that somehow the *status quo* is the preferred model for our society. However much it may be disrupted, through, for instance, the events of 11 September 2001, nevertheless it is possible, with the correct actions, to return to a new equilibrium. However much of the news media following these events focused on bringing the culprits to justice and, as a means of doing this, went to war against the Taliban in Afghanistan. The dominant discourse surrounding this war was that it was justified because of a need to restore some sense of equilibrium, bring those who committed the crimes to justice and destroy dangerous Muslim 'fundamentalism' (see Allan, 2002).

The media therefore are important systems for the transmission and reception of discourse, and discourse analysis enables us to investigate the values and ideas about the world and events which are limited, encouraged or prohibited.

Binary Oppositions

Another method of analysing the meaning and structure of texts is through the use of *binary oppositions*, as developed by the French anthropologist Levi-Strauss. He argued that many texts are structured by a series of binary conflicts between two qualities or groups and that meaning is generated out of their opposition to each other and the differences between them. For example, 'us/them' in relation to discussions about foreigners, either in sports or as 'illegal' asylum seekers. Refer back to Figure 2.11 *The Mirror* front-page; what does it say about 'us' especially in terms of the cricket match against 'Oz'? (also look at Figure 4.8 p. 75). Binary oppositions are often used in the analysis of specific film genres such as the western which is often portrayed as a conflict between culture or civilisation (cowboys, the railroad, towns, western values, law and order, family life) and nature or wilderness (indians, savage, pagan, nature, cruelty). Other examples might include typical gender representations:

Man	Woman
Active	Passive
External	Domestic
Public	Private
Producer	Consumer
Provider	Dependent

This means of analysing texts allows us to identify the opposing properties of a text as well as identifying a set of key characteristics for each side of the binary divide. For example, the manner in which men are seen as different to women in the way that they are portrayed in active public wage-earning roles outside of the domestic situation. (See also gender preferences in Chapter 4).

Binary opposites can also be used in the analysis of films, most obviously in terms of good/bad, hero/villain, weak/strong but also in more complex and *ideological* terms: nature/civilisation; masculine/feminine; Christian/heathen; democracy/dictatorship; progress/conservatism and so on. News is often structured in terms of conflict using binary opposites, for example the Glasgow University Media Group carried out a number of research studies looking at the ways various groups were categorised during industrial disputes (see p. 75). Hartley (1982) also analysed a news item about an industrial dispute involving health workers in terms of its binary opposites:

Children	Public Service Workers
Government	Strikers
Decent Trade Unionists	Irresponsible minority
Us	Them

If we consider the way in which some Muslim fundamentalists have been portrayed in the media since the events of 11 September 2001 we can see how both discourse analysis and binary opposites can be used to analyse media texts. The concept of 'orientalism' has been used by Edward Said (1985) to characterise European attitudes to the Orient, the Middle East and Asia. Said details the process by which European imperialists dominated their colonised subjects – not only through military force but also through the discourses that came to represent the colonised countries. He suggests that orientalism is a Western perspective which assumes authority over the Orient. It could be argued that the concept of orientalism has been influential in much of the Western media's coverage of organisations such as Al-Qaida and some other Muslim fundamentalist groups.

Said describes how the virtues of the West were established through the classification of differences between the 'civilised' West and the 'savage' Orient. This could also be applied to the portrayal of some Muslim groups:

Western	Foreign
Normal	Strange
Rational	Irrational
Civilised	Barbaric
Modern	Backward
Moderate	Extreme
Responsible	Dangerous
Superior	Inferior
Justice	Criminal
Us	Them

Activity 2.7

Take a recent news story and consider how the discourse has been framed. Are there any binary oppositions at work in the story? If so what are they and how are they valued, ie. good or bad, us or them, etc. How do these binary oppositions structure the story?

Multimodal

In the examples that we have looked at so far we have largely considered printed texts: newspapers, magazine advertisements, photographs, graphics and/or combinations of these. We have not considered moving images or sound, yet both of these also have a complex range of codes. It is becoming increasingly difficult to think of media texts in terms of only one particular media form (sound, images, text and so on). We increasingly live with *multimodal* texts that incorporate a range of media forms. Think, for example, of the way many computer games indicate that a game has finished. There may be a written message 'Game Over' that is superimposed on a computer-generated image but with the additional code of sound. Consider also the widespread, and taken for granted, use of visual logos that appear on a wide range of written material and objects from letterheads to carrier bags, buses, taxis and clothing. Increasingly television screens are adopting the aesthetics of computer displays and web pages. Television programmes such as news bulletins or 'youth' shows like *StreetMate* include captions at the bottom of the screen alongside dialogue and visual messages.

It is this increasing mixing and use of codes from one medium into another that is called *multimodal*. Not only do we have to understand written language, we have to be visually literate as well, to be able to understand the additional meanings that supplementary media modes bring to a text. An electronic text, such as a website, may incorporate many of the codes that we have looked at so far in terms of printed material but will also have additional codes of sound, possibly moving image and *interactivity* – or at least, the ability to move from one page to another, one site to another.

If we consider Figure 2.16 we can see that it incorporates many different types of codes: written, visual and audio. If we use McMahon and Quinn's three categories we can start to break down or *deconstruct* these signs and codes. For example, one of the first symbolic codes to notice is the use of colour, the dark blue background with lighter blues and white lettering and, perhaps most importantly, the bright primary colours of the 'creatures' themselves. The designers of this web page, the encoders, clearly thought that the combination of blue and white were the best colours to use. These colours are used throughout the website and in other areas of the creatures' 'world'. It may be because 'blue' has certain connotations associated perhaps with 'boys' and 'maleness' which the encoders might consider appropriate for something that is basically a computer game. These colours may also be

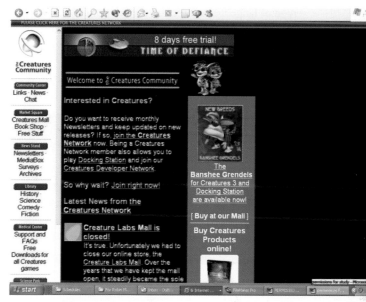

FIGURE 2.16
Web page **www.creatures.co.uk**
Source: © Creature Labs

partly determined by the technology, the computer systems and so the colours could also be considered as part of the technical codes.

The creatures are the main message, the preferred reading, of this web page. The whole website is devoted to them and their associated merchandising. Presumably the majority of those who access this website will be familiar with the creatures and their *iconography*, the identification of particular signs associated with particular genres (see Chapter 3). The symbolic codes that are used to give these creatures particular characteristics include their hair, its colour and style; their eyes, large and expressive; their body language and the objects that they are seen with.

There is also an additional set of codes, the 'buttons' at the top of the page that are symbols for various other sites such as latest news, press relations, etc. Those that are familiar with the site may already know what these buttons signify, others may need to click on the buttons to find out where they lead to or place their cursor over the button and be told where they lead. We generally understand that this is how a web page works in the same way that we have learned how to read a newspaper, use a video-recorder or watch television programmes. There are a set of conventions associated with this, and other web pages, that we increasingly take for granted and that the encoders increasingly assume we will be familiar with.

These buttons offer a graphic representation that symbolises their function, the ability to link to another web page, or a written text message that says 'latest news' or 'shopping trolley'. They fit any of McMahon and Quinn's categories in that they are symbolic, technical or written. Which category of codes do you think most accurately describes these buttons? How can we categorise these links? They are an important element of all websites and the way in which websites are designed, navigated and consumed. These links represent the interactivity of websites and are part of their architecture. We have started to use another type of language to describe the relationship between one site and another, to describe our relationship with the 3-D world of a website. Surfing is used to describe the manner in which we navigate from page to page. What does this imply about how we view and use the web and web pages?

We can see that the meanings of web pages like these are made up of a complicated synthesis of different types of codes from different media forms, or modes, as well as their interactions and interconnections.

Activity 2.8

Consider either this or another website of your choice. Starting at the top of the page slowly work down the page identifying all the components that are on the webpage. Try to categorise them using the framework provided by McMahon and Quinn. This was originally designed for printed material like newspapers and magazines. Does it also work for texts in website form? Think about the different components that you have identified, what do they signify and how do we understand their meaning? How do they work in relation to each other? What sort of audience pre-knowledge is assumed by the designers of the web page?

Narrative Codes

All media texts tell us some kind of story and the term *narrative* is the way this process of telling stories is organised – how stories are shaped, structured and then potentially decoded or understood.

Analysing narrative entails the idea that most narratives have a common structure, starting with establishing a plot, theme or problem: for instance, the creation of a *disequilibrium* through the murder by an unknown person at the beginning of a detective series. This is then followed by the development or elaboration of the problem, an *enigma*, an increase in tension, perhaps with the main suspect being murdered or new characters or 'twists' being introduced. Finally comes the *resolution* of the plot, theme or situation, in which the problems are conventionally solved and a new *equilibrium* is established. This resolution may happen when the detective 'reveals all' and the murderer is exposed, or when the hero triumphs and marries the heroine. Other well-known forms of resolution include the gunfight in a traditional western or the 'big bang' endings of action adventure films like the James Bond or *Die Hard* series.

Character Functions

In 1928, in a famous analysis of narratives, the Russian linguist Vladimir Propp used fairy tales as a basis for his model of over thirty fundamental character types, all of whom perform some kind of function in the way narratives are organised and developed. Some of these key character functions include:

- the *hero*, who seeks something;
- the *villain*, who hinders or is in competition with the hero;
- the *donor*, who provides some kind of magic talisman that helps the hero;
- the *helper*, who aids the hero and his or her quest;
- the *heroine*, who acts as a reward for the hero and is the object of the villain's schemes.

The importance of these characters is as much to do with who they are or what they are like as with the part they play in the development of the narrative and our recognition of their general function. We recognise the hero and heroine and identify with the (usually male) hero – 'us' – and the resolution that should bring them together. We are encouraged to take sides and oppose the villain – 'them' – and occasionally even boo or hiss when they appear on the screen, the stage or wherever the narrative is being played out.

Propp's character functions allow for individual changes in attitudes and/or beliefs – for instance, the main character's coming to the view that war is useless or corrupting in *Born on the Fourth of July* or *Apocalypse Now*; for the undertaking of a mythic 'quest' or search, perhaps for some personal justice as in *The Searchers* or *Saving Private Ryan*; and for conflict between hierarchies or within subcultures, in films like *Rebel Without a Cause*, *My Beautiful Laundrette* or *The Godfather* series.

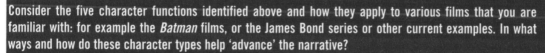

Activity 2.9

Consider the five character functions identified above and how they apply to various films that you are familiar with: for example the *Batman* films, or the James Bond series or other current examples. In what ways and how do these character types help 'advance' the narrative?

If we consider the James Bond film *The World is not Enough* (2000), we can see how these character types can be identified: Renard is the villain, James Bond is the hero, Q is the donor who provides the BMW car and other 'magic' gadgets to help Bond in his quest and M is the dispatcher who sends Bond off to stop Renard. The female characters are less straightforward although Electra can be seen as the false hero who is apparently at first on Bond's side. Dr Jones is both helper and towards the end of the film the heroine who Bond 'wins' as his reward. There does not appear to be an equivalent of the heroine's father.

Propp also identified thirty one functions that he argued were needed to advance a narrative. It might be the revelation of a secret, the death of a character, encountering a new threat, or successfully completing a task in pursuit of the hero's quest.

These narratives can be unambiguous and linear, as in traditional storytelling (from 'Once upon a time' to 'and they all lived happily ever after') or factual, as in the news ('The trial continues' or 'These are today's main stories'). Sometimes the narrative structure is altered, chopped up or manipulated, as in the film *Run, Lola, Run* (2001), to emulate a computer game and offer various possible endings. Sometimes the narrative can begin at the end and be presented as a series of flashbacks (as in *Pulp Fiction* (1994), *D.O.A* (1950, 1988), *Bad Timing* (1980), *Memento* (2001) or *Citizen Kane* (1941)). Occasionally the narrative is structured as a combination of both 'real time' and flashback, as in a live sports broadcast, where key moments in the development of the narrative of the event are highlighted as action replays or edited highlights.

In advertising there is often a simple before-and-after narrative that says: 'Before it/I was like this, but after using brand X, it is/I am like this.' Increasingly the narrative structures of some adverts have been made obscure and the key elements of character, time and narrator deliberately ambiguous, surreal, ironic or the subject of parody. Two of the most successful of these parodies in recent times, for instance, are the Häagen-Dazs luxury ice-cream and Boddingtons beer advertising campaigns.

Narration

Narration is the act of telling the 'story', and the media form which is used will affect how the narrative is told. One of the main differences between these forms is how *time* is handled; for instance, an 800 page novel can deal with a time span of many years (*Bleak House*) or a few hours (*Ulysses*), and equally the time taken to read the novel can also vary widely. A 30-minute radio or television programme can attempt to cover a similar range of time periods but has to do so in a finite, fixed or episodic, time slot. Consumption by the audience is also much more limited, although the video/DVD recorder does offer some degree of control and choice. To bridge this difference between the audience's 'real time' and the narrative's 'story time', various conventions are used. One of the most common historical devices for showing the passing of time on film used to be the speeding up of the hands of a clock or blowing away the pages of a calendar. Today these are both rather clichéd or heavy-handed, and as audiences we accept and understand more sophisticated conventions, such as the use of fade-outs or slow mixes from one shot to another, or even a single caption that may say 'two years later'. To complicate matters further, some media forms (*Brookside* or *Jonathan Creek,* for example) encompass complete narrative units (a single play or feature film) and also make extensive use of series, episodes and serial formats with ongoing, open-ended narratives.

Crisell (1994) suggests that in broadcast radio, as all the signs and codes are auditory only (words, sounds, music and silence) and sequential, then time is the major structuring agent for radio narratives, although the 'meaning' of radio texts is created by the contexts which the words, sounds, music and silences construct.

Activity 2.10

Record an episode of the long-running BBC Radio 4 soap opera *The Archers*. Analyse the programme by breaking down the episode into segments; then consider each segment individually and list its various components

- i.e. dialogue (How many people?)
- sound effects (How is a sense of situation established?)
- and the segment's relationship with both the preceding and subsequent segments (How are links created?)
- how is a sense of time passing created?
- how does the episode produce interwoven narratives?
- who are the narrators?
- how is a sense of closure created for the episode?
- compare and contrast the radio form of the soap opera genre with one of its television equivalents such as *Emmerdale.*

In order to be convincing, television soap operas often try to blur the gap between real time and story time; for instance, a *Brookside* episode may start in the morning with families meeting over breakfast, follow characters through the day and end with the families meeting again over the evening meal. By the evening the events being shown on the screen may be happening at the same time as the audience is watching them happen. Events in soap operas may parallel 'real' events and seasons; for instance, Christmas editions of popular soaps often show the characters themselves celebrating Christmas.

We often create the story ourselves by decoding the clues that we are given and then filling in the gaps to create the story, predicting and speculating about the outcomes of unfolding events. Previews and title sequences are particularly adept at giving just enough information for us to do this. Television title sequences can be seen as mini-narratives that act as trailers for the coming programme and mark the end of the previous segment or commercial break. The use of certain types of image and the importance of music and signature tune prepare us for the next narrative segment by introducing the character and signposting the type or genre of programme. Title sequences as used, for example, in *The Simpsons*, are familiar and reassuring elements of a programme's appeal, introducing each new episode by repeating the broader narrative of the series. In the television series *Quantum Leap*, each week viewers see the hero suffer a replay of the nuclear accident that now allows him to travel through time. These title sequences play an important part in the competition to attract and hold the interest of audiences and they can last for several minutes. In *Star Trek*, for instance, the title sequence has developed its own catch-phrase, 'to boldly go where no man has gone before', which has become part of the series' extensive mythology. In America the first commercial break, the next narrative segment, comes directly after this title sequence.

Even the most 'open' of narratives usually have a start and finish point, even if the structure within the narrative itself is sometimes unclear. A detective or police story that starts with a murder and then recaps the events leading up to it will often start with a title sequence and end with credits. In newspapers the headlines can be seen to encapsulate and mark the start of a particular narrative. The audience is being given a clear marker as to when each narrative is beginning or ending. However, because of the changing social contexts in which we consume media texts, it may be that we are increasingly creating our own narratives, stopping or starting partway through a radio or TV programme, film or magazine or, through the use of the remote control, 'zapping' and 'surfing' from one narrative segment to another, heightening intertextuality and creating our own 'synthesis' of 'hybrid' narrative structures.

Codes of Enigma and Action

There are two key codes involved in the sequencing of narratives, the *action* code and the *enigma* code. *Action* codes are often used as a shorthand for advancing the narrative: Tilley (1991) cites as an example the buckling of a gun-belt in the western as a prelude to the gunfight, or the packing of a suitcase which 'signals' panic or escape in a crime thriller. Other devices can include the starting of a car engine or the whistle of an approaching train. Increasingly television uses 'flashing blue lights' as action codes in a variety of fictional (*The Bill, Casualty, Holby City*) and 'real life' (*Crimewatch, 999, Street Crime UK*) programmes.

The *enigma* code 'explains' the narrative by controlling what, when and how much, information is given to the audience. This code captures the audience's interest and attention by setting up an enigma or problem that is then resolved during the course of the narrative. (Who was the murderer whose hand we saw in the opening sequence? What does 'Rosebud' mean in *Citizen Kane* (Figure 2.17)? Why was the phrase 'In space no one can hear you scream' used to promote the film *Alien*?) Headlines in a newspaper serve the same function of

FIGURE 2.17
Citizen Kane, 1941
Source: Kobal Collection/Mercury

FIGURE 2.18
Where's Lucky? dog adverts
Source: Ogilvy & Mather/Roy Mehta
(photo) and Vicki Maguire (text)

summarising the key elements ('Killer dogs foil cops acid party raid') and making a direct appeal to readers, as do the 'trailers' for films and new television or radio programmes: 'Another chance to catch up with *The Royle Family* on BBC1 tonight at 10.15' or '*Friends* is back in a new and exciting series.'

Advertisements are particularly good at using and compressing these enigma codes. They try to arouse the audience's interest but at the same time want to contain and limit what we know. Look at Figure 2.18 with its narrative enigma 'Where's Lucky?'. At first sight it seems to conform to the conventions of a notice about a missing dog, something that we are familiar with. However, during the summer of 2001 the missing dog notice appeared for several days in national newspapers, on billboards and eventually as a series of radio and television adverts. It quickly became apparent that this was not a notice about a missing dog but some kind of advertising campaign. People who called the number or accessed the website featured in the notice were given details of Battersea Dogs' Home in London.

Eventually it was revealed that the campaign was a form of 'teaser' advertising for a new Internet pet insurance service, similar in many ways to the 'Tell Sid' campaign in 1986 for the sale of shares in British Gas. The aim of the campaign was to get people, mainly ABC1 broadsheet readers, curious about the adverts to start talking to each other about them. It also created considerable publicity when the campaign was revealed as a hoax and later in the year when it was criticised by the Advertising Standards Authority. Members of the public had complained that they thought the campaign would undermine genuine attempts to find lost dogs (you can access a copy of the ASA's adjudication at its website **http://www.asa.org.uk/index**).

Activity 2.11

Consider Figure 2.19. How does the advert attempt to attract the reader's attention? What is the narrative contained in this advert? Is there an enigma? If so, what is it? The advert appears to show someone being 'saved', but what actually is being saved and by whom?

FIGURE 2.19
Source: Reckitt Benckiser

Narrator

It was a dark and stormy night and the captain gathered his men together one by one... 'Tell us a story, Captain,' they said, and so he began... 'It was a dark and stormy night...' and so on and so on.

The meaning of a narrative is often established by means of a narrator – the storyteller – who manages the relationship between the narrative and the audience. The process by which members of an audience align at least some of their own identity with that of the characters in the text and story, putting themselves in the characters' place, is known as *identification*. If the narrative is told in the first person, with 'I' as participant, individual members of the audience are directly drawn into the story and the relationship between the text and the individual may become more subjective as, to varying degrees, they identify with a particular character or performer. Examples include films such as *High Fidelity* and the 'video diaries' genre of television programmes as well as the Raymond Chandler books and films, such as *The Big Sleep* or *Farewell My Lovely*. 'I got up at nine, drank three cups of black coffee, bathed the back of my head with ice-water and read the two morning papers that had been thrown against the apartment door.'

On the other hand, if the narrative is spoken or reported by an observer, commentator or witness, the relationship between text and audience is more detached and objective and, as in news bulletins, documentaries or sports programmes, 'we' the audience are positioned as interested but usually impartial observers: 'Countryside Protesters took to the streets of London again today as...' Sometimes, however, the story is told by a silent, 'invisible' or detached third party represented by just the camera lens as observer. In this case the relationship between text and audience is less clear and each individual has to construct his or her own position or point of view.

The Pleasure of the Text

As audiences become more sophisticated and adept at recognising these codes of enigma and action, we begin to perceive patterns, predict and anticipate developments. There is then a creation of tension in trying to anticipate what is going to happen and then pleasure at predicting the resolution. We, as audiences, like to be able to recognise what is going to happen, the feeling of being 'in the know' that the promise of familiarity brings. It is this familiarity and continuity that for many of us makes narratives likeable, predictable and understandable. We know what is going to happen because it is the convention of this type of narrative or programme to be resolved in a certain way (the policeman gets his villian, the hero and heroine live happily ever after), but we will watch anyway, wanting to confirm our knowingness, our familiarity and understanding of the narrative structure: 'Ah yes! I was right, he is the secret father of her child.'

Part of this pleasure in predicting and recognising what is going to happen lies in an overlap between these fictional narratives and the 'real' narratives of our own lives. In the same way as we recognise our own lives as stories, so we recognise that these fictional stories reflect our own lives (or our projected desires and fantasies), the social world we inhabit and our place in it. The real and the fictional often have common values and attitudes, and perhaps the members of the audience can reflect on their own personal narratives to produce different meanings or different endings.

Equilibrium and Disequilibrium

Many writers have suggested that narratives work by generating a dynamic of equilibrium and disequilibrium. This suggests a model of narrative which starts with a state of equilibrium or 'harmony', where all is well and normal, which is then disrupted, often by an outside influence which causes disequilibrium and tension. For instance, a peaceful American suburban family or community is threatened from outside in many of Steven Spielberg's films (*Close Encounters* (1977), *E.T.* (1982), *Gremlins* (1984), *Back to the Future* (1985), etc) or in David Lynch's *Blue Velvet* (1986), before finally the threat is resolved and replaced by a new equilibrium. In other narratives the disruption may be more violent, as in the *Alien* series, or *Jurassic Park*. Some television programme narratives exist only in a world of apparent disequilibrium (*As Time Goes By*, *The Prisoner* or *The League of Gentlemen*).

The notion of equilibrium highlights questions about the ways narratives can speak ideologically about how social order is represented and how equilibrium functions to effect closure or the final ending within narratives: 'At the end of *The Outlaw Josey Wales* a new community has been created – a sharing and stable community of male and female, young and old, white and red' (Tilley, 1991).

Activity 2.12

Choose three recent films that you know well and analyse the ways in which disequilibrium occurs and is managed within the narrative. Compare the two states of equilibrium, the first at the beginning and the second at the end of the film. How has the equilibrium changed? In what ways has it remained the same? Have the characters' positions, status or relationships to each other altered in any significant way?

Study the two film posters in Figures 3.3 and 3.4, then consider the following questions:

- What visual and written codes are used?
- What information do they provide about the films?
- What other information might you have expected but is missing?
- In what ways do these posters create a sense of enigma?
- How are the film producers trying to create a sense of danger or disequilibrium?
- What genre of film do these belong to?
- What are the generic conventions that are at work in these posters?
- What differing representations of 'aliens' do they present?

This chapter has focused on introducing some of the basic *conventions*, the codes or grammars, of language and sign systems, which help us to construct the meanings of media texts. These provide the 'building blocks' by which certain meanings can be shared, interpreted and understood. They are often explicit but act as hidden or unspoken rules that we learn to accept, apply and recognise. They are part of culture and are therefore culturally specific, but as television and media networks become more available across the world, these conventions appear to be becoming more 'global' and linked to a 'homogenised' television and film culture dominated by American and Western values (see Chapter 8). They are involved in processes both of media production and of media reception and in many cases they are so familiar that they appear to be the only, the 'obvious', or 'natural', way of doing or understanding something.

Activity 2.13

1   Using the McMahon and Quinn categories of codes outlined on pp. 35 and 36, analyse a selection of newspaper front-pages chosen on the same day. Compare and contrast broadsheet and tabloid newspapers to highlight the conventions that are used to make tabloids more popular. (see also Activity 7.6 in Chapter 7).

2   Carry out an analysis of a film of your choice using the idea of binary oppositions and discourses.

Further Reading

Adbusters **www.adbusters.org**

Berger, J. 1972: Ways of Seeing. PENGUIN.

Bignall, J. 2002: Media Semiotics: An Introduction. MANCHESTER UNIVERSITY PRESS.

Casey, B., Casey, N., Calvert, B., French, L., and Lewis, J. 2002: Television Studies. The Key Concepts. ROUTLEDGE.

Chambers, D. 2001: Representing the Family. SAGE.

Dovey, J. 2000: Freakshow: First Person media and Factual television. PLUTO.

Ellis, J. 1992: Visible Fictions: Cinema, Television, Video. ROUTLEDGE.

Fiske, J. 1990: Introduction to Communication Studies. ROUTLEDGE.

Gauntlett, D. (ed). 2000: web.studies rewiring media studies for the digital age. ARNOLD.

Goodman, S. and Graddol, D. 1996: Redesigning English: new texts, new identities. ROUTLEDGE.

Goodwin, A. and Whannel, G. (eds). 1990: Understanding Television. ROUTLEDGE.

Hartley, J. 1982: Understanding News. METHUEN.

Izod, J. 1989: Reading the Screen. LONGMAN.

Kuhn, A. 1995: Family Secrets. Acts of memory and imagination. VERSO.

Kress, G. and Van Leeuwen, T. 2001: Multimodal discourse. The modes and media of contemporary communication. ARNOLD.

McMahon, B. and Quinn, R. 1988: Exploring Images. MACMILLAN.

McMahon, B. and Quinn, R. 1986: Real Images. MACMILLAN.

Morgan, J. and Welton, P. 1992: See What I Mean. EDWARD ARNOLD.

Rayner, P., Wall, P. and Kruger, S. 2001: Media Studies: The essential introduction. ROUTLEDGE.

Said, E. 1991: Orientalism. PEREGRIN BOOKS.

Tolson, A. 1996: Mediations: Text and Discourse in Media Studies. ARNOLD.

Wells, L. (ed). 2000: Photography: A Critical Introduction. ROUTLEDGE.

Williamson, J. 1978: Decoding Advertisements: Ideology and Meaning in Advertisements. BOYARS.

Zelizer, B. and Allan, S. (eds). 2002: Journalism after September 11. ROUTLEDGE.

CHAPTER THREE

Genre, Stars and Celebrities

The last chapter looked at the concepts of media *conventions* and media *narrative* and the ways in which they help and encourage us to construct the meanings of media texts. In this chapter we will consider media genres, in particular as a case-study, science-fiction, as well as looking at the ways in which stars and celebrities perform and operate in and across the media.

Genre

Familiarity through repetition is one of the key elements in the way media audiences understand and relate to media texts:

> *Repetition in the TV narrative occurs at the level of the series: formats are repeated, situations return week after week. Each time there is novelty. The characters of the situation comedy encounter a new dilemma; the documentary reveals a new problem; the news gives us a fresh strike, a new government, another earthquake, the first panda born in captivity ... The series is composed of segments. The recognition of the series format tends to hold segments together and to provide them with an element of continuity and narrative progression from one to the next.*
>
> *Ellis (1992), p. 147*

FIGURE 3.1
Crossfire, 1947
Source: The Kobal Collection/RKO

FIGURE 3.2
Stagecoach, 1939
Source: The Kobal Collection/United Artists

The concept of genre, developed particularly in the study of film and literature, is a way of classifying particular styles or types of media texts by identifying their common elements and distinctive features, the codes and conventions associated with particular genres. These are repeated again and again and over time, often across media, and act as rules used by both producers and audiences to encode and decode certain types of text. These common elements may be related initially to the 'look', style and settings of particular media texts, their *iconography*, for example the western or the *film noir* from Hollywood in the 1930s and 1940s (see Figures 3.1 and 3.2 (Crossfire/Stagecoach)). In films like these, for instance, their genres can be seen through the ways in which they use particular costumes, actors and their styles of performance, the lighting, action and narrative. Genre also allows us to classify other distinctive features associated with particular types of films or other media, including narrative structures, certain directors or actors, and character types. Hollywood western films, for instance, share a number of generic codes including narrative themes ('Indian' uprisings, people being cheated out of their land, prospecting for gold, family feuds), props (guns, horses, stagecoaches, cactus), and settings ('famous' Wild West towns like Tombstone or Dodge City, saloons, prairies, cavalry forts). There are also particular directors (John Ford), actors (John Wayne or Clint Eastwood), character types (the heroic loner or outsider, like Ethan in *The Searchers*), sets and locations (Monument Valley) and even theme music (*The Good, the Bad and the Ugly*). Recent directors associated with re-inventing genres of films include Martin Scorsese and Quentin Tarantino (American gangster films such as *Reservoir Dogs* or *Jackie Brown* and *Taxi Driver* or *Goodfellas*) and Tim Burton (Gothic horror films such as *Edward Scissorhands* and *Sleepy Hollow*).

Genre might also be used to describe modern day 'lads' magazines such as *Loaded, GQ* or *FHM* (see Figure 4.27). In these magazines the notion of genre is most obviously reflected in the similarity of covers, types of stories and features and the stars or celebrities who regularly appear in them. These magazines are targeted at 16–30 year old men, and, according to the *Loaded* website, talk 'in a humorous tone about the edited 'highlights' of a young man's life'. Most magazines aimed at this type of market will include a range of common, regular features. These include sex tips ('Find out what women really want'), pin-ups (recent editions have included photo-features on Jennifer Lopez, Geri Halliwell, Jordan, Natalie Imbruglia, Anna Kournikova, Kylie Minogue and Angelina Jolie), latest movie releases and 'TV happenings' as well as information on sports (particularly certain types of sports, for instance boxing or Formula One motor racing), interviews with particular male celebrities, fashion and the latest technology and gadgets ('The world's hundred best bikes' and 'Everything you need to know to go sub-aqua'). Other features include articles telling men how to buy underwear for women, one hundred sexiest music videos and an article on the world's hundred best beers.

Activity 3.1

Select a range of similar magazines, such as 'lads mags' or magazines aimed at a female readership of a similar age. Is it possible to identify a range of common genre characteristics for these magazines? You could also carry out a small survey amongst readers of these magazines and try to identify what it is that appeals to them about this genre of magazines and if they favour one magazine in particular. How do they think that it is different, or better, than the others? Why do you think magazine publishing companies such as EMAP publish several titles that appear to be in competition with each other?

The concept of genre can, however, be problematic when applied to all media texts because of the range, complexity and constant 'flux' of texts being produced at any one time. Many western films can be seen to encourage a strong ideological message about the triumph of law and order and the 'good guy' but this cannot be said of all westerns, as some, like the spaghetti westerns or films like *Little Big Man* (1970), *The Unforgiven* (1992), or *Dances with Wolves* (1990), appear to be more ambiguous in their ideological message and perhaps attempt to subvert or challenge the genre's traditional appeal. These films could be said to represent a sub-genre of the western as it adjusts to changed social and cultural circumstances.

Television

Different types of genres appeal to different audiences. With television and films this is partly because different types of narrative that are particular to different kinds of genres may be identified by gender characteristics. Fiske (1987) suggests that 'male' narratives tend to have a clearer sense of 'closure', any conflict or disequilibrium is more definitely resolved at the end of each segment, with the 'hero' overcoming the problem, and the status quo being re-established. These fictional narratives are found particularly in police crime or adventure series and can also be seen as integral to factual news bulletins, where order and equilibrium is restored at the end of every programme. Narratives in film genres tend to have a more distinct closure whereas some television genres often try to create some sense of narrative continuity. 'Female' narratives, Geraghty (1991) suggests, tend to be more open-ended, ongoing and not so clearly resolved. These types of narrative can often be found in long-running serials such as soap operas and this may explain why this genre tends to be popular with female audiences (see p. 126).

Television genres, like film genres, have distinctive codes and conventions associated with them. For example, quiz or game shows such as *Family Fortunes* or *Who Wants to be a Millionaire?* belong to a particular broadcast genre, and their common components are likely to include the following:

- a celebrity who hosts the show, often an ex-comedian;
- prizes;
- women as decoration and/or assistants;
- live audiences;
- 'real' people – members of the general public – as competitors;
- a sense of competition;
- excitement, tension and sometimes glamour;
- catch phrases, questions and music.

Activity 3.2

Watch several current quiz shows on television and amend and develop this list of components. Are there other ingredients that should be included? How do quiz shows like *University Challenge* or *The Weakest Link* fit the genre? To what extent do radio quiz shows fit? You can also start to identify other genres of popular television and compare their common characteristics.

For a long time television situation comedy was considered to be a single genre, but it may now be too restricting to cover the wide range and varied output of comedy that appears on television. It is now possible to identify a set of sub-genres of television comedy – alternative, sitcom, American, satire, stand-up – and it becomes difficult to categorise successful programmes like *The Royle Family*, *The Office* or *Marion and Geoff* into one particular generic pigeon-hole. These types of programmes owe their success to defying or reworking genre classification and therefore offer something new. Different production locations may also produce specific characteristics: for instance, British soap operas tend to be described as 'realistic' or 'gritty', whereas American soaps are more escapist, and Australian soaps may seem more idealistic.

The distinction between different television genres is becoming blurred. The apparent recent popularity of 'docu-soaps' may be partly explained by the manner in which they borrow certain conventions from soap operas (continuing story-lines, a sense of emotional involvement with particular characters and the sense of particular communities or individuals under pressure or close scrutiny) that are combined with the conventions of 'fly-on-the-wall' documentaries.

A related genre that has recently become popular is the 'confessional' chat show programme such as *The Oprah Winfrey Show* or *The Vanessa Show*. Dovey (2000) argues that we now live in a mediated confessional society and describes the phenomenon as 'first person media' where subjectivity, the personal and the intimate become prioritised. Examples include the growth of talk shows on television, some confrontational like *Jerry Springer* and *Ricci Lake*, others more gentle in their approach like *Esther* or *Trisha*. The confessional mode has become particularly popular through the range of so called 'reality' television programmes (see p. 109) such as *Video Diaries* and *Video Nation*. Many recent commentators, including Dovey, have suggested that it is regarded as a 'good thing' to disclose personal problems to certain 'significant' others. This used to be done in confidence through the church or family but is now increasingly done publicly on television and radio or in newspapers and magazines.

Activity 3.3

Consider the idea of a confessional society and undertake some research into the range of media opportunities that exist for both celebrities and 'ordinary' people to confess about aspects of their private lives. This may include problem pages in magazines and newspapers and radio phone-ins as well as television programmes. Can you identify any common characteristics about these shows and/or magazines and newspaper articles? Have we become increasingly 'media confessional'? If so, why do you think this is and what are the consequences?

Another recent hybrid television genre has developed around programmes like *Popstars* and *Soapstars* or *Big Brother* and *Survivor* where 'ordinary people' (people like us?) are placed in situations where they are in competition with each other – a mixture of quizshow (there can only be one winner), soap opera (we eavesdrop on how they cope with the stress and relationships of the situation) and documentary (there is supposed to be something educative, therapeutic or informative about these programmes.

In films and television some genres move in and out of fashion; for instance, until relatively recently, the western had been described as being dead; some years ago disaster movies were popular, and in the late 1990s there was a vogue for horror movies like *Scream*, and *The Blair Witch Project* and 'gross-out' teen comedies such as *American Pie, Kevin and Perry Go Large* or *Road Trip*. On television there has been a recent vogue for 'make-over' programmes such as *Changing Rooms, Home Front, Ground Force* and *Looking Good* that focus on home improvements as well as programmes like *BeachMate, StreetMate, Perfect Partners* or *Would like to Meet* that offer to 'match' partners.

Activity 3.4

Look through the television schedules and list the 'make-over' and lifestyle programmes broadcast in a typical week. In what ways can they be said to constitute a genre? Categorise the programmes in terms of what it is that is being made-over, to what extent can each of these categories be considered a sub-genre? Why do you think there are currently so many of these types of programmes on television? To what extent do these programmes and their presenters appear in other media forms?

It should be noted that genre is not just a static way of categorising 'types' of films or television programmes but that the notion of genre is important to both audiences and producers. Audiences are said to like the idea of genre (although they may not identify it by that term) because of the reassuring and familiar promise of patterns of repetition and variation. They know what to expect: if they enjoyed the first *Scream* film they will most probably enjoy *Scream 2*, *Scream 3* and so on. (See Chapter 6 for discussion of sequels.) Producers are said to use genres because they hope to exploit a winning formula and minimise risks. The concept of genre also helps institutions budget and plan their finances more accurately. It is important to note, however, that the formula approach may not always work; for example, *Scary Movie 2* was not as successful as *Scary Movie 1*, and most genres evolve and change over time.

The concept of genre is now widely used, both as a way of categorising forms of media production and output, from women's magazines to television quiz shows, and to explain how we, the audience, make sense of the 'flow' of media output by identifying and 'organising' certain types of television programme within an evening's viewing, or certain features within a daily newspaper or weekly magazine. The concept allows us to identify certain landmarks on the map of the media's total 'flow' in the same way as we go to different sections of a website, library or music shop.

It has been suggested that the dominance of genre, particularly in television, has had several consequences, one of which is to marginalise those programmes that do not easily fit into generic conventions, because it is argued that audiences will not recognise or accept them. Although this is true to some extent, there are instances where genres have been challenged or subverted: for instance, in television series such as *The Ali G Show* and *Twin Peaks* or the films *Pulp Fiction*, *Scary Movie* and *The Rocky Horror Picture Show*. In many cases the popularity of these texts is precisely because the genre conventions and characteristics have been deliberately parodied or mixed and made hybrid. This 'hybridity' could be seen as a consequence of the increasingly post-modern nature of film and television (see Chapter 1).

The other consequence relates to the power of generic structures, which can be ideologically limiting and in which the form can dominate over content. Traditionally western films required a 'happy ending' where the 'hero' succeeds in restoring order, defeating evil and is rewarded with a prize (often the heroine) and perhaps land and/or money (see section on narrative structure in Chapter 2). In police series such as *The Bill*, *Frost* or *Midsummer Murders* we are conventionally placed on the side of the police, who are the familiar characters that we are encouraged to identify with. In sitcom there is a need to maintain the status quo so that this original situation can be used again. This may mean that although an interesting problem might be set up, such as that of the mother's personal fulfilment and satisfaction in *2.4 Children* or Tom and Linda's lack of success in finding suitable partners in *Gimme, Gimme, Gimme*, it can never actually be resolved or allow for any real progression, because that would destroy the generic formula that has made the programme successful. In the case of Victor Meldrew from *One Foot in the Grave* the character had to be killed off for the series to finally resolve itself.

FROM OUT OF SPACE.... A WARNING AND AN ULTIMATUM!

THE DAY THE EARTH STOOD STILL

MICHAEL RENNIE   PATRICIA NEAL   HUGH MARLOWE

FIGURE 3.3
The Day The Earth Stood Still, 1951
Source: The Kobal
Collection/Twentieth Century Fox

2010
THE YEAR WE MAKE CONTACT

FIGURE 3.4
2010: The Year We
Make Contact, 1984
Source: The Kobal
Collection/MGM

Science Fiction

This section offers a brief analysis of a selected genre and some of its predominant conventions: science fiction.

Science fiction has been a popular film genre since Georges Méliès's 1902 film *Le Voyage dans la Lune*. Science fiction films often have strong *ideological* messages and *representations* (see Chapter 4) that reflect the concerns of the society at the time of their production and usually centre around some notion of 'conflict' between 'us' and 'them' and the positive or negative aspects of science and the future. Fritz Lang's *Metropolis* (1927) reflected concerns about 'new technology' and the dehumanising and exploitative potential of the new 'machine age', as well as featuring much of the genre's *iconography* (mad scientists and evil robots). Many of the science fiction films made in America during the 1950s – *It Came from Beneath the Sea* (1955), *The Invasion of the Body Snatchers* (1956) and *The Beast from 20,000 Fathoms* (1953) – featured invasion by aliens and are said to reflect America's anxieties about communist spies, the Cold War with the USSR and the danger of nuclear annihilation. *Barbarella*, in contrast, made in 1967, offered a more positive reflection of the values and interests of the 'swinging sixties'.

FIGURE 3.5
The War of the Worlds, 1953
Source: The Kobal Collection/Paramount

FIGURE 3.6
Close Encounters of the Third Kind, 1977
Source: The Kobal Collection/Columbia

The recent growth of the Internet and the advances in computer networks and telecommunications technology have been influential on recent science fiction films. Not only has the digital technology produced increasingly sophisticated and visual special effects, there has also been a continuing preoccupation with the relationships between humans and technology. Recent films such as *Johnny Mnemonic* (1995), *The Matrix* (1999), *AI* (2001), *Bicentennial Man* (2001) and *X-Men* (2002) all explore in various ways the theme of cyborgs and questions surrounding the effects of combining human intelligence with the new 'frontiers' of virtual reality and cyberspace.

According to Kennedy (2001), both *Blade Runner* and *The Matrix* offer post-modernist views of the world where the distinction between the real and representations of the real, the 'virtual', are blurred. Both films can perhaps also be seen to refer back to some of the original concerns of Mary Shelley's book *Frankenstein*, first published in 1817, in the way in which they both question the role of man in a new scientific age and the dangers of man acting as god. Part of the success of the film *The Matrix* may also be due to the way in which it combines elements from science fiction, martial arts and action-movie genres as well as featuring a strong female lead, Carrie Ann Moss as Trinity (see Figure 4.23, p. 90), and the way in which it draws upon cyberpunk culture and style.

Activity 3.5

Carry out a comparison between the women heroes in science-fiction films such as *Barbarella*, *Alien*, *Terminator*, *The Matrix* and *Tomb Raider*. Identify what characteristics they have in common and account for any differences between the characters. To what extent can these films and their heroines be considered to belong to one common genre called 'science fiction'?

One of the key films of the modern science fiction genre is *2001: A Space Odyssey* (1968), which combines optimism and spiritual development with exploration of new worlds. The film also set the standard for the iconography of the 1980s and 1990s science fiction films with its emphasis on the new technologies of spacecrafts, 'dangerous' computers with minds of their own and the use of music and image to create a sense of space and grandeur. Many of these conventions were used in the *Star Wars* films (1977 onwards), which were seen by many writers as the traditional western narrative relocated to outer space with state-of-the-art special effects added (see Nelmes, 1999). In the 1980s, dystopias, the opposite of the utopian 'perfect' or idealised societies, were common, with *Bladerunner* (1982), *Brazil* (1985) and the various *Robocop/Terminator* films. In the late 1990s, the science fiction genre seems to have become popular again with 'alien invasion' type films like *Independence Day* (1996) and *Men in Black* (2001) or the spoof *Mars Attacks!* (1997) and the continued popularity of the *Star Trek* series that ironically refers back to an earlier television version of the future as well as reinforcing a particular and pro-American ideological message (see also Ideology, Myth and Hollywood Cinema in Chapter 4).

FIGURES 3.7a and 3.7b
Star Trek
Source: The Kobal Collection/ Paramount

Activity 3.6

The *Star Trek* films and television series are part of a large multimedia merchandising industry. Identify the range of Star Trek merchandising (products and services) that is available. This may include books, audio cassettes, clothing, conventions and websites as well as films and videos.

- What particular aspects of *Star Trek* are most commonly used in the merchandising campaigns?
- Are there any images that are significantly more dominant than others?
- Are there any images closely associated with *Star Trek* that do not appear at all (the Klingons)?
- To whom is most of this multimedia merchandising addressed?
- Does this activity significantly increase at any particular time of the year (e.g. around Christmas)?
- Can you identify any other recent examples of merchandising based on the success of film or television genres (for instance, *The Lord of the Rings*, *Monsters Inc*, *Harry Potter*, etc)?

When we try to define the genre of science fiction we can start to see the limitations of the concept. If it is to include all those films that have what one commentator has called 'the fictitious use of science' in them we should include films like *Frankenstein* which, it could be argued, should belong to the horror genre. If we limit the definition we may exclude films like *Westworld* or *The War Game*, both of which also employ 'the fictitious use of science'. Blandford, Grant and Hillier (2001) suggest that the genre is composed of a series of sub-genres: Monster films such as *The Beast from 20,000 Fathoms* (1953) and *Godzilla* (2000); Action films such as *Mad Max* (1979 onwards), *Total Recall* (1990) or *Minority Report* (2002); and Apocalyptic films such as *Armageddon* (2000) that are founded on the promise of scenes of mass destruction. Although general definition of the science fiction genre is difficult, it is true to say that there are a number of films that contain certain sets of conventions – narrative structures, character types, gender roles, decor and setting, specific directors and even titles (consider *Star Wars, Starman, Star Trek, Stargate, Star Crash, The Last Starfighter*) – that we would recognise as belonging to a broad generic type and tradition of film.

There is often a complex relationship between different categories of genre and the stars and celebrities that are associated with them, for example Arnold Schwarzenegger and Bruce Willis have been associated with 'action' films, John Thaw with particular categories of television drama and Davina McCall with more popular 'reality' television shows such as *Big Brother* and *StreetMate*.

Film Stars

According to the Motion Picture Association of America the average cost of producing a Hollywood studio film in 2000 was $54.8 million. A substantial proportion of this sum goes towards paying top Hollywood stars to appear in the films. George Clooney or Tom Cruise can receive up to $25 millon per film. Julia Roberts received $20 million for the 1997 film *My Best Friend's Wedding* out of a total $73 million that the film cost to make. Most of these 'A' list stars will also be entitled to a percentage of the gross take.

The idea of film stars developed in the early years of the Hollywood film industry when the studio system was taking shape. The stars were seen by the studio heads as a means of marketing and gaining audiences for their films. Among the first stars were Charlie Chaplin, Mary Pickford and Douglas Fairbanks. As these and other new stars began to develop a following amongst the cinema-going public so the studios started to manipulate this loyalty by using stories in the popular press. The studio marketing and publicity departments began to see the stars as commodities and sell them like the films themselves.

Like genres, stars can be seen as part of the culturally variable set of expectations, orientations and values which circulate between media producers and consumers and they act as key signifiers. Like genre, part of the appeal of stars is their familiarity and repetition. Often this sense of familiarity is to do with the stars themselves, their 'real' and/or 'perceived' personage and the characters that they play. The notion of 'stars' enables film studios to promote and market their films as 'star-vehicles'. This is attractive to the film studios as it means that they are taking less of a financial risk with an unknown commodity – a new film release – if it can be tied to an existing performer or product that has proven financial success – the star or stars. A similar pattern is beginning to emerge in television where stars like David Jason or Ross Kemp are signed up to television companies and required to appear in a certain number of television series that are created primarily as vehicles for that star.

Tolson (1996) suggests that stardom is similar to genre, in that they are both an institutionalised form of reference. Stardom, however, is reinforced by a publicity machine and by public commentary and gossip, which inform our concept of particular stars and our reading of media texts.

> We read media texts through their signs, structures and modes of address, and through our mobilisation of a general knowledge of genres. But that reading is predicated on the possibility that, at least some of the time, these texts will have a cultural importance, a human significance, which the presence of a star can reaffirm.
>
> Tolson, p. 125

In other words the star is the physical manifestation of a set of values or debates that the text's character embodies. In their star images Bruce Willis or Julia Roberts, for instance, confirm the human significance of the characters that they have played in their films, from *Die Hard* to *Erin Brockovich*.

There are various elements in the construction of a star's persona:

First, what Christine Gledhill (1991) has called the 'real person' such as, for example, Sean Connery or Marilyn Monroe. This, however, in itself can be problematic because both Sean Connery and Marilyn Monroe changed their names, he dropping his first name (Thomas) and she changing her name completely from Norma Jean Baker. One of the most famous cases is probably John Wayne who was originally called Marion Morrison. There are many other examples like this, including Sylvester Stallone and Bruce Willis. Between the real person and the star persona is an artificial construction and a career in the film industry.

Second, there is the screen presence based on the characters or roles that the star may play and develop in a career in films. This is often linked to particular stereotype or genre, for example the Action Hero played by stars like Bruce Willis or Sylvester Stallone in a particular genre of films, the 'screwball' comedy of Jim Carrey or Goldie Hawn or the New York gangster/policeman roles of actors like Al Pacino and Robert de Niro.

Activity 3.7

Consider a star such as Tom Hanks and the films that he has appeared in (*Forrest Gump, Castaway, Saving Private Ryan*). To what extent do these films conform to some kind of stereotype or genre? If this exists to what extent is it responsible for the popularity and success of Tom Hanks? How do films such as *Philadelphia* or *Road to Perdition* fit with this image of Tom Hanks?

Third, there is the star's public persona or image which may vary between positive, carefully managed appearances as well as articles in gossip columns and appearances on television chat shows, and on the other hand negative aspects, particularly in their non-film activities such as personal relationships, addictions and deaths. This is what Ellis (1992) calls the 'subsidiary forms of circulation' which serve to maintain the hype surrounding the activities of stars. Gledhill suggests that this is always a mixture of public and private, drawing on the 'fiction' of the film roles and the 'authenticity' of the real person. Dyer (1998) suggests that this enables audiences to gain access to the inner thoughts and persona of stars. Dyer used the term 'rhetoric of authenticity' when talking about Judy Garland, to describe the ways in which her singing and acting 'personas' were seen by fans to reveal elements of her 'real person', the neurotic, insecure personality.

Activity 3.8

Think about the films that you have recently seen and the star actors that have appeared in them. What is it about these actors that make them 'stars'? How are they different to the other actors that appear in the same films? How do you define a 'star'? What is it that is special about an actor that makes them a 'star'? Is there still a 'star system'? If so why is it called a system? How are stars different from media presenters or celebrities?

Marriages and relationships are a particularly important part of the star's subsidiary form of circulation and are the focus of much 'celebrity' gossip, for example the marriage of Tom Cruise and Nicole Kidman and its subsequent break-up. The publicity surrounding the courtship and marriage of Michael Douglas and Catherine Zeta Jones in 2000 helped to reinforce both their individual personas as well as presenting them as a glamorous, happily-married Hollywood couple. They were paid £1 million by *OK!* magazine for its exclusive use of their wedding photographs. Increasingly stars like Michael Douglas and Catherine Zeta Jones are using the Internet as a means of promoting themselves and their latest films as well as reinforcing their personal personas and leaving messages for their fans. (See Figure 3.8).

All of these elements are artificial constructs but the second and third personas are often deliberately created by the studios or the stars' publicists and attempt to create a sense in the audience's mind that all three are entwined. In the same way that genre familiarity can help to shape particular media text, so the overall star persona can influence the manner in which media texts are produced and interpreted by audiences.

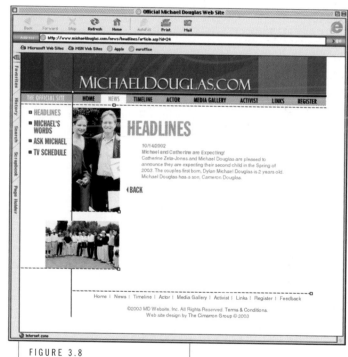

FIGURE 3.8
www.michaeldouglas.com website
Source: © michaeldouglas.com

Tolson uses the example of Sylvester Stallone and the *Rambo/Rocky* films and suggests that these became a metaphor for a certain type of masculinity in the 1980s – part of a debate about what it means to be a man in contemporary society. Stallone became the public embodiment of the ideals and values that his fictionalised characters (both on and off the screen) portrayed. Stallone as Rambo/Rocky became seen as an icon of contemporary masculinity, particularly a right-wing, anti-Communist pro-Ronald Reagan, muscular masculinity that surfaced at a time when there was a backlash against the perceived advance of liberal, feminist politics.

Activity 3.9

Is it possible to identify a similar dominant personification of 'masculinity' today? Is there a more contemporary example of the Stallone character? Or is there a different kind of masculinity in circulation today, such as that portrayed by actors like Hugh Grant? Which is the more popular? Why?

Like Stallone, Arnold Schwarzenegger has tried to move away from a particular type of character in his early films such as *Conan the Barbarian* (1982), *Conan the Destroyer* (1984), *Commando* (1986), *Predator* (1987) and the *Terminator* films (1984 onwards) to less stereotyped roles in films such as *Twins* (1988), *Kindergarten Cop* (1990) and *Junior* (1994). However, for both Stallone and Schwarzenegger, these early characters are still an important part of the way audiences view them and are still part of their public appeal and image. According to Dyer (1998), one of the key characteristics of the successful star is consistency of image, in which despite appearing in different films playing different people, or 'deepening' the characters that they play, they stay broadly the same in order to enhance recognition and identification. It might be suggested that one of the reasons for the decline of Sylvester Stallone as an 'A' list Hollywood actor is that the types of characters that he has played in his more recent films, attempting to move away from his earlier character type, contradict the audience's perception of him as a star. A star who seems to have successfully shifted her image is Julia Roberts. She seems to have moved from the 'sex symbol' type of characters portrayed in early films such as *Pretty Woman* (1990) and *Sleeping with the Enemy* (1991) to a more mature character with a social conscience, particularly in the film *Erin Brockovich* (2000) for which Roberts won an Oscar, and this has been developed in her recent nature documentaries on Mongolia and Borneo for American network television.

Stars like Sylvester Stallone and Julia Roberts, as well as other contemporary stars like Tom Cruise, Brad Pitt, George Clooney and Nicole Kidman, can all be seen as examples of what Tolson calls 'iconic stars': modern secular versions of the religious images that the term 'icon' is derived from. Films stars, particularly those from Hollywood, can often be seen as awesome or superhuman in the sense that they embody power. They come to be physical manifestations of central values and become recognisable around the world. Dyer (1998) suggests these 'maximised' types, like John Wayne the cowboy western star *par excellence*, epitomise a certain set of values and particular ideological preoccupations.

Michael Douglas has played a series of characters in films like *Wall Street* (1987), *Fatal Attraction* (1987), *Basic Instinct* (1992), *Disclosure* (1994) and *Falling Down* (1993) which all seem to contain undertones of a certain kind of political resentment. As an actor, however, Douglas is perhaps more ambiguous. On the surface he can also appear to be an icon of free market capitalism (for example the catch-phrase 'Greed is Good' from *Wall Street*) and it is not clear the extent to which we are supposed to sympathise with the characters he plays in some films. For instance, in *Falling Down* the hero is driven over the edge of mental stability by the pressures of modern life. His actions may be secretly desirable to some but the film is not a total endorsement of mindless vigilantism.

The young actor Sean Connery was a vital factor in the success of the original *James Bond* films. As part of the marketing of films like *Dr No* (1962) and *From Russia with Love* (1963), the producers tried to blur the distinction between Bond the fictional character and Connery who played the character in these films. The posters for the film *You Only Live Twice* (1967) proclaimed 'Sean Connery **IS** James Bond'.

The *Bond* films have become a metaphor for a set of values embodied and made real by the actors who have played the lead role. Pierce Brosnan and Sean Connery have successfully taken on the celebrity of the James Bond character and this has been reinforced in their public activities outside of the films: Connery's accent, his romances, his unconventionality and ruggedness all blurred the distinction between the character he played and the actor as a person. At the same time the character of James Bond was shaped by Sean Connery and became a specific construct at a particular time. Bennett and Woollacott (1987) suggest the Connery screen version of Bond significantly differs from the version of Bond originally written by Ian Fleming as a member of the establishment, public school and, like Fleming, an Eton educated schoolboy. It could be argued that the relative failure of other actors such as Timothy Dalton and George Lazenby to emulate Sean Connery's success with the James Bond character is in part due to their failure to marry up their own star personalities with that of the character of James Bond. Roger Moore's portrayal of James Bond seemed more ironic and ambiguous and it is difficult to judge the success or otherwise of his interpretation of the James Bond character.

Activity 3.10

The list of stars used above is predominantly male. Consider female stars who have created strong public personas; Madonna might for example be a good case-study especially as she crosses from both cinema and popular music. Others to consider might include Nicole Kidman, Demi Moore, Katherine Turner or Sigourney Weaver.

The list is also predominantly white. Is it possible to create a similar list of black film stars? If not, why not?

Film stars are complex signs whose significance is created partly by themselves acting out their personas, by taking on particular fictional roles, but also by their studios and publicists who promote their 'real', non-screen persona, by the popular press and by the audiences who buy into and use them for their own entertainment and pleasure.

Part of their fascination especially mediated in popular news concerns the contradictory elements in these multiple 'personas'. Stars appear to be 'ordinary people made strangely important'. For audiences, stars act as points of identification and as a result are invested with strong cultural significance. Like Kate Blanchett or Leonardo DiCaprio they may signify particular lifestyles or subcultures and attract forms of identification that may be less to do with a particular role they may have played but that result from the combination of their public, private and 'filmic' personas.

For audiences this implies that the meaning and value of a particular film is heavily related to the particular stars that appear in it. This is part of the 'knowledge' that audiences bring to films and that is exploited through the way in which films are marketed and appeal to them.

Activity 3.11

Select two male and two female stars from the list on p. 82, and, with the help of some background research, try to identify what individual qualities may have contributed to their box-office appeal. You will need to consider the kind of image and appeal produced by a combination of personal characteristics, on-screen performances and general publicity.

Stars and stardom are generally associated with cinema and in particular the Hollywood studios; however, we can also apply similar notions of stardom to pop music stars like Madonna or sports stars like David Beckham, Steffi Graf or Mike Tyson.

When the cinema was the dominant form of entertainment for the majority of people, film stars were seen as somehow 'special', larger than life, as people who transcended the ordinary, the everyday. Such escapism was a key ingredient in the success of the Hollywood studio system during the 1930s and 1940s. As television has become increasingly dominant so the emphasis has shifted onto 'ordinary people' and daily domestic life (see the section on Public Service Broadcasting, Chapter 7). This is partly evidenced in the popularity of soap opera stars, situation comedy performers and chat shows that show 'the human side' of super stars. Increasingly, however, on television, instead of stars appearing on chat shows like *Parkinson* or *So Graham Norton* in an attempt to show how 'ordinary', just like you and I they are, ordinary people are appearing in television programmes like *Big Brother* or *Pop Idol* in an attempt to become stars and celebrities themselves.

Television Celebrities

There has been a considerable increase in the cult of the celebrity in recent years. There are several possible reasons for this: the television celebrity can be seen as an alternative to the more distant and unapproachable film star; the increasing competition amongst an expanding market of television and radio stations, magazines and websites for readers and viewers; the cultural shift away from the dominance of the cinema to a more intimate and domestic television culture that requires a more approachable persona than that offered by the cinema star; and the public's increasing desire for publicity and the apparent trappings of 'fame and fortune'.

As we have seen, the star has often been a remote, iconic figure whose signification is complex and this can represent a range of wide, and sometimes controversial, issues. The celebrity, however, is usually 'safer', more intimate and reassuring and often presented as 'someone like us' with whom we can identify. This is often done by emphasising the celebrity's humble origins or upbringing. We are also often made to feel that somehow we are getting to know the 'real' person behind the celebrity. We may be told apparently intimate details of their life and upbringing in an interview or the celebrity may reveal a 'secret' sorrow or regret.

There are some other differences that we can identify between the concept of the Star and the Celebrity:

STARS	CELEBRITIES
Cinema	Television and other popular media
Distant	Familiar
Extraordinary	Ordinary
Enigmatic	Down to earth
Artificial (rags to riches)	Natural (Being themselves)
Iconic	Mediates/Interprets/Commentates/Comperes
Sporadic appearances	Frequent/regular
Indirect Mode of address	Direct Mode of Address
Recorded	Spontaneous

CHANGING ROOMS' HANDY ANDY KANE
LET'S US HAVE A PEEK AT HIS OWN HOME FOR A
CHANGE AS HE PRESENTS THIRD DAUGHTER OLIVIA

FIGURE 3.9
'Handy' Andy Kane
Source: Hello

There are, however, also some similarities between film stars and television celebrities. Both are constructed images and, like stars, celebrities have to find a balance between being 'ordinary' and being 'extraordinary'. In the case of the celebrity, the greater emphasis is perhaps placed on being more 'ordinary' (like you and I) whilst at the same time recognising that they are 'extraordinary' because they have after all managed to 'make it' – and are to a certain extent living out our fantasies. We perhaps imagine that like Will or Kate, we too could have won *Pop Idol* or *Big Brother* and move in a world of nightclubs, expensive restaurants and beautiful people or, like 'Handy' Andy Kane from *Changing Rooms*, could be paid to have our family featured in *Hello!* (see Figure 3.9)

Like film stars, television celebrities too have a 'subsidiary form of circulation' of their personas, often through tabloid newspapers or celebrity magazines like *Heat, Now, Closer, Hello!* and *OK!* that report on their relationships, marriages, socialising or businesses. Lacking the weight of acting roles or blockbuster films, television celebrities have in some way a much greater element of this 'subsidiary form of circulation' as it is this 'famous for being famous' that for many eventually enables them to become hosts of television or radio shows and gain appearances on television shows like *Celebrity Squares, Celebrity Ready, Steady, Cook, Celebrity Big Brother* or *The Celebrity Weakest Link*.

There is often a strong relationship between particular celebrities, the tabloid press and celebrity magazines. Richard Desmond, owner of United Newspaper titles such as *The Express* and the *Daily Star,* also purchased *OK!* so that he could cross-promote stories. *Heat* magazine in March 2002 ran a cover story about *Pop Idol* Will's 'secret past'. Newspapers like *The Sun, Mirror* and the *Daily Star* attempt to use celebrities to sell their newspapers but are also instrumental in making particular people celebrities in the first place. Tabloid newspapers, for example, were partially responsible for making the first series of *Big Brother* so popular. They helped create celebrities out of all the *Big Brother* housemates. Pictures were found from their pasts, such as the one depicting a nude Craig on holiday (front page of the *Daily Star* 13 September 2000) in order to give their own spin to the fuel crisis: 'TV Craig shows there's no shortage at his pump'. It is alleged that stories were created where none existed: 'Anna Begs Mel for Gay Sex' (front page of the *Daily Star* 8 September 2000). Because the contestants were all young and attractive, celebrity status came in the form of contracts for modelling (Tom), publishing (Sada), recording (Nichola) and presenting (Andy). It will be interesting to monitor the success (or otherwise) of other *Big Brother* housemates and of Will and Gareth after all the publicity they received during the final of *Pop Idol* in 2002.

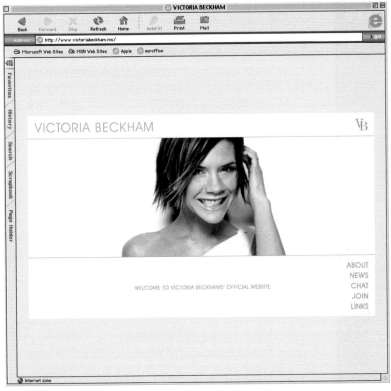

FIGURE 3.10
www.victoriabeckham.mu
Source: victoriabeckham.mu

The docu-soap *Driving School* made Maureen a well-known character and Emma from *Lakesiders* eventually got a recording contract as a result of her appearances in the show as well as appearances on various programmes such as *Celebrity Ready, Steady, Cook.* Although they both became very well-known personalities after the shows were broadcast it would be interesting to know whether their fame and success has continued. In contrast the appearance of Tony Blackburn in the 2002 series of *I'm a Celebrity – Get me out of Here!* is seen to have boosted his flagging career.

Some celebrities become well-known in areas outside of the media but then increasingly use the media as a means of developing their celebrity status. Victoria and David Beckham have increasingly become media celebrities as 'Posh'n'Becks' and, in a manner similar to Michael Douglas and Catherine Zeta Jones, promote themselves as a successful, glamorous (and ideal?) family; their children too seem to have celebrity status. As a famous footballer David Beckham still has a status and separate identity outside of their media activities but Victoria Beckham, who became famous through the Spice Girls, has undertaken various media roles since the popularity of the Spice Girls waned. She has had her own television programmes (interviewing celebrities), been a model and has also written her autobiography. They both regularly appear in the media either as stars on shows like *So Graham Norton* (where celebrities are paid to appear) or through other activities such as David Beckham's range of children's clothing for Marks and Spencer.

Activity 3.12

Select a current television celebrity and try to monitor their appearances in the media. Consider how many of these appearances are either self-promotion activities or appearances purely based on being famous. How often does the celebrity actually do something talented or creative? Suggest reasons as to why this particular celebrity is popular at this particular time.

Being a celebrity clearly has many advantages. The former MP Neil Hamilton and his wife Christine have appeared on *Have I Got News For You* and had a documentary made about them by Louis Theroux. They charge around £3,000 for each of their appearances on daytime television shows and for a while Christine had her own daytime satellite television show before appearing in *I'm a Celebrity – Get me out of Here!* However, part of what makes these people attractive to the audiences is the fact that we feel that we know all about them; they often become public property and this can have its disadvantages. Part of the attraction of celebrities is to see how 'ordinary people' cope with their fame, money and being in the public eye. Paula Yates often seemed to enjoy living her life in public but there were occasions when she wanted privacy. Barry George, the convicted murderer of Jill Dando was, it was claimed, 'obsessed with fame'.

Rojek (2001) suggests that the cult of celebrity highlights the 'gap between the theory and practice of democracy'; in theory we are all equal citizens and potentially can all become wealthy and famous whereas in fact only a few actually manage it. Those that do become celebrities, Rojek argues, act as a kind of compensation, a consoling myth, for those of us, the majority, who miss out on the trappings of fame. This is partly why celebrities need to be seen as ordinary people, so that the myth can continue. It could be said that it is a similar myth of 'fame and fortune' that underpins many people's fantasies about winning the National Lottery. This emphasis on celebrity also means, according to Rojek, that the realities of social and economic inequality in society remain hidden and ignored.

As the range of television channels available to us increase so television companies are increasingly looking for personalities to populate the airwaves, introduce and appear in television programmes and to draw loyal audiences. Television celebrities, like film stars, offer a set of expectations and values that circulate between producers and consumers and act as signifiers. For an audience, the appeal of these signifiers is, as with genre, through their familiarity and repetition that in turn offer signposts towards particular textual readings.

In the next chapter we look at both the content and the connotations of media texts, focusing in particular on the ideological messages they represent to us about the world.

Further activities

Look at some recent films and try to categorise them into genres by looking for their common, basic ingredients. What story types do these films have? What sorts of character do they have? What actors and actresses are particularly associated with them? Are there particularly distinctive sets, lighting or other 'production values' associated with them? How do they offer something new within the requirements of the genre? Are there current films that replicate the features of the earlier western genre? Compare a recent western film with one made at an earlier point in the century.

Select a television or film genre, such as *film noir*, and list its distinctive characteristics. Choose one particular film and analyse it in detail: how does it 'fit' into a particular genre; does it try to break the rules of the genre in any way?

Consider the extent to which the concept of 'genre' is useful in analysing and categorising media texts.

Summarise the ways in which the idea of genre might be helpful for media producers and for media audiences.

Further Reading

Bennett, T. and Woollacott, J. 1987: Bond and Beyond: the Political Career of a Popular Hero. MACMILLAN.

Blandford, S., Grant, B.K. and Hillier, J. 2001: The Film Studies Dictionary. ARNOLD.

Casey, B., Casey, N., Calvert, B., French, L. and Lewis, J. 2002: Television Studies. The Key Concepts. ROUTLEDGE.

Clute, J. and Nicholls, P. (eds). 1993: The Encyclopedia of Science Fiction. ORBIT.

Creeber, G., (ed). 2001: The Television Genre Book. BFI.

Dyer, R. 1986: Heavenly Bodies: Film Stars and Society. MACMILLAN.

Ellis, J. 1992: Visible Fictions: Cinema, Television, Radio. ROUTLEDGE.

Fiske, J. 1987: Television Culture. ROUTLEDGE.

Geraghty, C. 1991: Women and Soap Opera. A Study of Prime-time Soaps. POLITY PRESS.

Hunter, I. (ed). 1999: British Science Fiction Cinema. ROUTLEDGE.

Izod, J. 1989: Reading the Screen. LONGMAN.

James, E. 1994: Science Fiction in the 20th Century. OXFORD UNIVERSITY PRESS.

Kennedy, H. 2001: Introduction to The Matrix. University of Gloucestershire (unpublished).

Monaco, J. 1977: How to Read a Film: The Art, Technology, Language, History and Theory of Film and Media. OXFORD UNIVERSITY PRESS.

Neale, S. 1999: Genre and Hollywood. ROUTLEDGE.

Nelmes, J. (ed). 1999: An Introduction to Film Studies. ROUTLEDGE.

Rojek, C. 2001: Celebrity. REAKTION BOOKS.

Shippey, T. (ed). 1991: Fictional Space: Essays on Contemporary Science Fiction. OXFORD UNIVERSITY PRESS.

Tolson, A. 1996: Mediations: Text and Discourse in Media Studies. ARNOLD.

CHAPTER FOUR

REPRESENT- ATIONS AND REALISM

The concept of representation embodies the theme that the media construct meanings about the world – they represent it, and in doing so, help audiences to make sense of it in particular ways. For representation to be meaningful to audiences, there needs to be a shared recognition of people, situations, ideas and values. What require closer examination are the ideas and meanings produced by those representations. There may be shared recognition of the world as represented through familiar or *dominant* images and ideas, but there is sometimes little social consensus about how to interpret those representations, and always the possibility of *alternative* representations.

What kinds of media representation are more typical, and what explanations might be made to account for such patterns? Given that society is increasingly pluralistic in terms of the variety of social groups, interests and perspectives, emphasis will be given to key social identities such as gender and ethnicity, and also problems of achieving political unity.

Whose Representations?

Before considering what kinds of representation appear in the media, it needs to be made clear that any examination cannot be entirely innocent. Academic approaches to the study of human culture either start or end with broad explanatory models, or theories, which are used to make sense of all the information gathered in the course of research (see Chapter 10). Media studies embraces a number of such theoretical frameworks which have been applied over the years, not least in the analysis of media texts and representations. Here we first provide a brief outline of one model which has been influential in the analysis of media content. There is a fuller discussion of the key determinants of media output in Chapter 6 on institutions.

Hegemony

The underlying assumption of those subscribing to a hegemonic view of society is that there are fundamental inequalities in power between social groups. Those groups with most power are, in the main, able to exercise their influence culturally rather than by force. The concept has its origins in Marxist theory, where writers have attempted to explain how the ruling capitalist class has been able to protect their economic interests. According to this theory, hegemony refers to the winning of popular consent through everyday cultural life, including media representations of the world, as well as other social institutions, such as education and the family. To understand how hegemony may be achieved, it is necessary to consider the concept of ideology.

69

Ideology

Ideology is a complex concept but, broadly speaking, refers to a set of ideas which produce a partial and selective view of reality. This in turn serves the interests of those with power in society. It has its roots in the nineteenth-century writings of Karl Marx, who argued that the property-owning classes were able to rule by ideas which represented as natural the class relationships of production, therefore justifying their own wealth and privilege. These ideas could be found in all areas of social knowledge, such as religion: for example, the notion that it is 'God's will' that some are born rich and that the poor will be rewarded in the next life. Thus the notion of ideology entails widely held ideas or beliefs, which may often be seen as 'common sense', *legitimising* or making widely acceptable certain forms of social inequality. In doing so, ideologies are able to disguise or suppress the real structure of domination and exploitation which exists in society.

Modern writers (Marxist and others) have adapted and developed this idea so that all belief systems or world views are thought to be ideological. Although some ideas and beliefs seem more 'natural' or 'truthful', there is no absolute truth against which to measure the accuracy of representations. What interests those who analyse media representations is whose ideological perspective is privileged and how. This raises the issue of power inequalities. While Marxists have emphasised social class differences, others have increasingly pointed to gender and racial inequalities. What is agreed is that popular culture, especially media output, is the site of a constant struggle over the production of meaning. The media's role may be seen as:

- **circulating and reinforcing dominant ideologies; or**
- **(less frequently), undermining and challenging such ideologies.**

Let us consider a brief example of how the media may both reinforce and challenge dominant ideologies by comparing the representation of family life in two popular American television series, *The Waltons* and *The Simpsons*. *The Waltons*, (Figure 4.1), broadcast during the 1970s, depicted a close-knit extended family living in rural America during the depression years of the 1930s. The family managed to stay happy and overcome all of its problems through mutual love and support. Essentially, the series represents an idyllic, nostalgic and idealised vision of family life.

In sharp contrast, *The Simpsons* (Figure 4.2), broadcast since 1989, represents working class family life as riven with conflict and chaos. In particular, the selfish behaviour of the male members, Homer and Bart, is responsible for many of the problems of *The Simpsons*, unlike their heroic male counterparts, John and John Boy, who head *The Waltons* household. *The Simpsons'* popularity was/is unsettling for many Americans, not used to

FIGURE 4.1
The Waltons
Source: Ronald grant Archive

FIGURE 4.2
The Simpsons
Source: Corbis

the darker side of family life being a subject for comedy (as reflected in the comment of US President Bush in 1992 – 'I want families to be more like *The Waltons* and less like *The Simpsons*'). As such *The Simpsons* can be seen as a media text which is capable of subverting traditional values underpinning American institutions such as the family and education. However, it has to be noted that as a family *The Simpsons* do retain their unity, largely through the love and patience of Marge, the family matriarch.

Activity 4.1

Choose a modern US television animated series which you consider challenges or subverts traditional American values. In what ways do you think it is ideologically subversive?

Myth

Ideologies 'work' through symbolic codes (see Chapter 2), which represent and explain cultural phenomena. Barthes (1973) labels this symbolic representation as mythic, not in the traditional sense of being false (as in fairy tales), but in the sense of having the appearance of being 'natural', 'inevitable' or 'commonsense', so that it is not questioned. Advertising draws heavily on myth, using cultural signifiers to represent qualities which can be realised through consumption of the

FIGURE 4.3
How does this Hovis advert work as a myth?
Source: Hovis, CDP/Travis Sully.

advertised product or brand. Williamson (1978) has identified some of the value systems which are represented in the language of advertising. Particularly prominent in her analysis are adverts which she claims invite us to reunite ourselves with nature (even more relevant in the 'green' new millennium), and those which attribute the power of science and technology to products. In nearly all adverts, she sees two processes at work: first, an appeal to our belief in the 'magical' powers of products to solve our problems; and second, the divorce of production from consumption. Hidden from our view are the capitalist conditions from which advertised products originate (conditions which Marxist writers see as alienating and exploitative of workers: Figure 4.3).

Ideology, Myth and Hollywood Cinema

As an institution whose primary purpose is to entertain and where the financial costs of failure can be huge, it is not surprising that much of the mainstream film output of Hollywood studios can be seen as ideologically conservative. Ideological values of films are those which celebrate and reinforce the traditionally dominant values of American society: individualism, patriotism, equality of opportunity, justice, etc.

Such ideological values may be found in films across a whole spectrum of genres from comedy to science fiction. In achieving resolutions to narrative disruption a moral or ideological 'message' may be identified … such messages will usually appeal to the prevailing audience sentiments and values in order to achieve a 'feel good' factor and box office success.

The most successful film of 1996, *Independence Day* (see Figure 4.5), at face value is a simple science fiction fantasy in which an alien threat to the planet is overcome against the odds. The publicity surrounding the film mostly focused on the elaborate special effects including the spectacular destruction of American landmarks such as the White House. An ideological reading of *Independence Day* reveals a film that celebrates and endorses many traditional conservative American values and at the same time reaffirms the supremacy of the 'American Way'.

At its simplest, *Independence Day* represents the triumph of good over evil – a moral outcome typical of most Hollywood films. In this particular case, it is the triumph of the American people against an enemy invader. Patriotic emotions are stirred through the use of a range of iconic American signs starting with the American flag on the moon and continuing with the statue of American soldiers raising the flag in Iwo Jima in the Second World War and other landmarks symbolic of American 'freedom' such as the Statue of Liberty. America (and implicitly the rest of the world) is faced with annihilation by an alien force. This external threat (like other previous threats such as Russian communism during the Cold War), requires America to unite and defeat the enemy. The ideological notion of a racially integrated nation is supported through the casting of a black (Will Smith) and a Jew (Jeff Goldblum) as the two heroes who help to save America from the aliens. Racial conflict and division is absent from this patriotic film, as was the case in most American films made during the Second World War.

The male domination is completed by the third hero, the white (WASP) male President (Bill Pullman), who delivers a stirring patriotic speech on 4 July to the effect that it is America's duty to save the world. Meanwhile, women play subordinate roles supporting (and even marrying) their heroic men in their hour of need. The patriarchal ideology is reinforced by the fact that the President's wife is fatally injured through ignoring her husband's advice and not returning home from a business trip.

FIGURE 4.4 (RADIO TIMES)
How are these images mythic?
Source: Radio Times, 6–12 October 2001

Ultimately, *Independence Day* is about American supremacy (and superiority) in the world, and its ability to overcome any challenge whatever the odds. The ideological patriotism is anchored through the film's title – Independence Day (July 4) being the national holiday which celebrates America's 'liberation' from colonial rule. Furthermore, as a science fiction film which employs the most advanced computer generated special effects, and whose narrative equilibrium is re-established through administering a computer virus to destroy the enemy invader, *Independence Day* underlines America's technological superiority in the world. The closing scenes show the world rejoicing at the defeat of the aliens (including images of spear-carrying Africans in tribal dress and cheering Arabs against a backdrop of the Pyramids).

The September 11 destruction of the twin towers in New York created a wave of patriotic sentiment in America which has since been reflected in the kind of war film output released by Hollywood. Notable examples include *Black Hawk Down* (2001) and *Behind Enemy Lines* (2001), both of which are based on recent American involvement in war activity (Somalia and Bosnia respectively). Both of these films glorify American sacrifice without questioning the motives for American participation in the first place. The 'enemy' is represented as simplistically evil, without any clear moral or political motivation, and so we are meant to identify only with the American 'heroes'.

Activity 4.2

Analyse two recent Hollywood mainstream films in terms of what you see as the mythic values and ideological messages the films seem to contain. Focus particularly on the narrative disruption and resolution for each film. Consider also how they might relate to their historical context.

Genre and Ideology

As pointed out in Chapter 3, genres often contain ideological 'messages' as part of their narrative formulae. They may serve to reinforce or confirm the dominant values of society at any given time. However, these are not fixed or closed. New texts may subvert or challenge prevailing ideologies and myths, especially when they reflect wider social trends and shifts in people's thinking and values.

A good example of a genre which illustrates how social changes influence the ideological content of films is the gangster film. During the 'classic' era of gangster films, the 1930s, the characters portrayed were often based on real life gangsters who had grown rich during the years of prohibition and became targets of the American authorities like the FBI. Such gangsters as Al Capone and John Dillinger were not allowed to enjoy the fruits of their crime, so that audiences would clearly get the message that 'crime doesn't pay'. However, in that many of the gangsters acquired wealth and power from humble origins, the films also

FIGURE 4.5
Independence Day
Source: The Kobal Collection

FIGURE 4.6
Bonnie and Clyde
Source: The Kobal Collection

73

resonated with ideological elements of the American Dream – the ability to get rich in the 'land of opportunity'. Americans could admire the exciting and glamorous lifestyle of such anti-heroes even if they came to an early and suitably moral ending.

During the 1960s, the popularity of gangsters as anti-heroes was reflected in the success of *Bonnie and Clyde* (1967) (see Figure 4.6). The two (attractive) outlaws were represented as underdogs up against the forces of law and order, whose overreaction in spraying Bonnie and Clyde with bullets in the climactic bloody ambush contained echoes of American military behaviour in Vietnam. In 1972, *The Godfather* further developed the theme of gangster as morally acceptable in representing Italian mafia culture as a repository of mainstream American values – a close-knit family, loyalty and honour, etc. The family 'business' was depicted as integral to American economic and political life, although this was counterbalanced by revealing the ruthless violence employed against those who threatened the family's interests. *The Godfather* films were in tune with a shift in public perception of the morality of American political and economic life. During the 1970s there was disenchantment with government because of political scandal, and in some respects the Corleone family represented an attractive and glamorous alternative to other Hollywood heroes at the time.

Political Representations

Hegemony versus Pluralism

The extent to which the media shape or reflect political ideas and beliefs in society is very much open to debate. Those arguing for a hegemonic model of power believe the media play a vital role in helping political elites to win popular support and consent. This can be seen with the example of the press where wealthy newspaper proprietors have tried to directly influence the editorial content of their newspapers (see Chapter 6, p. 144). Until fairly recently, the British press have had an in-built majority support for the Conservative party which has usually been disproportionate to their real support among voters.

In contrast to the hegemonic view which sees media content as narrowly ideological, pluralists argue that there is diversity, debate and choice. Just as society is composed of a diversity of interest groups and points of view, so the media have to reflect their full range. If and when certain values and beliefs predominate in media output, this is due to their being shared and agreed upon by most of society. In this perspective media production is essentially responsive to audience demands. If audience needs and trends are ignored then the likely outcome (without alternative revenue) is commercial failure. As evidence of this, it might be pointed out that the newspapers' support for the Conservatives has steadily been eroded as a reflection of a general loss of public support for the party, so that at the 2001 General Election only two newspapers (the *Daily Mail* and the *Daily Telegraph*) openly advocated voting Conservative.

Propaganda or Impartiality

There is a general consensus that some media output qualifies as *propaganda*. This may be defined as the conscious manipulation of information in order to gain political advantage. However, it is possible to take a broader view as to what constitutes propaganda so that it includes other contexts in which communication is deliberately partial so as to deceive or persuade such as advertising. Political propaganda is most evident in countries where the state has a strong (often totalitarian) control over the media and so is able to promote favourably biased coverage whilst suppressing critical media coverage. Western media are often characterised as having a plurality or diversity of views including those which criticise or question those in power. In countries like Britain, it is thought that propaganda is largely confined to either political advertising, such as party election broadcasts, or politically partisan newspapers and magazines which seek to persuade audiences to support a particular political party (Figures 4.7 and 4.8). Another traditional form of press propaganda is that evident during war or crises over terrorism. In the Falklands War of 1982 and the Gulf War of 1991, tabloid newspapers like *The Sun* were vociferous in support of 'our lads' and against the 'Argies' in the Falklands War and the 'evil dictator' (Saddam Hussein) in the Gulf War (refer to Figure 3.5 in 2nd edition).

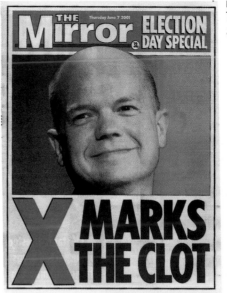

FIGURE 4.7
The Mirror, 2001
Source: The Mirror

Whilst print media may often be inclined to propaganda, this is less likely in the broadcast media in western countries. This is because there are regulations which are designed to protect broadcasters' independence from either state or commercial interference. In Britain, television and radio are required by law to be politically *impartial*. In practice this means broadcasters should, firstly, refrain from expressing their own political views or opinions, and instead, should base their political coverage on factual detail. The second principle underpinning impartiality is that political reporting should always be balanced by ensuring that opposing views are fairly represented. This does not necessarily mean equal coverage for all points of view, but those which are thought to reflect existing political opinion. Pluralist writers such as Hetherington (1985) see the broadcasters' professional commitment to detached and objective political reporting, especially in news coverage, at the heart of a democratic society – the very antithesis of societies dominated by state controlled propaganda such as found in the pre-1990 communist regimes of Eastern Europe or autocratic regimes such as Iraq under Saddam Hussein, Zimbabwe under Robert Mugabe, etc... It is fair to say that audience surveys in Britain support the perception that broadcasters are politically impartial. A large majority of the population continue to regard television as their most trusted source of information (see Svennevig 1998).

FIGURE 4.8
Front page of the Daily Mirror, Election day 1997
Source: The Mirror, 1 May 1997

However, those of a hegemonic perspective have been inclined to be far more critical of claims that broadcasting is impartial. The Glasgow University Media Group (1976, 1985, Greg Philo, 1999) have been the most consistent critics of what they see as the inbuilt systematic bias in British television news coverage. Since 1976, the research team have produced an impressive series of case studies in which they claim to have detected a consistent bias towards the political right whether it be in the coverage of industrial disputes, like the miners' strike of 1984/5, or that of Northern Ireland. They offer two explanations for such bias.

First, most journalists share certain 'consensual assumptions' about the world which are rarely questioned. With respect to industrial relations these would include: strikes are harmful and disruptive whereas uninterrupted working is a 'good thing'; management exercises control as a right, whereas workers' industrial actions are often illegitimate. Such ideas are particularly apparent when strikes occur in the public services such as education or the National Health Service.

The second main explanation for biased reporting is that those in power have privileged access when it comes to setting and shaping the agenda for reporting news stories. Not surprisingly, at the top of this pyramid of access comes the government and other 'establishment' organisations such as the police and the judiciary. In contrast, minority or alternative views are often marginalised, ignored, or deemed illegitimate. A good example of this is the coverage of Northern Ireland. Up until the 1994 IRA ceasefire, broadcasters rarely provided an opportunity for the IRA or indeed Protestant paramilitary groups to present their point of view. Groups like the IRA were labelled 'terrorist', a term with connotations of irrational random violence and lack of political legitimacy. Attempts made to investigate either the philosophy of members of organisations like the IRA (as in BBC's *Real Lives*, 1985) or whether the security forces had acted illegally (as in ITV's *Death on the Rock*, 1988) met with strong official resistance. *Real Lives* was temporarily banned by the BBC governors and shown only after re-editing; *Death on the Rock*, about the killings of three IRA members in Gibraltar by British agents, was subject to an enquiry (which subsequently cleared Thames TV, the programme makers). Nowadays, IRA/Sinn Fein leaders like Gerry Adams and Martin McGuinness (appointed as Education Minister for Northern Ireland in 2001) are treated by broadcast journalists as respectable and legitimate representatives whose views are regularly sought in covering the political problems of Northern Ireland.

Labelling any politically or religiously motivated violence 'terrorist' is an attempt to remove any sense of legitimate justification for such action, rendering it unacceptable to political democracies. This is particularly the case in the aftermath of September 11 since when the USA has waged a 'war on terror'. However, to quote the well-worn cliché, 'one person's terrorist is another person's freedom fighter'. As such, the media are the site of a continuous struggle by those seeking to impose their definition of terrorism whether it is in Palestine or Kashmir (see Schlesinger *et al*, 1989).

Activity 4 .3

Record a television news broadcast and choose a news story which involves a degree of political controversy. Find a second treatment of the same story in either radio or the press and subject both to the following questions:

1   Which sources are given priority (for example, who is interviewed and where)?
2   Which explanations are given priority (e.g. made into headlines, given order of priority)?
3   Does the story sequence encourage certain meanings and interpretations?
4   What terms of reference (language) or discourses (see Chapter 2, page 40) are used to describe or label the participants and their actions?
5   What physical or ideological points of view are produced by the camera shots or photographic images?

Media News Management

As the media's role as an agent of political communication has increased over the years, so the techniques by which politicians seek to manage and control such communication have become ever more sophisticated. Governments now employ numerous strategies designed to produce favourable media (especially television) coverage or 'spin'. These include: photo-opportunities, snappy soundbites, news conferences, exclusive interviews, media 'minders' and 'spin doctors'. The latter are employed to ensure that news stories are always presented and released in the most positive way.

At its most extreme, such news management can lead to accusations of media propaganda being made against journalists, intent on providing objective news coverage. Such claims are made by Philip Knightley in his book about media war coverage, *The First Casualty* (2000). He cites the 1982 Falklands War as the turning point, when the British government restricted access to a few journalists who were allowed to accompany the military providing they followed certain rules, including the acceptance of censorship by Ministry of Defence 'public relations officers'.

Similar restrictions operated during the 1991 Gulf War when again media coverage was largely dictated by what the military wanted to be revealed – a successful and triumphant campaign minus the images of casualties and destruction which might otherwise undermine public support for the war (as it did in America during the 1960s when the media were free to report the horrors of the Vietnam War).

FIGURE 4.9
Source: The Mirror, 2001

Most recently, the media have been criticised for their failure to question the NATO (led by America and Britain) war against Serbia in Kosovo in 1999. As with the Gulf War, the media largely accepted the official explanation for going to war – to liberate the Kosovan people from the evil dictator (Miloševic). Many of the official NATO reports of the extent of Kosovan casualties and suffering that were used to justify the attacks on Serbia were later revealed to be greatly exaggerated. Knightley argues that the inability of the media to reveal the truth about recent wars involving Britain shows how successful governments have become in managing news coverage. However, part of the problem for the media is gaining access to war zones in countries being bombed by western forces. This means journalists have a choice between reporting what is revealed at media briefings given by the western military or any equivalent process from within the country being attacked, whether that is Kuwait (in the Gulf War) or Afghanistan (in the war against the Taliban). Reports from within such countries are usually qualified by phrases like 'can't be independently verified' or 'subject to censorship by…' As to the justification for fighting such wars, it is far from clear that the British media will always support the government line. The bombing of Afghanistan was strongly criticised by *The Mirror* (Figure 4.9) as well as other newspapers, and the BBC World Service refused to use the label of 'terrorist' for those who destroyed the twin towers in New York on 11 September 2001, in order to try to maintain its reputation for independence in reporting global news.

Control of political reporting can never be complete. It is always possible to find some media coverage which allows space for alternative or oppositional views to be expressed. Just prior to the 1991 Gulf War, Channel 4 broadcast *The Gulf Between Us*, presenting an Arab perspective on the conflict. In the build-up to the Falklands War, the BBC broadcast critical views on the decision to send the task force in both

Panorama and *Newsnight*. Furthermore it is now possible to receive alternative political news and views on the Internet. A good example is the Independent Media Centre website (**www.uk.indymedia.org**), with centres in over fifty cities world-wide operating as an 'alternative Reuters' (the British-owned global news agency). During the protests against the World Trade Organisation in Seattle in 2000, nearly five hundred journalists and activists contributed text, photos and video clips to the site.

Stereotypes

A stereotype is a label which involves a process of categorisation and evaluation. Although it may refer to situations or places, it is most often used in conjunction with representations of social groups. In its simplest terms, an easily grasped characteristic (usually negative) is presumed to belong to a whole group, e.g. estate agents are insincere, devious and smooth-talking.

In ideological terms, stereotyping is a means by which support is provided for one group's differential (often discriminatory) treatment of another. If black Africans could be represented as uncivilised and savage in the nineteenth century, then slavery and exploitation of blacks by their white rulers could be justified. In contemporary society, old people are frequently portrayed as physically and mentally infirm, asexual and unable to adapt to social change. Such 'ageist' sentiments contribute to a lowering of the social status of the aged, including a lowering of their own self-esteem.

However, stereotyping is not a simple process. Tessa Perkins (1979) has identified many shortcomings in the way that stereotyping is normally assumed to operate:

- **stereotypes are not always negative (e.g. 'The French are good cooks');**
- **they are not always about minority groups or the less powerful (e.g. 'upper-class twits');**
- **they can be held about one's own group;**
- **they are not rigid or unchanging (e.g. the 'cloth-cap worker' of the 1950s became the 1980s 'consumerist home-owner who holidays in Spain');**
- **they are not always false, but can be supported by empirical evidence (e.g. 'Media studies teachers tend to be liberal/left-wing in their politics').**

Indeed, Perkins argues that stereotypes would not work culturally if they were so simple and erroneous.

Martin Barker (1989) goes further, to the extent of dismissing the concept of the stereotype as a 'useless tool for investigating media texts'. His first objection is that stereotypes are condemned both for misrepresenting the 'real world', e.g. for reinforcing the (false) stereotype that women are available for sex at any time, and for being too close to the 'real world', e.g. for showing women mainly in the home and servicing men – which many in fact do. However, this example bears out Perkins' point that for stereotypes to work they need audience recognition, i.e. to appear 'natural' and everyday. The ideological process, though, reinforces this 'naturalness' by failing to reveal any contradictions or inequalities in the representation, for instance, that women may feel trapped, undervalued and lacking economic independence in their domestic role.

Barker's second main objection is that the concept of stereotyping implies that it is wrong to see people in categories. Yet, within social psychology, it has long been recognised that categorisation is a fundamental cognitive process necessary to make sense of the world. Cultures constantly impose structure on events, experiences and people, particularly when faced with only limited information. Thus stereotypical judgements are made by everyone as part of creating order out of everyday life, as well as providing and maintaining a sense of group identity (for a fuller discussion of stereotyping see M. Pickering 2001).

Media representation may serve to inform, reinforce or challenge such stereotypes. This is partly for reasons of economy. Constraints of time and space, plus the desire to achieve rapid audience recognition, mean that stereotypical representations are constructed rather than fully fledged characters with individual identities. This is articulated effectively by Trevor Griffiths in his play *Comedians*, which is about an evening class for budding comedians led by an experienced comedian, Eddie Waters, who rails against the easy laugh achieved at the expense of minority groups:

WATERS [*driving home*]: If I've told you once I've told you a thousand times. We work through laughter, not for it. If all you're about is raising a laugh, OK, get on with it, good luck to you, but don't waste my time. There's plenty others as'll tek your money and do the necessary. Not Eddie Waters.

McBRAIN [*conciliatory, apologetic*]: So, a few crappy jokes, Mr Waters …

WATERS: It's not the jokes. It's not the jokes. It's what lies behind 'em. It's the attitude. A real comedian – that's a daring man. He dares to see what his listeners shy away from, fear to express. And what he sees is a sort of truth, about people, about their situation, about what hurts or terrifies them, about what's hard, above all, about what they want. A joke releases the tension, says the unsayable, any joke pretty well. But a true joke, a comedian's joke, has to do more than release tension, it has to liberate the will and the desire, it has to change the situation. [*Pause*] There's very little won't take a joke. But when a joke bases itself upon a distortion – [*at* PRICE*, deliberately*] – a 'stereotype' perhaps – and gives the lie to the truth so as to win a laugh and stay in favour, we've moved away from a comic art and into the world of 'entertainment' and slick success. [*Pause*] You're better than that, damn you. And even if you're not, you should bloody well want to be.

Griffiths (1976)

It is against the backdrop of criticisms of stereotyping of minority groups in the 1970s and 1980s that the concept of 'political correctness' developed. The avoidance of racist or sexist stereotyping has since become a sensitive issue not least for those responsible for producing media texts. It has opened up a critical set of debates concerning how the media encode meaning *and* how such texts are decoded by audiences. This is particularly the case in a **postmodern** culture where many images and ideas are intended to be ironic and playful and not interpreted at face value. This point is illustrated below with reference to the dumb blonde stereotype (Figure 4.10).

The Dumb Blonde

Some of the complexities of utilising stereotyped labels in analysis of media representations can be seen through a consideration of one example: the dumb blonde. A list of the main ingredients for a dumb blonde stereotype might include: blondeness, seductive body language, strong make-up, innocence or naivety, childlike voice, humour and wit, illogical thinking, etc.

The first problem is that not all these ingredients are consistent: childlike *and* seductive; witty *and* simple and empty-headed. In terms of whether the label is descriptive or evaluative, much depends on social perceptions of what kind of female image and behaviour is desirable. To be blonde is often defined as more attractive ('blondes have more fun'), while to be 'dumb' may be seen as both (sexually) appealing (to many men) and undesirable – being considered of low intelligence.

Gayle's Males

PIN-UP GAYLE TUESDAY, ALIAS COMEDY STAR BRENDA GILHOOLY, ON HER FAVOURITE SUBJECT: MEN

What I like most about men is that they are strong. Women by nature are pink and fluffy, aren't they? And men are out doing the hunting and the gathering. It's a law of nature that goes back for millions of years ... even longer than that, thousands actually. These feminist types don't understand that. Don't get me wrong, I don't hate them, in fact I feel sorry for them. I read somewhere that their feet are webbed and that is why they can't wear high heels.

I like men who treat a girl like a girl, you know, opening doors, stuff like that. So I think it's only right for a girl to make a bit of an effort. With all the micro-minis in the shops, I can't believe that women aren't out there wearing them.

I know it's not all that warm at this time of year, but my advice is to take the skirt off when you're indoors, otherwise you won't feel the benefit.

My boyfriend Grant is also my manager. He's very popular, what with his Armani suits and his steroids habit. He does have violent mood swings, but nobody's perfect are they? We had this terrible argument this morning and I thought my heart would burst. But then I realised that I had the wrong bra on.

Just because Grant looks after my business affairs doesn't mean we don't have fun. In fact I've got a pet name for him, I call him "pimp".

Grant lost his cool the other day. We were in this bookshop and it was awful because there was this book with all my former lovers in. Grant rang up the publisher and he was going to sue them. But they said that the Panini Premier League Sticker Album has actually been around for years.

I think you've got to be a proper woman for your man. You've got to be a cook in the kitchen and a whore in the bedroom. But you mustn't get them mixed up. The other day I got baked beans all over the bed and when the next door neighbour came round I opened the door in a basque and I said: "Ooooh, I'm £10 an hour."

I do like to be taken out. Me and Grant went to see Titanic the other night and I got really girly and upset because when the boat sank I just wasn't expecting it.

We love going on holiday — there's nothing better than lounging around with my top off and not a thing to occupy my mind. But as much as I love my job, everyone needs a break now and then.

I'm a very deep person, as a matter of fact. I believe in the old saying. "A girl's boobs are the window to her soul." I love to meditate. I'm quite good at it. Well, I'm quite good at the emptying the mind bit, it's getting it all back in afterwards that I find a problem.

Some men do feel threatened by me though, because I'm so successful. I've had my own series on the telly and it's not that many glamour models that make the crossover to talking.

I've got a video coming out soon which highlights the very complex relationship between men and women. I think I'll call it Disco Vixens On heat.

FIGURE 4.10
Gayle's Males
Source: Sunday Mirror 19.4.98

Childlike
High or breathy voice, rounded face, wide eyes; deliberate, self-conscious or awkward movements; naive responses, lack of concentration, an emphasis on 'fun' and 'play'; irresponsibility and emotional indulgence.

Inappropriate
Behaviour or appearance showing 'inability' to grasp (or refusal to obey?) rules of conventional (particularly middle-class) social contact. Includes over-dressing, unrestrained voice (volume/pitch) or especially 'excessive' laughter.

Unconventional
Unusual forms of logic, exaggerated gestures, unexpected responses; characteristics, behaviour and desires which do not concur with feminine roles; emphasising a unique individuality.

G. Swanson (1991)

What kinds of judgement may be made about women possessing the above characteristics, individually or in combination?

FIGURE 4.11
The Seven Year Itch, 1955
Source: The Kobal
Collection/Twentieth
Century Fox

FIGURE 4.12
Private Benjamin, 1980
Source: The Kobal
Collection/Warner Brothers

An examination of specific examples of dumb blonde types quickly reveals variations, which reflect both changes in the way the dumb blonde has been perceived over time and personal qualities brought to the role by individual performers. Marilyn Monroe is often considered to epitomise the dumb blonde, yet her own performances in the 1950s (both off and on screen) clearly accentuated sexuality and seduction (e.g. in the film *The Seven Year Itch*) (Figure 4.11). In contrast, Goldie Hawn's film and television performances in the 1970s emphasised the giggly or kooky facets of her personality (Figure 4.12). In recent years, the dumb blonde is as likely to be the source of parody (e.g. within adverts - Figure 4.13) as to be represented seriously (although Marilyn in *Home and Away*, the Australian television soap opera, or Raquel in *Coronation Street* could be said to maintain the essence of the type). Phoebe in *Friends* could be seen as a more contemporary version of the dumb blonde, although the character of Joey in the same series could arguably represent a male equivalent of the female dumb blonde.

Aptitude tests aid entry to elite academic institutions

FIGURE 4.13
MegaStar advertisement (Evening Standard 17.11.00)
Source: Megastar

Gender and Ideology

Before considering media representations of *gender*, it is necessary to establish what the term means. To be male or female can be defined biologically, but 'masculinity' and 'femininity' are socially constructed. This can be demonstrated by both cultural and historical comparison: ideas about what it means to be masculine or feminine vary between societies and change over time, even though there may be some aspects of gender difference which are found virtually universally, e.g. the mother–child bond, and these are more closely linked to biology.

Ideas about gender difference are produced and reflected within language. Both objects and abstract concepts can be seen as gendered. While this applies as part of the grammatical system in some languages like French, in English it is quite selective. Modes of transport – cars, ships, steam engines, etc – are given feminine labels as if to signify something possessed and controlled by men. Likewise, countries, nations and nature itself are ascribed a female status as representing caring, home and a sense of belonging and refuge. In contrast, ultimate power rests with a masculine God, and the word 'man' has been used to represent all humans, as in 'mankind', 'man in the street' or 'man-made'.

'Feminism' is a label that refers to a broad range of views containing one shared assumption – that there are profound gender inequalities in society, and that historically masculine power (patriarchy) has been exercised at the expense of women's interests and rights. This power may be expressed physically, but is more generally reproduced ideologically. Language is seen to be a form of social control in so far as the terms 'masculine' and 'feminine' carry very strong connotations of what is 'natural' for each sex, whether that refers to personal traits (like rationality or emotionalism) or to social roles (like businessman or housewife).

Appearance

One of the strongest cultural values concerning gender difference is that women are judged by their looks more than men. In the world of popular mediated culture this is especially noticeable. When comparing the social attributes of male and female Hollywood film stars between 1932 and 1984, Emanuel Levy (1990) concluded that physical looks and youth were far more important for the female stars (the list of stars being based on box office appeal). For men, attractive looks were a weak basis for longevity of appeal – indeed, many of the most successful men – Humphrey Bogart, Jerry Lewis and Dustin Hoffman, for example – were anything but handsome.

AMERICA'S MOST DURABLE FILM STARS (OVER FOUR YEARS ON THE POLL 1932–1984)

Men				Women	
John Wayne	25	Dustin Hoffman	7	Betty Grable	10
Gary Cooper	18	Robert Redford	7	Doris Day	10
Clint Eastwood	18	James Cagney	6	Barbra Streisand	10
Clark Gable	16	Mickey Rooney	6	Elizabeth Taylor	9
Bing Crosby	14	Frank Sinatra	6	Shirley Temple	6
Bob Hope	13	Sylvester Stallone	6	Joan Crawford	5
Paul Newman	13	Wallace Beery	5	Greer Garson	5
Jerry Lewis	12	Marlon Brando	5	Jane Fonda	5
Burt Reynolds	12	Lee Marvin	5	Bette Davis	4
Cary Grant	12	Woody Allen	5	Sandra Dee	4
Spencer Tracy	10	Harrison Ford	5	Julie Andrews	4
James Stewart	10	Will Rogers	4		
Steve McQueen	9	Randolph Scott	4		
Dean Martin	8	Richard Burton	4		
Abbott and Costello	8	Sean Connery	4		
Humphrey Bogart	8	Charles Bronson	4		
Rock Hudson	8	Al Pacino	4		
Jack Lemmon	8	John Travolta	4		
Elvis Presley	7				

Levy (1990)

Associated with appearance was age. The median age for female stars was 27, compared to 36 for men; and many men achieved stardom only after 40, e.g. John Wayne (at 42) and Charles Bronson (at 52). Given the ephemeral nature of youthful attractiveness, it is not surprising that few women stars have been able to sustain their box office appeal over many years. Those who have lasted longer have tended to possess 'something else' beyond glamour and beauty, e.g. Barbra Streisand's singing voice plus her ability to play career women. The list on the previous page shows the number of years the listed actors appeared in the American Motion Picture Poll (sometimes known as the Quigley Poll), a survey of which film stars had drawn the largest audiences according to cinema owners and film distributors.

Activity 4.4

1   Select two male and two female stars from the above list, and, with the help of background research, try to identify what individual qualities may have contributed to their box office appeal. You will need to consider the kind of image and appeal produced by a combination of personal characteristics, on-screen performances and general publicity.

2   Examine the current range of leading male and female film stars. Do they reflect similar differences in age and good looks as found in Levy's research? For example, in the 1997 Quigley Poll the top 10 stars were as follows: Harrison Ford, Julia Roberts, Leonardo DiCaprio, Will Smith, Tom Cruise, Jack Nicholson, Jim Carrey, John Travolta, Robin Williams and Tommy Lee Jones.

What is clearly apparent from Levy's research is the sheer inequality in number of male and female stars, a pattern that has persisted for several decades, and that also applies to other areas of the media like television, where it has been estimated that men outnumber women by two to one within programmes as a whole. One contentious area is that of television advertising (Figure 4.14a/b).

Television Advertising and Sex Role Stereotyping 1990

1 Overview
Men outnumbered women by a ratio of nearly 2:1. The vast majority of adverts had a male voice-over (89 per cent).

2 Physical attributes
Overall, one half of women were judged to be between 21 and 30 years old, compared with less than one third (30 per cent) of males. Among those judged over 30 years old, men outnumbered women by a ratio of 3:1 (men 75 per cent, women 25 per cent).

In terms of body type, most people were characterised as 'ordinary'. The slim, model or 'ideal' category was applied to only one in ten (11 per cent) men compared with more than one in three (35 per cent) women.

One third (34 per cent) of women were blonde compared with only one in ten (11 per cent) males.

Being 'attractive' (defined as the kind of person who might appear in a clothes' magazine) fitted the description for nearly two thirds (64 per cent) of females but under one quarter (22 per cent) of males.

One in five (21 per cent) females were judged 'beautiful' (for example, the Cadbury's Flake model) compared with only 4 per cent of males.

The conclusion is that women occupy a decorative role far more commonly than men. In the few examples of women characters predominating, they were almost all for 'personal maintenance' products.

3 Activities and roles

Occupation, when given or implied, revealed that men were almost twice as likely as women to be represented in some kind of paid employment (30 per cent of men, 16 per cent of women).

In only 7 per cent of cases was housework shown as the dominant activity for women. However, women were more than twice as likely to engage in household labour as were men (45 per cent of women, 21 per cent of men). Cooking was performed by a greater proportion of men (32 per cent) than women (24 per cent), but when men cook, it is portrayed as a special and skilled activity.

4 Relationships

In terms of marital status, most men could not be coded. Although women were more likely than men to be single (19 per cent female, 11 per cent male), they were much more likely to be married (27 per cent female, 18 per cent male). This would explain why their social integration was twice as likely to be with a partner (female 24 per cent, male 10 per cent) as with members of the same sex (11 per cent females, 26 per cent males). Same-sex adverts were most common in adverts for alcohol.

Women were twice as likely both to attract (25 per cent females, 13 per cent males) and to show they were attracted (26 per cent females, 12 per cent males). Moreover, while only 9 per cent of men

Men fight back over sexist TV adverts

by John Arlidge

HE'S A LAZY wimp who can't cook or fix the car and whose girlfriend is cheating on him. You can see him on TV, in the newspapers and magazines. He's 'advert man' and he's sick of being the butt of jokes.

Record numbers of men are complaining about the way they are depicted by advertisers. Figures to be released this week by the Advertising Standards Authority show that the number of complaints has doubled this year. Over the last six years protests have increased tenfold.

Men say they are fed up being depicted either as sex gods with unfeasible muscular bodies and chiselled jaws or – more often – as incompetent, brow-beaten slobs who cannot express themselves, hold down a job, clean the house, or keep a girlfriend.

Ads which men have objected to this year include a poster for Lambrini sparkling wine in which a girl tells a friend she has lost a lot of 'useless fat'. 'So you dumped him then?' comes the reply. A law firm promoted its divorce services with the slogan. 'All Men Are Bastards' and Lee jeans showed a woman resting her stiletto heel on the buttocks of a prostrate, naked man.

On television, Mr Muscle cleaning products are sold using a bespectacled wimp, and the man in the ad for Archers peach schnapps is outwitted by his manipulative girlfriend.

Claire Forbes of the ASA said: 'Public sensitivities have changed. What men may have regarded as funny or inoffensive a decade ago can cause serious or widespread offence today. That's reflected in the very sharp increase in the number of complaints we get.'

The ASA's findings are supported by a study from the Chartered Institute of Marketing. Of more than 1,000 adults questioned, two thirds said women in ads were intelligent, assertive and caring, while men were pathetic and silly. Only 14 per cent said men came across as intelligent.

Another survey of 140 men conducted by the London School of Economics found images of male models with perfect physiques made men feel angry, frustrated and physically inadequate. Rosalind Gill, a social psychologist at the LSE, said: 'Adverts now portray men as objects to be consumed – much like women have always been – and more than half the men we spoke to said they made them feel weak.'

By empowering women at the expense of men, advertisers hope to appeal to women. They insist portraying men as weak or useless is 'just a bit of fun'. But some industry experts say the joke is wearing thin.

Linda Hodgson, of the marketing consultants Corporate Edge, said; 'Advertisers are alienating men at a time when men feel the gap between the sexes is closing. It is time to move into a new phase where people are respected for their strengths rather than their sex'.

Caroline Marshall, editor of the advertising industry magazine Campaign, believes many women now find the depiction of men offensive. 'Women don't want to be seen to hate or walk all over men. They are unlikely to buy products advertised like that,' she said. 'I drink sparkling wine, but wouldn't buy Lambrini. I don't want to be associated with a product that makes women look cruel.'

john.arlidge@observer.co.uk

FIGURE 4.14b
Source: Guardian/
©John Arlidge

received some sort of sexual advance, nearly twice as many women (17 per cent) did so. In categorising the gain achieved by characters from the product being advertised, implied sexual success was almost twice as common for women (18 per cent) as for men (10 per cent).

Conclusion

The patterns that emerge lend strong support to the concern that women exist in what is essentially a man's world.

FIGURE 4.14a
Source: Adapted from research undertaken for the Broadcasting Standards Commission by Guy Cumberbatch et al, 1990

Activity 4.5

1   Conduct a content analysis (see Chapter 10) similar to the 1990 research in Figure 4.14a by recording thirty television adverts from different times of the day and coding the content according to the same criteria. Compare your findings to those of Cumberbatch.
2   What do you think of the shortcomings of using this method to analyse gender representations in television adverts?
3   How representative do you think are the claims made in the more recent *Observer* article (Figure 4.14b) about sexist TV adverts of men?

Looking at Women

The objectification of women's bodies in the media has been a consistent theme in critical analyses of women's representation. Laura Mulvey (1975) argues that the dominant point of view within cinema is masculine, especially where a woman is concerned. The female body is displayed and filmed for the **male gaze** in order to provide erotic pleasure (**voyeurism**), and ultimately a sense of control over her. She is rendered a passive object. This approach is carried to the extreme in pornography, where erotic pleasure from looking is the sole motivation for the production. This tendency has spilled over into newspapers in recent years particularly the tabloid newspapers, the most prominent example being Page 3 in *The Sun*. Some feminists feel that these images reinforce a 'fantasy of willingness: the Page three girl is waiting "to kiss the next man she sees"' (Joan Smith, 1990).

Despite a growth in the number of female editors of national newspapers, such as Rebekah Wade at *The Sun* (and formerly) *News of the World*, recent research by *Women in Journalism* (Meg Carter, 1999) shows that newspapers are inclined to apply different criteria to select pictures of women than for men. Women's photographs are often used to 'brighten up the page' whether in stories about sport, business or entertainment.

The dominance of a masculine perspective within news reporting in the press is apparent when it comes to the coverage of sexual crime. A survey by Channel 4's *Hard News* research team in the first six months of 1990 found more than six hundred articles on rape in the ten major national daily newspapers, an average of more than four a day. (*The Sun* topped the league, followed by the *Daily Telegraph*.) What concerned the researchers was the way in which rape tended to be misrepresented. Rape victims were stereotyped as either 'good' women who had been violated or 'bad' women who had led men on. Rapists were overwhelmingly portrayed as alien strangers in the guise of a 'sex fiend' or 'beast', despite the fact that in two out of three recorded rapes the rapist is known intimately by the victim. Regarding the crime itself, many newspaper reports dwelt on the details provided by the victim under courtroom cross-examination to the exclusion of other details, such as forensic or medical evidence.

The difficulties of dealing effectively with rape in the context of fictional 'entertainment' are very well illustrated by the controversy surrounding *The Accused* (a 1988 film based on a real court case) in which the actual rape itself is left to the climax of the film. Some concern was expressed that the prelude to the rape and some of the camera shots included in the attack might offer some members of the male audience voyeuristic pleasure, even though the film was praised for its overall treatment of the case. (For a discussion of women's responses to *The Accused* see Schlesinger *et al.*, 1992.)

Physical attacks on women have also been a feature of the 'slasher' sub genre of horror films in which attractive young females are stalked by a male 'monster' or psychopath before becoming victims of a frenzied violent attack. The cycle includes such films as *Texas Chain Saw Massacre* (1974), *Halloween* (1978), and *Dressed to Kill* (1980). *Pyscho* and *Peeping Tom* (both 1960) are often seen as the earliest examples to present violence against women in such a voyeuristic way. In the case of *Peeping Tom,* the voyeurism of the male killer is itself subject to scrutiny, and he is eventually challenged by a woman who refuses to be intimidated. Indeed, in this and other cases, it is not clear that masculine control over women is always a product of the camera's gaze at women. Women playing lead roles in *film noir* in the 1940s often projected power and mystery as well as sexuality, and in the role of '*femme fatale*' were able to exercise control over men. In a pop video by Madonna for her song 'Open Your Heart' (1986), she performs in a 'peep show' for a variety of male voyeurs, but the gaze is reversed so that the men are seen through Madonna's eyes – as pathetic and frustrated. Madonna is an example of a growing self-consciousness among female performers who are able to exercise greater control over their look and image.

Whether media images of female sexuality represent passive objects of (male) sexual pleasure or active subjects of female sexual control can sometimes be ambiguous. In December 2000, there was a lively controversy concerning the image of the naked Sophie Dahl in an advert for Opium perfume which attracted a number of complaints when it appeared on public billboards. Reactions to the advert tended to polarise between those who interpreted the image as 'porn chic' and those who thought it celebrated female sexual self-confidence and desire. The advert can be viewed on the Advertising Standards Authority website (**www.asa.org.uk**; go to the *Annual Report 2001:40 years of effective regulation*).

Looking at Men

Conventional approaches to looking at male subjects within the media tend to be limited to acceptable contexts in which traditional masculinity is not threatened. Television sports coverage provides numerous moments of close-ups of male bodies, but this is not given any sexual legitimacy by the camerawork or commentary, despite the fact that there is evidence that female viewers may gain pleasure from such images. Dorothy Hobson (1985) suggested that the strong appeal of television snooker for women is that the players exude a masculinity stripped of unattractive aggression and competitiveness. Until recently, it was only in gay culture that an open display and objectification of the male body for sexual pleasure was able to flourish. This has become less true in recent years, particularly as more women assert their own sexual desires and identities, and men have become more sensitive about how they are supposed to look.

Pop music has had many male singers willing to submit themselves to the female gaze, whether in girls' magazines or, more recently, in pop videos. Some have consciously feminised their appearance so as to create considerable ambiguity about their sexual identity, as typified in the 1970s glamrock era (e.g. David Bowie) and in the 1980s by Boy George and Michael Jackson. Growing consciousness of the masculine body has also been reflected in advertising, whether it be for aftershave or clothes, or in the rise of men's magazines such as *GQ* and *Arena*. One of the most successful men's magazines of the past decade has been *Men's Health*. In a similar vein to women's magazines, *Men's Health* seems to offer the promise of bodily perfection (providing its readers can fulfil its demanding regime of physical training and a disciplined diet). The male body becomes a site of continuous self-control and improvement, creating a sense of masculine achievement. However, whilst it may be argued that this reinforces a traditional notion of what it means to be masculine, (physical toughness, regimented self-discipline, etc.) it also raises questions (and provokes anxieties) about the ability to achieve the physical standards represented in the pages of magazines like *Men's Health*. The question

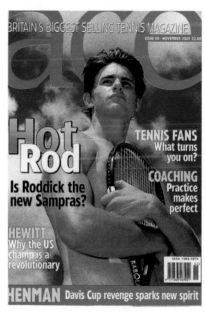

FIGURE 4.15
Source: Men's Health

FIGURE 4.16
Source: ACE

also arises concerning the extent that these images are for the male or female gaze (Figures 4.15 and 4.16). Related matters of audience identification and pleasure are discussed in the next chapter.

Gender Roles

In so far as the dominant narrative structure in cinema has involved a drive towards a final resolution of the problem or disruption posed early on in a story, it could be said that it is the male hero who usually makes things happen and is the agent who moves the narrative along. More often than not, the female serves either as reward for the hero's action or as the motivation for that action, e.g. 'the damsel in distress'. This masculine form of narrative is not confined to cinema, but has been a dominant feature developed across most areas of popular culture. Meanwhile, women's 'action' is more likely to be confined to the domestic domain, revolving around the search for a man or the care of the family. These have been prominent themes and emotions within women's magazines over the years.

I have argued that women's magazines collectively comprise a social institution which serves to foster and maintain a cult of femininity. This cult is manifested both as a social group to which all those born female can belong, and as a set of practices and beliefs: rites and rituals, sacrifices and ceremonies, whose periodic performance re-affirms a common femininity. These journals are not merely reflecting the female role in society; they are also supplying one source of definitions of, and socialisation into, that role.

Ferguson (1983)

Women's magazines could be seen as providing step-by-step instructions in how to achieve womanhood, with two roles being central to that status: 'wife' and 'mother'. Marjorie Ferguson (1983), surveying changes in women's magazines in postwar Britain, identified two main changes. First, there has been a shift from 'getting and keeping your man' to 'self-help'. This involves 'achieving perfection' (being a better mother, lover, worker, cook, and staying slim) and 'overcoming misfortune' (such as physical or emotional crises). Second, the role of paid worker or 'independent woman' has emerged from the mid-1970s in magazines like *Cosmopolitan*. Despite these changes, Ferguson argued the basic message continues to prevail – that women should identify with a femininity which 'focuses on Him, Home and Looking Good'. She considered only one mainstream women's magazine as challenging this orthodoxy, *MS*, an American production, which failed to succeed in Britain.

FIGURE 4.17
Source: more!/Emap Consumer Media

Not everyone accepts Ferguson's emphasis on the restricted agenda constructed by women's magazines. Janice Winship (1987) stressed the supporting role the magazines play, which is important given women's exclusion from the masculine world of work and leisure, and the lack of similar editorial content devoted to women (in any depth) in other areas of the media. Even in teenage magazines, readers are supplied with a broader range of options than before. For example, *Just Seventeen*, the market leader at the beginning of the 1990s, tackles problems such as domestic violence and sexual abuse, as well as offering advice on how to pursue an independent lifestyle. This shift is acknowledged by Angela McRobbie (1996), who in an earlier study had argued that adolescent girls' magazines like *Jackie* constructed an ideology of 'romantic individualism' in which a girl's main quest in life was a loving relationship with a man, a relationship in which she would acquiesce to his demands and needs. In contrast to the *Jackie* of the 1970s and early 1980s, McRobbie sees the 1990s *more* as much less idealistic in its representation of relationships with males. Instead, *more* encourages female readers to explore and satisfy their own sexual and social needs. Alongside a more egalitarian treatment of relationships with males, there is an emphasis on humour and irony rather than romantic escapism (Figure 4.17). Judging from the significant number of male readers of women's magazines (approximately one in five of *more*'s readers are male according to the National Readership Survey), there seems to be a latent demand for information and advice on how to succeed in personal relationships and other subjects which are not given space anywhere else in the media (see also A. Gough-Yates, 2003).

Advertisers have also begun to respond to changes in the role of women and shifting gender identities. Some have tried role reversals where traditional gender stereotypes are challenged (Figures 4.18 and 4.19), but rarely is such advertising the product of a female creative input, and there has been no reduction in the level of complaints of sexism in advertising (see Figure 4.20)

FIGURE 4.18
Source: Rainey Kelly Campbell Roalfe

FIGURE 4.20
Source: TBWA Ltd

FIGURE 4.19
Source: © Coty

CASE STUDY:
Women and Science Fiction Cinema

Traditionally, science fiction has been a masculine film genre, not least because of the domination of males in the leading roles whether that be as scientists, explorers, space commanders or other narrative heroes (see also the discussion of science fiction in Chapter 3). Women have largely featured as objects of male desire, typified by Altaira, the scantily clad blonde in *Forbidden Planet* (1956), whose narrative function is the 'princess prize' (according to Propp's narrative schema) (Figure 4.21)

FIGURE 4.21
Source: The Kobal Collection

The impact of feminism on female representations in science fiction cinema can be detected from the late 1970s and early 1980s, most notably in the *Alien* film series starring Sigourney Weaver as Ripley. In *Aliens*, she is the heroine who takes on the alien monsters. Her transcendence into the masculine role is symbolised by her short cropped hair and military style clothing. Such masculine attire is also noticeable in *Terminator 2*, where Linda Hamilton plays Sarah Connor in an action-heroine role (Figure 4.22). More recently, there is the example of a (post)modern action-heroine, Trinity (Carrie Ann Moss), in *The Matrix* (1999) (Figure 4.23). She is a cool, independent martial arts expert who is more than a match for the men in the film. However, it could be argued that these seemingly radical new representations of women are compromised by the narrative motivation which accounts for their heroism. Ripley in *Aliens* and Sarah Connor in *Terminator 2* are both emboldened by a maternal mission to protect their children (a surrogate child in the case of *Aliens*). In the case of *The Matrix*, Trinity eventually loses her steely detachment, and falls in love with the male hero, The One, played by Keanu Reeves.

Another example of shifting gender roles in science fiction has been developed in the *X-Files* where the rational, sceptical scientist Scully is a woman (Gillian Anderson) whilst the intuitive and irrational character, Mulder, is a man (David Duchovny). Nevertheless, it is Mulder's intuition and psychological powers which tend to triumph over scientific rationality in solving the various mysteries emanating from supernatural forces. Furthermore, Scully continues to be framed as an object of (sexual) desire, but at least retains her sexual independence.

FIGURE 4.22
Terminator 2: Judgment Day, 1991
Source: The Kobal Collection/ Pacific Western/Le Studio Canal Plus/Lightstorm

FIGURE 4.23
Matrix
Source: The Kobal Collection

There is no clear linear progression in the evolution of gender representations on the screen. In the case of science fiction, as far back as 1950 *Rocketship Xm* featured a female research scientist on board the mission to the moon, whereas fifty years later, *Independence Day* confirmed women's primary role as supporting men entrusted with risking their lives to save the planet.

Activity 4.6

Carry out a comparison between the women heroes in science fiction films such as *Barbarella*, *Aliens*, *Terminator*, *The Matrix* and *Tomb Raider*. Identify what characteristics they have in common and account for any differences between the characters. To what extent can these films and their heroines be considered to belong to one common genre called 'science fiction'?

Another masculine dominated genre, the television police series, has also been 'infiltrated' by women. *Cagney and Lacey* provided an alternative to the male 'buddy' police action series of the 1970s, such as Starsky and Hutch, and in Britain, Helen Mirren played a strong female detective succeeding in spite of male chauvinism in *Prime Suspect* (1991-6).

Some would claim the real breakthrough on television came with *Charlie's Angels* in the 1970s. Whilst these three independent female detectives were certainly novel at the time, the excessive sexual glamorisation of their appearance tended to counteract any sense of these being real characters. The updated film version of 2000 retains the emphasis on glamorous buddies, whilst at the same time parodying their sexual appeal. From Lara Croft in *Tomb Raider* to *Ally McBeal*, there is now a much wider range of leading female roles to identify with on the screen, but few female characters enjoy full independence in the masculine tradition. Women seen as turning their back on the family have long been represented as unfulfilled or even punished in Hollywood cinema. Relevant examples of this include *Fatal Attraction* (1987) (a neurotically obsessed single woman eventually suffers death), *The Hand that Rocks the Cradle* (1992) (a career woman nearly loses her husband and children to the nanny) and *A Stranger Among Us* (1992) (a female detective realises motherhood is superior to having a career). Another trend has been the re-emergence of the 'femme fatale', a seductive but dangerous woman, who manipulates men for her own ends. The detective writer played by Sharon Stone in the 1992 thriller, *Basic Instinct* (Figure 4.24), is just such a character, with the added twist that she is bisexual with psychopathic tendencies! Barbara Stanwyck represents an earlier example of a femme fatale who seduces Fred MacMurray into murdering her husband for insurance money in the classic 1944 film *Double Indemnity* (Figure 4.25).

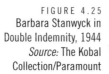

FIGURE 4.24
Sharon Stone in
Basic Instinct, 1992
Source: The Kobal
Collection/Carolco

FIGURE 4.25
Barbara Stanwyck in
Double Indemnity, 1944
Source: The Kobal
Collection/Paramount

It might be argued that British television soap opera has been the most effective in representing independent and assertive female characters. Since 1960, *Coronation Street* has had a succession of such characters, from Elsie Tanner to Bet Gilroy to Rita Sullivan. *EastEnders* has continued the tradition of strong, surviving women with the likes of Pat Butcher, Peggy Mitchell and Pauline Fowler. In contrast, strong and sympathetic male characters have been noticeable by their absence in British soaps. Rather the opposite is the case, with most men being exposed for their weaknesses or danger whether they be emotional instability, dishonesty or just plain incompetence.

Changing Images of Masculinity

Whereas representations of weak or inadequate men have always been a feature of British soaps, it has been argued that this has spread to other areas of television drama. Lucy Gannon, writer of *Peak Practice* and *Soldier, Soldier*, claims that because the ethos for the past few years has been to avoid portraying women in a negative way, then scriptwriters have usually opted for a male character when that person is amoral, wicked, etc in order to have their script commissioned (BBC Radio 4's *The Message*, 1 March 2002).

It is certainly true that media representations of masculinity have become much more varied since the mid-1980s. A good illustration of this was the Gillette advertising campaign of the late 1980s and early 1990s which displayed a full spectrum of masculine roles: father, lover, companion, sportsman, businessman, etc – action with feelings – men 'having it all'. The role of Fatherhood came to modern prominence in the 1979 Hollywood film, *Kramer vs Kramer*, which made the case for men being capable of taking responsibility for children. In this case, the man (Dustin Hoffman) is successful in proving that men can be effective as a single parent when the mother temporarily disappears.

FIGURE 4.26
To what extent does this image challenge traditional ideas of masculinity?
Source: Kouros, Yves Saint Laurent

In the 1980s, the label 'new man' came to be associated with a softening of traditional masculinity and the display of a more sensitive, vulnerable and caring image (see Figure 4.26). Part of this new representation involved the sexualisation of the male body, particularly in advertising for male cosmetics and clothing (Mort 1996) but in other respects it is easy to exaggerate how far representations of masculinity really changed. By the mid 1990s the 'new man' had been superseded by the 'new lad', a return to a not-so-new masculine culture celebrating sex, sport and alcohol, albeit with a postmodern 'twist' of irony and style.

Loaded magazine (Figure 4.27) with its provocative anti-PC motto 'for men who should know better', successfully tapped into this culture, and achieved a circulation of over 250,000 two years after its 1994 launch. Its popularity in turn inspired even more successful titles *FHM* and *Maxim*, and eventually most of these men's magazine titles resorted to employing sexually seductive images of contemporary sex icons such as Pamela Anderson and Britney Spears on their front covers in place of the masculine role models which had dominated the first wave of men's magazines.

FIGURE 4.27
Loaded, November 1996. An example of sexist stereotyping, or postmodern irony?
Source: Loaded/IPC Magazines

In their recent study, *Making Sense of Men's Magazines,* Jackson *et al* (2001) argue that the 'new lad' represented in magazines like *FHM* and *Loaded* seems to be a return to a fundamental masculine/feminine binary opposition in which female sexuality is something to be mastered and controlled. Their appeal lies in being able to deflect some of the masculine anxieties provoked by female independence and contemporary sexual politics. At the same time, the authors claim, the magazines have also opened up 'previously repressed areas of masculine experience, including men's appreciation of other men's bodies, fashion and health.'

A parallel set of 'new lad' representations can also be found in the spate of late 1990s British gangster films typified by the work of director Guy Ritchie. His two films, *Lock Stock and Two Smoking Barrels* (1998) (Figure 4.28) and *Snatch* (2000), are seen by Claire Monk (1999) as a 'regressive escape from the demands of maturity – and women.' The films represent a world of grown-up male adolescence in which macho posturing, male competitiveness and bullying feature strongly in an almost exclusively masculine environment. To add glamour and style to the characters, Ritchie provides them with quick witted and cheeky repartee. In *Lock Stock*, moral authority resides in the character played by Vinnie Jones, a 'hard man', whose masculine iconic status originated in football.

Gender and Sexuality

The cruder kind of stereotyping of gay and lesbian culture has increasingly been challenged in recent years. Gay men used to invariably be represented as camp or effeminate, as in a range of television sitcoms such as *Are you Being Served*, whilst lesbians were more inclined to be seen as butch and neurotic. British television soap opera began to include gay and lesbian characters from the late 1980s. A notable contrast to the dominant butch stereotype of the lesbian was provided by the character of Beth Jordache, a young, pretty and feminine lesbian (played by Anna Friel) in Channel 4's soap opera, *Brookside*. She was quickly identified as belonging to a new stereotype, the 'lipstick lesbian'. However, even she followed the conventional fate of lesbians in film and television drama by suffering a tragic fate (dying of a rare heart condition).

FIGURE 4.28
Lock, Stock and Two Smoking Barrels
Source: The Kobal Collection

The increasing visibility of gay and lesbian representations in the media is based on both cultural and commercial factors. A decline in homophobia is reflected in the success of gay and lesbian participants of the *Big Brother* series in 2000/1, and the rating success in America of the sitcom *Will and Grace*, demonstrated having leading gay characters doesn't harm viewing figures.

Channel 4's *Queer as Folk* (1999) broke new ground by being the first television drama series to focus on gay culture (Figure 4.29). There is clear evidence that the parameters of media representations of sexuality have significantly shifted, but it would be a mistake to assume sexuality is no longer an issue in those representations, especially in the more conservative media such as the tabloid press, where gay and lesbian homophobic labels are still employed.

Channel 4 glad to pioneer the first gay drama on British TV

Stuart Miller and **Janine Gibson** on a new series featuring three homosexuals which has provoked moral outrage over a plotline involving a boy of 15, but has won the praise of equality campaigners

FIGURE 4.29
Queer as Folk – Guardian 24.2.99
Source: Stuart Millar & Janine Gibson, ©Guardian

In conclusion, it has to be said that much of the above discussion has dwelt on the debates concerning dominant patterns of gender representation in the mainstream media. These are only patterns, and the more closely media texts are analysed, the more evident the variety of gender representation becomes, particularly once it is recognised that many texts are capable of activating more than one audience reading. Furthermore, in an increasingly pluralistic media, where narrow casting and 'niche' segmentation are ever more apparent, minority perspectives and lifestyles may be found, often providing alternative views that challenge the dominant ideologies and patterns of representation.

The British Nation: An Ideological Construction

What does it mean to be British? The extent to which the people of Britain can be considered a nation is deeply problematic. A shared sense of belonging and identity is certainly a real sentiment for many people living in Britain. However, closer scrutiny raises questions concerning divisions between various groups comprising the British population, not least nationalism within Scotland and Wales. And where England is taken as a national 'core', further divisions can be identified along ethnic, religious, regional and class lines. If there are so many alternative sources of identity, how has the national sense of identity achieved such a strong hold? Nations are, in part, 'imagined communities', and their historical and contemporary formation is the result of complex social and political processes. The modern media have contributed towards the symbolic representation of what it means to be British. In doing so, it is possible to argue that they have helped to create and recreate an imaginary community which is ideological in the sense that it disguises the real divisions and conflicting interests which contradict 'national unity'.

At the heart of the sense of being British is the idea of historical tradition, and this is most strongly personified by the monarchy. The Queen, as head of state, symbolises national unity as well as being a historical point of reference, reminding us of our 'great' history and heritage. Standing above day-to-day politics, she is often seen as epitomising what is good about Britain. Her ritual role is strongly supported by a largely deferential media. Within broadcasting she is exempt from the critical scrutiny normally applied to anyone with her power and status. The annual Christmas address to the nation, broadcast on all national television and radio channels, is supplemented by frequent documentary features which celebrate her role (see also Figure 2.11).

An alternative perspective is voiced by writers like Rosalind Brunt, who perceive the monarch to be a barrier to real democratic freedom and self determination;

> *In so far as ideologies are never simply ideas in people's heads but are indeed the myths we live by and which contribute to our sense of self and self-worth, then I think it actually matters that the British have no real identity as 'we the people' but continue to consign ourselves to a subordinated position as 'subjects' of the Queen. Not that we see it that way; the commonsense view is that the British are freer than their monarch; we can go anywhere we please without a police escort and 'I wouldn't have her job for the world!' In this way we happily consent to the monarch's continuing to act on our behalf...*
>
> *Brunt (1992)*

How can the Queen be seen as an ideological force? As she is the country's richest landowner and a member of a privileged elite, the Queen's status as unifying the nation is seen as mythic. The media, not least television, appear to have conspired in perpetuating this myth by acting as public relations agents on behalf of the royal family. The BBC has a 'Royal Correspondent' who usually provides a news report based on the activities of the royal family when on public duty without the critical scrutiny which may be applied to other powerful public figures, unless a story is followed up after being first broken in the tabloid press, e.g. the reports of Prince Harry's consumption of alcohol and drugs early in 2002.

Rituals of royal births, marriages, anniversaries and deaths provide opportunities for media and national celebration (Figure 4.30) or mourning as in the case of the death of Princess Diana in 1997. Whilst television and press coverage of the funeral encouraged the nation to mourn together, it did not necessarily reflect the degrees of detachment or disinterest in the country. The British Film Institute's own survey of 500 diarists (John Willis and Rob Turnock, 1998) revealed 40 per cent of their sample thought the coverage over the top or excessive, and 50 per cent were not profoundly affected by Diana's death. In fact, many of the diarists commented that television's coverage was a significant influence in stimulating the scale of the emotional public response.

FIGURE 4.30
Radio Times 19.6.99
Source: Reproduced with permission, Radio Times 19–25 June 1999

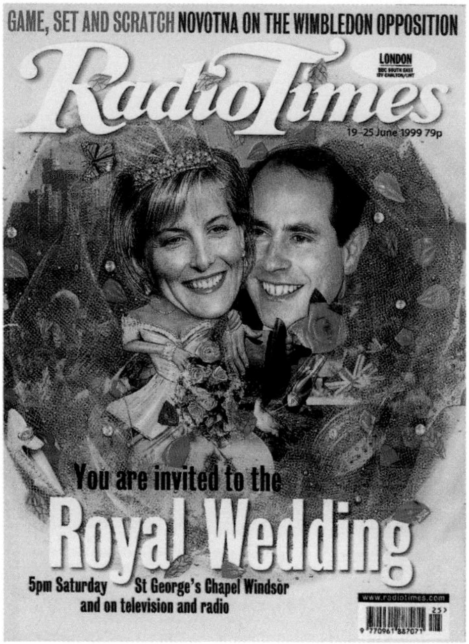

Ironically, the reaction of the tabloid press to the perceived aloofness of the Queen prior to Diana's funeral (Figure 4.31) was damaging to her image. It is also the case that in using stories about the royal family in order to boost circulation, the tabloid newspapers have steadily eroded the traditional idealised and mythic representation of the monarchy which had developed during and after the Second World War. In the past fifteen to twenty years, there has been a steady stream of stories claiming to expose adultery and deceit within the royal marriages as well as questioning the expense and tax-free privileges of the monarchy and their lifestyle.

The Guardian Friday September 5 1997 3

The death of Diana

'We have broken with convention for this unique day for this unique person.'
Lt Col Malcolm Ross, comptroller of the Lord Chamberlain's office

The Mirror
YOUR PEOPLE ARE SUFFERING
SPEAK TO US MA'AM
VOICE OF THE Mirror: PAGE 11

THE Sun
THE SUN SPEAKS ITS MIND
WHERE IS OUR QUEEN? WHERE IS HER FLAG?

THE EXPRESS
SHOW US YOU CARE
Mourners call for the Queen to lead our grief
TOUCHED BY DIANA

Daily Mail
LET THE FLAG FLY AT HALF MAST

Yesterday's front pages made unhappy reading for the royal family, which after a week defending protocol and tradition realised it had misjudged the mood of the nation

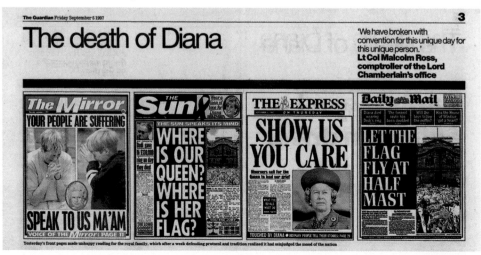

FIGURE 4.31
Death of Diana
Source: Guardian 5.9.97

What media texts may be seen as representative of genuine contemporary British (or English) culture? Surely, we could recognise British culture in a British film (as opposed to Hollywood)? Aside from the fact that few films are authentically British, with respect to both financial investment and artistic input and control, a list of recent British film successes reveals a very wide diversity of cultural representations. For example, there are the 'heritage' films like *A Room With a View* (1985) or *Sense and Sensibility* (1995) which tend to focus nostalgically on the lives of the upper middle classes in previous generations. These period films fit many outsiders' (usually American) perceptions of British culture – a traditional, educated and civilised way of life – and they are filmed with great attention to period detail. More contemporary British films which dwell affectionately on the lives of the upper middle class include *Four Weddings and a Funeral* (1994) (Figure 4.32) and *Notting Hill* (1999). In contrast, films like *Trainspotting* (1996) (Figure 4.33) and *East is East* (1999) represent Britain as much less unified, and divided by cultural differences and social problems.

FIGURE 4.32
Four Weddings and a Funeral (1994)
Source: The Kobal Collection

FIGURE 4.33
Trainspotting (1996)
Source: The Kobal Collection

Activity 4.7

Choose two of the following films and compare what makes them distinctly British in terms of their representation of British Culture:

Trainspotting (1996)
Lock Stock and Two Smoking Barrels (1998)
Notting Hill (1999)
Billy Elliot (2000)
Bridget Jones's Diary (2001)
Harry Potter and the Philosopher's Stone (2001)

A key factor in helping to shape media representations of national identity is in the construction of binary oppositions 'us' and 'them'. International competition or conflict provides a good opportunity for 'British values' to be asserted in contrast to an enemy, real or imagined. The Second World War inspired countless stories celebrating the triumphant British spirit in the face of overwhelming odds, including many films like *Battle of Britain* (1969) and *The Dam Busters* (1954), which are still regularly recycled on television. Such transparent patriotism was invoked in 1982 by the popular press during the Falklands War (most notoriously with *The Sun's* headline 'Gotcha!', in reference to the sinking of the *Belgrano*), in 1991 during the Gulf War, and in 2001 in the war against the Taliban in Afghanistan

(although not unanimously – see Figure 4.9 on page 77). Perceived attempts to dilute British national identity or sovereignty, especially via the European Union and the euro, also provoke a patriotic response, particularly in the tabloid press. An example was the reaction to the decision by the EU to introduce a worldwide ban on British beef until BSE, so called 'mad cow disease', was brought under control. Many newspapers portrayed the British government's stand against the EU in terms of a declaration of war (Figure 4.34). Much of the anti-European stance of many British newspapers such as *The Sun* and the *Daily Mail* is based on a belief that British identity will be destroyed and lost through closer integration with Europe. Although Germany is now a close European ally, football matches between England and Germany are still reported in terms reminiscent of the Second World War. For instance, following England's 5-1 victory over Germany in September 2001 in a World Cup qualifying match the headlines included:

FIGURE 4.34
Source: Daily Express

'Germany Blitzed' (*Sunday Mirror*)
'Our Finest Hour' (*Express on Sunday*)
'Don't Mention the Score' (*News of the World*)

Hollywood: America versus 'Others'

In creating enemies or threats to the American way, Hollywood films have come up with a range of possibilities. Starting with its own native Americans (the US cavalry versus the Indians), American films have demonised Russians and Chinese (during the Cold War), Colombians (the war on drugs) and most recently, Arabs (as Islamic terrorists). Even prior to the Twin Towers destruction of 11 September 2001, Arab Muslims have frequently been represented as religious fanatics intent on bombing America, in films such as *True Lies* (1994), *Executive Decision* (1996) and *The Siege* (1998). Rather than attempting to understand anti-American sentiment among Arab peoples, these films resorted to crude negative racial stereotyping against which heroes such as Bruce Willis or Arnold Schwarzenegger could protect America.

Race and Ideology

Racial difference is based on biologically determined human variations which have long ceased to exist in the world. Colonisation and inter-racial mixing mean that there are no simple racially distinctive groups left. However, perceived physical and culture difference is the basis for social definitions of racial or, more specifically, ethnic difference (an ethnic group having a shared culture usually linked to national or religious identity). The belief that other racial/ethnic groups are inferior is at the root of racism/ethnocentrism, and such ideologies can usually be traced back to imperialism and colonialism as a means of justifying the colonial conquest and exploitation of other social groups.

Most western societies today are multicultural, largely as a result of immigration from ex-colonies linked to the demand for cheap labour. How far this multiculturalism is adequately reflected in the media is questionable. A further issue concerns the extent to which the media resort to racial stereotyping when representing ethnic and racial minorities.

Race and Entertainment

Having dark skin has long been thought to signify difference not just of colour but also of 'nature' from a white perspective. The idea that black people are more physically expressive than whites is deep-rooted in western culture. Blacks have been able to achieve most visibility in the media via music and sport, both of which reinforce the notion of 'natural rhythm'. The fact that their disproportionate achievements in such areas may be a product of poverty and the lack of alternative avenues to gain success is rarely considered. In such roles, black people remain unthreatening and only reinforce existing stereotypes. Indeed, early performances by blacks in Hollywood cinema consciously played up to white prejudices – e.g. the eyeball-rolling servant and 'mammy' stereotypes in films like *Gone with the Wind* (1939).

Within both pop and jazz music, much of the creative drive and inspiration has been provided by Afro-American musical culture. Yet many black musicians have been marginalised. More often than not, white versions of black music have predominated, frequently watering down the emotive, sexual or social power of the music in the process. For example, rock and roll, the new 'youth rebellion' music of the 1950s, was simply black rhythm and blues sung by white performers like Bill Haley and Elvis Presley. This was seen by many American whites as an unwelcome infiltration of their culture by the back door, as they tried (unsuccessfully) to suppress the 'nigger music'.

It is not only in pre-war Hollywood that patronising and demeaning images of blacks were produced. The tradition of 'blacking up' by white singers such as Al Jolson in *The Jazz Singer* (1927) was sustained on British television up to 1976 with *The Black and White Minstrel Show*. Likewise, the 'simple' and 'quaint' delivery of English by ethnic minorities has been a constant source or ridicule, as in *It Ain't Half Hot Mum* (Indians living under colonial rule), *Fawlty Towers* (Manuel, the half-witted Spanish waiter) and *Mind Your Language* (a foreign student class containing several crude stereotypes). All of these are 1970s British television sitcoms, frequently repeated over subsequent years.

Much racism in comedy is unconscious, and is rarely perceived as racism by the white audience – 'It's only a laugh.' Indeed, the pleasures of comedy are complex and the reasons for laughing not easily explained by either audiences or comedians. One function served would seem to be the sense of collective identity produced by laughing at 'others' – those who are perceived as different and possibly a threat. Too often, when blacks appear alongside whites in comedies, racial issues become a main focus for the humour, for example *Rising Damp* and *In Sickness and In Health*, rather than these being comic characters who just happen to be black or white. Furthermore, the audience may well end up laughing with, rather than at, the racial bigotry expressed by characters such as Alf Garnett (see Pickering 2001).

Race and Social Problems

Portraying black people as problems

The main way in which black people are treated in newspapers is as a social problem. Black people are portrayed as constituting a threat to white British society, first through their immigration to this country and then, when settled here, as posing a law and order problem. This is done in a number of ways: through dramatic presentation of stories involving banner headlines and prominent positioning, provocative or damning quotations and statements from people portrayed as authoritative figures, popular stereotypes, repetition of unreliable stories, and the creation and manipulation of popular fears.

Gordon and Rosenberg (1989)

Given that 'bad news is good news' when it comes to choosing stories in the press and broadcasting, it is not surprising that incidents involving violence and crime and ethnic minorities are given prominence. What matters is the explanatory framework offered to enable the audience to understand such stories. This might be shaped by the political values of a newspaper, particularly in the case of British tabloid newspapers like *The Sun* and the *Daily Mail* (Figures 4.35 and 4.36). In this case the stories relate to the recent controversy surrounding asylum seekers and refugees, and their impact on British society. Where such stories coalesce in a short timespan, the media can be said to be contributing to a **moral panic** demanding some kind of political response (in this case stricter immigration controls).

FIGURE 4.35
The Sun, London, 14 March 2000
Source: ©News International Newspapers Limited

Two wives, 15 children, two homes

£32,000 A YEAR ASYLUM SEEKER

AN asylum seeker with two wives and 15 children has received more than £32,000 in benefits while his case is being considered.

The Algerian family, headed by Mohammed Kinewa, who is in his 60s, arrived 15 months ago.

They have also been given the use of two fully-furnished four-bedroomed houses with satellite TV – one for each wife and her children.

They receive £617.72 a week in benefits alone. The yearly estimated cost rises to more than £50,000 when council tax relief, educating the school-age children, translators, solicitors, and English classes for the family are taken into account.

One wife said yesterday that after deciding to flee their war-torn country they had chosen Britain because 'it is a kind country'.

Shadow Home Secretary Ann Widdecombe said yesterday: 'I'm appalled we are

bearing such costs, particularly given that polygamy is not lawful in this country.

'I hope Mr Kenewa's case will be dealt with as quickly as possible so that either he can be sent back to Algeria or maybe start working and begin earning some money to support his enormous family.'

Currently the Home Office is sitting on a backlog of 104,000 asylum applications stretching back 19 months. Ministers have

FIGURE 4.36
Daily Mail 13.3.00
Source: Daily Mail

FIGURE 4.37
In 1991, the police in Los Angeles were captured by an amateur video operator in the process of beating up Rodney King, a seemingly defenceless black man. On the basis of the video evidence, the police were brought to trial, but were (initially) found not guilty, a verdict which sparked widespread disturbances
Source: Mike Bygrave, Guardian Weekend, 13 February 1993/Rex Features

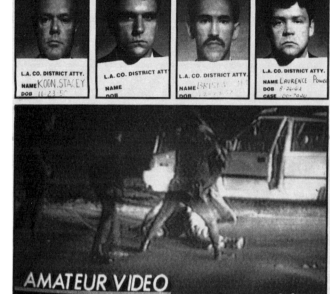

Despite the xenophobia and racism implicit in these front pages all journalists in the media are bound by a professional code of conduct which forbids racist reporting, and most would claim they simply report the facts without prejudice. However, unconscious or inferential racism may be detected in the language used to tell a story: 'riots' imply rampaging mobs who need to be controlled; 'uprisings' imply rebellion against injustice. The desire for simple stories with single causes and themes of 'good' and 'bad' often means that long-term causes and morally ambiguous actions may be overlooked or not understood by the journalists themselves (Figure 4.37).

The Los Angeles riots of 1992 were widely seen as a rerun of previous examples in inner-city black 'ghettoes' (except this time the initial outcry was based on the broadcast of an amateur home video showing white police officers beating Rodney King, a defenceless black man). What was not revealed was the fact that blacks were now a minority in the inner city of Los Angeles (Hispanics and Latinos were by far the majority), and much of the violence and looting was directed against Korean immigrants who owned most of the stores in the 'ghetto'. Meanwhile, the amateur video images of the police beating have become an icon for racial inequality in the USA and elsewhere, being incorporated into Spike Lee's 1992 film, *Malcolm X.* The broadcast of the video on television helped to bring about a criminal trial of the officers involved and it was the not-guilty verdict which finally led to the riots.

Another example of television images provoking a strong public response can be found in the dramatic television news pictures of famine in Ethiopia during 1984, which stimulated the subsequent 'media event' Live Aid the following summer (Figure 4.38).

Third World Images

As with the reporting of racial problems within western countries, the causes of problems like famine are grossly simplified for audience consumption, the one difference being that sympathy and pity are offered. Yet the emphasis on aid as a solution only serves to reinforce the sense that Third World countries (especially in Africa) are largely helpless, and depend for their survival on 'our' help; it also obscures the history of colonial exploitation and subsequent economic dependency which have played a significant role in the failure of Third World economies to become self-sufficient.

An alternative to the image of poverty or war is that of the 'exotic' and 'colourful'. Television holiday programmes are inclined to dwell on these qualities when featuring long-distance tourist packages, complete with a backdrop of the locals' friendly smiling faces and atmospheric native music. An exception to this was BBC2's *Rough Guide* series, which attempted to provide a social and political context within which tourist attractions could be experienced. The 'Singapore Girl' of the airline advert is a reassuring and (sexually) seductive image promising the western male 'service with a smile', effectively effacing the widespread hardship and sometimes sexual exploitation faced by many young women in South East Asian countries like Thailand and the Philippines (Figure 4.39).

FIGURE 4.38
British media at work in a relief camp at Haiya in the Red Sea Hills, Eastern Sudan, in December 1984. People in the camp put the child on the ground for display, aware that publicity for their plight might eventually bring some help.
What are the problems in using images of starving children to highlight famine in Africa and other parts of the world?
What alternative images might be used to represent problems of poverty and exploitation in Third World countries?
Source: photograph by Wendy Wallace

FIGURE 4.39
A magazine feature on Sri Lanka. How does this travel feature represent Sri Lanka to the potential western tourist?
Source: Observer Magazine/Panos Pictures

Changing Representations of Race: Hollywood Cinema

As society changes, so do the media. The shift in how black people in the USA have been represented in Hollywood films reflects wider social changes in American society. In their own way, the films themselves will have contributed to the changing perceptions of black and white identities in the USA.

The pre-war period was characterised by the use of black characters as light relief – as song-and-dance acts or wide-eyed simpletons. These patronising images drew heavily from white perceptions of black life in the southern plantations. In the post-war period, a growing number of films reflected the growing consciousness of racial injustice, particularly the segregation policies of the south. In *The Defiant Ones* (1958), two convicts, one black and one white, are symbolically chained together and forced into cooperating in their bid to stay free. The film starred Sidney Poitier, who later appeared in numerous films in which he challenged, and usually overcame, white prejudices, for example *In the Heat of the Night* (1967) as a black detective working with a white police force in the southern states of the USA.

FIGURE 4.40
Shaft, 1971
Source: The Kobal Collection/MGM

It was not until the 1970s that films began to feature predominantly black casts and thus move closer to capturing black American culture. However, the emphasis was on large doses of violence and sex, in a bid to be commercial. The cycle which began with *Shaft* (1971) (Figure 4.40) came to be known as 'blaxploitation' films. While containing some ethnic authenticity (e.g. the argot), and often reflecting a stylised sense of black pride, the films also could be said to reinforce white perceptions of the black man as aggressive gangster or drug dealer.

A few black actors, such as Eddie Murphy and Richard Pryor, became 'stars' in the 1980s. Nevertheless, most of their roles could be seen as 'safe' for white audiences in the sense that they could be said to be 'deracinated'. This means that they tended to play isolated black characters whose black culture is used only as an entertaining decoration, for example Eddie Murphy's street-talking, wisecracking detective in *Beverly Hills Cop*, *Beverly Hills Cop II*, *48 Hours* and so on.

At the start of the 1990s there was a surge in American films made by and starring blacks. This was precipitated by the commercial success of *Do the Right Thing* (Figure 4.41) and *House Party* in 1989 (both made over $26 million profit), and the growth in young (mostly male) black film-makers eager to represent the many facets of black culture largely ignored by white-dominated Hollywood. Many of the films, such as *Boyz n the Hood* (1991) and *Menace II Society* (1993), tell coming-of-age stories of young black Americans caught up in the violence and criminality of inner-city neighbourhoods. Hip hop and rap music are employed to emphasise the anger and aggression felt by many of the characters (often played by rap music stars such as Ice-T and Ice Cube). Hailed by some writers as representing a 'new black realism' (Diawara, 1993), others criticised the films for focusing on 'the violent, destructive features of ghetto life: drugs, the cocaine wars, gangs, gangsta rap, drive-bys and gang warfare' (*Denzin*, 2002).

FIGURE 4.41
Do The Right Thing, 1989
Source: The Kobal Collection/40 Acres and a Mule

Growth in Visibility on Television

In both American and British television, there has been a steady growth in the number and range of ethnic representations on the screen: news readers (Trevor McDonald), chat show hosts (Oprah Winfrey) and police series (*Hill Street Blues*). One development has been the emergence of the ethnic minority sitcom. In the 1970s, early examples were *The Jeffersons* (USA) and *The Fosters* (UK). Beginning in 1984, *The Cosby Show* has been the most successful, but not without some controversy. In many respects, it represents a recoding of some of the traditional black stereotypes shared by white Americans. The family is a strong and cohesive unit with the perfect father figure. Both parents are successful professional workers (doctor and lawyer) who, although affluent, are not frivolous in their consumption. There is a strong emphasis on the value of education (particularly in the spin-off series *A Different World*, set in a black college). From time to time, the theme of racial pride is foregrounded with references to black history and culture, and yet the family is clearly well integrated into a multiracial America.

Critics of *The Cosby Show* have argued that it fails to address questions of racial or class conflict, and that its representation of black culture and lifestyle is very superficial and idealised. The series is seen as reassuring white American audiences that the American Dream is alive and well, and that black people can be successful through hard work and discipline (see pp. 130–131 for audience responses). On British television, ethnic minority representation in soap opera has been a contentious issue. *Coronation Street*, Britain's most successful soap opera, failed to feature a black character in a prominent role until 1999, despite being set in an area which would in reality be multicultural. In contrast, *EastEnders* has included a range of ethnic minorities (Bengali, Turkish, West Indian, etc) and has tackled the issue of racism, albeit as a transient 'story'.

Christine Geraghty (1991) suggests that there have been three strategies adopted by soaps in handling black characters. First, there is 'the exotic' – the one-off character who is used to add drama to a story, but whose blackness does not become an issue itself. For 'the singleton', Geraghty's second category, being black means being used as a vehicle for stories about racial issues, which tends to produce a separate and marginalised status for the character. Finally, there is 'incorporation', where blacks share similar problems to those of other members of the community, and clearly belong to that community as insiders. This allows the characters to be much more varied in their representation, and to be active in developing the narrative.

Despite being one of the few dramas to include significant characters of ethnic minority origin, no one could claim *EastEnders* comes close to representing the real ethnic conditions and cultural diversity of London's East End. It is still dominated by white English families of cockney extraction.

FIGURE 4.42
Source: The Voice

In fact, surveys of British television regularly confirm the continuing marginalisation of ethnic minorities from mainstream broadcasting, especially in popular programming such as game and quiz shows (see Cumberbatch 2001). With the mainstream media failing to represent ethnic minorities adequately, such groups have found their interests more effectively served by independent media production. The growth of incremental and community radio stations has included ethnically based services such as Sunrise Radio (for Asians in West London) and Choice (for the Afro-Caribbean community in South London). Newspapers for Britain's black population include *The Voice* (Figure 4.42). Independent black media production in the USA has been gaining strength, particularly in response to a growing black middle class. An early success story was the Tamla Motown record label established by Berry Gordy in 1960 which during the 1960s produced a string of hits for artists such as Diana Ross and the Supremes, Marvin Gaye and Stevie Wonder. More recently, labels like Def Jam have helped rap and hip-hop acts to flourish. This is in stark contrast to the British music industry, where record companies (almost exclusively controlled by whites) have been accused of failing to develop black talent (with the possible exception of Island Records, for whom Bob Marley recorded).

Independent television producers catering for ethnic minority audiences in Britain do have two channels (BBC2 and Channel 4) that are committed to creating space in their schedules for such groups. Consequently, there has been a variety of programmes targeting Afro-Caribbean and Asian audiences, including the very successful all Asian comedy show, *Goodness Gracious Me*.

Realism

Chapter 2 discussed how the media *mediate* reality via various recognised codes and conventions. Because of the intervening technology, it is impossible to gain first-hand direct experience of the world via the media, no matter how 'transparent' or 'virtual' their representation of reality. Even live television coverage of events, such as a football match, involves continuous selection through the choice of multiple camera frames and angles as well as interpretation via the accompanying commentary and discussion which anchor the meaning of the pictures.

Activity 4.8

Record a short segment (of 10–15 minutes) of a live television broadcast of a football match and list the range of camera shots used to represent the action. Say why you think these particular shots have been chosen. In what ways do you think the television viewing experience of the game contrasts with the experience of actually seeing the match from within the ground?

Part of the process of creating meaning is the degree to which we, as audiences, can recognise and identify with what is being portrayed – the media text's credibility or realism. We expect what we see, listen to or read to have some connection with our own lives and experiences and the world we inhabit, or to appear to be based upon some sort of recognisable reality of the world 'out there'. This then helps us to identify and understand the text and its meaning. We often judge how successful this illusion or story is by measuring the text against our own experiences, our own 'situated culture' (see Chapter 1) and biography. What is 'real' therefore can become a subjective and controversial concept, where a text that one person perhaps considers to be realistic may not be considered so by someone else with another perspective. A programme that describes all football fans as 'hooligans' may appear convincing to someone who knows nothing about football fans except what they read or see in the media, but to someone who has been supporting a football club for many years this may seem to be a very unfair and one-sided portrayal.

In assessing the realism of a media text there is no single measure which can be applied. Four distinctive criteria have been identified as contributing toward a sense of realism. Firstly, there is the *surface realism*. This means 'getting the details right'. For example, a period costume drama should have the characters wearing the clothes appropriate to that period, and the houses should not be adorned with modern accessories like television aerials or satellite dishes. Considerable expense is often incurred ensuring that such period drama precisely recreates the right environment and look such as in the British heritage cinema or the popular television police series *Heartbeat* set in the 1960s complete with steam trains and British motorbikes (although the programme's signature tune is from the 1950s!).

The second criterion refers to the *'inner' or emotional realism* of the characters and their motivation. This allows the audience to identify with the situation and characters portrayed and in particular 'feel' or 'share' the emotions that are an essential part of the story-telling process; for instance, the sadness in tear-jerkers like *Love Story* (1970), *Ghost* (1990) and *Titanic* (1997) or the fear and suspense in films like *Jaws* (1974) or *Jurassic Park* (1993).

A third criterion of realism concerns the logic or *plausibility of the plot* or characters that appear appropriate to the text's particular terms of reference. Viewers often complain if well-established characters in soap operas suddenly shift their typical behaviour pattern and act 'out of character'. In their search for publicity and higher ratings, some British soaps like *Brookside* and *Emmerdale* have introduced a high quota of intensive dramatic incident such as a plane crash, murders, and drug-based crime, which have led to criticisms that these incidents undermine the sense of realism achieved by the soaps' claim to represent ordinary everyday lives and situations. Related to this is the notion that there is some degree of consensus as to the nature of 'reality' and 'truth'. Media texts which challenge certain 'commonsense' or taken-for-granted assumptions, such as the honesty and integrity of the legal and medical professions, may be rejected by audiences as implausible or 'far fetched'.

The fourth criterion of realism refers to the employment of technical and symbolic codes that correspond with those recognised and expected by the audience. We have learned to accept the use of music in the background as a 'mood enhancer', but only so long as it is discreet. Audience or 'canned' laughter is the norm for situation comedies. These codes and conventions change over time, especially as technical advances shift our perceptions of what seems 'real'. Originally, silent films were accompanied by a live piano player who musically 'signalled' the climax of a scene or speech, or the development of the narrative was indicated by captions. The actors wore heavy make-up and performed very theatrically. Contemporary cinema audiences now expect to experience a radically different form of realism made possible by sophisticated technological innovations such as the use of computer-generated special effects and 'surround sound' theatres. Indeed, the marketing hyperbole would lead us to believe we are on the verge of experiencing 'virtual reality'.

Therefore, it is important to recognise that audiences do not apply a unified set of standards to differing media texts in terms of their realism. Depending on the respective media form or genre, we apply varying *modality judgements* of the realism of a text. Although we know that science fiction and cartoons are not 'real', we suspend disbelief and adjust our perceptions in accordance with the accepted codes and conventions of such media categories and genres. Consequently, an animated cartoon comedy like *The Simpsons* is able to achieve a level of realism equal, if not superior to, television situation comedies which employ 'real' human subjects. However, if the generic codes are not adhered to with some degree of consistency, then audiences may well reject the realism of the text. This is particularly apparent when genres are blended together and it is not clear which mode of realism is dominant. For example, *Coprock*, a 1980s American television police series, alienated audiences by incorporating song and dance numbers into the gritty police narrative. More successful in juxtaposing codes from several genres, such as soap opera, gothic horror and murder mystery, was *Twin Peaks* which became a cult television serial. Its constantly shifting modes of realism meant it could be defined as a surreal text.

This kind of generic playfulness is a feature of the postmodern tendency found in many contemporary media texts. It can also be detected in the ironic, parodic reworking of conventional genres such as the television chat show (*Mrs Merton, Dame Edna Everage*, etc). Audiences are increasingly invited to witness the processes of media construction such as in the regular shots of the production crew in the *Big Breakfast Show*, the effect of which is to seemingly expose the 'full' illusion of realism (although such 'exposure' is still carefully controlled). Nevertheless, the dominant aesthetic is still one in which media construction is disguised and the audience (usually very willingly) is drawn into an ensuing seamless reality.

News and Documentary Realism

Despite the differing modes of media realism, audiences generally accord most credibility to representations of reality produced in broadcast news and documentaries. This credibility is rooted in the perceived accuracy and reliability of the reporting (its factuality). As mentioned earlier, legally, broadcasters are required to be impartial in covering news and current affairs, which means refraining from favouring one particular point of view or exercising any undue editorial bias. Whether this impartiality is actually achieved is controversial and much debated. Nevertheless, British broadcasters clearly do wish to be seen as providing an authoritative and truthful news service, whose traditional high status is emphasised through its regular occupation of key positions in the prime-time television and radio schedules.

Activity 4.9

Examine how television and radio create the impression that their news is factual/objective and authoritative by analysing:

a) the title sequences – including the music, graphics, images, and voice-over announcement;
b) the newsreader – status, appearance, accent, mode of delivery and camera framing;
c) the studio set – the furniture, lighting, backdrop and props.

In terms of representing the 'truth', documentaries are generally accorded the highest status. To 'document' a subject implies keeping a factual record for future reference. However, the founder of British documentary film-making, John Grierson, argued that documentaries should combine information with education and propaganda. He oversaw the production of over forty documentaries on aspects of British life in the 1930s and 1940s. The idea was to engineer social reform by highlighting some of the deprivation and hardship endured by working-class people, as in *Coalface* (1935), as well as providing a degree of poetic sensitivity to ordinary lives, as in *Night Mail* (1936).

It wasn't until the 1950s that the more detailed and naturalistic approach to documentary film-making developed, particularly in France where the style was labelled *cinéma vérité* – literally 'cinema truth'. The intention was to observe and record the reality of everyday life as it happened without the usual organisational planning and structured direction and editing. The approach was made possible by new lightweight mobile cameras with synchronised sound recording.

Meanwhile, by the 1960s, television had become the principal medium for documentary production and the genre was typified by the use of an authoritative presenter and/or voice-over, recorded interviews with experts and ordinary people, and visual 'evidence' via location shots, archive film, photographs, etc. The seamless editing and smooth narrative flow of such documentaries, which are still prevalent in today's television, contribute to creating a sense of irrefutable truth and authenticity which disguises the editorial values and choices which shape the making of such documentaries (Figure 4.43). On the basis of Robert Fisk's discussion, list what you think are the relative strengths and weaknesses of television documentary realism and the realism of newspaper/magazine feature reporting.

During the past twenty years the *cinéma vérité* style of documentary film-making has become increasingly popular in television. Known as **fly-on-the-wall**, this approach represents the subject apparently unmediated by a film crew, a presenter or reshooting. Those participating in this type of documentary tend to speak for themselves, and their words or actions are apparently merely recorded and observed, not reflected upon or mediated by a presenter. Examples include Paul Watson's *The Family* (1974), a six-week series focusing on a working-class family living on a council estate in Reading, and Roger Graef's *Police* (1982), also shot in Reading. In helping to define the distinctive fly-on-the-wall approach, Roger Graef listed certain 'ground rules' to be applied in the production. These included:

a) filming events exactly as they happen;
b) agreeing in advance the specific subjects to be filmed;
c) showing the edited version to the participants, but only to ensure any factual errors may be corrected.

Michael Duffield had worked for *Panorama* and made a host of prizewinning documentaries. And his heart was devoted to the theme of the films we found ourselves making: the despair and contempt and sometimes hatred felt by growing numbers of Muslims towards the West. It was he who had refused to stop filming when Israeli troops repeatedly tried to arrest us on the streets of Gaza. It was he who found the brave little Palestinian family of Mohamed Khatib outside Jerusalem – whose tiny home was to be bulldozed away so that the Jewish settlement surrounding it could be further enlarged.

But there was something about Michael's approach towards films – the approach of all directors – that troubled me. It was not the theatricality I identified in documentary film-making – cruelly and wrongly in Michael's eyes – but the refusal to acknowledge it. I was to learn a lot – "not enough" I hear Michael remark as he reads this – about film-making. And I learnt to admire what it can achieve. I also learnt to be deeply suspicious of it.

"If you try to tell that story to my 82-year-old Mum, she'll be so confused she'll fall off her chair," Michael would say each time a Palestinian or a Bosnian had finished a long and complicated political explanation on film. Michael's 82-year-old Mum – a lady whom I did not have the honour to meet – began to dominate my life. The moment a UN officer tried to outline the problems his soldiers experienced in Lebanon with the "de-facto forces" of Israel's "South Labanon Army allies", the second an Egyptian fundamentalist embarked on the history of his movement, I experienced a clear picture of Michael's 82-year-old Mum crashing to the floor. She wouldn't understand the detail, was what Michael was saying. Just as viewers would get the "wrong idea" if I wrote this article. I found this a strange argument.

If it was not shaped for television, reality had to be made digestible. It had to meet certain requirements, the first of them being simplicity. And it also had to show what the director regarded as the reality, even if the occasional item of furniture tended to contradict this. [...] We had, in effect, to move the furniture in order to accommodate the "reality" of the camera. Just as we had to shoot and re-shoot street scenes to accommodate the different camera angles needed to establish the verisimilitude of the film. [...] "Don't look at the camera" became a kind of law. Because, of course, the camera is not supposed to be there. In hospitals in Gaza and Sarajevo, in the Chatila camp, in the "ethnically cleansed" villages of northern Bosnia, we were always telling people not to look at the camera.

Michael returned to his maternal explanation "How do I explain to my 82-year-old Mum that you're driving through the streets of Beirut if I haven't got a clear shot of you driving there?" he asked. "If you're going to Baalbek, my 82-year-old Mum wants to see you going there. I can't afford eight film crews lining the road from Beirut to Baalbek in the hope that just one of them manages to get a good shot of Lord Fisk as he passes on his way. So we have to ask you to do it like this." [...]

But what really concerned Michael, I think, was the idea that by discussing the technical side of the film, we would be revealing the camera's drawbacks and limitations, the failure rather than the success of the technology in which we – making these films – expected the public to believe. How else can one explain the problems we had in choosing those who would or would not appear in the films? In Beirut and Gaza and Sarajevo, we would talk to crowds of Lebanese, Palestinians or Bosnian Muslims, seeking out not only those who had a story to tell and who were prepared to tell it – but who could tell it simply, and preferably in English. Given the fashion for dubbing, Michael's decision to allow men and women to speak in their original language with subtitles was honourable. But the process of seeking out those whom we wanted to appear in the film involved their ability to speak coherently in their own language, let alone in English. We judged them on their performance in private conversation. Or, as Michael would say on such occasions, we would "audition" them. [...] Men and women who looked and sounded convincing could appear in the film. Those who did not rarely got before the camera. In television terms, this made obvious sense. But not in journalistic terms. [...]

An equally important issue arose when we wanted to include Arab fighters in the Bosnian film. We found a young Algerian guerrilla who had been wounded in the battle for Sarajevo and who was happy to meet me and chat about his life. But he refused to appear on film. His story appeared at the top of a page in the *Independent* but is not even mentioned in the film. He would not appear on television; so it could not acknowledge his existence.

Even when I talked to Muslims who spoke both fluently and passionately, the sheer expense of filming – we were using real film-stock, not video – became a burden. In newspaper interviewing, you let people talk for as long as they like, make them feel relaxed and at last they'll answer all your questions. But at £20 a minute, we could not allow our television interviewees – whether they be Shia women, Palestinian doctors or Israeli families – to ramble on. I would have to interrupt, interject, cut into their monologue to bring them back to the point. [...]

But when it was used spontaneously, Steve's camera possessed an awesome power – an "authenticity", Michael called it – which I had to acknowledge. Here Michael came into his own. In Gaza City, Israeli troops were shooting down demonstrators and repeatedly ordering us to turn off the camera; which Michael refused to do. One of the Israelis walked right up to us with his hand outstretched towards the camera lens, saying in Arabic and English: "Yalla [Go] ... Finished for today. Take your things and go away. It's finished. It's over. It's a closed military area." The reason for his fear of the camera – which we did not know as we filmed him – was that he and his men were vandalising and then blowing up the homes of 17 Palestinian families. [...]

And that, of course, is the point. "The film is cut for the power and duration of the pictures," Michael wrote to me before I scripted my commentary for the series. "...the commentary should be written to fit – not the other way round." In writing journalism, we are in control. In film journalism, we can decide what we want to record, but the camera dictates the way in which we do it. We are, in a sense, prisoners of the technology. [...]

Michael took a more aggressive view. "Why should you claim that films are artificial? This is part of the myth of written journalism. When you send your report to the *Independent*, they put it into type, they put a box and lines round it, they choose a picture for it which you didn't take. And you have to 'clean' quotes because people don't speak in proper sentences. You have to put in full stops and commas and paragraphs. That's what we're doing when we have to use lights or film you in your car. Like your reports, film has to end up as a language. Film is a compromise between words and realism." [...]

FIGURE 4.43

Source: Independent on Sunday Review, 5 December 1993 Robert Fisk

However, in practice there is variation between documentary teams, and critics have argued that while seeming more 'natural' and unmediated, these documentaries are subject to considerable editorial control during post-production. With a shooting ratio of up to 50 hours of recorded video to one hour broadcast, the onus is on the editor to generate as much dramatic interest and entertainment as possible. For example, in Paul Watson's *Sylvania Waters* (1993), a series built around Noele Donaher, a *nouveau riche* Australian woman and her family, Ms Donaher complained that the producers had unduly focused on her domestic arguments and highlighted her casual racist remarks about black/Asian Australians. To many Australians it did seem as though the British production team had set out to reinforce certain negative stereotypes about them.

Sylvania Waters also employed a title sequence and incidental music which were similar to those used in Australian soap operas. Although this was meant to be ironic, it reflects the growing convergence and overlap of documentary and drama on television. As early as 1966, Ken Loach had applied *cinéma vérité*-style filming to a drama about homelessness, *Cathy Come Home*. The documentary feel of the film created a stronger sense of realism and contributed to its strong impact on audiences (which in turn contributed to the establishment of Shelter, the charity for the homeless). More contemporary drama employing a *vérité* naturalism includes *NYPD*, *This Life* and *ER*. *NYPD* and *This Life* use hand-held cameras, which seem to react 'spontaneously' to the characters and situations, natural atmospheric sound effects which sometimes make the dialogue difficult to follow, and jump-cut editing. The intention is to achieve a sense of voyeurism, of watching a slice of 'real life' policing on the streets of New York.

Reality Television

A growing range of media texts have emphasised that they feature 'real life' and 'real people'. The term 'reality television' has been increasingly applied to all those programmes which seemingly allow people access to appear as themselves using actual or reconstructed scenes. The surge in such programmes was originally stimulated by the growth in availability and technical sophistication of the video camcorder since when CCTV and the webcam have given an extra technical dimension to programme makers.

In practice reality TV is a generic hybrid embracing a wide range of mixed generic codes which feature people in a diverse range of roles including:

a) **professionals employed in the police and emergency services via either dramatised reconstructions of real events (*999* or *True Crimes*), or real video action recorded by video journalists and/or the police (*Police, Camera, Action*)**

b) **subjects of entertainment or humour in spontaneous or contrived comic situations (*You've Been Framed* or *Trigger Happy TV*)**

c) **characters within a professionally produced observational documentary serial – sometimes labelled 'docusoaps' (*Driving School, Airport*)**

d) **amateur directors offering a personalised account of an event or way of life (*Video Diaries, Video Nation*)**

e) **participants in an extended game or challenge within a controlled environment (*Big Brother, Pop Stars*)**

Apart from the availability of new technologies, the growth of reality television is largely attributable to economic factors – the programmes can deliver high ratings at relatively low expense. Their popular appeal has also been boosted by other media interest. They are now part of the entertainment agenda and circulation war of the tabloid newspapers. Programmes like *Big Brother* and *Pop Stars* have become 'event tv'. For example, *The Sun* and *The Mirror* both championed individual participants as *Big Brother 2* neared its climax in the summer of 2001.

Despite the use of real people and authentic action, many critics have argued that much of this 'reality television' fails to be genuinely informative or revelatory. At its worst, video footage of ordinary people's personal experiences or emotions may be exploitative in pandering solely to audience voyeurism. Andrew Goodwin (1993) is scathing of the claims of those programmes featuring the police and emergency services which he says cite educational and investigative value as an excuse for depicting graphic details of real or reconstructed crimes and disasters. He also argues that the viewer is placed firmly on the side of the police and rescue workers, and that the optimistic, upbeat message reassures viewers of the good work performed by such people.

With respect to the docusoaps of the late 1990s and more recently reality/gameshows, such as *Big Brother*, critics have accused producers of selecting and exploiting subjects who will make 'good television' in terms of having strong characters, and engineering situations designed to maximise audience entertainment (conflict, romance, etc).

However, this is to ignore the fact all television involves mediated reality, and a degree of selectivity and editorialising is a constant factor in television production. Furthermore, audiences are aware that some degree of manipulation is integral to such programmes. Indeed, the viewers themselves are increasingly part of this process, as more reality tv becomes interactive, inviting audience participation (via votes, websites, phone-ins, etc). Some have even argued this represents a new form of democratic popular entertainment. Certainly, part of the appeal of such programmes is that they provide an opportunity for viewers to reflect on modern anxieties and moral dilemmas within an entertaining and accessible format. Against this, however, they have attracted consistent criticism as being programmes which are exploitative of their subjects and audiences, modern day 'freak-shows' (for a further discussion see Dovey 2000).

Activity 4.10

Choose two distinct examples of 'reality tv' and consider

a) how and why the people were chosen as subjects for the programmes;
b) from whose point of view the subjects have been represented.

Further Reading

Cottle, S. 2000: Ethnic Minorities and the Press. OPEN UNIVERSITY PRESS.

Denzin, N. 2002: Reading Race. SAGE.

Dovey, J. 2000: Freakshow: First Person Media and Factual Television. PLUTO.

Ferguson, R. 1998: Representing Race: Ideology, Identity and the Media. EDWARD ARNOLD.

Geraghty, C. 1991: Women and Soap Opera. POLITY.

Glasgow University Media Group. 1985: War and Peace News. OPEN UNIVERSITY PRESS.

Gough-Yates, A. 2003: Understanding Women's Magazines. ROUTLEDGE.

Jackson, P., Stevenson, N. and Brooks, K. 2001: Making Sense of Men's Magazines. POLITY.

Kilborn, J. and Izod, J. 1997: An Introduction to Television Documentary. MANCHESTER UNIVERSITY PRESS.

McDonald, M. 1995: Representing Women. EDWARD ARNOLD.

McNair, B. 2000: An Introduction to Political Communication. ROUTLEDGE.

O'Sullivan, T. and Jewkes, Y. (eds). 1997: The Media Studies Reader. EDWARD ARNIOLD.

Philo, G. 1999: Message Received. LONGMAN.

Pickering, M. 2001: Stereotyping. PALGRAVE.

Pines, J. (ed). 1992: Black and White in Colour. BFI.

Ross, K. 1996: Black and White Media. POLITY.

Stead, P. 1989: Film and the Working Class. ROUTLEDGE.

Strinati, D. and Wagg, S. (eds). 1992: Come On Down: Popular Media Culture in Post War Britain. ROUTLEDGE.

Tasker, Y. 1998: Working Girls: Gender and Sexuality in Popular Cinema. ROUTLEDGE.

Winston, B. 2000: Lies, Damn Lies and Documentary. BFI.

CHAPTER FIVE

Audiences

The first chapter of this book emphasised how the media play a prominent part in people's everyday lives. Given the time spent by audiences consuming the media, it is hardly surprising that much speculation and debate has focused on the exact nature of the relationship between audiences and media output. In reviewing the progress of this debate, it is possible to identify distinct phases of audience analysis. What makes these phases distinct is the degree to which the balance of power and influence is attributed to the media, in terms of production and content, or to audiences in the reception of that production.

Phase 1: From Mass Manipulation to Uses and Gratifications

Mass Manipulation Model

Concern about media 'effects' on audiences, especially harmful influences, has been expressed almost continuously since the turn of the century. The idea that the media are a powerful social and political force gathered momentum in the 1920s and 1930s, when the political propaganda of first Soviet Russia and then Nazi Germany seemed capable of seducing and persuading ordinary citizens in ways not thought possible prior to an age of mass media.

Audiences came to be seen as comprising a mass of isolated individuals vulnerable to the influence of the powerful new media such as cinema and radio – hence the label 'mass manipulation'. Propaganda of a different sort, advertising, was later perceived in the same way by writers such as Vance Packard. His best-selling book, *The Hidden Persuaders* (1957), claimed to expose some of the ways advertisers were employing subliminal techniques to manipulate ordinary people, unaware of such techniques, into consuming goods.

Children and teenagers have consistently been considered susceptible to the harmful influence of popular entertainment. From time to time, moral panics (see Chapter 4) have been generated, often orchestrated, via the media, especially tabloid newspapers. Each medium in turn has been accused of corrupting young people, whether it be Hollywood crime films in the 1920s, pop music in the 1950s, 'video nasties' in the 1980s, video and computer games in the 1990s, and, most recently, rap music (for glorifying guns) and the Internet (ranging from chatlines to pornography). The heightened social concern and anxiety associated with moral panics often stimulates more stringent controls over the media to protect 'the innocent' from any damage. In the case of video nasties, the 1983 Video Recordings Act was passed. This introduced strict regulation of videos via the British Board of Film Classification (BBFC). However, concern over young people's access to violent videos rose again in the early 1990s. A number of highly publicised crimes of aggression in which a violent film was implicated (most notably the linking of the James Bulger murder with a video, *Child's Play 3*) resulted in further restrictions being enacted in 1994. The British Board of Film Classification now has to take into account:

> *any harm that may be caused to potential viewers or, through their behaviour, to society by the manner in which the work (film) deals with: criminal behaviour, illegal drugs, violent behaviour or incidents, horrific behaviour or incidents, or human sexual activity.*

Soon after this tightening of the regulation there was considerable controversy surrounding the granting of an 18 certificate to Oliver Stone's film *Natural Born Killers* (1994), which was accused of glamorising violence and precipitating copycat murders in America and France. More recently, the *Scream* horror cycle of films has been implicated in murder trials (Figure 5.1).

'Scream' movies are blamed by teenage girl's copycat killer

by
Andrew Osborn
Brussels

AN American judge once described Scream, the 'ironic' cult horror film, as a 'very good source to learn how to kill someone'. Now the film has spawned yet another copycat killing – one so cold-blooded it has shocked a local community in French-speaking Belgium.

In the movie the sleepy American town of Woodsboro is terrorised by a 'slasher' who wears a black tunic from head to toe and a ghoulish mask inspired by Edvard Munch's painting The Scream. The film and its sequels have attracted a cult following and fancy-dress shops now stock replicas of the mask and robe.

Unfortunately, the films have also inspired a spate of copycat killings and attacks, usually by impressionable American teenagers.

The film obviously struck a chord also with lonely Belgian lorry driver Thierry Jaradin, 24, who chose 15-year-old schoolgirl Alisson Cambier as his victim.

She dropped by Jaradin's house, a few doors away from her own in the town of Gerpinnes, to exchange some videotapes and have a chat. Jaradin made amorous advances towards her, but when they were rejected his retribution was brutal.

Excusing himself for a few seconds, he stepped into an adjacent room where his Scream costume was waiting, together with two enormous kitchen knives. Clamping his hand over Alisson's mouth to muffle her screams, he stabbed her 30 times, ripping open her left side. He then lowered her blood-soaked corpse on to his bed, slipped a rose into one of her hands and telephoned his father and a colleague to confess. He later told police that his crime had been premeditated and had been motivated by the cinematic trilogy.

Alisson's family and the people of Gerpinnes are now in a state of shock. 'Alisson was a dazzling, young, affectionate teenager who should have celebrated her sixteenth birthday on 16 November,' said one neighbour.

Her family has also been distressed by allegations that she was in love with Thierry. 'Alisson was not in love with her killer,' Jean-Jacques Cambier, her father, told the daily newspaper La Dernière Heure. 'People are misinterpreting facts and talking to me about a love affair which never existed.'

There was nothing in Jaradin's background to suggest that he was capable of committing such a terrible crime. He had no criminal record or history of psychiatric problems.

FIGURE 5.1
Scream – Observer 18.11.01
Source: Andrew Osborn, ©Observer

Television has also been singled out by many critics as being responsible for anti-social and psychologically harmful outcomes. Marie Winn's book *The Plug-in Drug* (1977) is typical in its claim that children watch television in a 'trance', their eyes having a 'glazed vacuous look'. Using the drug metaphor, with its notions of addiction and passivity, is a familiar ploy, most recently employed in the context of video and computer games. Consequently the mass manipulation model is sometimes referred to as the hypodermic-needle or magic-bullet theory because it implies such a direct causal and linear influence.

Despite these continuous alarms about the power of the media over audiences, much of the concern has been based on flimsy anecdotal evidence. In the case of *Natural Born Killers*, the BBFC followed up the alleged ten cases of copycat killings and in only two cases had the accused seen the film in question, and these two involved one with a record of violent crime, and another who had repeatedly expressed his intention to commit the murders prior to seeing the film.

Children and Media Violence

The last sixty years have seen a mountain of academic research investigating the possible harmful effects of media violence on children. As early as the 1930s, the Payne studies in the USA assessed the effects of cinema on audiences, and concluded that films did in fact cause harm to children by disrupting sleep, encouraging delinquency and crime through imitation, and so on (Peterson and Thurstone, 1933). A key problem for such research is demonstrating a cause and effect relationship. Influences on social behaviour such as aggression are complex and multivariable. It is impossible to isolate one variable, such as television, and remove all the other social factors which might influence aggressive behaviour. Media violence might affect aggression but it will be in conjunction with a range of other (possibly more profound) influences that help shape the thinking and behaviour of a child, such as parents, peer group, school, etc.

In addition, there are a number of issues which further complicate the possible relationship between media violence and children's aggression.

1 **Who is affected?**
Moral panics concerning children or teenagers and media violence are based on adults' concerns for the vulnerability and susceptibility of younger audiences in relation to the assumed harmful effects of the media. However, when asked, teenagers usually identify children as the vulnerable group, and older children see younger children as at risk. This is the phenomenon known as **displacement** whereby concern about the effects of the media are always attributed to someone else (the more educated versus the less educated, the middle class versus the working class, etc).

2 **What counts as media violence?**

The Independent Television Commission's research into finding out what people define as violent on television is clear in its conclusion – 'What constitutes violence on the screen is measurable against real life. One is recognised from the other' (ITC, 1998). Children do not tend to perceive cartoons or video games as violent, as they are seen as removed from real life. Thus television representations of real-life violence, as found in the news, for example, are much more likely to disturb children than most fictional violence. Much depends on the **context** of media representations of violence, both on-screen and in the viewing situation.

Children's responses will be affected by their **modality judgements**, their ability to differentiate between the mode or level of reality represented in a media text. These are often based on generic codes. For example, horror films will be judged by their narrative plausibility. David Buckingham (1996) found that *Child's Play 3*, implicated in the James Bulger murder trial, was described by many children as a comedy. Much more upsetting was a BBC spoof documentary, *Ghostwatch*, broadcast on Halloween night in 1992 (Figure 5.2). Over fifty years earlier, Orson

Welles had caused much greater panic in America through his radio broadcast of *War of the Worlds* in 1938. An estimated one million plus (who either failed to hear the intro or tuned in during the performance) believed their country was being invaded by Martians, as a result of the play being produced in the form of a spoof 'live' news report with eye-witnesses, sound effects, etc. Then, as now, audiences trusted the credibility of broadcast news as a reliable source of truth.

3 What kind of effects?

Speculation about possible media effects has tended to emphasise the direct harmful influences that can accrue from violent media content. However, there are important distinctions to be made about the kinds of effects that are involved. First, there are short-term **behavioural** effects, such as when children imitate what they have seen. Second, there are **emotional** effects such as being frightened, aroused, or excited. Finally, there are **ideological** effects, how media representations of violence may effect ideas and attitudes – what is acceptable, who has a right to apply violence to whom, etc. Ideological effects are more likely to be long term and therefore virtually impossible to quantify through research.

Halloween spoof riles BBC viewers

THE BBC yesterday refused to disclose how many calls had been received from angry viewers after a spoof Halloween-night TV documentary been proved too realistic.

But a spokesman conceded there had been a "substantial reaction", with many people convinced the gory scenes in Saturday night's Screen One special, Ghosts, were real.

Most callers simply rang to ask if the 90-minute show — starring Michael Parkinson, Sarah Greene and Mike Smith, all playing themselves — was a genuine documentary.

But BBC staff said many others were angry at realistic scenes including an interview with a young girl apparently possessed by spirits and with blood dripping down her face.

"People thought it was real," said one.

"We've had anything from being sworn at to people who say they are going to write to the director-general."

Last night the BBC insisted the programme had been clearly billed as a drama in the Radio Times and other listings magazines, and in an on-air announcement before the start.

In the show, Michael Parkinson played the anchorman of a Watchdog-style current affairs programme and Mike Smith hosted a spoof phone-in on ghostly manifestations. Meanwhile, a mock outside broadcast team investigated "Britain's most haunted house" — a council house in Northolt, west London — where the fictional Early family had complained of paranormal experiences.

These included objects flying around rooms, dark figures and mysterious puddles — all owing a great deal to the BBC's special effects department.

FIGURE 5.2
Source: Guardian, 2 November 1992. © Guardian

Much of the psychological research (such as Bandura and Walters, 1963, Newson, 1994) has tended to focus on harmful behavioural effects. However, as David Buckingham (1996) points out, this is too simplistic, as it is likely that children simultaneously experience 'positive' and 'negative' responses. For example, children may find a horror film frightening or a news story distressing, but a beneficial outcome is that they are learning to cope with such fears or anxiety. How children respond will also be dependent upon the social context including factors such as family, class and gender. Television viewing and other media reception needs to be seen as social activity involving other people. Later in the chapter, we will consider the importance of the context in which audiences receive and use the media as well as the motivations for consuming media texts (not least of which is pleasure and entertainment).

Most of the research claiming proof of direct effects, especially on young audiences, is rooted in behaviourist psychology or social learning theory. The assumption is that children learn through conditioning. 'Good' behaviour is rewarded, and this is reinforced by seeing positive adult role models.

Supporting evidence cited frequently centres on experiments in which children are exposed to a media stimulus and their response is then measured. An example is Bandura and Walters' 'Bobo Doll' experiment of 1963, in which children were shown films of adults acting aggressively towards the doll, behaviour later imitated by the children when left alone with the dolls. Such experiments have been criticised for failing to reflect normal viewing conditions under which the media are consumed. Children do not usually encounter such a strictly controlled media diet, and the aggression shown may well result from a desire to please the experimenter. Furthermore, children can distinguish between real and simulated violence both in media content and in their own play.

Other psychologists, drawing on developmental psychology, have instead emphasised how the media, particularly television, affect cognitive development, how children learn to think and make sense of the world. While this is a complex and multifaceted subject, much of the work stresses the active learning which accompanies media consumption. Máire Messenger Davies' book, *Television is Good for Kids* (1989), describes many positive learning outcomes which have been identified in various academic studies. These include: the development of television literacy skills, such as understanding visual narrative, editing conventions, etc; improved memory of events due to visual aids, which also stimulate imagination; being able to differentiate between different degrees of realism (so-called 'modality judgements') across narrative forms; the acquisition of knowledge, understanding and practical skills; and not least the play value, usually involving social games in which favourite television programmes are 'remade' or re-enacted.

These claims need to be qualified on the grounds that psychological frameworks of research, whether behaviourist or developmental, have often lacked an adequate account of the social context. Children's response to the media will vary according to social group membership such as family, class and gender. Television viewing needs to be seen as only one form of social learning within the immediate and broader cultural environment, including other forms of media. Little empirical work has been undertaken on the ideological 'effects' of media representation, such as gender or ethnic stereotypes, on children (see D. Buckingham (ed), 2002).

Political Persuasion

One of the most influential studies of media effects on audiences was *The People's Choice* in 1944, which focused on political persuasion. Lazarsfeld, Berelson and Gaudet set out to discover what influence the media exerted over voters during the American presidential campaign. Using a panel sample over a period of six months, they concluded that voting intentions were very resistant to media influence. This was due to a combination of individual cognitive and wider social processes. A majority of the sample already had well-formed political attitudes, and this predisposition was reinforced through selective exposure, whereby people read newspapers which were likely to support existing views. Even when confronted with politically challenging ideas, these could be resisted via selective perception – filtering the message to fit existing attitudes, or interpersonal discussion. The research identified opinion leaders – people whose political views were trusted – and suggested that they were a much more significant influence than the media, whose information could be mediated via a process the authors called the *two-step flow*. In other words, media content is always subject to the influence of the audiences' immediate social environment. The overall conclusion was that the media's 'effect' on the audience was one of reinforcement rather than change or direct effect.

Although subsequent research in Britain supported these findings, the potential for media influence on political behaviour seems to have increased in recent years as the strength of voters' loyalty to one party has declined. At the same time, the British tabloid newspapers have become more politically partisan. There has always been a close relationship between a newspaper's political bias and the voting behaviour of its readers. W. Miller's research (1992) into the British general elections of 1987 and 1992 identifies a disproportionate swing towards the Conservatives during the campaigns among readers of the Conservative-supporting tabloids. By the 1997 election, there was less support for the Conservatives in both the newspapers (especially *The Sun* which switched to Labour – see Figure 6.2) and among the electorate. Figure 5.3 shows the strong relationship between the newspapers' political sympathies and their readers' voting preferences. The top five newspapers in the chart all endorsed Labour and three of the bottom four (the exception being the *Financial Times*) supported the Conservatives. Nevertheless, a significant percentage of voters ignored their newspaper's political preference. It is difficult to demonstrate a direct political influence, especially as many readers choose a newspaper because of its perceived political values. Again, like the problems of examining the longer-term ideological effects of screen violence, it is much more difficult to measure the cumulative effect of newspapers' editorial bias on such issues as law and order or whether Britain should abandon the pound and adopt the euro.

As a causal agent of direct social and political influence, it is likely that the media's power is quite modest. Persuading consumers which brand of jeans or breakfast cereal to buy pays dividends for the advertiser, but advertising which attempts to alter more deep-rooted and complex forms of behaviour, such as drug-taking or forms of sexual practice, has been found to have minimal impact (Figure 5.4).

Instead of the media being seen as an all-powerful force working directly on the audience in isolation, during the 1960s there emerged the view that:

a) audiences are creatively active in interpreting media content;
b) audiences comprise individuals whose membership of social groups should not be ignored.

Newspapers and voting in 1997

How readers voted %

	Labour	Tory	LD	Didn't vote
Daily Mirror	71	6	8	16
Guardian	69	0	25	6
Star	58	11	9	22
Independent	39	12	35	15
Sun	38	23	9	31
Times	29	37	22	12
Daily Mail	29	45	15	11
Financial Times	24	24	13	39
Daily Express	22	53	11	14
Daily Telegraph	20	61	10	9
Don't read a paper	41	18	17	23

FIGURE 5.3
Source: ©Guardian

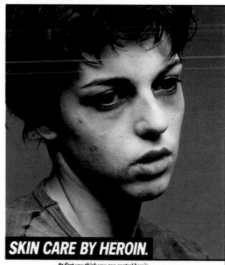

FIGURE 5.4
This 1987 anti-heroin poster failed because the boy proved too appealing for some girls, who wrote in for the poster.
Source: the Central Office of Information

Therefore, the concept of 'effect' has come to be seen as problematic within media studies because:

a) it implies audience passivity and media causality;

b) there can be confusion between short-term effects, such as during elections, and long-term ideological effects of a much more subtle but profound nature, e.g. on gender identities;

c) it is virtually impossible to measure media effects – the media cannot be isolated from all the other potential influences at work within society.

For some researchers, this was a shift in perspective within audience research, summarised by James Halloran's (1970) much-repeated phrase: 'We must get away from the habit of thinking in terms of what the media do to people and substitute for it the idea of what people do with the media.'

Uses and Gratifications

(a) Television

The basic tenet underlying this new approach to studying audiences was that individuals actively consume and use the media in order to meet certain needs. Blumler and Katz (1974) undertook group discussions about media use in which subjects' statements were listed and categorised, and consequently listed four broad needs fulfilled by viewers' watching of television:

1 Diversion – a form of escape or emotional release from everyday pressures;

2 Personal relationships – companionship via television personalities and characters, and sociability through discussion about television with other people;

3 Personal identity – the ability to compare one's own life with the characters and situations within programmes, and hence explore personal problems and perspectives;

4 Surveillance – a regular supply of information about 'what's going on' in the world.

This list of uses and gratifications for television viewing was found to be just as significant twenty years on when the British Film Institute undertook a tracking survey of five hundred people's viewing patterns between 1991 and 1996 (Gauntlett and Hill, 1999). For many respondents, television was seen as 'a good friend' as illustrated by the following comment;

> I would miss most of all the feeling of having company actually with me in the room. I have 'friends' on radio too, but seeing the people I like is even better. I do not like going out but I like to think I can still keep reasonably up-to-date with what is going on 'out there'. TV not only provides me with 'company' but it also causes me to react mentally, and, therefore, keep emotionally active, without having to face any consequences. I would miss seeing it all.
>
> *(78-year-old widow)*

Further parallels with Blumler and Katz's work, arising from the BFI survey, were that television was valued as both a source of conversation and a means by which individuals could make connections between their personal identities and media representations. In the latter case, this might mean finding people on the screen who shared a similar situation to their own, e.g. being physically disabled. In more extreme cases, the audience might identify with a particular programme as a fan, e.g. *Star Trek* fans ('trekkies'). Such fanbases can, and have, developed into 'virtual communities' through the Internet.

Blumler and Katz's concept of 'diversion' or 'escape' was developed by Richard Dyer (1977) in relation to cinema and television entertainment. In trying to answer the question of how 'escapism' works, he offers three suggestions of how real life is suspended or temporarily erased. First, it may be obliterated in so far as the content completely ignores reality, as within dance, music, magic, slapstick comedy, etc. Second, it may work via contrast. Here, the mediated reality provides a pleasing positive alternative for the audience, e.g. within soap operas like *Coronation Street* which supplies a sense of close community. Finally, Dyer identifies incorporation, where reality is shown to be better than imagined, thus creating a sense of optimism. An example of this might be the annual television telethon which promotes a sense of a caring and altruistic society.

Activity 5.1

Undertake a survey of uses and gratifications by:

1 recording informal conversations about specific programmes or genres with a sample of television viewers;
2 listing the most common motives mentioned for viewing such programmes;
3 clustering together similar statements under a collective heading (e.g. for quiz shows: excitement appeal, basis for social interaction, etc);
4 presenting the list of headings to a further sample as a self-report survey allowing for a graduated response to each heading (e.g. from 'very much' to 'not at all' or 1 to 5).

(b) Radio

Another application of uses and gratifications is demonstrated through the work of RAJAR, the organisation responsible for research into radio audiences. It identifies two key aspects to listeners' requirements from radio. First, there is the *functional* need for information (news, travel, weather, etc). The second requirement is *emotional.* This is characterised in terms of the relationship audiences may have with a presenter or a particular programme. These needs may operate simultaneously. For example, a breakfast show will provide news, travel, timechecks, etc, but also an emotional 'feel-good' factor provided by the presenter's friendly, light-hearted and upbeat delivery.

Nevertheless, 'uses and gratifications' as an analytical model for understanding audiences does have its limitations. At its crudest, it implies that audiences comprise individuals whose conscious search for gratification elicits a functional media response which supplies their needs. This approach overlooks the extent to which audience needs are partly a product of media supply (learning to enjoy what is available), and the social context from which audiences originate, e.g. class, national and ethnic subcultures.

The tendency to concentrate solely on why audiences consume the media rather than extending the investigation to discover what meanings or interpretations are produced, and in what circumstances, is a related area of critical debate. These issues form the focus of *reception theory*, discussed in the next section.

Phase 2: From Textual Determination to Audience Reception

Audience Positioning

During the 1970s, new theoretical frameworks emerged which could be applied to analysing the relationships between media content and audiences. Drawing heavily on semiotics (Chapter 2) and structuralism, media texts were seen as structured according to well-defined codes and conventions (see Chapter 2 for a fuller discussion). Rather than recognising the polysemic nature of such texts, some writers chose to emphasise how audiences (or subjects) were positioned or 'fixed' by the text.

Much of this was applied to film, and in Britain was articulated most strongly in the academic journal *Screen*. The main thrust of the argument is that the structure of film language produces a perspective or point of view for the audience. The spectator is drawn into the flow of the narrative through various strategies of camera work and editing. One example is the shot/reverse shot, where the perspectives of two characters are interchanged so we as an audience are able to see and 'stand in' for each subject and identify with their view. Another example is the glance/object shot. Here we are shown a close-up of a character as he or she looks off screen. A second shot reveals what the character can see and thus simultaneously situates us in his or her position. Through the editing of camera shots and perspectives the spectator is able to gain a privileged view of events, and yet unconsciously has been 'sewn in' to the narration, a process referred to as 'suture'. It is as if we are invisible onlookers, an effect most films never deny, in order to produce a sense of witnessing their 'objective reality'.

As noted on page 85, it has been argued by writers like Laura Mulvey that the spectator perspective achieved by dominant Hollywood cinema is essentially masculine. The camera shots and editing conventionally reproduce a male gaze, a subject position and point of view with the woman as object. Given strong characterisation in association with this process of spectator suture, the sharing of the character's experiences and emotions leads to effective audience identification. This works powerfully when identification and attraction are combined in a sexual or romantic context such as *The Bodyguard* or *Notting Hill*. (For a further discussion of narrative and point of view, see pp. 48–49).

Mode of Address

This refers to how media texts 'speak to' their audiences and establish a fundamental relationship between media producers and audiences. It implies a less determinate outcome than audience positioning and identification. As argued by Martin Barker (1989), ' "Identification" suggests that we are spoken for. "Dialogue" suggests we are spoken to.'

Cinema

Spectators are rarely acknowledged within Hollywood films. The dominant mode of address is impersonal. There is little sense of an author or identifiable source beyond the film credits. This does not mean there are no points of view supplied; indeed, some films contain a first-person voice-over to guide us through the story, e.g. The *Shawshank Redemption* (1997). Nevertheless, there is normally a sense of reality being pre-existent, 'out there', an enigma waiting to unfold before us.

Occasionally, the impersonal mode of address is broken when characters look into the camera to directly speak to the audience, thereby undermining the illusion of transparent 'reality'. This is most common in comedy, where the audience is invited to share a character's feelings towards events. An early example is that of Laurel and Hardy, where Hardy's looks of exasperation with Laurel are frequently directed to the camera. More recent examples from Hollywood include *Kuffs* (1991), *Fight Club* (1999) and *Wayne's World* (1992).

Television

Robert Allen (1987) has characterised television viewing as centrifugal, in contrast to cinema, where watching a film is centripetal. By this he means that whereas the cinema screen draws in the audience to witness another world, television's programmes are directed outwards to viewers:

> *In those instances in which contestants are selected from the studio audience, they are plucked from among 'us'.*

> *By splitting off one or more characterised viewers from the rest of the studio audience, the game show sets up a circuit of viewer involvement. When Bob Barker asks the contestant to guess how much the travel trailer costs, we almost automatically slip into the role of contestant, guessing along with him or her. If we guess correctly along with the contestant, the bells and whistles go off for us as well as for him or her. But we can also distance ourselves from the contestants and take up the position of the studio audience as they encourage the contestants and, on 'The Price Is Right', at least, shout out what they believe to be the correct guess. As we watch a game show, we constantly shift from one viewer position to another, collapsing the distance between contestants and ourselves as we answer along with them, falling back into the role of studio audience as we assess contestant prowess and luck (or lack thereof), assuming a position superior to both when we know more than they. The viewer-positioning strategy of the game show encourages us to mimic the responses of the characterised viewer in the text.*
> *Robert Allen (1987)*

Two factors help to explain this situation. First, television texts tend to refuse resolution – the news, soap opera, sitcoms, etc, are continuous, daily or weekly and as a result, open-ended. In conjunction with this, viewing is intermittent or casual, and thus television needs to 'work' to attract our attention. Apart from obvious strategies like strong music, studio applause and laughter, etc, one increasingly prominent feature is the use of direct address. The viewer is openly and personally acknowledged. Allen considers this to be a rhetorical mode of address in that television is 'pretending' to speak on behalf of the viewer. Presenters, reporters, comedians, and so on look directly into the camera as if in a face-to-face conversation, yet of course it is only one-way communication. Hence the use of phrases like 'we', 'you the viewer', or 'what the viewer at home wants to know'.

It has traditionally been assumed that the audience comprises members of families situated within the living room as part of a wider community or nation of viewers. This is underlined by the family viewing policy which regulates against explicit language or controversial 'adult' material being represented before nine o'clock in the evening. The sense of a national audience tends to be inscribed within representations of certain annual rituals, such as the Queen's Christmas address to the nation or sporting occasions like the FA Cup Final. Moreover, in international competitions, like the World Cup or Olympic Games, British commentators and presenters shift from a detached and neutral form of address to a more partisan and emotional delivery when describing British participants. As television audiences become more fragmented it seems likely that different types of viewer will be more specifically addressed. Already, there is clear variance in the modes of address contained across breakfast television, late-afternoon children's television and late-night weekend programmes. Furthermore, differing channels may adopt distinctive styles of delivery and modes of address in accordance with both their perceived audience and the organisation's sense of its own identity, particularly with the advent of genre-based channels on satellite and cable television. This latter point is particularly pertinent when considering radio.

Radio

When traditionally the BBC maintained a monopoly situation as Britain's only national radio service, it adopted a mode of address which was designed to reflect its public service ideals – to be authoritative and set high standards. This meant speaking a form of English which used correct standard grammar, had no regional accent and was delivered in a formal tone – what came to be called 'BBC English' or (more technically accurate) 'received pronunciation'. Only gradually in the post-war period did this verbal style decline and leave space for more varied forms of address, for example on Radio 1 (post-1967).

With the shift away from national to local and regional radio services, and the conscious targeting of distinctive audiences, there is a greater need for radio's mode of address to fit its perceived audience identity. The use of accent and vernacular language, the tone and pace of delivery and the structuring of a dialogue with the audience (e.g. via the phone-in programme) are all differing ways by which the listener is addressed. One telling clue to a station's sense of identity and consequent mode of address is its choice of signature jingle, which is repetitively broadcast between programmes or segments within programmes. These jingles are often given as much thought and attention as the rest of the station's schedule.

Activity 5.2

Compare the mode of address adopted in the following:

1   the different breakfast television services offered on BBC, ITV and Channel 4;
2   the different news programmes broadcast on BBC Radios 1 to 5 and your local ILR station(s);
3   quiz/game shows on radio and television.

Newspapers and Magazines

The front page or cover of newspapers and magazines is the key to creating both a sense of identity and a point of contact with the potential reader:

> On any magazine stand each women's magazine attempts to differentiate itself from others also vying for attention. Each does so by a variety of means: the title and its print type, size and texture of paper, design and lay-out of image and sell-lines (the term the magazine trade aptly uses for the cover captions), and the style of model image – but without paying much attention to how a regular reader will quickly be able to pick out her favourite from others nestling competitively by it. Cover images and sell-lines, however, also reveal a wealth of knowledge about the cultural place of women's magazines. The woman's face which is their hallmark is usually white, usually young, usually smoothly attractive and immaculately groomed, and usually smiling or seductive. The various magazines inflect the image to convey their respective styles – domestic or girl-about-town, cheeky or staid, upmarket or downmarket – by subtle changes of hairstyle, neckline and facial pose.

There is one other important and defining characteristic of this cover image: the woman's gaze. It intimately holds the attention of 'you', the reader and viewer. The gaze is not simply a sexual look between woman and man, it is the steady, self-contained, calm look of unruffled temper. She is the woman who can manage her emotions and her life. She is the woman whom 'you' as reader can trust as friend; she looks as one woman to another speaking about what women share: the intimate knowledge of being a woman. Thus the focus on the face and the eyes – aspects which most obviously characterise the person, the woman – suggests that inside the magazine is a world of personal life, of emotions and relationships, clearly involving men and heterosexuality, but a world largely shunned by men. This is all women's territory.

Janice Winship (1987)

Activity 5.3

With reference to Janice Winship's analysis of how women's magazine covers vie for readers' attention, compare the mode of address employed by three different women's magazine covers.

Ⓐ

Broadsheet newspapers are distinguished from tabloids in Britain by their more impersonal, formal and detached mode of address. The tone is subdued and measured, in contrast to that of the emotive 'loudness' of papers like *The Sun* and *The Mirror*. Even here there are important differences. As described by Peter Chippendale and Chris Horrie (1990), *The Sun* under Rupert Murdoch cultivated a sense of the 'cheeky cockney' who, while happy to stick two fingers up at the establishment, was keen to show it was speaking on behalf of its readers. It continues to hail its readers whenever possible through encouraging participatory action or gestures, including various xenophobic stances towards foreign 'enemies' like Argentina or the European Community (see also *The Mirror's* patriotic mode of address in Figure 2.11).

As with radio, the more specialised the target audience, the more distinctive will be the mode of address. Some magazines, like those dealing with computer interests, will incorporate a style and argot which exclude access to those without the necessary knowledge and expertise.

Parallel to the work of those privileging the ways in which media texts position audiences was the contribution made by members of the Centre for Contemporary Cultural Studies at Birmingham University under the leadership of Stuart Hall. His own encoding–decoding model, discussed below, was very influential in examining the relationship between text and audience (Figure 5.5).

To some extent, the encoding process tends to contain a sense of textual power at work. Using

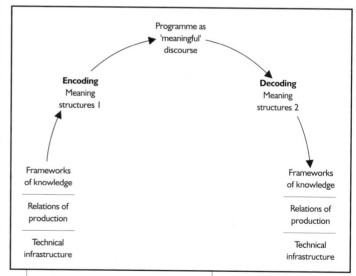

FIGURE 5.5
Source: S. Hall (ed.), Culture, Media, Language, Hutchinson, 1980

a hegemonic theoretical framework, Hall argues that media texts such as television programmes contain dominant ideological discourses. This is due to the fact that media producers' own professional routines and practice contain certain assumptions and ideas about how programmes should be made (the 'relations of production'). They draw agendas and meanings – 'definitions of the situation' – from the wider society, which are ideological in nature (the 'framework of knowledge'). Finally, television's own codes and conventions are employed to complete the encoding process, and the effect is to naturalise or make transparent the meaning of the programme for the audience (to deny its own ideological construction).

However, because the communication is achieved in a coded form and is polysemic, there is no guarantee that the audience's decoding (how they make sense of the programme) will 'fit' or be consistent with the encoded meaning. Despite this possibility, polysemy does not equate with there being a random plurality of possible interpretations. Instead, Hall argues that texts are structured in such a way that they contain a dominant or preferred meaning which limits the scope for different audience interpretations. The more closed the text, the more obvious is the preferred meaning. Thus an advert whose images are heavily anchored by rhetorical language will be 'read' with considerable consistency by audiences, whereas the relative openness of a television soap opera may make the '**preferred meaning**' more problematic.

The concept of 'preferred meaning' has been subject to some criticism. The main objections raised are as follows:

a) **Preferred meanings are more applicable when analysing factually based texts like news reports or television documentaries. Fictional narrative is more likely to contain competing perspectives and values.**

b) **It is not clear whether preferred meanings are a property of the text (they are there whether we see them or not), something identified by 'expert' analysis, or what is agreed by most members of the audience. Ultimately, who decides what is the preferred meaning?**

c) **Are hegemonic values so dominant that professional practice within the media cannot undermine and challenge such ideologies through producing 'progressive', radical or 'subversive' texts?**

Despite these problems in acknowledging that the audience plays a key role in producing the meaning of media texts, Hall's encoding–decoding model is a significant shift away from the overdetermined subject as represented in some of the approaches outlined and discussed above. Hall's model identifies three types of audience decoding:

1 A *dominant hegemonic* position, established when the audience takes the full preferred meaning offered by the text.

2 A *negotiated* position, established when there is a mixture of adaptation and opposition to the dominant codes.

3 An *oppositional* position, established when the preferred reading is understood but rejected, drawing on alternative values and attitudes (Figure 5.6).

It is possible to include a fourth audience response – that of *aberrant decoding*, where the text is read in a largely unanticipated manner, the preferred reading not being recognised. A good example is a 1998 magazine advert for Audi cars which simply showed a toy bunny (previously used in adverts for Duracell batteries) lying flat on an open road with the caption 'keeps on going'. The readers were meant to recognise the joke that the (everlasting) 'Duracell bunny' has failed to outlast the Audi car, signifying the durability of a car that will keep on going (the preferred meaning). However, many people interpreted the image as representing the aftermath of a car accident involving a child (an aberrant decoding). The advert was subsequently withdrawn when many people complained to the Advertising Standards Authority.

Hall's encoding–decoding model is essentially a theoretical construction, but it helped in redirecting attention as to how audiences interpret media texts. We might apply the model to the controversial media character Ali G (created by the comedian Sacha Baron Cohen). The preferred meaning of Ali G's character is that he is a parody of Asian (and white) young males who adopt exaggerated black 'street' persona and style in a bid to appear cool, but in practice appear ridiculous. A negotiated reading might be to recognise the parody but be critical of a white (Jewish) man playing the role because it is rather patronising. An oppositional reading might be based on the view that Ali G's character reinforces crude stereotypes that many white people have about the attitudes and lifestyle of young black British men (in other words white audiences not in on the joke will produce aberrant readings).

FIGURE 5.6
Jill Posener's book features the work of graffiti artists who specialise in producing political messages, especially on advertising billboards
Source: Jill Posener

Reception Theory

'The unity of a text lies in its destination not its origin' (Eco, 1981). Eco's famous quotation is a recognition of the fact that whatever an author may intend when writing a text, it is the reader's interpretation which really matters in terms of the end results. During the past fifteen years, considerable research, largely of an ethnographic nature, has gone into uncovering what meanings audiences produce from media texts and under what conditions. This research has been defined by certain principles:

The Active Reader

The concept of audience identification has been reviewed as a result of some of these audience studies. Total audience identification rarely occurs while audiences are engaged with media narrative. Instead, there is likely to be a constant shift between *implication* – when the audience imagines how they would behave in the situation represented – and *extrication*, the release from that involvement. What helps to prevent over-involvement is a sense of critical distance brought to the proceedings, for example judgements made about how 'real' the story is, or the quality of acting.

In writing about children's responses to the British soap opera *EastEnders*, David Buckingham (1987) concluded that they were 'by turns deeply involved, amused, bored, mocking and irreverent', and regularly moved between these positions. This is expressed in another way by Ien Ang (1985), in writing about women's pleasure in watching *Dallas*: 'The "flight" into a fictional fantasy world is not so much a denial of reality as playing with it.' This 'playing' with reality in soap operas may include direct responses (e.g. sending letters) to the characters and episodes not because reality is confused with fiction, but because the audience has chosen to treat the serial as 'real' in order to gain more pleasure.

Cultural Competence

In 1978, David Morley investigated how different audience groups (largely based on socio-economic class differences) decoded and made sense of a television current affairs magazine programme, *Nationwide* (Morley, 1980). While he found differences that in part fitted Hall's encoding–decoding model – of dominant, negotiated and oppositional readings – many of the responses failed to fit. This was, first, because additional social variables like gender and ethnicity were at work, and, second, because for many of the sample the programme either was irrelevant or failed to make much sense. Morley later reflected that it is more appropriate for audience research to recognise the knowledge, experiences and taste which different people bring to their media usage: what has been called **cultural competence** or **cultural capital**. This is a key concept, as it helps to explain varying audience preferences and pleasures. As Richard Dyer (1977) has argued, this means that the decoding model based on agreement or opposition to encoded ideologies needs to be replaced by one that recognises audience enjoyment or boredom. This in turn opens up space for audience readings of texts which are unanticipated or work against the grain of any presumed preferred reading, as will be seen in some of the research reported below.

However, before considering different readings of media texts it is important to recognise that audiences' consumption of the media is often markedly patterned according to social factors such as gender, age, class and ethnicity (Figures 5.7 and 5.8).

Gender Preferences

Various studies have confirmed that males generally prefer factual programmes (news, current affairs and documentaries), sport, action-based narrative where there is a minimum of dialogue and emotion (for a discussion of 'masculine' versus 'feminine' narrative see p. 87) and realist fiction. David Morley (1986) found that men often disapproved of watching fiction on the grounds it was not 'real life' or sufficiently serious. They were consequently inclined to define their own preferences as more important. It is clear from audience ratings figures that large numbers of males do watch 'feminine' programmes such as soap operas, but to admit as much seems to present a threat to their sense of masculinity.

These observations were also echoed in Ann Gray's research on women's use of video, based on interviews with thirty women she contacted via a video library in Yorkshire. All the women took pleasure in texts which focused on personal relationships, believable characters and a strong story. Men were perceived as disliking texts in which emotions were openly displayed.

> *Love Story …I've seen that about half a dozen times, I think it's just as good, no matter how many times you watch it – it can still make you cry. Men find them soppy, don't they? I think probably because they're frightened that they might actually feel some little bit of sympathy or feeling … men don't like to show their emotions very much, do they? (Barbara)*
>
> *Gray (1992)*

FILM	Total attendances (millions)	7–11	12–14	15–17	18–24	25–34	35+	Male	Female	ABC1	C2DE
1996											
Indepence Day	10,058	–	9	9	23	27	32	61	39	60	40
Toy Story	8,032	22	11	8	17	23	19	53	47	55	45
Seven	4,985	–	–	–	42	39	19	60	40	59	41
1997											
The Full Monty	13,013	–	–	9	19	28	44	44	56	60	40
Men in Black	10,267	11	10	12	20	27	20	57	43	56	44
Jurrasic Park (Lost World)	8,175	13	10	10	13	23	31	57	43	53	47
1998											
Titanic	16,791	–	7	8	16	22	47	46	54	56	44
Dr Dolittle	4,661	–	–	8	21	26	45	57	43	58	42
1999											
Star Wars: Episode 1– The Phantom Menace	12,130	12	6	6	16	27	33	60	40	62	38
Notting Hill	7,674	–	–	6	15	22	57	40	60	69	31
A Bugs Life	11,489	18	7	5	11	21	38	45	55	53	47
2000											
Toy Story 2	10,687	20	10	7	11	25	27	50	50	58	42
Gladiator	7,733	–	–	7	16	26	51	58	42	68	32
Chicken Run	9,270	16	9	5	9	18	43	47	53	67	33

FIGURE 5.7
Source: CAA/Caviar (Cinema and Video Industry Audience Research)

A further distinction Gray made was that of education. She found that women with a minimum experience of education (i.e. leaving school between ages 14 and 16) were much more likely to be critical of their own tastes, using phrases like 'soppy' or 'silly', whereas those women with experience of higher education were more inclined to retain a critical distance from what were perceived as more 'trashy' or 'trivial' media texts.

In terms of narrative themes, Gray summarised the contrast in responses between male and female preferences (as reported by the women) as follows:

Male	Female
heroic	romantic
public	domestic
societal	familial
physical	emotional

FIGURE 5.8
Apartheid in TV Guardian 6.2.03
Source: ©Guardian

How race divides American viewers

White favourites	Black favourites
1 CSI: Crime Scene Investigation	1 One on One
2 Friends	2 Cedric the Entertainer
3 ER	3 Girlfriends
4 Everybody Loves Raymond	4 Half and Half
5 Will and Grace	5 The Parkers
6 Law and Order	6 My Wife and Kids
7 CSI: Miami	7 Bernie Mac
8 Survivor: Thailand	8 Fast lane
9 Scrubs	9 NFL Football
10 Still Standing	10 CSI

Will and Grace

Alex Kingston in ER

These divisions cut across traditional 'masculine' and 'feminine' genres, so that women could enjoy a war film which strongly featured a character's emotions (rather than actions). Nevertheless, it is fair to say that gender thematic preferences are closely linked to particular film and television genres.

Christine Geraghty (1991) argues that there are four elements which explain the appeal of so-called 'women's fiction' – a label embracing soap opera, romance and melodrama:

1 an emphasis on a central woman whom the audience is invited to support;
2 a division between the public and private sphere, with women understanding and controlling the private sphere;
3 an emphasis on building and maintaining relationships;
4 an element of fantasy in which values linked to the personal private sphere are privileged.

A **Activity 5.4**

Undertake a survey of favourite television programmes and films according to gender (remember to balance your sample by age). Categorise the preferred programmes and films by genre – e.g. soap opera, factual documentary, sitcom, etc for television, and action, science fiction, romance, etc for film.

Do your findings confirm or refute those outlined above (Morley, Gray and Geraghty)?

Much of the above discussion on gender preferences assumes a heterosexual audience. Given the paucity of explicit gay and lesbian media representation, it is not surprising that such groups have tended to find pleasure in those texts perceived as providing an alternative gay or lesbian reading to the dominant heterosexual discourse. An example of this is soap opera which has a strong following amongst gay men. Many of the female characters have gained cult status because of their perceived campness. In the 1980s, *Dynasty* was popular with American gays, especially the character Alexis, played by Joan Collins, because of her excessive costumes and emotional intensity. Likewise, British soap women like *Coronation Street* barmaids Bet Gilroy (Julie Goodyear) and Raquel (Sarah Lancashire) have also appealed to gays because of the melodrama and kitsch surrounding their tragi-comedy lives.

Lesbian audiences have found pleasure in series like *Prisoner: Cell Block H* and *Bad Girls*. Both dramas are set in women's prisons with implicit (or explicit) representations of lesbian sexuality. A particular lesbian cult television series is *Xena: Warrior Princess* (Figure 5.9). Kirsten Pullen's (2000) analysis of Xena websites reveals that a significant number are devised by lesbian fans of the series. They generally focus on the relationship between Xena and Gabrielle which is perceived as having a homoerotic subtext. This is rejected or ignored by the other Xena websites which prefer to dwell on the more conventional aspects of the action narrative, or in the case of male fans, the heterosexual appeal of Xena. The Internet has precipitated an explosion of cyber fanculture, enabling audiences to share ideas and information pertaining to such media texts and characters as Xena, Buffy and the *X-Files*, etc (see Matt Hill's discussion of fancultures, 2002).

The most popular forms of media text seem to succeed because they contain a degree of openness and ambiguity which allows very different groups in society to decode them in a pleasurable way. In the pop world during the late 1980s the two most successful artists, Michael Jackson and Madonna, not only created music with 'crossover' appeal, focusing on dance, but also contrived images of gender and race which were polysemic to say the least! Madonna's performances provided sufficient support either for a view of her as a strong, liberated woman or as a sexual plaything:

FIGURE 5.9
Xena website
Source: www.xenafanfiction.com

'She's sexy and she doesn't need men… she's kind of there all by herself.'

or

'She gives us ideas. It's really women's lib, not being afraid of what guys think.'
(quoted in *Time*, 27 May 1985)

'Best of all, her onstage contortions and Boy Toy voice have put sopping sex where it belongs – front and centre in the limelight.' (quoted in *Playboy*, September 1985)

Fiske (1987)

Michael Jackson's physical appearance has generated considerable controversy – has he attempted to dilute or deracinate his blackness? Further questions concern his sexual identity, especially in the light of adverse publicity surrounding his relationships with young boys. Like Madonna, he has consciously played with his image, not least in his videos. In his best known video, *Thriller* (1983), he calls his own identity into question via a blend of generic codes – horror, musical, pop video and 'teen pic movie'. *Thriller* is a classic example of intertextuality at work.

Ethnic preferences

The only black performers in America to rival Michael Jackson in black/white crossover appeal in the late 1980s were Bill Cosby and Eddie Murphy. *The Cosby Show* regularly topped the television ratings and attracted much academic speculation as to its racial message (see p. 103). In an attempt to discover how black and white audiences in America responded to it as a black situation comedy, Justin Lewis (1991) conducted interviews with fifty black and white viewers of the show of mixed social-class origins. Most of the subjects' reading of the specific episode watched were consistent with that of the programme's 'preferred reading' (a gently progressive feminist narrative in which women proved they could outperform men in the mechanics of fixing a car). However, Lewis found significant racial differences in their perceptions of the Huxtables as a black family. The dominant white perspective was one of colour blindness. Cliff Huxtable (Cosby) was seen as 'typical' or 'everyday', an observation reinforced by his upper-middle-class status and home (like those of many white families on American sitcoms). The show was thought to be different from other black television sitcoms in its absence of 'black humour' and style – defined as being loud and slapstick in nature. Lewis concluded that for most of the white audience *The Cosby Show* served to sustain the ideal of the 'American Dream', i.e. that colour is not a barrier to upward mobility.

In contrast, black interviewees were very sensitive to the show's reference to black culture, for example anti-apartheid posters on the wall. Lewis comments that this is indicative of how the show treads a thin racial dividing line: 'The symbols of black culture are strong enough to incorporate a black audience and weak enough to entice a white audience.' Moreover, blacks approved of the show because of their awareness of how few positive black representations appear on American television. That is not to say they were not also conscious of absences in the form of social realism. The lack of struggle and racism was regretted by many blacks, but this reservation was largely suppressed by the desire to have positive black representations made available. Since *The Cosby Show*, few American television shows are succeeding in crossing over audiences (Figure 5.8), with *The Simpsons* being the only comedy crossover hit.

As an example of an internationally consumed media text, *Dallas* has been subjected to considerable academic analysis involving a number of audience studies in different countries. Far from *Dallas* being a case of 'cultural imperialism' (see pp. 234–235), whereby American capitalist values are spread throughout the world, the audience research makes clear that *Dallas* is made sense of via the local cultural framework of interpretation that people bring to the programme. In Israel, Katz and Liebes (1986) discussed a *Dallas* episode with several ethnic groups including Israeli Arabs, Moroccans and Russian Jews. The more traditional ethnic groups, e.g. Israeli Arabs, tended to see the 'message' of *Dallas* as being that wealth cannot bring happiness and that rich Americans are immoral. Meanwhile, in Holland, Ien Ang (1985) found some female viewers enjoyed the programme through adopting an ironic attitude, treating it as 'trashy' and inferior. Some even applied a Marxist/feminist perspective and enjoyed it for its excess of sexism and capitalism, which could be viewed as evidence to support their own criticisms of American cultural values.

Clearly, much of the audience research summarised above has provided important insights into the limits of power that media texts may exert over their audiences. Furthermore, it is now accepted that the meanings audiences produce will to some extent be shaped by their own cultural competences and social origins. However, there is a danger that the pendulum swings too far the other way and audience power over the text is exaggerated. As with uses and gratifications, there may be a tendency to attribute consumer sovereignty to the audience and hence ignore the wider constraints which determined the production, circulation and reception of media texts. In the context of the hegemony–pluralism debate, this is a case of veering towards a pluralistic position.

Likewise, in celebrating the ability of the audience to resist dominant ideologies, there is frequently a conflation of *alternative* with *oppositional* readings. The fact that the polysemy or ambiguity of texts allows a variety of meanings to be produced is not the same thing as the text being actively challenged for its ideological content. As Justin Lewis points out with *The Cosby Show*, its hegemonic or ideological power actually depends upon its ability to strike a chord with different audiences in a variety of ways.

The Context of Reception

Much of the academic controversy surrounding the encoding and decoding of media texts has had to be significantly qualified in the light of recent research into how audiences receive the media. The assumption that full attention is given when listening to the radio, reading magazines, etc, has been discarded in favour of schemes which differentiate between levels of attention. One example is Jeremy Tunstall's (1983) definition of levels as *primary* (close attention), *secondary* (the medium in question is relegated to the background) and *tertiary* (although the medium is present, no conscious monitoring of it is taking place). These varying levels of attention are in turn influenced by the specific nature of the medium in terms of technology, audiovisual codes, and so on, and the social context in which it is received.

Andrew Crisell (1986) argues that the defining characteristic of radio as a medium of communication is '**flow**' (a term borrowed from Raymond Williams, 1974 – see below), analogous to water pouring from a tap when switched on. There is a lack of clear programme boundaries, because listeners tend to dip in and out as it suits them. More often than not this sporadic listening is accompanied by other activities such as driving the car, or making the breakfast, and so radio seems to be clearly a secondary medium. It is used in conjunction with the routines of daily life in a way that no other media can achieve. This is because it does not require visual concentration and is extremely portable. This quality of mobility has led some people to claim that radio is capable of considerable intimacy, since it can function as a 'personal companion' accompanying us into very private situations, not least in bed! The Walkman, or 'personal stereo', delivering radio and music, has been criticised on the grounds that its wearers retreat behind the headphones into their personal space, which excludes everybody else (see Michael Bull, 2000).

Activity 5.5

Ask a sample of radio listeners to keep a diary of their daily listening, including details of:

1   what radio programmes are listened to;
2   for how long (on average);
3   under what conditions, e.g. alone, in the car, at work, etc.

In contrast to radio, cinema requires an audience commitment in every sense of the word. A deliberate decision to visit a cinema and the cinematic environment itself contribute to the sense of this activity as a special occasion. The viewing conditions deny almost all alternative activities apart from watching the screen: the large screen size, the powerful sound system, the darkness and collective audience concentration, etc, all of which make cinema a primary medium. What is to some extent ambiguous is the degree to which the conditions privilege a private/personal or collective response to the film. The audience usually comprises a large public gathering, but the opportunities for social interaction are minimal.

Print media by their nature require some degree of close attention, if only to read the words! Nevertheless, reading newspapers and magazines is qualitatively different to reading a book. Selectivity, skimming and scanning all reflect the sense of leisurely engagement which characterises much newspaper and magazine reading. Having said that, there is very little in the way of contemporary research into this area.

It was Raymond Williams (1974) who first described television programming as a 'flow'. Unlike the singular text foregrounded at the cinema, television emits a constant fragmentary stream, including adverts, trailers, continuity announcements, etc. An excellent example of this pattern can be found on MTV, where the core form of the pop video informs the style of the accompanying adverts, title sequences and features. As mentioned in Chapter 2, John Ellis (1982) has refined the notion of flow to one of *segments*: relatively self-contained scenes conveying an incident, mood or particular meaning. He argues that these segments, which rarely last more than five minutes and usually contain a kind of climax, link closely to the context of television viewing.

Television is above all a domestic medium. It is watched in the home and consequently is part of the domestic atmosphere, providing mood and comfort. The flickering set in the corner is almost equivalent to the 'warmth' of a fire and, from the 1950s, replaced the radio as the focus of the living room. Given that a large variety of social activity takes place in the home it is not surprising that much television viewing is intermittent in nature.

This is borne out by the results of Peter Collett's research (1986), which involved installing a specially designed television cabinet that contained a video camera directed at those watching television. From the resulting 350 hours of videotape Collett concluded that people have their eyes on the screen for only about 65 per cent of the time they are in the room. For the rest of the time, they are engaged in eating, sleeping, talking, ironing, and so on. It also confirmed the social nature of much viewing: 'Even the more popular programmes like soap operas and the news are punctuated with conversation and idle chatter. People exchange views on the plot, complain about the mismanagement of the weather, or comment on the newscaster's hairdo.'

Family Viewing

One trend that television has contributed towards is that of families staying at home for their evening entertainment – part of the privatisation of family life. The specific dynamics of how television interacts with family relationships and domestic life is a subject of much recent research. Using cross-cultural evidence, the following extract indicates how domestic time usage is affected both by general cultural values and the nature of television itself as a structuring social activity:

Cultures also have their own general sense of time, and there are tendencies to regulate social activity accordingly. Let me illustrate how cultural orientations toward time can influence family television viewing: time means something very different in Denmark compared to Pakistan. In Denmark, nearly all families eat the evening meal at almost precisely the same time – 6:00 p.m. The evening television news is broadcast at 7:30, so that it won't interfere with dinner. The systematic, predictable pattern of the Danish orientation toward time, including the scheduling and viewing of television shows, is an extension of this very orderly culture. In Pakistan, on the other hand, television programs often appear on the state system at times that differ from the published schedules, or fail to appear at all. Audiences generally are not surprised or angered by these irregularities…

But in the long run television also influences perceptions and uses of time within cultures that are very different. Mealtimes, bedtimes, chore-times, periods for doing school homework, and patterns of verbal interaction, among other activities, are influenced by the scheduling of television shows. Television is transforming the lives of some rural Indian families by changing their routines away from regulation by nature to regulation by the clock and by television. As Behl reported in her article, Sunday has become a 'TV holiday' and 'TV time' in the evening has replaced time that was previously used for transacting business and 'integrating thought' in rural Indian culture. The reports from India and China demonstrate another phenomenon that has occurred in all cultures with television – the speeding up of home activity, especially the preparation and consumption of the evening meal. Parts of the day become redefined and structured around the scheduling of TV shows, and certain behaviors (such as differing mealtimes for men and women in rural India) are consolidated in the interest of preserving time for viewing.

Lull (1988)

As to whether television integrates or divides families, there is no single pattern. In some families, television acts as a point of common reference and discussion, whereas in other families, it offers a means of avoiding social contact or even potential conflict. A growing pattern which has contributed to a decline in family viewing of television is that of the multiset home. In 2000, 43 per cent of British homes contained three or four television sets and, with the growth in choice of channels, it seems inevitable that individual viewing will only increase. This trend applies particularly to children and teenagers. In a recent study, *Young People, New Media* (Sonia Livingstone, 2002), it was found that of those aged six to seventeen, 63 per cent had a television set of their own. In addition, 68 per cent had a music centre, 34 per cent a video games console and 21 per cent a VCR. The authors describe the growth of a media-based **bedroom culture** (Figures 5.10 and 10.a) which provides an easy escape from family culture (and parental control). This individual media culture is likely to extend further as the PC/Internet also becomes part of the bedroom media technology.

Further fragmentation of audiences is also a product of the growth of niche or segmented media. Mass audiences for television are on the decline as specialist digital channels target specific audiences, **narrowcasting** as opposed to broadcasting. Audience research into digital television homes shows distinctive patterns of viewing by particular groups, as illustrated in Figure 5.11.

FIGURE 5.10
Source: Susan Thompson

	Age of eldest child	
	4–9 2001 %	10–15 2001 %
Television	56	75
Radio	50	70
Games console	40	43
Video recorder	28	35
Computer	10	14
Satellite/cable	7	10
Computer with internet	4	6

FIGURE 5.10a
Equipment in eldest children's bedrooms
Source: ITC The Publisher's View 2001

Dads and Lads

When Sky Sports appeared, it was the answer to the prayers of this important audience group. These men love and trust Sky more than any other television brand. It gives them exactly what they want – dedicated sports coverage, lively news and the technology that puts them in control. Sky Sports Extra and Sky News Active are great and much more than just a gimmick – more than half of the group have used these services. They save the effort of having to boot up the computer to look at the internet.

These channels have fundamentally changed the viewing lives of this broad range of men. In return, they have driven the take-up of multichannel TV and are pouring huge amounts into the coffers of Sky. They are the group most likely to consider gambling or playing games through the TV.

Having only one digital set is a big issue for this group. They will watch as much sport as they can, but the rest of the household object to having the main TV dominated by football. The howls of protest are even louder when they hit the interactive button.

News is also important to these men and Sky News remains the best rolling news service for them. If there is nothing else on, they will have a look at Sky News or Sky Sports News. They often flick over to these channels for a quick look during the ads.

They watch the big shows with the rest of the family but, when they have a bit of time on their own, these men love late night on Channel 4 and Channel 5, terrestrial comedy shows such as Have I Got News For You? and They Think It's All Over, and the truly factual shows on BBC2 and C4 (Why Buildings Collapse, Great Military Blunders or Escape from Colditz).

They love Radio Five Live (and often don't realise it's BBC) and commercial radio and wander over to BBC local radio for the football matches on Saturday and Sunday. They are the group most likely to have a WAP phone – and actually use it to access the internet.

This group is still growing slowly. So what will it take to make the rest of the sports addicts subscribe? Cost is still a big barrier, but there are signs that this is reducing slowly. The key battle remains over the rights held by terrestrial and digital channels.

Men without digital are being held back by the amount of football on terrestrial TV at the moment. A big change in the size of this group is only likely if there is another haemorrhaging of sports rights to digital TV.

Pop Tarts

Being part of the gang is the essence of life. They are young women in their teens to early twenties, for whom chatting about pop, celebrity, style, TV and men is the best way to pass their time. They have got to be on top of what's going on.

TV is an essential source of social currency and the shows, zones and channels they love are those which create a lifestyle and an attitude that they and their friends buy into – a combination of light-hearted entertainment, edgy drama of which their parents would disapprove and glossy sets of which they dream of being a part.

The characters featured in their favourite shows are almost part of their gang.

What is fantastic about digital TV is that it allows access to channels 'for them' all week. E4, bits of Sky One, the MTV channels, The Box and Trouble provide the fun, glamour and edginess that make them essential viewing. Music channels allow them to use the TV just like the radio. If they don't like the video, they just flick to the next channel, there are so many of them to choose from.

Channel 4 is the only terrestrial channel that offers this group a regular slot filled with shows handpicked for them – and they love it. T4 is good fodder for a Sunday morning veg, even if they've already seen Hollyoaks during the week. They drop into the other terrestrial channels to pick out the programmes they love – the soaps, of course, but also Top of the Pops, CD-UK, The Pepsi Chart, Friends repeats, Buffy and most recently Popstars.

They consume media of every sort – and lots of it. They use the internet whenever they can, mostly for email and chat, listen to lots of commercial radio (sampling on average four stations each week) and buy more than two magazines from Sugar and More at the younger end, to Heat and Hello! for the older girls. Everyone has a mobile and text messages fly back and forth – on average five each day.

FIGURE 5.11
Source: Broadcast, 16 march 2001

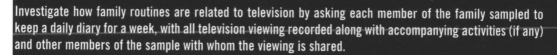

Activity 5.6

Investigate how family routines are related to television by asking each member of the family sampled to keep a daily diary for a week, with all television viewing recorded along with accompanying activities (if any) and other members of the sample with whom the viewing is shared.

Gender and Television Viewing

In what David Morley (1986) calls the 'politics of the living room', the question of who exercises the most power and control over programme choice is firmly linked to gender. His own research, based on eighteen families in South London, confirmed that where men are in paid employment, they have the most control over what is watched. This was symbolised by their domination over the use of the remote control handset. (Peter Collett (1986) recorded one instance where the man carried the remote control with him even when he left the room to make coffee!)

Another difference Morley discovered was that men preferred to watch television attentively, in silence and without interruption, whereas women were more inclined to engage in conversation or perform other domestic activities while viewing. Men's approach to viewing was generally more deliberately planned, closely scrutinising the evening's schedule. These differences reflect more general distinctions in gender roles and identities, particularly in relation to work and leisure. Men make quite a sharp demarcation between work outside the home and leisure within it. Women, however, are more inclined to define home as a site of labour and therefore watch television more distractedly and with a sense of guilt (hence their greater enjoyment of viewing when the rest of the family is absent). Finally, as the main 'breadwinners' in most families, men see it as their 'right' to exercise first choice and in the event of any dispute may invoke this as a justification for prevailing over what is watched.

However, in the more recent BFI study (Gauntlett and Hill, 1999), there was found to be much less male domination over choice of television viewing, although men were still more inclined to hold the remote control and make unilateral decisions about what to watch on the main television set (Figure 5.12).

The authors attribute this to 'women allowing men the mild feeling of power which may come with physically holding the remote control device' whilst not allowing programme choices to be dictated to them.

Such patriarchal patterns are not necessarily universal. James Lull (1988) reports that in China there is no dominance of night-time viewing by males, and that in Venezuela it is women who control viewing (especially with respect to the viewing of the *telenovelas* – soap operas) as a reflection of their greater control of domestic space. Finally, in India, television

Who usually decided what was watched on television in a mixed household	
Joint decision, or household dispersed to multiple TV sets	81%
Man usually decided	11%
Woman usually decided	6%
Children usually decided	2%
Who usually used the TV remote control in a mixed household	
Man usually had remote control	46%
Woman usually had remote control	22%
No pattern	20.5%
Children usually had remote control	11.5%

FIGURE 5.12
TV Living
Source: D Gauntlett & A Hill TV Living (Routledge)

viewing has actually helped to increase democracy in the household at the expense of traditional patriarchy.

Gender and Media Technology

The main theme of Ann Gray's (1992) research into women's response to video in the household is that gender is a key determinant in the use of, and expertise in, specific domestic technologies. In the case of the video cassette recorder (VCR), men's influence prevailed in a number of ways, ranging across the initial decision to purchase or rent a VCR, the mastery and control of the timer programming and the ownership of videotapes (men being more inclined to develop their own personal archive). When it came to time shifting, many of the women failed to operate the timer with any confidence. This was partly due to lack of motivation and a sense that it was masculine terrain.

The gendering of video technology as masculine is a key issue emphasised by Gray and others and recognisable in some of the commercial advertising stressing the 'hi-tech' nature of VCRs. This is in contrast to 'feminine' technology like microwave ovens, dishwashers and washing machines, which are no less technically demanding. Apart from VCRs, other new technology defined as masculine includes computers and video games.

Sherry Turkle (1984) has argued that computer culture appeals to masculine pleasures because of its abstract formal systems and its ability to offer a safe and protective retreat from personal relationships. 'Hackers' are preoccupied with winning and take risks, qualities traditionally perceived by women as 'non-feminine'. Meanwhile, video-games software seems to emphasise masculinised images of action–adventure scenarios in which a single male hero tackles overwhelming odds. The games focus on a quest which is attained via technological intervention. Female games players responding to a survey on **www.Womengamers.com** in 2001 complained about the lack of acceptable female characters and gender-neutral games, and objected to the level of sexism within many computer games (arising from the domination of males in the gaming industry).

Activity 5.7

Compare two households, as in the case study on p. 137, in terms of information and communications technology (ICT) in the home.

1 Profile each household in terms of occupation, housing, age and education where possible.
2 List the ICT owned and its physical distribution in the house (see list below).
3 How is ICT regarded in general by each member of the household?
4 Identify which member(s) of the household 'own' and control which items of ICT (e.g. use of remote control). Include the number of each item possessed or rented.

ICT:	Television (Teletext?)	DVD/video recorder
	Satellite/cable receiver	Camcorder
	Video-game console	Computer/CD ROM/Internet
	Radio (Walkman?)	Music centre/hi-fi/CD

For the national figures for some of these see Figure 1.4 (p. 6).

C A S E   S T U D Y :
Media Technology in the House

Family A
1. Father (42) manager of fire safety.
   Mother (41) receptionist.
   Daughter (19) shop assistant.
   Daughter (16) studying A levels at college.

2. ICT (owned and physical distribution in the house).
   1 widescreen television – living room.
   3 standard televisions – bedrooms (parents and both daughters).
   4 video recorders – 1 in living room. 1 in each bedroom.
   1 DVD player – living room.
   Sky Digital – living room.
   2 Playstations – 1 in parents' bedroom. 1 in daughter's room.
   1 laptop computer – mobile.
   4 radio/CD Walkman – each person.
   3 music centre/hi-fi/CD – 1 living room. 1 in both daughters' rooms.

3. How ICT is regarded in general by each member of the household.

The father has control over television downstairs, including video-player, DVD and Sky Digital. Laptop is owned by him. He takes control over remote control, especially for football and films on Sky, and takes big advantage of the Teletext. He also owns, and frequently plays on, the Playstation in the bedroom, particularly racing games. He is the controller of all ICT in the household as he knows how it works. He is also very protective of the DVD. The mother partly has control of all ICT downstairs but not as much as the father. She is not confident in using ICT within the household, especially the VCR/DVD, except the television and music hi-fi/CD player, which she uses often downstairs – maybe more than the others.

Daughter, 19, has little control of ICT downstairs but has own control of hi-fi/CD in her own bedroom which she uses regularly. More than often though she will be in control of her own television and VCR. Daughter, 16, has little control of ICT downstairs when parents are around, but otherwise when alone confidently uses Digital, VCR, hi-fi systems and widescreen TV downstairs. She has regular use of hi-fi/CD system in bedroom which is rarely used by anyone else and regularly watches and uses television and VCR in bedroom.

Each member of the family views their own ICT but has a smaller usage of other ICT around the household. Laptop is owned by father, but is shared between each family member, but used mainly between father and daughter, 16.

The whole family will watch *Hollyoaks* at teatime and *EastEnders* in the evening.

Family B
1. Mother (42) doctors' receptionist.
   Father (55) head engineer at docks.
   Son (16) student at college.
   Daughter (13) at school.

2. ICT (owned and physical distribution in the house).
   Father: television (Teletext and Sky Digital), VCR situated in living room as well as separates including CD player, tuner, tape deck; clock/radio alarm in bedroom, Walkman and radio situated in garage; WAP mobile phone.
   Mother: CD player, TV in kitchen, Walkman.
   Son: Television (Teletext), VCR, DVD player, CD player, tape deck and radio. CD Walkman, radio alarm, Dreamcast games console, Playstation games console, WAP mobile phone.
   Daughter: TV with Teletext, CD player, tape deck, radio, karaoke machine, VCR, CD Walkman, radio alarm, WAP mobile phone.
   General: 3 TVs, 2 VCRs, 2 CD players, 1 PC.

3. How ICT is regarded by each member of the household.

The televisions owned by the whole family were bought by the father and are situated in the living room, dining room, kitchen and spare room. These are all places that the family congregate, especially to watch *EastEnders*. Therefore, the television is watched by all members, yet only the son and father know how to fully operate everything. This also applies to the hi-fi equipment situated in living room. All the electronic equipment is usually used and operated by the son or father. The mother's main 'ownership' is of the television in the kitchen. She mainly watches soaps such as *Emmerdale* and *Coronation Street*. She has no idea how to work 'Sky' or the video recorder.

The son and daughter mainly watch the television and the Sky remote passes mainly between them for MTV2 or *Kerrang!* (son) or *Sabrina* (daughter).

Each member of the family has a stereo and listens to their own types of music. The mother's stereo is in the kitchen and the father's is in the bedroom. The son and daughter have a stereo each in their rooms. The one in the living room is shared by all and is usually on the radio (95.8 Capital FM) when the family is socialising.

All the family use the Internet: the father for researching his hobby (boating), the son for homework, music (*Kerrang*) and films (IMDB.com), the daughter for chatrooms and least frequently the mother for e-mails.

Both son and daughter's ICTs are similar and usually used in the evening when they need to relax, do homework or have friends round.

Most items 'owned' by the father tend to be situated in the front room and are considered as being for use by the whole family.

Further Reading

Barker, M. and Petley, J. (eds). 2001: Ill-Effects: The Media/Violence Debate. ROUTLEDGE.

Buckingham, D. 2000: After the Death of Childhood. POLITY PRESS.

Buckingham, D. (ed). 2002: Small Screens: Television for Children. LEICESTER UNIVERSITY PRESS.

Gauntlett, D. and Hill, S. 1999: TV Living: Television, Culture and Everyday Life. ROUTLEDGE.

Geraghty, C. 1991: Women and Soap Opera. POLITY PRESS.

Gray, A. 1992: Video Playtime. ROUTLEDGE.

Lewis, J. 1991: The Ideological Octopus. ROUTLEDGE.

Livingstone, S. 2002: Young People and New Media. SAGE.

Lull, J. (ed). 1988: World Families Watch Television. SAGE.

Morley, D. 1992: Television Audiences and Cultural Studies. ROUTLEDGE.

Nightingale, V. 1996: Studying Audiences: The Shock of the Real. ROUTLEDGE.

Peterson, R.C. and Thurstone, L. 1933: Motion Pictures and Social Attitudes. MACMILLAN.

Schlesinger, P., Dobash, R.E., Dobash, R.P. and Weaver, C. 1992: Women Viewing Violence. BFI.

CHAPTER SIX

Media Institutions and Production

This chapter examines the media as contemporary social institutions with specific determinants and processes of production (whose historical antecedents are discussed in Chapter 7). After providing an overview of institutional determinants, the analysis focuses on two case studies of media production: pop music and local newspapers.

Media as Institutions

One of the key themes of this book is that the media form a significant part of the everyday cultural life of modern industrial societies. As audiences, our routines are often structured around viewing, reading and listening to media output, and we regularly refer to specific media texts in social encounters. There is a sense in which the media are part of the social fabric. When certain social practices take on a regularity and structure which are apparent to ordinary people, then they may be called an institution. This is not to be confused with the more common usage of the term as referring to a specific organisation or building (e.g. a prison).

There is a helpful framework for examining the constituent elements of institutions.

It may be useful to think of all social institutions in terms of the varying degrees to which they represent historical and continuing social responses to conflicts at the level of:

1 *Economy,* concerned with the production and distribution of raw materials, manufactured goods and wealth.
2 *Politics,* concerned with the exercise of power and processes of social regulation.
3 *Culture,* concerned with the production, exchange and reproduction of meaning.

O'Sullivan et al (1994)

The emphasis in previous chapters, especially Chapters 2, 4 and 5, has been on the third element in the list, the making of cultural meaning. While this is a critical ingredient in the analysis of institutional processes, the intention here is to focus on the economic and political dimensions and how these shape media production, distribution and consumption.

Institutional Determinants: Economic

Despite the fact that media texts are important sources of cultural meanings, they also share many of the characteristics of industrial commodities like motor cars or washing powder. Assembly-line production, marketing, research and development, etc can all be found in media industries. The capital investment for a typical Hollywood feature film in 2003 was likely to be well over $50 million, and that did not include the marketing costs which in some cases could be as much as the production budget. Up to 2000, the most expensive Hollywood production was *Titanic* (1997) which cost $200 million to produce (but made over $1800 million at the box office). For Hollywood studios, such costs can be justified only by success at the box office, manifested as profit in the form of revenue from admissions, video/DVD rights and other sources in domestic and global markets.

With such high financial stakes, it is not surprising that companies make every effort to minimise their risks in what is at times a very uncertain and risky market. For Hollywood, this has meant the increasing tendency to produce sequels for successful films like *Star Wars* and *Scream* until public interest declines. A further strategy is to rely more on research-based marketing from the initial packaging of a film (title, synopsis, stars, etc) to the selection of the final cut on the basis of test screenings of alternative climaxes. For example, the ending to *Fatal Attraction* (1987) was eventually chosen (against the director's wishes) by a vote of preview audiences. However, one of the simplest ways of maximising profits in media production is by extending control over the market.

Concentration of Ownership

In all industrial markets there is a tendency for the bigger, more successful companies to take over smaller companies in a search for even greater growth. When the takeover involves a direct competitor in the same sector then the process is referred to as **horizontal integration**, for example a newspaper publisher buying out a rival publisher. **Vertical integration** is when a company takes over another company which is responsible for other stages of the production cycle, for example a newspaper company buying out a newsagent's chain or a paper manufacturer. Such processes of integration occur almost daily in the media sectors, as can be detected by a quick survey of the industry's trade magazines such as *Broadcast, Campaign* and *Screen Digest*. What they mean in practice is that mainstream media production is characterised by a growing concentration of ownership. In all the media industries, a few (between five and six) very large companies control a sizeable share of the market. When these companies own shares in several media sectors and on an international scale, they are referred to as multimedia conglomerates (see Doyle, 2002).

Often these companies are seeking to achieve vertical integration in order to guarantee a means of distributing the media product to the audience. This has long been a feature of the film industry where production companies have controlled the means of distribution and exhibition of films, but this has become even more significant with the development of new media technologies of distribution, e.g. high band cable and the Internet. In 2000, the merger between AOL and Time Warner (Figure 6.1) was largely motivated by the opportunity of making available to AOL's millions of Internet subscribers the huge Time Warner catalogue of films, music, television programmes and so on, providing another future source of profit. However, at the time of writing, AOL Time Warner's huge financial losses for 2002 mean that the process of integration and growth may be reversed.

FIGURE 6.1
AOL Time Warner
– Guardian
11.1.00
Source: David
Rowan, Guardian

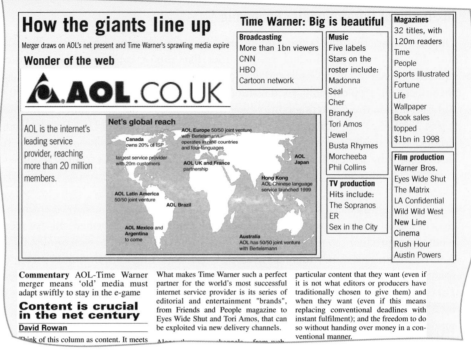

How the giants line up

Merger draws on AOL's net present and Time Warner's sprawling media expire

Wonder of the web

AOL.CO.UK

AOL is the internet's leading service provider, reaching more than 20 million members.

Net's global reach

Canada owns 20% of ISP

largest service provider with 20m customers

AOL UK and France partnership

AOL Europe 50/50 joint venture with Bertelsmann operates in nine countries and four languages

AOL Japan

Hong Kong AOL Chinese language service launched 1999

AOL Latin America 50/50 joint venture

AOL Brazil

AOL Mexico and Argentina to come

Australia AOL has 50/50 joint venture with Bertelsmann

Time Warner: Big is beautiful

Broadcasting
More than 1bn viewers
CNN
HBO
Cartoon network

Music
Five labels
Stars on the roster include:
Madonna
Seal
Cher
Brandy
Tori Amos
Jewel
Busta Rhymes
Morcheeba
Phil Collins

TV production
Hits include:
The Sopranos
ER
Sex in the City

Magazines
32 titles, with 120m readers
Time
People
Sports Illustrated
Fortune
Life
Wallpaper
Book sales topped $1bn in 1998

Film production
Warner Bros.
Eyes Wide Shut
The Matrix
LA Confidential
Wild Wild West
New Line Cinema
Rush Hour
Austin Powers

Commentary AOL-Time Warner merger means 'old' media must adapt swiftly to stay in the e-game

Content is crucial in the net century

David Rowan

Think of this column as content. It meets

What makes Time Warner such a perfect partner for the world's most successful internet service provider is its series of editorial and entertainment "brands", from Friends and People magazine to Eyes Wide Shut and Tori Amos, that can be exploited via new delivery channels.

particular content that they want (even if it is not what editors or producers have traditionally chosen to give them) and when they want (even if this means replacing conventional deadlines with instant fulfilment); and the freedom to do so without handing over money in a conventional manner.

These media conglomerates are in a much stronger position to take advantage of the growing international media markets (see Chapter 8 for a discussion of globalisation) as well as exploiting opportunities to sell their own products across the various sectors of the corporation. Such multimarketing is a growing media phenomenon. The profits made from a film's release may be multiplied through sales of the accompanying music soundtrack, video and DVD sell-through, paperback novel, television spin-off rights, etc.

Perhaps the greatest profits are to be made in licensed merchandising, whereby the media brand is attached to various consumer products such as toys, clothes or food and drink. For example, it is estimated that in the past twenty years the *Star Wars* films have earned more than $3 billion in merchandising. The Disney Corporation is probably the most adroit in capitalising on merchandise related to its films. Such merchandise is usually made available in the shops *prior* to the release of a film, thus building anticipation and interest in the film. British media companies have also begun to exploit their popular characters, a good example being the BBC which has sought to exploit its success with children's television characters such as the *Teletubbies* via licensed products such as clothing, food, toys, etc, not to mention the global television sales and accompanying videos. BBC figures show that by September 2002, the revenue for *Teletubbies* merchandising had reached £1.2 billion (including 4.5 million videos and 5.5 million books).

A similar example of media secondary marketing is integral to the concept of **synergy** – the selling of two or more compatible products simultaneously. In the late 1980s, a series of 'classic' pop songs from the past were used to create the desired atmosphere and mood for the advertising of Levi 501 jeans on television. Apart from the massive boost to sales of 501 jeans, the revived songs invariably recharted, often reaching number one. This pattern has been repeated with films such as *Robin Hood, Prince of Thieves* (1990; Bryan Adams, 'Everything I Do', topping the singles chart for nine weeks), *The Bodyguard* (1992; Whitney Houston's 'I Will Always Love You') and *Titanic* (1997; Celine Dion's 'My Heart Will Go On').

Finally, media conglomerates are also able to take advantage of their cross-media ownership to promote products within the company. For example, Rupert Murdoch's British newspapers have been consistent supporters of his satellite station, BSkyB, and its services. Indeed, at one time the chief executive of BSkyB, Andrew Neil, was also editor of the *Sunday Times*.

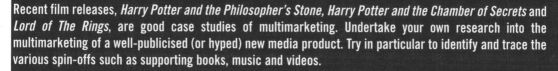

Activity 6.1

Recent film releases, *Harry Potter and the Philosopher's Stone*, *Harry Potter and the Chamber of Secrets* and *Lord of The Rings*, are good case studies of multimarketing. Undertake your own research into the multimarketing of a well-publicised (or hyped) new media product. Try in particular to identify and trace the various spin-offs such as supporting books, music and videos.

Ownership and Power

What has concerned many people about the trend towards concentration of ownership and the rise of international conglomerates is the potential for using media outlets to exercise power and influence. Marxist writers have particularly emphasised how, under capitalism, the property-owning class promote and defend their own interests at the expense of the rest of society – the thesis of political economy. The search for profit is seen as the key arbiter of what is produced in the media, first in the economic sense of achieving surplus revenue and second in the ideological sense of promoting those values and beliefs which support capitalism. (This echoes the hegemonic model outlined in Chapter 4.)

There is little doubt that the major companies do exercise their economic muscle in squeezing out, or taking over, new competition. This might involve, for example, undercutting the competitors' prices and advertising rates, or increasing the marketing and promotion budget. When the *Daily Star* was launched in 1978, *The Sun* implemented all these strategies and almost managed to deliver its new rival a fatal blow. In 1993, Rupert Murdoch initiated a newspaper 'price war' by slashing the price of *The Times* (by 50 per cent) and *The Sun* (20 per cent) by which, although it cost him millions of pounds in the short term, he managed to squeeze his rivals, in particular *The Independent* whose future is in doubt. Ironically, the first casualty of the circulation battle was Murdoch's own paper, *Today*, which closed in November 1995. From the consumer's point of view, the net result is less choice and diversity.

As to the ideological effect of concentrated ownership, it is difficult to arrive at a conclusive judgement. Curran and Seaton (1997) argue that with respect to the press, owners have sought to promote business interests in general, usually by ensuring their newspaper supported the Conservative Party. In return, newspaper editors and proprietors have been given honorary titles (e.g. Sir Larry Lamb, ex-editor of *The Sun*, and Sir David English, ex-editor of the *Daily Mail*).

FIGURE 6.2
Front page of The Sun, 18 March 1997. In 1997 The Sun switched its support to the Labour Party after having backed the Conservatives for the previous twenty years. The decision (taken by the proprietor, Rupert Murdoch) reflected the perception that the Tories had lost favour with many of The Sun's readers, but also that the Labour Party no longer posed a threat to News Corporation's commercial interests
Source: Sun, 18 March 1997

The proprietor most notorious in recent times for his interventionism is Rupert Murdoch. His admiration for Margaret Thatcher was strongly echoed in *The Sun* despite the fact that the majority of its readers were not Conservative voters. When Murdoch acquired *The Times* and the *Sunday Times* in 1981, the editors of both titles came under strong pressure to endorse Thatcherite policies, and duly obliged or resigned (Harold Evans resigned from *The Times* in 1983). Prior to being elected Prime Minister in 1997, Tony Blair carefully wooed Rupert Murdoch and was rewarded with his support at the general election (Figure 6.2), although the switch in *The Sun's* support from Conservative to Labour was no doubt influenced by the loss of popularity of the Tories among the readership of *The Sun*. Such is the perceived political power of Rupert Murdoch in Britain, Australia and even America emanating from his ownership of the media that his critics have argued that politicians have refrained from threatening his business interests in these countries. This is despite the fact that Murdoch has often flouted the rules in extending his media empire. For example, in Britain BSkyB is virtually a monopoly provider of digital satellite television via its control of the satellite decoder technology. In Australia, the rules were actually changed to permit him to own newspaper titles despite being a foreign citizen (previously only national citizens could own Australian newspapers and Murdoch, originally from Australia, had become an American citizen – in order to acquire American newspapers and interests!).

FIGURE 6.3
Source: Daily Mirror, 6 November 1991

Even so-called 'independent' newspapers do not seem to be immune from proprietorial pressures. While the *Observer* was owned by Lonrho, its editor, Donald Trelford, often allowed the paper to carry stories favourable to the activities of Tiny Rowland, Lonrho's chairman (e.g. Rowland's attempt to take over the Fraser Group, owner of Harrods department store). Figure 6.3 shows the front page of *The Mirror* the day after the death of its proprietor, Robert Maxwell, was announced in 1991. Within days *The Mirror* was savagely criticising its former 'saviour' owner in the light of revelations about his corrupt misuse of *The Mirror* pension funds (Maxwell had suppressed all criticism of his business dealings whilst he was the owner of the paper).

Meanwhile, *The Mirror* came in for another form of ownership pressure in July 2002 when a major American investor in Trinity-Mirror, the company that owns *The Mirror*, threatened to sell its shares in the company if *The Mirror* continued to prominently publish features written by journalist John Pilger which were highly critical of America's foreign policy.

The Limits of Ownership Power

The profit drive in media industries is not always consistent with upholding dominant ideologies. Rupert Murdoch, famous for shifting his publications towards the political right, has allowed some of his titles to advocate minority or ideologically ambiguous views. In 1991, the Scottish edition of *The Sun*, anxious to boost its relatively poor sales north of the border, switched its political support to the Scottish Nationalists. In 1993, *Today* newspaper, still in search of a clear identity, moved leftwards towards the Labour Party. Furthermore, *The Simpsons*, the hugely popular cartoon series produced by Murdoch's Fox Television, has been attacked in America for having as its 'hero' a streetwise educational underachiever who belongs to a dysfunctional family.

In the music industry, few companies have hesitated to release and promote songs containing politically radical or unorthodox ideas if there was a reasonable chance of such songs being commercially successful. In the late 1960s, CBS records in the USA had a large roster of 'countercultural' artists, many of whose music expressed anti-Vietnam war sentiments, and yet CBS itself was part of a corporation with military investments.

Unlike many other consumer commodities, media products can never be uniformly standardised. This makes total control of the market virtually impossible to attain. Nowhere is this more apparent than in the film industry, where the size of the budget, the casting of stars and the intensity of publicity cannot guarantee a profitable outcome, such is the unpredictability of the audience response. Contrast the fate of *Ishtar*, a comedy film starring Dustin Hoffman and Warren Beatty which lost $37 million in 1987, with *Rocky*, which starred the then unknown Sylvester Stallone in 1976 and made $56 million, having cost only $1.5 million to make. Even more startling is the example of the *Blair Witch Project* (1999), which cost a paltry $35 000 to produce (almost a lavish home movie) and made over $140 million at the box office. There are numerous similar instances from across the media of audiences supporting or rejecting media products in a seemingly capricious manner. Prominent recent examples include *Viz*, a locally produced comic whose circulation topped 1 million in the early 1990s, *The Darling Buds of May*, a gentle comedy-drama which topped the television ratings in 1991–92, and Classic FM (radio), all of whose popular appeal took most media analysts by surprise.

It is far easier for major companies to dominate the market when the capital costs of investment (especially in technology) are high. The potential for would-be rivals to BSkyB is minimal, given the hundreds of millions of pounds necessary for starting up a digital satellite service. The collapse of BSkyB's main rival in providing digital subscription television, ITV Digital, in 2002 is a good illustration of this (see page 213). In contrast, making a pop record or launching a fanzine is within the means of many people who might wish to take a small step into such media markets. Given the size and complexity of much media production today, the actual *control* of such production usually lies with groups of professionals who have the requisite technical expertise. Such professional autonomy is discussed in the next main section.

Market freedoms are not unfettered. Not only are there monopoly controls to prevent a single company exercising complete control in the market, but all the media are also subject to regulatory frameworks, often backed up by legal sanctions (see *The Limits of Freedom*, below).

While acknowledging the variety of institutional determinants of media production, most commentators would probably stress the *economic* forces as being of greatest significance. However, the phenomenon can be interpreted in different ways. As we have seen in Chapter 4, hegemonic theorists would relate it to the structure of economic inequality in society and the perpetuation of powerful group interests, particularly via the direct or indirect influence of owners. Pluralist thinkers, on the other hand,

145

would rather emphasise the sovereignty of the audience and their demands, with media production acting as a barometer of changing tastes and preferences. Diverse audience interests are reflected in a diversity of media choice. If there is a demand, media corporations will respond.

But how effective are the media in fulfilling the 'demands of the market' (if these can ever be known)? As stated above, the larger media conglomerates have the power to squeeze new competition and thus keep control of the market. Furthermore, audiences are not of equal commercial interest to media producers.

Advertising Revenue

Apart from revenue gained from sales of newspapers, magazines, videos, etc, the other main source of revenue for the media is advertising (Figure 6.4). For commercial television and radio, advertising is the lifeblood of the industry. What concerns advertisers using the media is reaching the target audience, i.e. those people most likely to buy the product in question. Consequently, there is little point advertising Armani clothes in *The Sun* or MFI furniture in the *Financial Times*. The size of audience is obviously of interest, especially on television, where advertising rates tend to be calculated in direct proportion to numbers of viewers as revealed in the ratings. As a consequence, the profitability of ITV and Channel 4, as well as independent radio, is dependent on the ability to achieve and maintain good viewing and listening figures. This in turn has implications for the type of programming scheduled. Those programmes which have a broad popular appeal, for instance soap operas, police series, sitcoms, invariably predominate over programmes which are seen as attracting minority audiences.

The second criterion for advertisers is the social profile (or demographics) of the audience in terms of social class, gender and age. Of least interest to most advertisers are older working-class people, who have the lowest disposable income. This is particularly significant for those media productions with a well-defined audience profile. Generally, the more 'upmarket' (AB as defined by market research) the audience, the easier it is to attract advertisers and hence achieve profitability. Consequently, there is greater choice for younger, more middle-class audiences. Figure 6.5 shows how in 2001 there was a greater choice of (broadsheet) newspapers for their predominantly middle-class readers (ABC1) than the 'red-top' tabloid newspapers read mainly by the working class (C2DE).

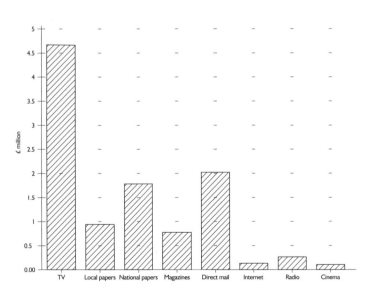

FIGURE 6.4
Advertising expenditure by medium
Source: Advertising Association, 1995

This distribution of revenue from advertising also has implications for the political bias of national newspapers. Because newspapers like *The Mirror* need large circulations to flourish, they have tended to sideline hard political news and focus on entertainment values and celebrities (see Chapter 3), although this

PRESS – NATIONAL NEWSPAPERS

	Circulation Tabloid/ B'sheet	Adult Readership (1) '000s	Adult Readership (2) '000s[1]	%	Men %	Women %	Adult Readership Profiles (2) 15–34 %	35–54 %	55+ %	ABC1 %	C2DE %
POPULATION PROFILES					49	51	34	35	32	52	49
NATIONAL DAILIES											
The Sun	T	3,388	9,567	21	57	43	42	33	25	35	65
The Mirror	T	2,085	5,617	12	53	47	30	33	37	37	63
The Daily Express	T	966	2,058	4	51	49	21	33	47	64	36
The Daily Telegraph	B	989	2,239	5	56	44	17	33	51	86	14
Daily Record (Scotland)	T	588	1,584	3	53	47	35	37	28	31	69
Daily Star	T	552	1,499	3	71	29	49	37	14	31	69
The Times	B	676	1,558	3	61	39	31	41	28	88	12
The Guardian	B	357	1,069	2	56	45	37	43	19	88	12
The Independent	B	201	576	1	59	41	32	47	21	89	11
Financial Times	B	180	594	1	74	26	32	51	17	93	7
NATIONAL SUNDAYS											
News of the World	T	3,776	10,201	22	52	48	41	35	24	36	64
Sunday Mirror	T	1,777	5,646	12	52	48	33	34	33	39	61
The Mail on Sunday	T	2.249	5,873	13	49	51	25	38	36	67	33
Sunday People	T	1,360	3,230	7	54	46	27	34	38	34	66
The Sunday Express	T	900	2,196	5	50	50	21	34	45	67	33
The Sunday Times	B	1,224	3,146	7	58	42	36	43	22	87	13
Sunday Post (Scotland)	T	645	1,581	3	44	56	15	29	56	36	64
Sunday Mail (Scotland)	T	694	2,721	4	50	50	32	40	28	36	64
Sunday Telegraph	B	778	1,999	4	53	47	20	33	47	82	16
The Observer	B	399	1,096	2	59	41	34	42	24	85	15
The Independent on Sunday	B	211	629	1	58	42	36	46	18	82	18

FIGURE 6.5

Note(s): [1]Rounded to nearest £.

Source(s): (1) A.B.C. data, July 2000 – June 2001. (2) National Readership Survey (NRS Ltd.), July 2000 – June 2001.

trend was temporarily reversed in the months following the Twin Towers attack of September 11th. More in-depth political coverage and comment is left to the more upmarket tabloids (like the *Daily Mail)* or the broadsheets, whose more affluent middle-class readership prefers conservative political values. In the past, this has meant the closure of a Labour-supporting paper like the *Daily Herald* (which folded in 1964 with a circulation five times that of *The Times*) and the Liberal *News Chronicle* (whose circulation equalled that of the *Daily Telegraph* when it closed in 1960). Even *The Mirror's* commitment to the Labour Party seems threatened following the death of Robert Maxwell in 1991 and the attempt to make the paper an attractive commercial proposition to new owners in the face of intense competition from *The Sun.*

There is every danger that, in the future, the more advertisers are keen to pinpoint their target audiences via the media, the more those audiences unattractive to advertisers will tend to be ignored. This is because a key trend is towards *narrowcasting* (or niche targeting) in the media – i.e. supplying differentiated, customised services to specialist audience groups and as with other market-based services, those with most disposable income exercise greatest choice.

Activity 6.2

From listing the adverts which appear within different television programmes (at varying times of day) on ITV and Channel 4, see whether there is any pattern which indicates a target audience for that programme (age, gender, class, etc).

A similar exercise can be undertaken with newspapers and magazines, whose readership is usually better defined in terms of social profile.

Institutional Determinants: Professional Autonomy

Although ownership of media companies makes possible power over production from the point of view of allocating resources (capital investment, budgets strategy, etc), the day-to-day management of media organisations in the operational sense lies with media professionals. Of course, in small-scale 'independent' enterprises the owners and controllers of production may well be the same people, but most organisations require a division of labour based on specialised areas of skill and technical expertise.

Such skills and expertise are often elevated to an occupational ideal, making it possible to lay claim to professionalism. Most media organisations require new recruits to undertake considerable in-house training on top of any formal qualifications already obtained. The ethos of the organisation – what it stands for and how it goes about things, together with the 'house style' of production – are central to the process of occupational socialisation. The ensuing collective thinking and practice provide a degree of solidarity from which external threats (owners, the government, the public, etc) can be negotiated or resisted. This also has implications for the boundaries of creative freedom within media production. The 'correct' or conventional way of doing something becomes enshrined in professional practice until, and if, someone is bold or strong enough to break or question the 'rules' (see Chapter 9 on Media Practice).

The freedom to deviate from the accepted codes and conventions will very much depend on a previous hierarchical position. In cinema and television, producers and directors exercise the greatest control over the content and style of films and programmes. Some film directors have been seen as '*auteurs*' or artistic authors, able to imbue their films with a personal vision or look, e.g. Orson Welles, Alfred Hitchcock, David Lynch and Tim Burton. However, media production, not least in film, is essentially a cooperative venture, necessitating considerable mutual assistance and interdependence (Figure 6.6).

In newspapers and magazines, editors are in the strongest position to influence the shape and direction of the immediate publication. Some individual editors have made a recognisable impression on their newspaper's or magazine's identity: *The Sun* between 1981 and 1994 under the editorship of Kelvin MacKenzie is one example:

> But it was in the afternoon, as the paper built up to its creative climax of going to press, that the real performance would begin. MacKenzie would burst through the door after lunch with his cry of 'Whaddya got for me?' and the heat would be on. He had total control – not just over the front page but over every page lead going right through the paper. Shrimsley was remembered as a fast and furious corrector of proofs, but MacKenzie was even faster, drawing up layouts, plucking

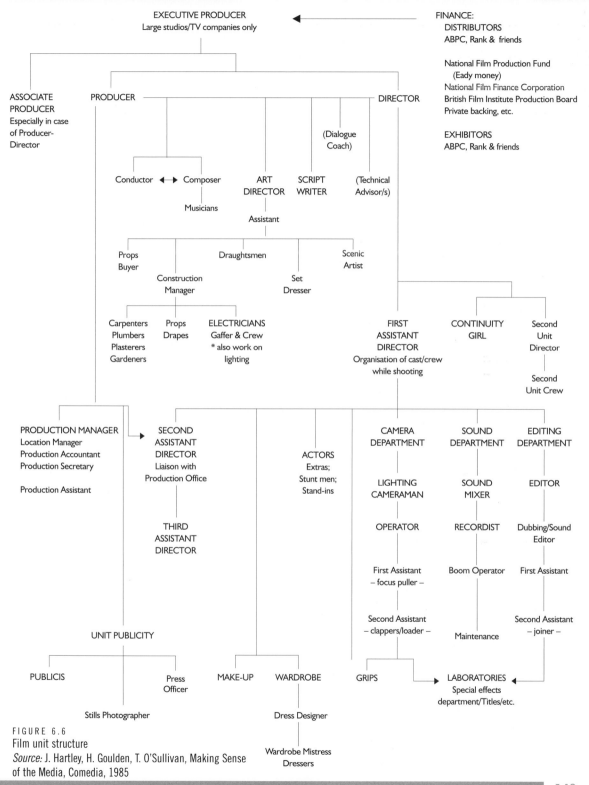

FIGURE 6.6
Film unit structure
Source: J. Hartley, H. Goulden, T. O'Sullivan, *Making Sense of the Media*, Comedia, 1985

headline after headline out of the air, and all the time driving towards the motto he hammered into them all: 'Shock and amaze on every page'.

True to the code of sarff London, MacKenzie also wanted to be surrounded by 'made men', who had proved themselves by pulling off some outrageous stunt at the expense of the opposition. One way of becoming a made man was to phone 'The Mirror' and ask for the 'stone' where the final versions of pages were assembled for the presses. The trick was to imitate another member of 'The Mirror' staff to fool the stone sub into revealing the front-page splash. One features exec became a made man by walking across Fleet Street into 'The Express' and stealing some crucial pictures from the library. Hacks refusing to get involved in this sort of behaviour were suspect – falling into the category of those who were not fully with him, and could therefore be presumed to be against him.

Chippendale and Horrie (1990)

The Limits of Freedom

The ability of media professionals to achieve autonomy is subject to two key constraints:

1 *Profitability.* Few owners of the media are content to maintain a 'hands-off' policy if there is not a healthy flow of profit or at least the prospect of one. 'Creative' film directors are only indulged by Hollywood studios if their last film was a blockbuster. Virtually no part of the media is now immune from economic pressures. The BBC's decision to axe *Eldorado*, its expensive and short-running soap opera, in 1993, was largely due to a need to bolster its falling share of the ratings (and thus strengthen its case for the continuation of the licence fee). Despite paying a huge fee for the rights to show football highlights from the Premiership, in the autumn of 2001, ITV very quickly changed the Saturday evening scheduling from 7.00pm to 10.30pm when the ratings were deemed below what could be achieved with programmes like *Blind Date*.

Equally, media professionals may be trapped by success. Productions with popular appeal become formularised, with writers, editors, actors, etc working in assembly-line 'factory' conditions, allowing little scope for experimentation or risk-taking (e.g. television soap operas).

When it comes to a showdown between proprietor and professional, the former nearly always prevails. Even the ebullient Kelvin MacKenzie of *The Sun* was known for his subservience to Rupert Murdoch, and prior to his death Robert Maxwell was intolerant of any dissidence within his corporation. Curran and Seaton (1997) can find only one occasion when journalists actually succeeded in decisively defeating their proprietor (when the *Observer's* staff resisted Lonrho's boss, Tiny Rowland, who tried to change the newspaper's liberal stance towards South African politics).

2 *Regulation.* On the one hand, professional independence is actually bolstered by self-regulation. Like doctors and lawyers, media professionals operate within codes of ethical practice designed to prevent unacceptable standards of production or irresponsible behaviour. If members adhere to such codes, then there are less likely to be attempts made to impose conditions from outside the industry (e.g. by the government).

However, not surprisingly, there is limited state or public faith in any organisation's or industry's attempts to police itself, and all the media are subject to a variety of external controls either enshrined in the law and/or administered by external, independent bodies.

Institutional Determinants: External Regulations

The media appear to operate relatively freely in democratic western countries like Britain, compared with those under more repressive regimes in the world. Nevertheless, there is a plethora of laws and regulations which act as constraints on British media production. Most of these have been historically invested in by the state and are kept in reserve for when the media step out of line. We need to distinguish between general laws which apply to all the media and more specific regulations relevant to individual media institutions.

Political Controls

The government rarely intervenes directly to censor the media, as this would be perceived as anti-democratic. It reserves that right for national emergencies or crises such as wartime. For example, in 1939 Winston Churchill banned the *Daily Worker*, a communist newspaper, as it was seen as a threat

---

MoD guidelines for the Gulf War

Fourteen categories (covering 32 subjects) of information cannot be published or broadcast without talking to the Ministry of Defence. These include:

- Numbers of troops, ships, aircraft and other equipment: specific locations of British or Allied military units; future military plans.
- Photographs showing locations of military forces. Photographs of wounded soldiers.
- Information about casualties should not be broadcast until next of kin contacted.
- Specific information on British ships and planes which have been hit.
- Information on how intelligence is collected.

Not the full story ...

First World War (1914–18)

Strict censorship began in August 1914. A government-appointed officer, Colonel Sir Ernest Swinton, wrote 'eye-witness' reports for the press, but they gave few details.

Newspaper proprietors Lord Northcliffe and Lord Beaverbrook were among those working closely with the government.

Second World War (1939–45)

The Ministry of Information employed, at one stage, 999 people to turn 'news' into an anti-German crusade. No British soldier could be named. The true extent of Japan's attack on Pearl Harbor was hidden until after 1945.

Vietnam War (1954–75)

The first television war: American journalists reported for the first time without direct censorship from the army. The US military issued general guidelines which journalists were expected to follow, but media criticism, especially of the 1968 Tet Offensive, helped turn American public opinion against the war.

Falklands War (1982)

Twenty-nine carefully selected British reporters were kept under strict Ministry of Defence control. Reporters, who had to agree to censorship, were told what was happening after the event. Some reports had to pass through three stages of vetting before they could be released.

FIGURE 6.7
Government reporting guidelines in wartime
Source: Guardian, 29 January 1991. © Guardian

to a united war effort. More recently, during the Falklands and Gulf Wars, the Ministry of Defence (MoD) vetted all news reports. This frequently led to censorship in the case of reporting the 1982 Falklands War, whereas in the 1991 Gulf War the MoD guidelines generally produced self-censorship in reports (Figure 6.7). (See also the discussion on news management, pp. 76–77.)

The Official Secrets Act, passed originally in 1911 and updated in 1988, allows the media to be prosecuted for disclosing information about the security services, defence and the conduct of international relations. It is no defence to claim any leak of information is in the public interest. In the 1980s, a number of famous prosecutions occurred under the Act, including that of the journalist Duncan Campbell, whose 1986 *Secret Society* television series for the BBC contained an episode on Britain's satellite spy system (called Zircon), which was banned. The affair included MI5 arriving at the BBC office in Glasgow in a dawn raid. The Official Secrets Act is criticised by many as being a means by which the state hides its actions from proper public accountability. Equally controversial is the Prevention of Terrorism Act. Journalists who make contact with 'terrorist' or illegal organisations risk prosecution. In 1988, it was extended in the form of a specific ban on the broadcasting of the voices of any representative of proscribed Northern Ireland organisations and their political offshoots. It was still possible to report the words of such representatives but only if dubbed or with subtitles. Broadcasters largely adhered to the spirit of the law, thus seriously curtailing opportunities for organisations like the IRA to put their point of view on television and radio until late 1995 when the ban was lifted following the IRA ceasefire of that year.

Anti-Monopoly Controls

It is often claimed that fears of excessive concentration of media ownership are counter balanced by the existence of legislation designed to maintain fair competition in the market place. Broadcasters, in particular, have been subject to strict control. For many years there were restrictions preventing any one company owning more than one ITV franchise or owning both a national newspaper and television station. However, these controls are continually being eroded. Rupert Murdoch's takeover of national newspapers (he owned five national titles in 1993) and his monopolisation of British satellite television have been allowed to proceed without resistance from the Monopolies and Mergers Commission. From November 1996, the rules on cross-media ownership were relaxed, allowing the growth of larger British media groups owning television and radio licences as well as newspapers, providing that their market share of television does not exceed 15 per cent, and that diversity of provision is maintained in any one region or locality. Further relaxation of the ownership rules is anticipated in the future as pressure mounts to allow British-based media companies to be strong enough to compete with foreign media conglomerates in the global competition for markets.

Apart from British restrictions on monopoly power, the European Commission may also intervene. In 2000, it blocked the proposed takeover of EMI by AOL Time Warner because it would mean their combined share of the music market would be nearly 25 per cent.

Moral Standards

In 1990, the Obscene Publications Act was extended to include all the media. It is designed to uphold standards of taste and decency and any material thought liable to 'deprave and corrupt' audiences is subject to prosecution. In the case of pornographic videos, DVDs, websites and magazines, this may be relatively straightforward, but it is frequently difficult to achieve any consensus on what is likely to 'deprave and corrupt'. This raises issues concerning not only what qualifies as obscene but also how it can be demonstrated that audiences will be corrupted.

Libel

There have been numerous well-publicised cases of individuals being awarded damages against media organisations found guilty of issuing unjustified or harmful statements about the individual in question. The satirical magazine *Private Eye* is perhaps the most frequent offender as a result of its willingness to criticise and make fun of the rich and powerful. The problem is that it is predominantly the rich and powerful who are most able to take advantage of the protection offered by the libel law, through their ability to pay the huge court costs which such cases often incur. Robert Maxwell's success in not being exposed as a corrupt businessman before his death was certainly aided by the frequency with which he threatened his accusers with legal proceedings.

The media are also subject to more specific forms of control, either by separate legislation or by regulatory bodies.

Cinema/Video/DVD

The British Board of Film Classification issues certificates for all cinema, DVD and video releases, applying the categories U (Universal), PG (Parental Guidance), 12A, 15 and 18, plus UC for DVD and video, meaning it is particularly suitable for children. Controls are stricter for video because of the possibility of young children viewing films rented by adults or older children (for more details see the website, **www. bbfc.co.uk**).

Newspapers

The Press Complaints Commission (PCC) exists primarily to consider complaints made by the public about the accuracy and standards of reporting in newspapers. It also issues guidelines for responsible behaviour and monitors how well the press adheres to these guidelines (for more details see the website, **www.pcc.org.uk**). There has been criticism of the ineffectiveness of the Commission and regular calls for stronger legal provision to prevent what is seen by some as excessive behaviour by some newspapers (especially following the death of Princess Diana in 1997 for which some of the blame was attributed to harassment from newspaper photographers).

Probably the most contentious issue is that of individual privacy. The PCC states that 'everyone is entitled to respect for his or her private and family life, home, health and correspondence'. However, it also says that newspapers and magazines may intrude into someone's private life if it is in the 'public interest'. By this it means the public have a right to know (see Figure 6.8). A further complication is added by the European Convention on Human Rights which became law in 2000. It too has a clause which protects the rights to individual privacy, but also contains one which upholds the right to free speech. Numerous people in the public eye, such as media celebrities and politicians, have begun to pursue legal cases against the media (especially the press) and it may mean that the ability of journalists to investigate and report on what is defined as an individual's private life will be significantly curtailed.

The Public Interest

There may be exceptions to the clauses marked ✳ where they can be demonstrated to be in the public interest.

1. The public interest includes:
   (i)   Detecting or exposing crime or a serious misdemeanour.
   (ii) Protecting public health and safety.
   (iii) Preventing the public from being misled by some statement or action of an individual or organisation.

2. In any case where the public interest is invoked, the Press Complaints Commission will require a full explanation by the editor demonstrating how the public interest was served.

3. In cases involving children editors must demonstrate an exceptional public interest to over-ride the normally paramount interests of the child.

FIGURE 6.8
Source: Press Complaints Commission

Broadcasting

Television and radio are subject to the strongest controls of any media, for technological and political reasons (see Histories and PSB in Chapter 7). The BBC's licence is renewed every ten years and the licence fee set by the government, which also appoints the board of governors. Their role is to ensure that the BBC fulfils its obligations as laid down by law and if necessary to intervene if individual programmes are deemed to exceed the BBC's remit, e.g. the banning of *Real Lives* (see p. 76).

Non-BBC television services, including ITV, Channels 4 and 5, cable and satellite, are licensed and regulated by the Independent Television Commission (ITC). A similar role for radio is played by the Radio Authority. Both the ITC and the Radio Authority publish codes to which licensees must adhere, covering programmes, advertising and sponsorship. Viewers or listeners may complain to either body, which, if deciding the complaint is justified, may take action, such as requesting a broadcast apology.

The public can also complain to the Broadcasting Standards Commission (**www.bsc.org.uk**) whose role is to consider complaints about violence, sex, taste and decency, as well as accusations of unfair treatment or invasion of privacy. The Commission can insist on a public apology if the broadcasters are found guilty.

Advertising

The Advertising Standards Authority (ASA – **www.asa.org.uk**) tries to ensure that advertisers live up to their much-quoted ideal of producing adverts that are 'honest, decent, legal and true'. It issues codes covering matters like cigarette advertising, monitors the flow of adverts being produced and responds to public complaints – sometimes by demanding the change or removal of an advert. For instance, in reponse to complaints it requested the removal from poster sites of the 2001 Opium advert featuring Sophie Dahl (see p. 86). Such requests are normally heeded, but this was not the case in 1992, when Benetton ignored the ASA in a campaign which had depended on images of an increasingly provocative nature (such as newly born babies, a white baby sucking a black woman's breast, etc). Benetton caused most offence when it used a picture of a man suffering from AIDS at the moment of his death. Many people complained that it was immoral to use such an image within a commercial context, in this case promoting a brand name of clothing. The advertising agency countered that its advertising highlighted important social and moral issues and stimulated public debate.

The government has proposed that by late 2003, a new regulatory body for media and communications will be established. Called OFCOM (the Office for Communications), it will replace the five existing regulatory bodies including the ITC, Radio Authority and the Broadcasting Standards Commission, but its precise powers remain undefined. It will have to encompass not only traditional media but also new computer-based systems and their online networks.

The Internet

Technically, the Internet has proved very difficult to regulate. This is because it is global, and its content may originate anywhere. There have been some prosecutions based on breach of copyright such as the Napster case (see p. 168). Where it is too difficult to identify and trace the author of offending websites, one strategy has been to hold the Internet service providers responsible for any content deemed to be offensive such as child pornography or racism. However, it may prove to be virtually impossible to scrutinise and regulate the constant stream of new material being supplied on a daily and growing basis.

Regulation Versus Economics: the Case of Television News

Both the BBC and ITV have been required to adhere to the principles of public service broadcasting when producing news output. As discussed in Chapter 7, this has meant a commitment to due impartiality so that no particular political bias or point of view is given prominence. A further requirement is that the main terrestrial channels include a news programme during prime-time viewing (between 6.30-11.00pm). This is because television news is considered to be an important part of modern democracy, through which the public and citizens can be kept reliably informed of political issues and developments. There is little doubt that audiences rely on and trust television significantly more than other media when it comes to news coverage.

As television channels have become more and more conscious of their audience ratings (ITV to attract advertising revenue and the BBC to justify the licence fee), then there has been growing pressure to reschedule the news to make way for more popular programmes. This has already happened with current affairs series like BBC's *Panorama*, moved from 8.00pm on Mondays to 10.15pm on Sunday (a 'graveyard' slot), and ITV's long running *World in Action* axed in 1998 after thirty five years. More controversially, ITV dropped their *News at Ten* in 1999, offering instead two news programmes at 6.30 and 11.00pm. After criticism from the ITC, ITV partially restored the *News at Ten* (for three nights a week). Meanwhile, the BBC itself pushed back its own flagship *Nine O'clock News* to 10.00pm, thereby going head-to-head with ITV's *News at Ten*.

The other strategy to attract more viewers is to make the news more entertaining – to 'dumb down' as some critics have claimed. Applying the newspaper analogy, the argument is that television is moving from a broadsheet to a tabloid news agenda, that there is a growing focus on personalities, human-interest stories and the world of entertainment to the exclusion of more serious and important political stories, especially of a global nature (see John Langer, 1997, on the tabloidisation of television).

To test this hypothesis, a recent research project analysed more than seven hundred evening news bulletins on the four main terrestrial television channels taking one year in four between 1975 and 1999 (Steven Barnett *et al*, 2001). Stories were categorised into broadsheet (political, economic or social affairs), tabloid (consumer issues, crime, sport, showbusiness, etc) and foreign. Whilst confirming that ITV and the early evening news broadcasts had become more tabloid in news content, this was not the case for the BBC's *Nine O'clock News* and the *Channel 4 News* (Figure 6.9). The authors concluded that instead of there being a general decline in the seriousness of news coverage on television, there is now more diversity tailored to specific audiences and distinctively branded. This is becoming more apparent with the growth of 24-hour digital television news channels such as *BBC News 24*, *Sky News*, and *CNN*.

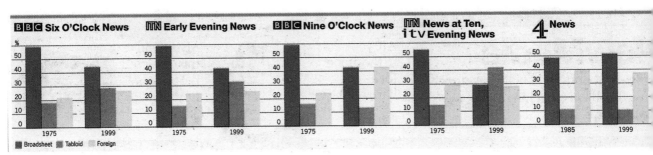

FIGURE 6.9
Source: ©Guardian

However, the research is open to debate on methodological grounds. The actual *treatment* of stories, in terms of both information and presentation, was not analysed. Is a story best approached via the human interest angle or through the broader social and political context which might help explain the underlying causes? Is the coverage image led or shaped by the written word? i.e. is there more concern with the visual impact of the pictures, which is more likely to engage the viewer's attention, than with a journalist's 'talking head' providing lots of factual (but less exciting) detail?

Activity 6.3

Compare a 'broadsheet' television news programme (BBC's *Nine O'clock News* or *Channel 4 News*) with a 'tabloid' news programme (ITV's *News at Ten*, *Channel 5 News* or *Sky News*) from the same evening. In comparing the two programmes consider the following:

1   The choice and agenda of stories – what differences in news values are applied?
2   The use of pictures – how important are these in the selection and coverage of stories?
3   The treatment of stories – where both programmes cover the same story, how do they differ in their treatment of the story?
4   The presentation and style – what differences are there in the overall style of presentation, e.g. the presenters, the set, production, etc?
5   The audience – are they speaking to the same audiences?

Do your findings support a broadsheet/tabloid distinction between the tv news programmes?

Independent Production

What is Independent Production?

To be independent implies autonomy and freedom from external constraints. In the context of media production, it is most often seen as meaning not under the direct control of a larger organisation, be that commercial or state. As such, independence carries a positive status, and may even be invoked in order to lay claim to being more trustworthy or authentic. *The Independent* newspaper's advertising campaign used the phrase 'It is ... Are you?' when the paper was launched in 1986. This was designed to draw attention to both the absence of a corporate owner, such as Murdoch's News International Corporation which owns *The Times*, and its editorial policy of political neutrality.

However, complete independence in media production is unlikely, as the support or cooperation of other organisations in the cycle of production and distribution is necessary if any kind of significant audience is to be reached. What is more, there are no totally agreed criteria by which any media organisation can be labelled 'independent'. 'Independent television' most often refers to the ITV companies holding the commercial regional franchises, which now essentially means two large media corporations, Carlton Communications and Granada (who at the time of writing were planning to merge), whereas 'independent film and video' has normally been associated with small-scale, grass roots production, often involving voluntary labour. Nevertheless, to varying degrees there are some principles to which most independent media production conforms. These include:

a) **A democratic/collectivist process of production. This may take the form of a co-operative, characterised by an absence of hierarchy and participative decision-making, etc. Often audiences may actively participate in the production as with fanzines or, more commonly now, webzines, through the Internet (e.g. www.indymedia.org).**

b) **A targeting of minority or community audiences. Audiences perceived as being ignored by mainstream commercial media include local, ethnic, political and subcultural groups. Such groups tend to be marginalised in terms of power, influence and access in society and lack economic resources (and hence media profitability).**

c) **A commitment to innovation or experimentation in form and/or content – often called 'alternative' media. This 'radicalism' can be manifested in experimental design and rule breaking within media conventions, as well as in a campaigning, political mode of address, which challenges the consumerist status quo, e.g. environmental action, anti-capitalism.**

All three elements work in contrast to mainstream or dominant media production practice, that which is widely accepted and recognised as 'the norm', and which is most available for audiences to consume. Only when independent production 'takes off' in popularity does it come to the attention of a wider public, as happened with the adult comic *Viz*. Most of the time, the content for such media is produced and distributed haphazardly or within very narrow social channels access to which must be actively sought by audiences, for example through mail order, specialist word of mouth or the Internet.

From the radical press of the nineteenth century, through workers' film societies of the 1930s, to the 'underground' hippie press of the 1960s and up to the pirate radio stations, there has been a thriving tradition of independent media production initiatives. The dynamics of such movements can be examined more closely by considering some specific examples.

Football Fanzines

Fanzines can be traced back to the 1940s when, in the USA, specialist magazines were distributed to fans of various cults of the day like science fiction. The contemporary essence of fanzines is that they are produced by and for fans; consumers are producers and vice-versa. Prior to the recent boom in Football Fanzines, music fanzines such as *Sniffin Glue* flourished in the late 1970s and early 1980s in the wake of the punk/New Wave movement. It was estimated that in the 1988-89 season, approximately one million copies of football fanzines were sold, although most individual magazines averaged between 250 and 1,000 circulation (Shaw in Hamilton (ed). 1992). A few of the less parochial titles, such as *When Saturday Comes*, have gained access to high-street newsagents. What, then, is their appeal?

A key factor is that they provide a public forum for the views of fans hitherto ignored, especially by those running the game who are often perceived as being 'out of touch' and bent on making money and thereby ruining the traditional experience of supporters. The official view of the club is usually expressed via the club programme, which voices very different sentiments to those expressed in fanzines. When BSkyB attempted to take over Manchester United in 1998, grassroots resistance from the fans was mobilised via both fanzines and their new media equivalent, **webzines** or **e-zines**. This was instrumental in persuading the government to veto the proposed deal.

Another attractive ingredient for the fans is the 'inside' humour, which draws on folklore, gossip and affectionate lampooning of players and rival fans (Figure 6.10). Fanzines for unfashionable and poorly supported clubs generate a participative *camaraderie* and a sense of collective identity despite – or because of – the sometimes primitive production techniques and forthright editorial line.

FIGURE 6.10
Source: Over Land and Sea, January 1992

Independent Film and Video

Whereas fanzines can be produced at minimal cost with low-tech facilities, film production requires considerable capital investment (although the advent of digital production in the past few years has made it much more affordable). Added to that are problems of distribution and exhibition not faced by the major production companies, which have automatic access to cinema chains (particularly when there is vertical integration, see p. 141). Consequently, truly independent film production, in which a company finances, produces, distributes and exhibits its own films, is very rare. *The Blair Witch Project* (1999) (Figure 6.11) does show what can be achieved independently of the major Hollywood studios. Virtually a 'home movie' produced by two film school graduates with a group of friends, it was exhibited at an American film festival, where Artisan Entertainment bought the distribution rights. Audience interest was largely sparked through an intriguing Internet website (**www.blairwitch.com**), a marketing strategy hitherto neglected by the major Hollywood studios. The fact that independent film and video production exists at all is usually due to some kind of subsidy or patronage. In the past, this has been from state-supported bodies like the Arts Council or the British Film Institute, but increasingly it has been television that has provided the key investment for independent British films. Until deciding to pull out of film production in 2002 because of mounting losses, Channel 4's backing (via FilmFour) was vital for the stream of British film productions such as *My Beautiful Laundrette* (1985) and *A Letter to Brezhnev* (1985), followed by the even greater commercial success in the 1990s of *Four Weddings and a Funeral* (1994) (cost £2 million, earnings £72 million), *Trainspotting* (1995) and *The Full Monty* (1997) (cost £2 million, earnings $150 million). These examples show the possibility of representing aspects of British culture not usually found in the Hollywood-dominated contemporary cinema.

FIGURE 6.11 The Blair Witch Project
Source: Ronald Grant Archive

However, most of these films employed conventional narrative forms and cinematic styles, albeit on a modest scale compared to Hollywood. This is not surprising, since the primary motivation in making these films was commercial, to avoid excessive costs and, if possible, to make a profit.

Channel 4 was also instrumental in funding the Workshop Movement, a group of politically motivated film-makers. This more radical independent cinema is often rooted in local communities or interest groups eager to provide an alternative voice to that of mainstream cinema and television. Sometimes it has been possible for such productions to gain exposure via a loose-knit network of independent film distributors and exhibitors. With the increasing use of video as a means of communication, this has become less of a problem. For example, *The Miners' Campaign Tapes*, produced during the coal strike of 1984–85 and representing the miners' perspective, were viewed nationally and internationally due to the flexibility of the video format. Workshops have tended to focus on documentary forms of film-making as a means of projecting their own social and political concerns. A good example of a workshop incorporating many elements found in such organisations is that of Red Flannel, a women's film and video workshop based in South Wales and funded by Channel 4, the Welsh Arts Council and the South East Arts Association. It sees itself giving a voice to the women of the Welsh Valleys, hitherto largely neglected. An example of its work was *Mam* (1988), a historical documentary about working-class women and their patriarchal powers in the valley communities (Figure 6.12).

The Life-cycle of Independents

Given the precariousness of most independents in terms of insecure funding, small audiences and fragile staffing, it is not surprising that longevity is not easily achieved. More often than not, an independent will wither or collapse once a key supportive component is removed, such as a local authority grant or creative, leading member of the organisation. However, there are occasions when independents flourish and 'break through' into the mainstream market. A spectacular case is that of *Viz*, a comic originally distributed in a few local Newcastle pubs, but eventually achieving a circulation in excess of one million. Growth and commercial success are frequently accompanied by takeover bids from larger competitors. In the case of the American film industry, the successful independent companies of the 1990s were taken over by the major studios. For example, Miramax, which had produced *Reservoir Dogs* (1991) and *Pulp Fiction* (1994), became part of the Walt Disney Corporation. Another independent film company, New Line, became part of Time Warner, but still retained a separate management and identity, focusing on smaller budget and more innovative types of film (New Line's biggest investment being *The Lord of The Rings* trilogy 2001-03).

This semi-independent status is not unusual in both the film and music industries where smaller, largely autonomous companies are given the opportunity to take more risks based on a proven ability to make profits with limited resources. Alternatively, independents themselves may become companies with diversifying interests to ensure their survival. For example, the *Viz* publishers, John Brown Co., expanded into other areas of the periodicals market such as gardening and home decorating. Finally, some independents manage to maintain economic viability while retaining the core principles which stimulated their original conception, the time-honoured example in Britain being *Private Eye*, the satirical magazine which has survived decades of litigation.

the Wars' in the Oral History Journal.

HOW WE MADE THE FILM

The core of the film rests on the interviews we did with women in the Valleys. We met many of them through the screening groups we had set up in the Valleys. Out of these groups there also emerged a core of women who were interested in working with us on the film and acting as consultants. They formed a production group which saw the film through to its final stages. As well as the contacts made from the screening groups we also visited Old People's homes in the Valleys.

We then found a lot of our archive material from the BFI, the BBC film library, St Fagans, the Miner's library, Swansea and local libraries and museums. We also spoke to women historians like Dee Beddoe and Angela John and spent a lot of time talking to as many women as we could find, as well as employing a Welsh speaking feminist historian who found a lot of interesting material in the Welsh language.

'Mam' was very much a Red Flannel joint effort, all members of Red Flannel worked on its research and we had regular meetings where all our information was brought together and knocked into shape.

By the end of the research period we had a pretty thorough understanding of womens role in the developing history of the Valleys, but we wanted women themselves to tell the story, through their own memories and experiences.

From the very many women we spoke to during the research period we finally chose our film interviewees. We chose on the basis of firstly personality, women who could speak articulately and engagingly about

the past, secondly we needed a good age range so that the film could cover a long period in time. Lastly, it was important that their personal stories reflected what was the common experience.

The script was developed through the following process:

– Screening and discussions on questions raised under 'background'

– Formation of production group

– Sound interviews

– Archive research: feature films, documentary, stills

– Background reading: historical, sociological, economic, literature

– Choosing material for dramatisation and documentary development

– Creating basic structure of film

– Drama improvisations

– Shaping of documentary material into cohesive sequences

– Final scripting

The production group carried on working with us during the editing of the film, so that our decisions could be informed by their opinions.

Red Flannel feel that because of the long term involvement of Valleys women during the making of 'Mam', via screenings, discussions and within the production group, that the final result is a truer representation of their lifes, than a film made under normal mainstream constraints would allow.

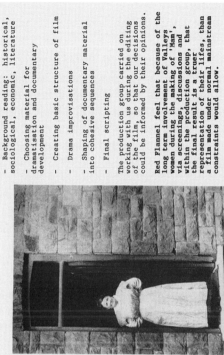

FIGURE 6.12
Mam, 1988
Source: Red Flannel Films Publicity

CASE STUDY
The Music Industry

Majors versus indies: a historical overview

'To be totally ruthless about it, our job is to see the trends coming on the street, steal them, and sell them back to them'. This comment, made by a record company executive in the mid-1980s and quoted by Garfield (1986), might be said to epitomise the dynamic tension that exists between popular music as a culturally creative activity and as a form of cultural commodity marketed by industrial corporations. This tension has been mirrored to some extent in the contrasting roles of major and independent record companies (majors and indies) ever since pop music, or rock and roll, first became big business in the 1950s.

As an emergent musical style (based fundamentally on black rhythm-and-blues), rock and roll was launched on independent record labels in the USA. Small companies like Sun Records (whose roster included Elvis Presley) were willing and able to support new music for which there was initially a local, then a national, and finally an international market. The major record companies, after first ignoring what was perceived as a 'passing fad', eventually responded by signing up many of the new stars, like Presley (who switched from Sun to RCA in 1956), as well as supplying their own much less authentic versions in a bid to halt their declining market share, based mainly on older-established musical styles. Whereas prior to rock and roll in the early 1950s the top eight major companies enjoyed an average 95 per cent share of the singles market, by the early 1960s this had fallen to less than 50 per cent. Having stabilised during the 1960s era of pop and rock, the majors eventually regained a dominant market share of over 80 per cent by 1973. Peterson and Berger (1975) have indentified this pattern as a cyclic phenomenon, whereby the 'degree of diversity in musical forms is inversely related to the degree of market concentration'. In other words, when the major companies are in a dominant market situation it is because there is little variety of musical choice, but this is only temporary, as new musical styles burst on to the scene to be taken up by the indies and, much later on, by the majors. This could be seen as a process of generational renewal, whereby each new wave of teenagers rebels against the perceived conformity of the existing musical styles.

Soon after Peterson and Berger published their thesis, the cycle they described seemed to be back in full swing, when punk and new wave made a significant impact during the years 1976–79. Once again, independent labels, like Rough Trade and Chrysalis in Britain, played a key role. However, the cyclic model, although containing some legitimacy as a historical description, provides an over-simplistic view of the relationship between majors and indies, which is much less valid today. Even in the 1960s, for Britain many of the new beat and rhythm-and-blues groups, such as the Beatles and the Rolling Stones, were signed to majors from the start of their careers, while in the USA, some of the major labels like CBS were quite willing to 'experiment' with new acts during the hippie or counterculture period of the late 1960s. In actuality, there has always been an element of co-operation as well as competition between majors and indies in the music industry. Few indies have the resources to manufacture and distribute records, tapes, etc, other than on a localised scale, and so they have usually depended on the majors to gain access to a national or international market. Meanwhile, the majors have frequently relied on the indies as a source of new talent, a sort of 'research and development' role.

In previous decades the music market tended to be dominated by relatively few musical forms (e.g. the early 1970s was characterised by 'teenybop' singles and 'progressive' rock albums), but in recent years there has been a growing fragmentation. This is reflected in the diversity of charts published which monitor sales. Apart from the traditional Top 40, there are charts for dance, indy, metal and other forms of music. Consequently, it is much more difficult to control the market, as many of these musical styles are quite specialised, thus allowing independent labels with the requisite knowledge and reputation to carve out a niche in the market. This is not entirely new, as illustrated by the case of Atlantic (soul music) in the 1960s and Island (reggae music) in the 1970s. Some indies may even become a showcase for a local area's new talent, as Factory Records was for Manchester in the late 1980s.

Keith Negus (1992) argues that instead of seeing majors and indies as separate and oppositional organisations, it is more appropriate to distinguish between major and minor companies:

Majors increasingly split into semi-autonomous working groups and label divisions, and minor companies connected to these by complex patterns of ownership, investment, licensing, formal and informal and sometimes deliberately obscured relationships. This has resulted in complex and confusing, continually shifting corporate constellations which are difficult to plot, as deals expire, new relationships are negotiated, new acquisitions made and joint ventures embarked upon. At the end of 1990 the trade magazine Music Week reported that 82 different labels were operating 'under the banner' of the PolyGram group in the UK alone. Which companies are owned, part owned or licensed becomes difficult to ascertain. If it can be done, what it means in terms of working practices becomes equally harder to infer, as the distinctions between an inside and outside, and between centre and margins, has given way to a web of mutually dependent work groupings radiating out from multiple centres.

These organisational webs, of units within a company and connections to smaller companies, enable entertainment corporations to gain access to material and artists, and to operate a co-ordinating, monitoring and surveillance, operation rather than just centralised control. The corporation can still shape the nature of these webs through the use and distribution of investment. But it is a tight–loose approach, rather than a rigidly hierarchical form of organisation; tight enough to ensure a degree of predictability and stability in dealing with collaborators, but loose enough to manoeuvre, redirect or even reverse company activity.

Negus (1992)

Music Week comes to similar conclusions:

When the PJ Harvey album Rid Of Me, *their first release on Island Records, entered the national chart at number three in May, its success consolidated the group's position as one of the best new acts in Britain.*

The chart position marked a vital breakthrough for Polly Harvey and her band. But it also had a wider significance for it was a prime example of just how much independent and major labels are now working together to develop new artists.

Nevertheless it still raised questions about the relationship between the two sectors. Like how much do the majors need independent acumen to help them develop new acts? And how much do independent labels need major muscle to secure commercial success both at home and abroad? And furthermore, what can the smaller labels do to protect their interest in the bands they discover and nurture?

In the case of PJ Harvey, of course, Island was involved almost from the beginning. An Island scout had seen the group's sixth gig and preliminary talks with the band had already taken place before the release of their debut Too Pure single, 'Dress'. And, when they ultimately signed to Island early in 1992, it was agreed that their first album, Dry, should appear on Too Pure, with whom the band had a longstanding verbal agreement.

The advantages of such an arrangement were immediately obvious. Secure in the knowledge that they had a longterm future with one of the country's most respected major labels, Harvey and her band were still able to grow their music organically, free of many of the commercial pressures that might have applied had they signed immediately to a major.

Island Records stood to benefit too. Too Pure's fully independent status meant that Harvey's profile could be developed modestly and inexpensively through the independent charts and a music press that is perceived to be biased in favour of the independent artist.

Music Week, 24 July 1993

Activity 6.4

Compare the Top 40 singles/album charts with the independent charts (e.g. in *New Musical Express* or *Music Week*), and identify the musical acts and styles with which the independent labels are achieving chart success.

A further qualification to the conventional image of independents, as groundbreaking pioneers of new music, is that many independents thrive on mainstream pop music. PWL with its string of hits by artists like Kylie Minogue and Rick Astley in the 1980s is a good example, as is the more recent example of Jive records, whose most successful artist is Britney Spears. Jive was taken over by the major BMG in 2002.

Nevertheless, many independents continue to play a key role in developing new acts, especially in music genres where they have the expertise and willingness to cede *creative control* to the artist, whether that be nu-metal or dance music.

The growing power of the majors
During the 1990s, all of the significant independent companies became victims of takeovers by the majors. For example, Polygram took over A & M, Motown and Island records. Britain's biggest independent company, Virgin, succumbed to a £550 million takeover by EMI in 1992 (although in 2000 Richard Branson relaunched Virgin as V2, an independent label). This process of **horizontal integration** has led to the music market being dominated by five companies, Sony, Warner, Polygram (Universal), EMI and BMG. Their global market share is somewhere between 70–75 per cent (*The Guardian*, 25 January 2000).

There has also been vertical integration, whereby large hardware manufacturing companies have taken over the music software companies and the music labels. The prime example of this is Sony's $2 billion takeover of CBS in 1994. This was prompted by a desire to ensure that when Sony launched their new music format, the mini-disc, they would be able to provide sufficient music on the format. Sony's betamax video format had lost out to Matsushita's VHS in the video format war of the 1980s.

With respect to music formats, the rise of the compact disc (Figure 6.13) has benefited the major music companies. At the beginning (the early 1980s) the CD owners were older and more affluent. Such consumers tend to be more conservative in their musical tastes and thus are attracted to the well-established artists usually on major labels. Furthermore, profit margins are much higher on CDs than on vinyl or cassette (Figure 6.14). Indeed, the majors were accused of accelerating the decline of both vinyl and cassette by issuing music only on CD. Thus vinyl is now virtually obsolete, functioning only as a specialist music format for 12-inch singles or else as a collector's item.

At the heart of the majors' commercial strategy has been the exploitation of **copyright**. As the audience for music now cuts across several generations, back catalogue has become much more significant. Approximately 40 per cent of weekly album sales are accounted for by re-releases of old music often in the form of compilation albums, Greatest Hits, The Best of, etc. This is one of the reasons the majors are attracted to the big-name artists. Another reason is that their new music seems less of a risk of failing in a global music market where the biggest artists, such as Madonna and U2, are virtually guaranteed sales

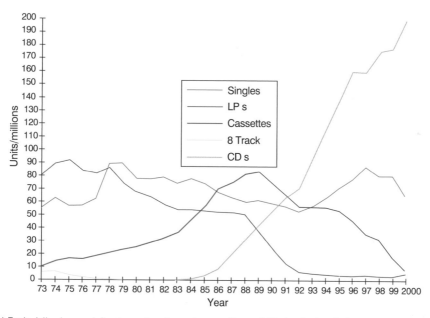

* Trade deliveries are defined as sales of records, cassettes and CDs invoiced to dealers, distributors and mail order houses

FIGURE 6.13
UK sales of records, cassettes and CDs, 1973–2000
Source: British Phonographic Industries Surveys

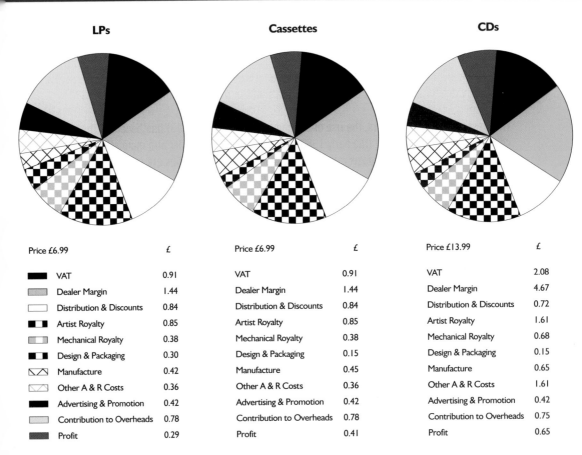

LPs		Cassettes		CDs	
Price £6.99	**£**	**Price £6.99**	**£**	**Price £13.99**	**£**
VAT	0.91	VAT	0.91	VAT	2.08
Dealer Margin	1.44	Dealer Margin	1.44	Dealer Margin	4.67
Distribution & Discounts	0.84	Distribution & Discounts	0.84	Distribution & Discounts	0.72
Artist Royalty	0.85	Artist Royalty	0.85	Artist Royalty	1.61
Mechanical Royalty	0.38	Mechanical Royalty	0.38	Mechanical Royalty	0.68
Design & Packaging	0.30	Design & Packaging	0.15	Design & Packaging	0.15
Manufacture	0.42	Manufacture	0.45	Manufacture	0.65
Other A & R Costs	0.36	Other A & R Costs	0.36	Other A & R Costs	1.61
Advertising & Promotion	0.42	Advertising & Promotion	0.42	Advertising & Promotion	0.42
Contribution to Overheads	0.78	Contribution to Overheads	0.78	Contribution to Overheads	0.75
Profit	0.29	Profit	0.41	Profit	0.65

FIGURE 6.14
Price breakdown: LPs, cassettes and CDs
Source: British Phonographic Industries Yearbook, 1993

through their recognisable brand image. This is a much safer investment strategy in an industry where it is notoriously difficult to continue launching successful new products.

Furthermore, copyright extends to royalties accruing from performance, whether that is radio airplay, covers by other artists, use in adverts, or even being played in a hotel lobby (Figure 6.15). A song used as a film soundtrack such as 'Love is All Around' (*Four Weddings and a Funeral*) can generate millions for the music company and composer. As members of integrated entertainment corporations, music companies are in a good position to exploit this synchronisation or **synergy** - to select music from the company's own artists for use in promoting the company's own film. For example, *Austin Powers the Spy who Shagged Me* (1999), a New Line film (a Warner subsidiary), featured a soundtrack of Warner artists such as Madonna, Lenny Kravitz and REM.

In it for the money

The flow of funds around the music industry

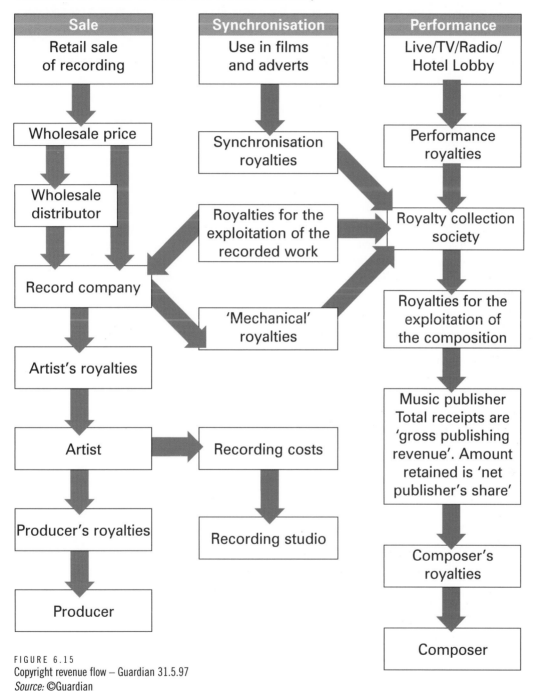

FIGURE 6.15
Copyright revenue flow – Guardian 31.5.97
Source: ©Guardian

Piracy and the Internet

Whilst the majors strengthened their grip of the market during the 1980s and 1990s, their profitability has been undermined by the growth of piracy. It is estimated that, globally, one in three compact discs are manufactured illegally. The figure is much higher in some parts of the world such as Russia and China, where the policing of illegal recordings is minimal. The advent of the CD recorder has meant anyone can copy CDs, but what has really alarmed the music companies is the access to pirated music provided by the Internet.

With the advent of MP3 music files, compressed digital music can be downloaded onto CDs or MP3 players. The music is made available via shared files software in which any Internet user can supply or receive music. The problem for the music companies is that the music is free, and thus infringes copyright rules. The companies have tried to combat this illegal trading through the courts, the most famous example being the prosecution of Napster, the most popular of the file-sharing software options up to 2001.

To try to exploit this new means of distributing music, the majors have begun to establish their own subscription online music services. The first was Bertelsmann (BMG) which teamed up with Napster in 2001. The new service, MusicNet, eventually involved a fusion of music companies (Warner, BMG, and EMI), Internet service provider (AOL), and distribution technology (Napster, CD Now and RealNetworks). A rival service is Pressplay, a joint venture involving, among others, Sony, Universal, Yahoo and *MP3.com*. These new services are designed to sell the music online through downloading or streaming and they represent a new form of vertical integration in the industry – for example, Warner's plans to make its catalogue of music available through its parent company AOL. However, such initiatives have been undermined by the emergence of new file-swapping services on the Internet and the music industry seems unable to stem the growth of piracy. The industry's own research into the problem (as reported in the *Financial Times*, 28 January 2003) calculates that around the world 4.5 million people are accessing almost 1 billion pirated music tracks at any one time. An estimated 10 per cent of CD sales were lost through Internet piracy in America in 2002.

Much of the appeal of digital technology is that it enables the user to assemble their own CD albums rather than accept the selection of the music company. DIY CDs are becoming available in music retailers that are more prominent on the Internet. The majors are exploiting this opportunity to sell their music online through supporting retailers such as **www.Musicmaker.com**, who specialise in custom-made compilation CDs. The independent companies are also trying to utilise the Internet. In Britain, four hundred and fifty independent companies have joined forces via AIM (Association of Independent Music) to offer their music online using the e-commerce shopping system. These labels account for a quarter of the British market, and so provide meaningful competition to the majors. Whether legal or not, it is clear that the Internet is now a key medium for music sales (see p. 178 on Internet marketing).

Mediating the market

Approximately 90 per cent of all recorded music released on to the market fails to make a profit. Given this poor rate of success, together with the considerable fixed costs in terms of pressing plant, recording studios, etc, it is not surprising that much effort is directed towards stimulating consumer demand for the music in the search for the bestselling album or smash single which will offset the majority of failures.

Between those making the music and those purchasing the end product there exists a range of **gatekeepers** – filters sifting out the likely hits from the flow of excess production. Keith Negus (1992) prefers the concept of *cultural intermediary*, since it engages with the fact that music, unlike conventional industrial manufacturing, is a product with symbolic cultural value which affects how it is perceived by producers, distributors and consumers alike. The 'intermediaries' are those who help to shape the three key decisions identified by Simon Frith (1983) – 'who records, what is recorded, and which records reach the public'.

Of course, the music itself is not the whole 'product'. Performers add cultural meaning and value depending on their perceived image. For those with 'star' appeal, the actual music may be of secondary significance to the audience. Furthermore, music is often embedded within distinct subcultures which facilitate processes of identification and group solidarity among participants, especially in adolescent and teenage groups. Therefore, the analysis of music mediators which follows is necessarily contingent on the kinds of artist involved and their potential market niche.

A&R (artists and repertoire)

In the music company, at the front line of discovering and developing musical talent is the *A & R (artists and repertoire)* representative, whose responsibilities include: signing artists (perhaps 'poaching' them from other companies); examining the company catalogues for potential hits; and developing the musical policy and direction of a company's record labels. Negus (1992) describes A & R culture as predominantly white, male and college-educated (dating from the late 1960s/early 1970s). Consequently, there tends to be a conservative ethos in musical policy among the well-established, mainstream record labels – the rock-music aesthetic still being preferred at the expense of new styles, which are often viewed with suspicion or hostility.

When a band or performer has been signed to a record company, the producer plays a key role in organising and co-ordinating the actual recording of the music. Achieving 'the right sound' often involves skilful engineering during the mixing or post-production stage. Some producers' reputations have exceeded the artists' in being able to create a recognisable sound, e.g. Phil Spector in the 1960s ('the wall of sound'), Georgio Moroder in the 1970s (disco), Paul Oakenfold in the 1980s (remixing tracks to enhance the dance element) and William Orbit in the late 1990s (best known for Madonna's *Ray of Light* album). New technology, in the form of synthesisers, samplers, drum machines, etc, linked to a computer, has made possible DIY music production for a modest outlay, undermining the necessity of employing expensive studios owned by the major companies. The success of KLF in the early 1990s is testimony to the possibilities of using such new technology creatively in music production.

Marketing

Working in conjunction with the A & R team is the *marketing department*, which usually has a 'product manager' overseeing the packaging of an artist. This requires giving close attention to the appropriate image of the artist in relation to their target audience.

Pop music is as much image as music, and given the competitive nature of the business, the vital elements much sought after are 'uniqueness' and 'authenticity'. These qualities are frequently cited by fans to justify their support for particular artists. To claim that audiences are manipulated or duped by skilful marketing alone is to underestimate the critical scrutiny applied by the majority of such audiences to the music, performances, interviews, lifestyle and so on, of the artists. That is not to deny the existence of some degree of artifice and fantasy, especially within the traditional core of adolescent and pre-adolescent female fans, whose loyalty and identification is notoriously fickle.

Increasingly, music companies are contriving or 'manufacturing' the image and identity of an artist or group when targeting this very young market (see discussion below).

One of the greatest challenges, both in terms of music and image management, is making the transition from the teenage to the adult market. George Michael achieved this very successfully following the break-up of Wham! Other examples include Kylie Minogue who replaced the wholesome image sustained by her role in *Neighbours* with a more knowing and voluptuous performance in her post-*Neighbours* music career, and Robbie Williams who went from Take That member to successful solo performer with mass-market appeal. Marketing images is further explored below in the discussion of the press, television, video and the Internet.

A key part of the marketing strategy of the majors is to ensure a single released from an album achieves a high chart entry in order to promote the album. One way this is achieved is via heavy discounting whereby the music shops are supplied with cut-price or free copies of the single during the first week or fortnight of the single's release. A second strategy is to pre-release the track on radio up to a month before being available in the shops. Finally, the record company can multi-format the single, for example, releasing two slightly different CDs as well as a DVD version all of which will be bought by the keenest fans. These combined methods often result in the single going straight to number one but then just as likely disappearing from the charts within three to four weeks. This has contributed to a much more volatile singles chart whose value as a barometer of real consumer demand has been significantly devalued. Furthermore, the cut-price discounting represents a form of subsidy by the majors of between £100,000-£200,000 per single, making it much more difficult for the independent labels to compete and build a record's popularity over time.

To make matters worse for small independent companies, loss of independent retailers (see below) has made it harder to get the music into the shops in the first place.

Distribution

Apart from producing and marketing, the other key function for a record company is to ensure effective *distribution* of the music. Larger record companies employ a strike force whose aim is to ensure good visibility for the company's output in the high-street retailers, the shops from which the charts are

FIGURE 6.16
Source: Paul Hickinbotham

compiled. Various strategies may be applied to persuade shops to co-operate, such as issuing glossy packages and point-of-sale displays, and joint advertising.

As with record companies, the trend for *music retailers* is horizontal integration, so that in Britain the multiple stores like Woolworths, Virgin and HMV have emerged as the dominant outlets for music distribution and consumption. In some cases, record companies are able to guarantee outlets for their music via vertical integration, an example in Britain being EMI–HMV. In contrast to the multiples and their flagship megastores are the specialist independent record shops, which focus on specific musical styles as well as catering for the beleaguered lovers of vinyl. Such shops often generate the initial sales for new music ignored by the conservative multiples until, and if, such music gains a chart entry (Figure 6.17).

There is little doubt that the music company plays a significant role in determining the outcome to the questions of who records and what is recorded. Most companies negotiate contracts with artists that cede rights over the end product – what is released, when it is released, how it is promoted, etc – to the company on their terms. Even artists with massive international appeal may find their artistic freedom curtailed by their music company, as George Michael found to his cost. He failed in his attempt to sue Sony for neglecting to promote his album, *Listen Without Prejudice* (1990), and was unable to release any music for over five years until he was able to transfer to a new company, EMI.

The music press

The answer to the third question as to what music reaches the public is more at the mercy of other mediators. The relationship between the *music press* and the music business is, on the whole, symbiotic. Most music journalists are dependent on the rest of the industry for news, interviews, access, etc, while the companies and artists are keen to gain as much favourable publicity as possible. Indeed, it is not unusual for careers to cross over in both directions: Neil Tennant of Pet Shop Boys began as a writer for *Smash Hits*. It is generally acknowledged that unfavourable reviews are not particularly influential in damaging sales, but that very positive reviews are helpful in the drive to 'break' new acts – in helping to stimulate a 'buzz' around an act.

In recent years, the range of music press has broadened to encompass the growth in musical diversity and audience taste. The long-standing teenage 'pop' magazines like *Top of the Pops* act as quasi-consumer guides for a mainly female teen audience (although this role has become subsumed

Individual retailer market share – Albums. 2000	
	% of units
Music specialists	**51.3**
HMV	18.4
Virgin	10.0
Our Price (now V2)	5.2
MVC	4.7
Andys	1.1
Tower	0.9
Other specialists	11.0
Chains/Multiples	**20.1**
Woolworths	13.2
WH Smith	5.8
Boots	0.9
Other multiples	0.2
Supermarkets	**11.9**
Asda	4.1
Tesco	3.6
Sainsbury	2.3
Safeway	0.5
Other Supermarkets	1.4
Mail order and clubs	**8.3**
Britannia	6.4
mail order	1.9
Internet	**3.2**
Other outlets	**5.2**
TOTAL	**100**

FIGURE 6.17
Number of shops selling records,
tapes and CDs
Source: Taylor Nelson Sofres
'Audio Visual Trak Survey'

by the more general magazines like *Sugar*). The attitude is unashamedly one of being a fan, unlike that of the music magazines targeting an older, more musically knowledgeable (and usually male) readership, such as *New Musical Express*. NME's identity and musical policy have undergone various shifts over the decades, but of late have focused on the independent or college-based music scene with only a limited interest in dance, hip-hop, metal, etc. To cater for these more specialised audiences there are contemporary titles such as *Kerrang!*, *Hip Hop Connection* and *Mixmag*, readership of which implies a commitment and knowledge well beyond the casual consumer. An even more partisan and dedicated audience can be found in the purchasers of the numerous music fanzines whose original inspiration can be traced back to the punk movement of the late 1970s.

The growing popularity of the Internet has meant that dedicated fans can almost always follow their favourite artists or music on the thousands of dedicated music websites and e-zines. Finally, there is the new wave of glossy, more adult oriented music magazines which are as much about past as present music. These include *Q* and *Mojo* whose readers span 18 to 50 and whose interests are often based on artists who rose to fame in the 1960s, 1970s or 1980s.

The agenda set by these magazine is also paralleled in the broadsheet daily newspapers, each of which has at least one (usually male) pop music critic whose taste and selection reflects the age, education and class of the readers. Very different in approach is the tabloid press, whose rising interest in pop music (*The Sun* having established its first pop column, 'Bizarre', in 1982) ties in with the growth in entertainment news values of such papers. Journalists on the tabloids are more interested in the private lives of the artists than the music, and so their publicity value is certainly double-edged, as many pop stars have found to their cost. Whatever the attitude of newspapers and magazines, the target for music companies and artists is maximum public exposure to coincide with the release of an album or single, and, via the company's own press officer and marketing department, considerable resources are directed to that goal.

Activity 6.5

Survey the range of music-based magazines available in the main high street newsagents. From an examination of the front covers, musical content, adverts, price and design, build up a descriptive profile of the music styles represented and the likely target readership of the magazines.

Your conclusions can be validated by writing to the magazines and requesting a 'media pack', which includes synopsis of the readership profile, circulation and editorial policy.

Radio airplay

Given the fact that pop music is essentially aural in nature, and that most consumers like to hear a sample of music before buying it, it is not unreasonable to identify *radio* as the key form of mediation between artist and audience. Following scandals of bribery (or 'payola') in the American music industry in the early years of rock and roll, mainstream radio has been at pains to demonstrate its independence in the selection of what is played over the airwaves. Most radio stations in Britain use the playlist as a means of choosing which music is played most frequently. For Britain's most popular radio station, Radio 1, there are three playlists:

- **an A list of 15–20 tracks guaranteed 30+ plays per week**
- **a B list of 6–14 tracks guaranteed 15+ plays per week**
- **a C list of 5–10 tracks guaranteed 5+ plays per week**

In recognition of the much greater volume of albums sold than of singles, there is also an album list where six new album tracks receive a minimum of four plays per week. Records on the playlist account for approximately two thirds of Radio 1's mainstream shows.

In choosing tracks for playlists, the perceived needs of the station's audience are uppermost in the radio producers' minds. The Radio 1 playlist panel of disc jockeys and producers is anticipating the taste of those aged between 11 and 15, who account for the biggest proportion of singles buyers.

It is unique in including music from across different genres or formats (see Figure 6.18) from rap to nu-metal to pop. Radio 2 also has a playlist which is more conservative in sticking to pop/MOR (middle of the road) artists such as the Corrs or well-established rock groups like U2.

On independent radio, a similar but more cautious policy exists in compiling playlists. It is rare for an unknown artist to be selected for a playlist until the release enters the charts. Research by Gallup (1993) suggests that the majority of top 75 singles arrive in the charts without being originally playlisted. The purpose of the playlist is to help sustain sales of music once a chart position has been obtained.

For independent radio, playlisted music is increasingly the only means of airplay for new releases. Its desire to maximise the audience for advertisers' benefit has led to the widespread practice of adhering to a musical format based on a mix of past and present hits selected by computer so that each song differs from the last in terms of tempo, mood and origin, but that none of the music is likely to alienate the target audience. Many stations split their frequencies in order to differentiate between music by generation – the AM service usually providing a more easy-listening format (often called 'gold') for older listeners. The formatting of radio services is a trend emanating from the USA, which has developed the system to a fine art.

USA radio formatting

There are over ten thousand radio stations in the US, and in a bid to achieve a distinctive audience profile which might be attractive to advertisers, stations have increasingly adopted specialised formats, the most prominent of which are listed below.

Adult Contemporary (AC) is America's most popular radio format and aims for the 25-to 54-year-old group, advertisers' most desired group, by playing less abrasive contemporary hits. This means no hard rock, no raucous upbeat dance tunes, no pre-rock, no supper club singers. There are at least five main subspecies: full service stations are descendents of the huge MOR mainstays of the past and play soft hits with emphasis on news, talk and personalities; gold-intensive stations play 80 to 90 per cent oldies with tiny current playlists of the safest hits; life encompasses everything from love songs to easy listening and aims for the upper end of the AC age bracket; music intensive have playlists of twenty or thirty records and are the most aggressive about playing new artists and crossovers; adult alternative stations feature an AC base with emphasis on other types of music such as jazz or soft rock.

Album Oriented Rock (AOR) grew out of progressive rock radio in the late 1960s and had a broader musical scope in the past. Nowadays it seldom strays from white rock, rarely playing more than one track from an LP during a two-month period. Presentations still try to preserve the 'rock and roll outlaw' attitude of the format's early years, though the music is now safe and predictable. The last remnants of AOR's free-form roots are the dozens of college stations which are increasingly important in exposing new music.

Contemporary Hit Radio (CHR) is the descendent of Top 40, which by the 1980s had a shopworn image. CHR made a comeback in 1983–85, bucking the narrowcast trend by picking up hits from Urban and AOR stations.

Classical has a long and lucrative history, with sufficient population to support its minority appeal. Listeners are few, but their economic standing is an ad agency's dream.

Contemporary Christian Radio is a relatively recent development arising from a growing Christian music industry. Some stations are like other Adult Contemporary stations ('Christians need traffic reports too'); others maintain a more religious atmosphere.

Country is one of the oldest formats and, in total number of stations, the largest. Loyalty is to artists rather than the latest record. Country remains a heavily oldies-based format, but rarely reaches back before 1970.

Easy Listening Radio is an umbrella term encompassing nostalgia, big band, and other non-rock material. Though easy listening ratings are excellent, it means an older (45-plus), less-profitable audience to ad agencies.

Gold is a blanket term for a format playing exclusively post-1955 oldies, pioneered by WCBS in New York twenty years ago. A second gold rush has materialised (the first came in the wake of 'American Graffiti' in the mid-1970s). The biggest oldies phenomenon remains 'classic rock', concentrating on the 1967–75 heydey of progressive rock; loads of Cream, Doors and so on.

Gospel is divided into black and white stations, both concentrated in the South and serving constituencies too small to register in the ratings.

Hispanic stations specialising in modern and traditional Latin forms of music are bound to increase in importance as the nation's Hispanic population rises.

Jazz is rarely found as a full-time format. Similar to classical in attracting upscale, loyal listeners, but doesn't have the same prestigious image.

New Age music – instrumental atmospheric records largely popularised by the Windham Hill label and characterised by unbelievers as 'aural wallpaper' – has been a quiet industry phenomenon. Most stations also include jazz, AC or soft AOR programming.

Quiet Storm is named after the Quiet Storm programme on WHUR in Washington in the mid-1970s which played softer R and B ballads and mellow jazz. Increasingly popular.

Urban Contemporary is a synonym for black radio but, with more and more white artists in traditionally black musical domains, it is a more accurate term. Urban stations have made great strides in the ratings. Economic prosperity has not kept pace, however, as ad agencies persist in viewing Urban Listeners as denizens of the underclass.

FIGURE 6.18
From *Facing the Music* by Simon Frith. © 1988 by Simon Frith. Reprinted by permission of Pantheon Books, a division of Random House, Inc.

Activity 6.6

Identify which music radio formats are available in your area. Are there any formats or music genres that have been ignored?

British radio has followed the American pattern in that all commercial licences are based on particular formats. Because of the need to attract listeners most sought-after by advertisers (21–50, middle-class), then a few formats dominate the larger stations – mainly adult contemporary, CHR, gold, rock and easy listening. Some of the smaller incremental stations in larger cities do offer additional formats such as Kiss (dance), and Choice (urban black music).

Choices in music radio are developing through digital radio and the Internet. These are enabling more specialised music formats to broadcast, such as Christian music, soul or country. The fact that digital radio stations are available via digital television (especially Sky digital) has significantly boosted audience share. For example, Total Rock puts its weekly audience at over one million (based on research by BMRB).

The fact that pirate radio continues to flourish is testimony to the failure of mainstream radio to provide a full range of music to listeners. It is estimated that in London alone there are likely to be as many as fifty pirates operating at any one time (*Independent,* 7 July 1998). In the capital, pirate radio is predominantly black, reflecting the relative absence of licensed stations playing black music. Prior to being granted a licence by the Radio Authority in 1991, Kiss FM had been a successful pirate station in the capital. In 2000, So Solid Crew, the successful black garage band, launched their own pirate station, Delight FM, which helped them acquire a record deal with Relentless Records.

Meanwhile, the BBC, with its commitment to public service broadcasting, continues to offer the only stations (Radio 1 and 2) with real musical diversity, especially in the evenings. BBC radio presenters have the freedom to play music of their own personal choice. From time to time, Radio 1 presenters have been responsible for breaking new acts such as when Mark Radcliffe's extensive air play in 1996 for a song called *Your Woman* by an obscure artist called White Town led to it reaching number one (despite recording the song in a bedroom and having no marketing!). Radio 2, with the largest music radio audience in Britain at over twelve million, has also impacted on the charts, as illustrated by the success of Gordon Haskell's 2001 Christmas single and follow-up album both extensively played on the BBC station.

Television and video

Television exposure is much sought after by companies and artists as a means of enhancing audience awareness and hence sales. Until Channel 4 pioneered youth programmes based on music, from *The Tube* to *The Word*, BBC's *Top of the Pops* was the main television showcase for pop music. While being consistently criticised for its musical conservatism and exclusive concern with the singles chart, its impact on sales is undeniable.

Other opportunities on television are generally restricted to weekend children's television and music showcases like the annual Brit awards (the music equivalent of the film Oscars). A notable exception were the ITV music talent series *Pop Stars* (2001) and *Pop Idol* (2002), the exposure from which ensured the successful launch of Hear'Say (*Pop Stars*) and Will Young and Gareth Gates (*Pop Idol*).

To gain access to television, especially cable and satellite music channels, the key marketing device is the music video. Its potential as a promotional tool was first fully realised when Queen's 1975 video for their song 'Bohemian Rhapsody', broadcast on *Top of the Pops*, played a vital role in sustaining the song for nine weeks at number one in the singles chart. The 1980s saw a huge expansion in music videos linked to the rise of MTV in America (launched in 1981). It particularly suited performers with a strong and attractive image which could be enhanced by video. Artists like Madonna were very successful in exploiting the potential for music video to help create or change their image. As MTV rapidly developed into a global channel, then the investment in a striking music video could easily pay off in terms of increased sales, even when the production costs rocketed, as in the case of Michael Jackson's $2 million 1983 music video *Thriller*.

The extent to which the music video has foregrounded image at the expense of music is debatable. It seems apparent that artists able to produce more imaginative or compelling videos, such as Madonna, do gain an advantage, not least in boosting sales of the videos themselves. This might become even more important as the DVD audio format develops in the future. However, it is questionable how much close attention they receive. It has been suggested that, for most of the audience, music videos, especially on MTV, are used as background entertainment, rather like radio. Also like radio, music video television channels have developed into formats often utilising magazine brands, so-called **masthead television,** so that there are now channels for pop (*Smash Hits*) nu-metal (*Kerrang!*), indy/alternative (MTV2), etc. Audiences for these niche channels remain extremely small in Britain, usually below fifty thousand.

The pop video as a generic form overlaps with television advertising through the use of fast edits, special effects, unusual camera angles, etc. Indeed, it is a form of advertising in itself. Meanwhile, television adverts have been increasingly prone to apply music soundtracks drawn from the past. The Levi 501 jeans campaign is a notable example. Its resurrection of 'golden oldies' has led to a succession of chart successes for songs like 'I Heard It Through the Grapevine', 'When a Man Loves a Woman', etc. This has led to accusations of commercial values corrupting the original meaning and power of the songs themselves. (An extreme example is the use of Bob Dylan's 1960s protest anthem, 'The Times They Are a-Changin', to promote a Canadian bank). Indeed, the ties between advertising and pop music have become ever more interwoven. Most major tours involve corporate sponsorship, star performers regularly endorse commercial products, and most recently, album and single releases have been sponsored, for example Häagen-Dazs ice cream launched a successful double CD of love songs via EMI and the Spice Girls' single 'Step to Me' was available only through a Pepsi promotion.

Cinema

Another form of **synergy** is the use of music soundtracks to accompany films. Although this is not a recent phenomenon – Bill Haley's 'Rock Around The Clock' hit single featured in the 1955 film *Blackboard Jungle* – it was not until the spectacular success of the Bee Gees' disco-based music score for *Saturday Night Fever* in 1977 (Figure 6.19) that the commercial potential of such soundtracks was fully realised. (This is discounting pop 'musicals', films designed to showcase pop stars performing their songs, such as the Beatles' *A Hard Day's Night* and *Help!* In the past twenty years, there have been dozens of films released which contain a sufficient sampling of music to justify an album release, or whose opening-closing credits feature a song targeted at the singles charts, e.g. Whitney Houston's 'I will always love you' from *The Bodyguard* (1992).

FIGURE 6.19
Saturday Night Fever, *1977*
Source: The Kobal Collection/Paramount

This trend has been accelerated by the integration of film and music companies such as Warner and Sony/Colombia (see pp. 141–142). If the film is set in the recent past, it provides an opportunity to repackage old hits and sell them to a new audience, such as *The Wedding Singer* (1998) which, set in 1985, enabled Warner to use a range of 'New Romantic' hits of the period from its back catalogue. Increasingly, the music has little to do with the films' narrative and genre and more to do with the profile of the film audience. For example, *A Knight's Tale* (2001), set in medieval England, used a set of classic rock songs by artists like Queen and David Bowie which might appeal to a new generation of young male music buyers, whilst *Mission Impossible 2* (2000) plays safe with a hard rock soundtrack featuring Limp Bizkit and Metallica.

The Internet

This relatively new electronic medium has the potential to supersede all the existing forms by which music is mediated to audiences (so-called **disintermediation**). It has already become a significant means of distributing music if still mainly illegally (as discussed above), but it also provides the means to either bypass the major music corporations altogether or else become yet another medium by which the majors can increase their profitability in the industry.

For new artists faced with the daunting challenge of acquiring a record deal, the Internet now offers quasi-A&R websites such as **Peoplesound.com** which showcases more than three thousand five hundred unsigned artists and allows its millions of visitors to compile free CDs of the music. However, at the time of writing, no notable artist has launched exclusively on the Internet. A few have managed to sell several thousand copies of singles and entered the lower reaches of the specialist charts such as dance. The first exclusive Internet release by a major group, Public Enemy's *There's a Poison Going on*, in 1999, failed to chart.

A key problem is that few people have the time to sample unknown artists. Potential fans need to have some sort of guidance or prior knowledge to seek out music that is likely to be appealing. Instead, the majors are waking up to the marketing possibilities of fan websites. Capital records in America set up a Radiohead website which included a special instant 'messaging buddy' as a means of spreading information on the band's album releases and concerts during 2001. The result was a number one album 'Kid A' and a sell-out tour without any radio airplay, video, hit single or advertising.

It is now standard for artists to have official and unofficial websites to market and develop fan bases. Many include audio and video clips as well as news updates, quizzes and competitions. More general music websites such as Dotmusic now provide the range of news and reviews previously the preserve of music newspapers such as *New Musical Express* (NME). Dotmusic has an audited user figure of 1.25 million users a month in contrast to NME's weekly circulation of fifty thousand, less than a sixth of its 1970s peak. Music retailers are also threatened as Internet sales steadily climb (not counting the huge amount of piracy, discussed on p. 168). Live concerts featuring major artists are beginning to receive webcasts. Madonna's London concert of November 2000 received 4.5 million streams during the concert and millions more in the following weeks. The only real obstacle to the growth of such events is technical. Currently, restricted broadband Internet access means the quality of pictures is substandard.

The Internet provides yet another example of the struggle between the conservative major companies and the more enterprising independent companies to control and exploit new technology as a means of producing, distributing and marketing music to audiences and fans.

The manufacture of success

It has always been the case that the music industry has attempted to minimise the risk and maximise the profit by carefully producing the right product that will succeed in the market. In recent years, the degree of manipulation has significantly increased as companies have sought to contrive groups with all the right attributes to succeed in the pre-teen or adolescent pop market. As far back as the 1960s, the case of the Monkees is a forerunner of the modern trend. They were auditioned and packaged to be an American version of the Beatles with the bonus of their own television series to showcase their music. During the 1990s, a series of boy bands like Take That and Boyzone were similarly manufactured with ever-growing precision to create an appealing packaged image for the singles and then album charts.

The process was transferred to girl groups with the advent of the Spice Girls, carefully selected with distinctive 'personalities', then taught how to sing and dance for almost a year until they were launched with their first single 'Wannabe' in 1996, which topped the charts in 31 countries. They even had their own marketing slogan, 'girl power'. Their first managers, Chris and Bob Herbert, went on to manufacture a more streetwise version of Take That, 5ive, who had a string of hits between 1997 and 2001.

The Spice Girls' second manager, Simon Fuller, who was eventually sacked by the band, next conceived a boy/girl group, S Club 7 (Figure 6.20). The campaign to ensure they would succeed demonstrates how sophisticated the modern marketing of a pop group is. The key elements comprised:

The group's name – a club whose members can interact with the official website, receive personal newsletters, etc.

A range of distinctive identities – to broaden potential audience appeal; differentiated by age, gender, ethnicity, individual personalities – 'the romantic', 'the black clubber','confessed shopaholic', etc.

FIGURE 6.20
S Club 7
Source: ©Redferns Music Picture Library/Nicky J. Sims

A television series – *Miami 7,* set in America, to help develop a British and American fan base and enable their songs to be broadcast (on BBC1).

A slogan – 'everybody is a somebody' said in conjunction with an S traced in the air.

Needless to say the group were extremely successful. Fuller then went on to launch S Club Juniors, a group of 11-14-year-olds explicitly targeting a pre-teen audience of 7-11-year-olds. The group were marketed through such children's media output as the *Cartoon Network* on television and magazines like *Star Pets*.

In 2001, a new variation of manufacturing pop groups was introduced via *Popstars* in which a panel drawn from the music industry selected who would belong to a new group over several weeks of primetime television viewing. The group's name, Hear'Say, their music and marketing were all controlled by their management and music company. In this case, the manufacturing process was to some extent transparent. Hear'Say disbanded in 2002 after a short period of chart success.

The alternative route to success

The above discussion focuses on the mainstream commercial means by which modern music is successful. The major companies seem to be ever more effective in controlling the music market. However, there are always alternative avenues by which new music and artists can flourish from grassroots to eventual commercial success.

Pop music has always had an undercurrent of subcultures or cults which have emerged relatively spontaneously. In the 1960s, it was 'folk protest' and hippie psychaedelic music; in the 1970s, Northern Soul, gay disco and reggae; in the 1980s, hiphop and rap, etc. In the latter case, the music sprang from the black inner-city neighbourhoods of American cities such as Los Angeles. A good example is the career of Niggaz with Attitude (NWA), formed by Eric Wright in 1986. He paid $7,000 for ten thousand 12-inch records sold at first around the local neighbourhoods. By word of mouth, the record eventually sold 500,000 copies. Wright set up his own label, Ruthless, and then NWA's first album, 'Straight outta Compton', sold over one million records without any radio or television support. By 1991, they were the first rap band to top the US album charts. At first resisted by the music industry and television, eventually rap music was embraced – *Yo MTV Raps* became the most popular music television show, and major labels took over the successful independents. Ruthless records is now part of the Sony group.

FIGURE 6.21
Source: garagenation.com

In Britain, it is dance music (Figure 6.21) that has most successfully flourished at the grassroots level via a thriving club scene, DJs, mixers, DIY music production, pirate radio, etc. Probably because it is difficult to identify and then market star dance music artists, and because the musical styles constantly mutate and cross over, dance music continues to largely elude control by the major music companies.

Activity 6.7

Try to identify a current example of a musical subculture or style which could be said to be 'alternative' – to be largely uncontrolled by the major companies. How does it generate its popular appeal?

Local Newspapers

Studies of news media have tended to focus on national or mutinational institutions and their output, but for many people one of the most immediate and 'close-to-life' examples of news consumption is the local newspaper that provides the news, events and values of their particular community. Research by Gunter *et al* (1994) showed that 70 per cent of the public get their information about world news through television and about 20 per cent through newspapers, whilst 40 per cent of the public said that they get their local news through newspapers compared to about 35 per cent through television. If we consider the size of the geographical area served by local newspapers in comparison to local radio and television, it is clear that local newspapers have a much tighter 'local' focus than most BBC or independent radio or television stations. Local newspapers serve a function that neither commercially-run local radio, usually based upon national music charts or golden oldies, nor local television, with its limited local slots sandwiched between the network output, can easily provide.

However, despite this apparent advantage, the number of local weekly newspapers has been in sharp decline for some considerable time.

Ownership and Control

Franklin and Murphy (1991) and McNair (1996) have examined some recent developments in the local newspaper market, and their research suggests that there is a change taking place in the nature of local newspapers, most significantly in the structure of ownership and economic organisation of the local press. They identify an increasing concentration of ownership of local press into a small number of large media groups, intent on expanding their horizontal integration (see p. 141) by taking over competitors and creating regional monopolies. Today, according to the Newspaper Society (**www.newspapersoc.org.uk**), the top twenty publishers account for 85 per cent of all local and regional titles in Britain and 96 per cent of total weekly circulation.

The Newspaper Society estimates that there are today around one thousand three hundred local and regional newspapers in Britain. This includes nearly one hundred daily morning and evening newspapers and nineteen Sunday newspapers. However, the main category of local and regional newspapers is the weekly, accounting for nearly one thousand two hundred of the titles. These weekly newspapers are divided into those that readers pay for and those that are available free, the freesheets.

The regional newspaper groups are now being bought up by other, larger cross-media groups who are keen to develop their cross-media interests, and see a 'synergy' between owning both local and national newspapers as well as having interests in local radio and television services in particular areas. The top three local publishing groups are all part of larger media groups: Trinity Mirror is part of The Mirror Group; Newsquest Media Group is owned by a large American media company, American Gannett; and the Northcliffe Newspaper group is part of Associated Newspapers.

As part of this concentration of ownership of the local press, Franklin and Murphy identify an increasing homogenisation, or 'sameness', in local newspapers, where small independent companies have been bought out by larger groups that want to eliminate competition, reduce costs and streamline production. For many newspapers this has resulted in a loss of 'local' identity, and many 'local' newspapers, like those of the Portsmouth and Sunderland Newspaper group, are now printed at regional centres away from their communities, and are often only one in a series of 'local' newspapers whose only difference is their front and back pages, while the articles and features on the inside may often be identical.

The consequences of this homogenisation can easily be seen by looking at the 'alternative' or independent local press that has tried over the years to establish various titles as voices for alternative views in society, often youthful and/or left-wing, such as the *Manchester Free Press*, *Leeds Other Paper*, *East End News*, *Northern Star* or *New Manchester Review*. Only a few of these titles have survived, usually by focusing on listings and 'lifestyle' rather than maintaining a radical alternative editorial line. Their success, as various commentators have noted (Franklin and Murphy, 1991; Whitaker, 1984), has been generally at the expense of any radicalism, and rather than extending choice and variety the 'alternative' newspapers that have survived have been absorbed into the mainstream values, attitudes and styles of big-business newspaper production and ownership. One of the few successful 'alternative' newspapers that has managed to retain some radical idealism is the *Big Issue*, which through its network of unemployed street vendors is available throughout Britain.

One of the main areas of growth for local newspaper publishers has been the introduction of weekly freesheets. These local newspapers are often distributed free directly into people's homes or left at central points such as railway and bus stations or in shopping malls. They are partly the result of advances in new printing technology and low staffing overheads as well as the expansion in advertising revenue. Freesheets can present serious competition for many established weekly 'paid-for' newspapers (Goodhart and Wintour, 1986, and McNair, 1996). Many of the original freesheet companies were bought up by existing local newspaper groups, or else the latter launched their own freesheet in direct competition, having the advantage of an established editorial and printing network. Many local newspaper groups often published both 'paid-fors' and freesheets in the same area.

Freesheets are primarily vehicles for advertising with little editorial or journalistic content and this means that they are very much at the mercy of economic trends. For example, in their heyday in the late 1980s there were over one thousand freesheet titles. However, during the economic recession of the early 1990s, many of these freesheets closed down due to a decline in advertising revenue. Today it is estimated that there are around six hundred and fifty freesheets. One of the recent successes of the freesheets has been the *Metro* series introduced by Associated Newspapers (owners of the *Daily Mail*) intitially in London and then Manchester and Birmingham and other large urban areas. These freesheets appear more professional and offer more news and content than the earlier versions of freesheets that seemed to offer very little except advertising in various forms.

Local newspapers traditionally used to be the entry point into the newspaper industry, where young cub reporters served their apprenticeship, their ambition being to move on to the national press of Fleet Street, or into local radio and/or television and then perhaps on to national news. This traditional route was overseen by the National Council for the Training of Journalists, set up in 1952 as a result of criticism at the way in which newspapers were training journalists. Today, however, newspaper owners and editors are looking for alternative ways of training journalists. Increasingly learning to become a journalist is less about the acquisition of knowledge and more about gaining competencies through NVQs. Beharrell (1993) points to this change in the training of journalists as one of the reasons for the change in style and content of local news reporting. Beharrell suggests that the modern reporter, trained in a climate of 'commercial reality', will rely upon previous success in the types of story that appeal to both the editor and readers. Stories become shorter in length, less detailed or informed, and instead simpler and more emotional. Local newspapers have tended to become more populist in character, relying on a 'house (or group) style' that consists of a diet of human-interest stories and moral panics, a style that is no longer the result of a professional ideology of balance and impartiality but rather a campaigning sensationalism that is aimed at increasing sales.

For many people the local newspaper is likely to be the single most important source of news and information within their area, especially as the local newspaper may reach over 80 per cent of households and be kept around the house for several days, rather than being thrown away the next day as often happens to daily newspapers. Local newspapers have an important relationship with the communities they serve, recording the 'organised output of symbolic events, decisions and official accounts produced by a local establishment in sectors of the state, business and the formal voluntary sector' (Franklin and Murphy, 1991). Advertising is vital for the industry and through the newspapers it also provides information about local services and products available in the community.

It is interesting to note that the five top daily local and regional newspapers in terms of circulation are all based in Scotland. The newspaper with the highest daily circulation is the *Daily Record* although it is debatable whether this is truly a local newspaper as, although it is based in Glasgow, it is owned by Mirror Group Newspapers and is very much a Scottish version of *The Mirror*. There are also two other newspapers that cover all of Scotland, *The Scotsman* and *The Herald*. The other top local daily newspapers are from Aberdeen and Dundee. This is perhaps an indication of the service that local and regional newspapers provide for their communities, especially in communities that are a long way away from the large concentrations of national media outputs found in London.

Source	Total	Percentage
Courts	105	12.0
Coroner	10	1.0
Police	98	11.5
Other emergency services (fire, ambulance)	11	1.5
Council (and regional authorities)	199	23.0
Business	73	8.5
Government	32	3.5
MPs	11	1.5
Schools/colleges	33	4.0
Clubs/voluntary sector	107	12.5
Charitable appeals	36	4.0
Political parties/pressure groups	13	1.5
Churches	25	3.0
Public protest	14	1.5
Investigations	9	1.0
Other	89	10.5
Total	**865**	**100.5**

FIGURE 6.22
Local Press: sources of news
Sources: Glossop Chronicle, Bury Times, Westmorland Gazette, Cumberland and Westmorland Herald, Burnley Express, Rochdale Observer, Rossendale Free Press, North Wales Weekly News, Wigan Observer, Lochaber News, Oban Times, Warrington Star, Stockport Express Advertiser, Lothian Courier

A report on the sources of eight hundred and sixty five stories in fourteen British local newspapers, accounting for over 67 per cent of all news stories, revealed five main sources of news: local and regional government, voluntary organisations, the courts, the police and business (Figure 6.22). Franklin and Murphy suggest that this reliance upon these limited sources means that the local press tends to reinforce the status quo and celebrate the values of a stable, well-ordered and, as much as possible, conflict-free community.

The Newbury Weekly News

A local 'paid-for' weekly newspaper that has served its local community since 1867 is the *Newbury Weekly News*. This is a broadsheet that was started during the explosion of small newspapers that resulted from the abolition of the various taxes (stamp duty, paper tax and advertising duty) on newspapers in the 1850s and 1860s (see Chapter 7, p. 196). This meant that both the cost of production and the cover price of newspapers fell. For the first time, a legal, mass readership was possible, and legitimate newspapers like the *Newbury Weekly News* became an economic possibility and profitable reality. Originally, it contained only a small amount of local news and syndicated material from London-based newspapers. As the size and prosperity of Newbury grew, so the demand for local news and information on trade and agriculture developed.

Ownership of the *Newbury Weekly News* is in the hands of a private company, whose shareholders include members of families who have controlled the newspaper since it started. The company also produces a weekly freesheet, the *Advertiser*, and monthly and quarterly supplements aimed at the local business, youth and leisure sectors. The company that owns the *Newbury Weekly News* is unusual in also owning its own presses, which give the paper increased flexibility for deadlines as well as providing additional income through commercial printing for outside organisations.

One of the advantages of being independent is the 'organic' nature of the relationship between the newspaper and the community. The company claims that any decisions concerning the running of the *Newbury Weekly News* are made by a management team consisting of local people, living within the community the newspaper serves, who should therefore be able to keep in touch with the conditions and feelings of the community. Editorial decisions are internal, and unlike the editors of local newspapers that are members of large groups, the editor of the *Newbury Weekly News* does not have to worry about outside or group interests, although there are still commercial, and circulation, pressures to consider.

Readership

The *Newbury Weekly News* regards its readership as 'everyone who lives locally'. A survey it commissioned in 1989 suggested the paper reached over 70 per cent of adults in the area and up to 80 per cent in Newbury itself. In 2002 the circulation was over twenty six thousand, a reduction from its 1987 peak of about thirty two thousand.

As there is no direct competition the *Newbury Weekly News* states that there is no overt 'segmentation' of readership, and that specific groups are not targeted in terms of age, socio-economic grouping or gender but are simply defined by locality; if you live in the Newbury area you are seen as a potential reader of the newspaper.

The traditional nature of the paper and its readers is perhaps reflected in the debate about its page size. When most newspapers are moving to tabloid, letters to the *Newbury Weekly News* indicate a strong support among its readers for it to retain its traditional broadsheet format. The *Advertiser*, its freesheet sister, is tabloid and has a slightly higher circulation. It is particularly popular in the neighbouring town of Thatcham with its higher concentration of new housing and 'non-professional' households. The *Newbury Weekly News* is predominantly middle-class in tone and content and for a small extra investment the *Advertiser*, like many freesheets, allows the newspaper company to address a more distinctly working-class readership.

Activity 6.8

Try to establish a reader profile for your local newspaper. What categories of news and features are used and what does this tell you about:

1   the local community?
2   the newspaper that serves it?
3   how the newspaper defines its sense of community?

Competition

Competition for the *Newbury Weekly News* is limited, and one of the clues to its apparent success is its unique role as the only truly local newspaper for a fairly specific geographical area. Newbury and its surrounding villages exist on the edge of various other regions – southern, western, London or south Midlands – but no other newspaper seems to offer the specific local service of the *Newbury Weekly News*. Other local newspapers, daily and weekly, that are available in the area come from towns several miles away, such as Reading, Swindon or Basingstoke, and are part of larger newspaper groups and therefore very different in character. These papers reflect the news and needs of their larger, more urban, communities.

Activity 6.9

Choose a period of time, say one week, and try to monitor across the range of different media that serve your locality the quality and frequency of 'local' news about your neighbourhood or community. List all press, radio and television sources. Where else does the local news come from?

Although freesheets from other newspaper groups are delivered in the area it is unlikely that any new newspaper will appear to challenge the hegemony of the *Newbury Weekly News*; the last competitor was seen off in the late 1890s. There is no alternative or community press borne on the back of supposedly cheaper technology to challenge the *Newbury Weekly News*, and the local council does not produce its own PR-minded municipal free papers, as Franklin and Murphy suggest may occur in some urban areas.

Activity 6.10

Carry out a survey of what media are available in your local area. How do the different media define and represent your locality or region? Try to assess the extent to which they represent the views and issues of your locality. What participation do the local media offer to the members of the communities they are addressing?

An ILR station, 2TEN FM, has been available in Newbury for many years. Based in Reading, it is part of the GWR regional network and has some local programming, but generally offers either chart or 'golden oldie' music. Its 'footprint' includes an area that is served, in local newspaper terms, by at least four different weekly local newspapers and two daily local newspapers. In 1992 the BBC opened a local radio station, Radio Berkshire, which offered a limited local service and aimed to cover the whole county, a potential audience of nearly seventy thousand. Owing to financial pressures it briefly merged with the local BBC station based in nearby Oxford to form Thames Valley FM but this was deemed unsuccessful as it diluted the local focus for the Newbury area. When Meridian took over the local ITV franchise in 1993 it set up a local TV studio in Newbury, which has had its own local news programme at 6.30pm every evening. This has presented some competition to the *Newbury Weekly News*, mainly because it has the immediacy of a daily programme and the attraction of pictures over print. However, since Meridian was taken over by Granada Media the news-gathering facilities in Newbury are being downgraded and centralised at Meridian's main newsroom in Southampton, some fifty miles away.

The most recent challenge to the *Newbury Weekly News* came when the commercial radio station KICK FM was launched in 1996. This was a smaller radio station than 2TEN FM and focused on the same geographical area as the *Newbury Weekly News* as well as involving people from the local community in the making and presentation of programmes. In due course the *Newbury Weekly News* joined the consortium that owned KICK FM and helped provide the business experience that the Radio Authority requires when granting licences. This does mean, however, that like many other newspaper groups, it is part-owner of one of its main competitors for local advertising revenue.

Revenue

Classified advertising is an important source of income for all local newspapers. Advertising provides the *Newbury Weekly News* with about 80 per cent of its revenue. Without this source of income the cover price would be around £1.50 per copy, rather than the 40p charged in 2002. Most of the advertising comes from local people and businesses and so the economic health of the paper is bound up with that of the town's businesses. During the late 1980s when Newbury was a 'boom' town, there would be up to a dozen pages advertising job vacancies; in 2002 the Situations Vacant adverts (although they call it 'Recruitment') cover about four pages. There has been a similar decline in advertising for house and car sales, as well as in the amount of advertising taken out by local shops and businesses.

Advertising is part of the service a local newspaper offers its readers. It is a source of local information regarding services and 'what's on'. The balance between advertising and editorial, however, needs to be finely judged: if the newspaper contains too much advertising, readers become dissatisfied; too little, and the newspaper loses money or has to raise its cover price. The *Newbury Weekly News* tried to keep that balance at about 65 per cent advertising to 35 per cent editorial. As the advertising pays for the editorial, the amount of advertising revenue available will affect the size and news content of the paper. At its height in the late 1980s, editions of the paper could have up to seventy two pages, but in the mid-1990s they fell to around fifty six pages plus various supplements. There is a risk in becoming too thin, as the newspaper may start to lose readers if it is not considered good value.

News Values

Editorially the *Newbury Weekly News* tries to reflect the community that it serves – a conservative one, despite having had a local Liberal Democrat MP since 1993. Newbury is a prosperous, middle-class town, rated one of the four wealthiest districts in the country in a survey carried out in 1993 by the School of Advanced Urban Studies at Bristol University. Although claiming to be impartial, the *Newbury*

Weekly News echoes these local values and ambiguities, and its pages frequently reflect the issues that concern the more established or prosperous members of the community. The stereotypical reader will be a middle-aged member of a middle-class family. They will have elderly parents and are therefore concerned about the quality of local health services, they will have children and so are interested in the quality of local education, they will also be worried about local traffic and safety issues, law and order and local levels of crime. Their hobbies and interests will also be reflected in the newspaper's content and advertising: these include the arts and entertainment, shopping, gardening and holidays.

The paper's editorial pages reflect the concerns of its middle-class readership, what Franklin and Murphy call the 'rituals of the community': weddings, Christmas concerts in local schools and churches, exam and degree results, and, of course, births, deaths and engagements. A regular feature on the letters page is 'Old memories revived', with newspaper cuttings going back one hundred and twenty five years, helping to reinforce a sense of history for both the newspaper and the community. There is also a junior weekly news section and a monthly woman's page.

Activity 6.11

Look through a copy of your local newspaper and identify the main sources of news. How many of the stories will have been sent in and how many are the result of investigation or research by a journalist from the newspaper? How does your newspaper compare with Figure 6.23?

Letters to the editor can take up two or three pages and usually include contributions from local councillors, political activists and other local 'notables'. Beharrell (1993) notes that although the letters pages tend to reflect the concerns of the more vociferous members of the community, these are often local variations of national news stories such as the health service or public spending, although in recent years high-profile stories like the peace camps at Greenham Common, possible nuclear accidents at the American airbase and the controversy surrounding the Newbury bypass have all featured. The other significant feature of the letters pages are public expressions of gratitude for help or information, or congratulations for successes, public or private.

Franklin and Murphy note that one of the functions of the local press is to respond to national news events in a local way, reflecting the local dimension. After the massacre in nearby Hungerford in 1987, the *Newbury Weekly News* tried to deal with the incident as a local matter with personal dimensions, rather than in the more lurid and sensational way the national tabloids approached it. The *Newbury Weekly News* claims to have received only one complaint about its treatment of the story, whereas reporters from the national newspapers supposedly alienated many of the local population in their hunt for 'good' copy.

The *Newbury Weekly News* is apparently a successful newspaper because it reflects a large proportion of the community that it serves and that provides it with its market. In appearance it is a traditional newspaper, with perhaps slightly old-fashioned values, that assumes its readers are well informed and want to know both sides of a story (see Figure 6.23). Like the town it serves, it has an air of 'quiet respectability' (Beharrell). The *Newbury Weekly News* is the type of newspaper that Franklin and Murphy see as becoming increasingly rare in England, although remaining still strong in America, where the locally owned newspaper offers a focus for the community's particular sense of itself, defined in terms of the local economy, the local political system and local social relationships. The *Newbury Weekly News* can be seen as a newspaper that tries to combine high moral and journalistic standards with a vested interest in maintaining the status quo and the comfortable 'middle-England' background of many of its readers and the community itself.

Activity 6.12

Carry out a content analysis of the letters page of several editions of your local newspaper. What are the most common types of letter and who writes in most frequently? Does your local newspaper edit or in any way control the letters it publishes? How does your local newspaper compare with the Newbury Weekly News and the letters pages of other types of newspaper?

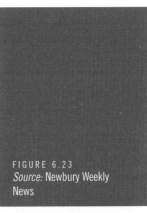

FIGURE 6.23
Source: Newbury Weekly News

The lack of a real rival to the *Newbury Weekly News* means, at the moment, that it is unlikely to be bought out by a larger group trying to eliminate competition, and so as long as the community stays the same, or as long as the paper can change as the community changes, it should survive as a local, independent weekly newspaper.

Further activities

1 Draw up a profile of your own local newspaper, looking at such issues as: who owns it; what type of reader it is aimed at; what other local media are in competition with it; what proportion of its revenue comes from advertising and how might that affect the content of the newspaper and the types of story it contains. How successful is your local newspaper and what are its criteria for success?

2 Compare your local newspaper with another contrasting example, e.g. rural with urban, or independent with one that is part of a large group. Look at such aspects as news values, style, political bias and content.

3 Consider what a community radio station could offer your neighbourhood. In what ways would it offer an 'alternative' to the existing media available locally? Try to define specific community groups based on

● location and neighbourhood, or
● language and culture, or
● a specific interest or cause.

Draw up an outline for a possible Restricted Service Licence (RSL) proposal for your area. What event would it focus on? What are the possible sources of funding? What types of programmes and presenters would the RSL have? Write to the Radio Authority and ask for a licence application form, and try to supply answers to the questions they ask (address at the end of this chapter).

4 Conduct a survey of those who listen to your local radio stations. What stations are available? Who do they target as their listeners? How is this reflected in the programme content and the style of presenters? If you have a local ILR station, try to find out if it is part of a larger group and what, if anything, your particular station has in common with others in the same group.

Further Reading

Allan, S. 2000: News Culture. OPEN UNIVERSITY PRESS.

Beharrell, M. 1993: Protest, Press and Prejudice: RAF Greenham Common 1982-92. INSTITUTE OF EDUCATION, UNIVERSITY OF LONDON.

Curran, J. 2002: Media and Power. ROUTLEDGE.

Curran, J. and Seaton, J. 1997: Power without Responsibility. ROUTLEDGE.

Doyle, G. 2002: Media Ownership. SAGE.

Fountain, N. 1988: Underground: The London Alternative Press 1966-1974. COMEDIA.

Franklin, B. 1997: Newszak and News Media. ARNOLD.

Franklin, B. and Murphy, D. 1991: What's News? The Market, Politics and the Local Press. ROUTLEDGE.

Goodhart, D. and Wintour, C. 1986: Eddy Shah and the Newspaper Revolution. CORONET.

Harcup, T. 1995: A Northern Star – Leeds other paper and the Alternative Press 1974-1994. CAMPAIGN FOR PRESS AND BROADCASTING FREEDOM.

Langer, J. 1997: Tabloid Television. ROUTLEDGE.

Lewis, P. and Booth, J. 1989: The Invisible Medium: Public, Commercial and Community radio. MACMILLAN.

McNair, B. 1999: News and Journalism in the UK. ROUTLEDGE.

Tunstall, J. 1996: Newspaper Power: The New National Press in Britain. CLARENDON PRESS.

Whittaker, B. (ed). 1984: News Ltd: Why you Can't Read All About It. COMODIA.

Music Industry

Frith, S. 1983: Sound Effects. CONSTABLE.

Frith, S. and Goodwin, A. (eds). 1990: On Record. ROUTLEDGE.

Garfield, S. 1986: Expensive Habits: The Dark Side of the Music Industry. FABER AND FABER.

Gillett, C. 1983: The Sound of the City. SOUVENIR PRESS.

Longhurst, B. 1995: Popular Music and Society. POLITY PRESS.

Negus, K. 1992: Producing Pop. EDWARD ARNOLD.

Negus, K. 1996: Popular Music in Theory. POLITY PRESS.

Histories

CHAPTER SEVEN

The last chapter focused on the theme of media institutions, their regulation and their everyday relationships with the present – the here and now. This chapter aims to develop a range of issues about the *historical* development of the modern media and the conditions that have shaped their respective development as they have emerged and changed over time. These themes should not, however, be confined to this chapter. Attention to the historical development of media institutions and organisations is an essential component of media studies. In short, studying the historical formation and evolution of the various media – how they have emerged and under what conditions – makes possible a more informed understanding of their present dynamics, and their likely patterns of development and change.

History, or rather the study of history, is often associated with lists of dates, lists of apparently undeniable, historic events and 'facts'. For example, a timeline of British media might look something like this:

1476	William Caxton prints the first printed English book.
1702	The *Daily Courant*, the first English daily newspaper, is published.
1785	The first issue of *The Times* is published (as the *Daily Universal Register*).
1896	The first moving picture show to a paying audience in London.
1922	The British Broadcasting Company (radio) is formed.
1927	The first full-length talking film is released.
1936	BBC Television starts broadcasting.
1946	Cinema attendance in Britain peaks at 1 635 million visits a year.
1962	The first communications satellite, Telstar, goes into orbit.
1969	Colour transmissions are introduced on BBC and ITV.
1973	The first independent local radio station opens (LBC).
1982	Channel 4 is launched.
1989	Sky Satellite Broadcasting launched.
1997	Channel 5 launched.
2002	45 per cent of British homes access the Internet.

As Carr (1961) and others have argued, however, historians are involved in more than just the 'cult of facts', the uncritical compilation of lists of self-evidently important dates. Historical study always entails a sense of why and how certain events and processes, and their dates, are *selected* as significant, and how their relevance should be *interpreted*. Popular ideas of history, for example, tend to be bound up with notions of 'progress', 'development' or other taken-for-granted ideas of 'industrialisation' or 'modernisation'.

Activity 7.1

In the light of this discussion, research and plot your own timeline, mapping media development in Britain from the date of your birth to the present day.

A Sense of History

The development of organised systems of mass communication has had important consequences for both personal and public perceptions of the past and history. Our own biographies are connected to 'media generations', bound up with remembered media events and shared experience of particular media at certain phases of their development. Life before television, for instance, when viewed from the early 2000s, seems a strange and rather alien, bygone time. The ages before film or pre-photographic records appear even more 'historical' and 'out of sight':

> *The modern world almost seems to have begun with the birth of film, at any rate in retrospect. Because we're used to seeing film images of the First World War, the First World War seems to be part of the modern period. But anything more than twenty years earlier than that belongs to an era which we easily feel to be lost.*
>
> *Chanan (1980), p. 16*

Activity 7.2

The quotation from Chanan suggests that film and visual media have had an important impact on our sense of history.

List some of the most memorable media images associated with your own life. Conduct interviews or surveys among other members of your household or family, particularly from different generations, about their memories of earlier media and media coverage of significant events.

Local media archives and visits to national museums such as The Museum of the Moving Image, The National Museum of Photography, Film and Television and The National Sound Archive provide invaluable resources for this kind of work.

As you work through the chapter you may find it useful to return to this activity.

The Battle of Trafalgar

When the Battle of Trafalgar reached its conclusion in favour of the British fleet on 21 October 1805, it was more than a fortnight before the news of the victory, and of the death of Admiral Lord Nelson, was published in Britain. The first account of the events reached the pages of *The Times* on 6 November (Figure 7.1). Admiral Collingwood's full despatch was published there on the following morning, 7 November 1805.

GLORIOUS AND DECISIVE

VICTORY

OVER THE

COMBINED FLEET,

AND

DEATH OF LORD NELSON.

We know not whether we fhould mourn or rejoice. The country has gained the moft fplendid and decifive Victory that has ever graced the naval annals of England ; but it has been dearly purchafed. *The great and gallant* NELSON *is no more*: he was killed by almoft the laft fhot that was fired by the enemy. The action took place off Cadiz, on the 21ft ult.; the enemy were thirty-three fail of the line, Lord NELSON had only twenty-feven.

The following account we have received by express; we can pledge ourfelves for its truth:

TIMES OFFICE, 11 o'Clock, A. M.

A Lieutenant of a man of war arrived this morning, with an account of a moft glorious victory achieved by the Britifh fleet, under the command of Lord NELSON.

The enemy's fleet confifted of THIRTY-THREE fail of the line, with frigates, &c. They came out of Cadiz on the 19th of October, and two days afterwards were en-countered by the Britifh fleet, confifting of only TWENTY-SEVEN fail of the line, (feveral having been detached under Rear-Admiral LOUIS) with fome fmaller fhips. The battle continued during four hours, and ended in the capture of NINETEEN of the enemy's ships of the line, befides one which blew up in the action.

The *Victory* being clofely engaged with feveral of the Enemy's Ships, a Mufket-fhot wounded Lord NELSON in the Shoulder, and thus terminated a Life of Glory.

A number of Prizes drifted on a lee-shore, in a gale of wind, a day or two af-terwards, and probably many have been wrecked. Admiral COLLINGWOOD had ordered that every ship which could not be brought away should be destroyed. Two, however, effected their escape into Cadiz.

Admiral VILLENEUVE is a prisoner. On our side two Captains, we believe DUFF and COOKE, and three or four hundred men were killed. We have not lost a single ship.

FIGURE 7.1
Source: The Times, 6 November 1805. Reproduced by permission

The news, having travelled variously via the British Consul in Lisbon and overland by coach, did not reach London until early November … The story of Trafalgar was read in the newspapers of the day by at most a few thousand people.

Carter (1971), p. 9

Needless to say, such events would not be covered in quite the same way today. From the Falklands to the Gulf War, Bosnia, and Afghanistan and in coverage of numerous other international conflicts and events, developments in the media have greatly increased the speed of transmission, the size of audiences and the amounts and types of information made available to them.

Activity 7.3

Compare the reporting of Trafalgar with that of any more contemporary international conflicts. What major differences would you identify in the patterns and forms of media coverage? How would the Battle of Trafalgar be covered by today's media?

For useful references see: Knightley (1978), Harris (1983), Taylor, J. (1991), Taylor, P. (1992), Brothers, C. (1997), McLaughlin, G. (2002), and Zelizer, B & Allan, S.(eds 2002).

Demand and Supply: The Conditions of Media Development

The growth of mass communications is a dual process. On the one hand it describes the development of an industry, on the other the evolution of an audience. The relationship between the two is one of supply and demand for two basic social commodities: leisure facilities and information.

Golding (1974), p. 14

Before looking at some detailed case studies of the historical development of particular media, it is useful to consider some general factors that have shaped and historically structured this relationship of supply and demand. In essence, this entails an analysis of certain general conditions which have had important implications for media producers and processes of production (supply) and for media consumers and their access to reception of media output (demand).

Demand

Historically, the *demand* for information and entertainment has been influenced by three key factors: the amounts of *time* available, the affluence or *spending power* of social groups, and a variety of other educational and *cultural* considerations.

The time available for media consumption has helped determine the meaning of leisure and hence the formation of various media markets. One study of the press in the first half of the nineteenth century, for example, notes that you not only needed time, but also light to read a newspaper by:

> To say that conditions were against the growth of a working class reading public would be to put it mildly. In the towns, a fourteen-hour working day was commonplace: those in even the most favoured trades did not get home until 6 or 7pm; not until the 1860s was the Saturday half-holiday introduced. Another major problem was the absence of light: the window tax was not abolished until 1851 … and in most houses tallow dips or candles were the only source of illumination apart from the fireplace. So the worker confined reading to Sundays – hence, of course, the popularity of Sunday newspapers.
>
> Cranfield (1978), pp. 120–1

Legal and technical changes in many forms of employment from the late nineteenth century onwards have resulted in decreased working hours, the widespread availability of statutory holidays, and more *time* being generally available for leisure or non-work activities. As we noted earlier in this book (see Chapters 1 and 5), media consumption has grown as a significant component of this 'discretionary' time. But at the beginning of the twenty-first century, there are still important differences in the leisure time available to men and women, old and young, rich and poor and between many other social and cultural groupings.

The *amounts of money* that different groups have been able to spend on media products have also been a key variable in conditioning the demand side of media markets. In short, if people are not able to afford to buy magazines, newspapers, films, DVDs, CDs or to invest in the licence or subscription fees for broadcast, online and other media, for example, this will have obvious consequences for the media organisations involved and their ability to operate viably or profitably. Consumer spending on entertainment, information and the media in Britain continues to represent a significant part of the UK economy overall and expenditure on advertising is often used as a key economic indicator.

There have been, and continue to be, important differences in media expenditure patterns – 'media spending power' – between low-income and high-income groups in British society. Actual expenditure on magazines and books, newspapers, cinema, DVD and computer-based software and hardware varies sharply with income. Different levels of income and other resources are basic factors in wider social inequalities and have had important consequences for the kinds of cultural demand that different audiences have been able to make on media markets and media institutions historically.

Cultural factors are perhaps a final set of historical issues to be considered in the development of the demand for various kinds of entertainment and information. These are often held to be the product of larger divisions of social class, gender, ethnicity, age or occupation, and have given rise to *differential* styles and patterns of media use, consumption and lifestyle. Part of the history of the media in Britain from the late nineteenth century onwards concerns the emergence of more distinct and differentiated groups of consumers, increasingly privatised and mobile. The post-1950s period, for example, saw rapid growth in media forms and industries – music, fashion, films, etc – aimed at and responding to a range of youth and ethnic audiences and subcultures. More recently, accelerating segmentation of demand has been claimed across gender ('new' women and men) and generation ('grey power'). Another important historical factor is literacy – the educated ability to read and write. While Britain is assumed to have high literacy rates at this time, this has not always been the case. For the development of print, publishing and the press industries, particularly popular newspapers and magazines, literacy and the ability to read was the vital cultural precondition, especially in the nineteenth century. In a similar way, some current debates also focus on 'computer literacy' and access to online resources and networks as a pre-condition for participation in the world-wide web.

Supply

The historical growth and regulation of media industries and institutions have determined how the various demands for forms of mediated information, knowledge and entertainment have been met. The ability to *supply* forms of media output has at a general level been subject to three principal forms of constraint: commercial, legal and technological conditions. These forces are explored in contemporary detail in Chapter 6.

Commercial markets and their operations have been significant in a number of ways. First, some of the principal historical dynamics of media development have resulted from the motives associated with commercial investment for profit. This broad aim has structured the operations of media producers and the contours of media markets in important ways. Since the late nineteenth century, investment in media industries has often been a high-risk business, and commercial success has been popularly characterised as 'giving the public what it wants', supplying the 'mainstream' or popular, profitable forms of demand. In practice this is an oversimplistic view, which neglects the ways in which demands are structured by what is supplied, and how, at any given moment, there are a range of dynamics in play. Although in the early part of the twenty-first century there are ways in which these blunt distinctions are held to be increasingly outmoded by the sophistication of 'deregulated' hi-tech, digital media, commercial logic remains an important and central historical determinant or condition of media production. An important, related issue here concerns commercial ownership and control. The history of media industries in Britain since the turn of the century involves studying the power of those who have owned them; from the press barons – Northcliffe or Beaverbrook – to modern-day media proprietors and owners, such as Rupert Murdoch. Media industries tend to have developed highly concentrated patterns of ownership, and questions of ownership and control have great significance for the historical analysis of the rise of commercial forms of broadcasting and other media (see Chapter 6 and the case study on Public Service Broadcasting later in this chapter).

Activity 7.4

Start to map the growth of local media histories for press, cinema, radio, TV and so on, in your own locality or region. Research the ways in which time, affluence and other cultural factors have shaped the local historical demands for media consumption. What additional factors and issues need to be considered?

Statutory and legal controls have also played an important part in determining how media institutions and industries have been able to develop and operate. Alongside commercial considerations, a significant dimension in the history of the media in Britain is that of their regulation by law, by government and by the state. Given the ability of the media to deal in information, opinion and images, it is no surprise that, from their earliest days, media producers have attracted the attentions of established authority and governments, which have sought to control, repress or regulate their output and operation. Early print systems, for example, in the sixteenth and seventeenth centuries were subject to very strict regimes of licensing and pre-publication censorship – everything that was to be published was required to be officially approved or censored beforehand. As the last case study in this chapter will outline, the growth and development of broadcasting in Britain, first in radio and then in television, has been powerfully structured by the requirements of government policies and legal codes, which have conditioned and constrained broadcasters in a number of significant ways.

Technologies and inventions, whether in the form of the development of the telegraph, the telephone, radio, or the communications satellite or computer systems, have rightly been regarded as key factors in the historical growth of media industries.

> *Technological changes further complicate the pattern of media supply, based often in underlying industrial and economic developments. Necessity, in the form of wars, imperial expansion, and commerce, has mothered a large proportion of the inventions which punctuate the history of the mass media. The steam printing press, wireless telegraphy, the cathode ray tube, satellites have all in turn recast the supply of media material and thus the range of options within which audiences exert their demands.*
>
> *Golding (1974), p. 18*

While the development of new media technologies has undoubtedly had important consequences for the overall historical growth of media industries and forms, it is important to recognise that the history of the media entails more than a linear account of 'great inventions'. As Williams (1990) has noted, accounts of the impact of modern technologies are often characterised by an over-emphasis upon the technologies and inventions themselves. This belief in the inevitable power of technologies to cause widespread social change and effects is known as *technological determinism*:

> *It is an immensely powerful and now largely orthodox view of the nature of social change. New technologies are discovered, by an essentially internal process of research and development, which then sets the conditions for social change and progress. Progress, in particular, is the history of these inventions, which 'created the modern world'. The effects of these technologies, whether direct or indirect, foreseen or unforeseen, are as it were the rest of history.*
>
> *Williams (1990), p. 13*

Activity 7.5

Look back at the research on forms of local media production that you started in the last activity and consider the ways in which commercial, legal and technical factors have shaped their history.

Research the technological history of a selected medium. Compile a map of the key inventions which have been influential. How have these inventions subsequently been institutionalised and regulated by other historical forces?

To counter this view it is important to note several points. First, processes of invention are complex and interwoven and have been shaped in a number of ways by commercial or military factors (as in the case of wireless transmission, the cathode ray tube, satellite and Internet technologies, for example). Secondly, once inventions have been made, there is a process whereby their social applications and uses are discovered. The potentials of inventions are realised in actual historical periods where social, economic and other forces operate to make them actual and regulate them in particular ways. The principal failing of accounts which adopt a technologically determinist view of media history is the tendency to cut the technology off from the many other forces and conditions which shape its invention and deployment. Some new technologies have not been taken up and have failed (such as the eight track sound system), while others have taken off in unanticipated ways (such as the personal stereo). The Internet is a focus for much recent work (see Chapter 8 for further discussion).

The remainder of this chapter is devoted to three case studies. These are chronologically organised and begin with two brief snapshots focused on aspects of the press and press development in the nineteenth century and the emergence of cinema in Britain from the 1890s to the 1920s. Both these case studies are brief outlines which should provide opportunity for further research. Finally, there is a more fully developed account of the development of Public Service Broadcasting in Britain, from the 1920s to the present day.

CASE STUDY:
Radical and Popular Press in the 19th Century

Two hundred years ago, the press was the most important single medium for the communication of ideas, opinion and knowledge, and the newspaper was the first recognisable modern mass medium. Newspapers were not a nineteenth century invention, although their production, forms and readerships changed and expanded considerably during that period as they became industrialised. The first daily newspaper, the *Daily Courant*, was published early in the eighteenth century (1702), and before that there were pamphlets, '*Mercuries*' and '*Intelligencers*', which carried reports of international events, limited forms of opinion and propagandist argument. By the end of the eighteenth century, the press had fought for the right to report parliamentary proceedings, and in spite of the fact that newspapers were controlled by means of the stamp taxes – duties paid per copy which kept the prices high – the foundations for a national, commercial press had been established.

The Times, published first as the *Daily Universal Register* in 1785, epitomised the new, respectable middle-class commercial press. By 1803 it had turned away from direct government subsidy, developing a stance which was independent of the government but generally supportive of establishment interests. This idea of 'independence', partly based on the view that newspapers should play an important intermediary role between governments and the governed, represented a significant historical shift, congruent with the formation of the new industrial and professional middle classes and their authority. In 1800 some 2 000 copies of *The Times* were being produced daily. By 1817, with the installation of new technologies – the steam-driven press – production increased to over 7 000.

Between the late 1790s and about the middle of the nineteenth century, the ascendancy and authority of this new model for the newspaper was powerfully challenged by another kind of press which served to articulate the demands of a very different culture and class. In this period, the radical press, also referred to as the 'pauper' or 'unstamped' press, emerged to play a part in voicing popular, oppositional opinion. As many social historians have noted, these papers played an important role in radicalising working-class ideas and politics, acting as agents or catalysts in the broader context of the development and experience of an industrialising, capitalist system and culture. The period between the 1790s and the 1830s was marked by considerable political turbulence and instability. This was accompanied by rapid population growth centralised on cities, the growth of the factory system, economic depressions, poverty and disease. 'Revolutionary' ideas from the Continent, calls for political agitation or industrial unrest, demands for voting rights, reform and the fundamental necessity for a free press were all fiercely debated and advanced by the radical press and its producers. For those in power, these publications were a subversive threat requiring suppression.

The first wave of these papers broke the law by their very existence and circulation. They were 'unstamped' – that is, they had not paid the required duties or taxes – and were the products of unlicensed presses. Important writers of this period include Tom Paine (1737-1809) and William Cobbett (1763-1835). Their works were usually in the form of a pamphlet, often the script of a speech. Paine's *Rights of Man* sold 50 000 copies within a few weeks in 1791; Cobbett's *Address to Journeymen and Labourers* sold 200 000 in 1826. Other radical publications, from the many titles in the period, include the *Black Dwarf* (1817), which specialised in sarcasm and attacks on government and royal personalities; *The Gorgon* (1818), which advocated practical reform of voting rights; and the *Penny Politician* (1818), which was published under the masthead 'Let's Die Like Men and Not Like Slaves' and attacked the whole system of industrial production and corrupt politics.

The high point of this early period was reached with the Peterloo Massacre (1819), when armed and mounted troops forcibly broke up a mass meeting about parliamentary reform held at St Peter's Fields, Manchester. Eleven people were killed as a result. During this period, the radical press faced the Gagging Bills (1819–20), laws which extended and increased the stamp taxes and strengthened the legal offence of seditious libel. Many of the writers and publishers of radical papers were arrested and served lengthy periods in jail, in some cases continuing to write from prison. Against these odds, the papers had succeeded in establishing a radical reading public and providing a rallying point for oppositional politics. The attempts at their suppression were a sign of this success, as were the many counter-propaganda publications they gave rise to (the *White Dwarf*, for example).

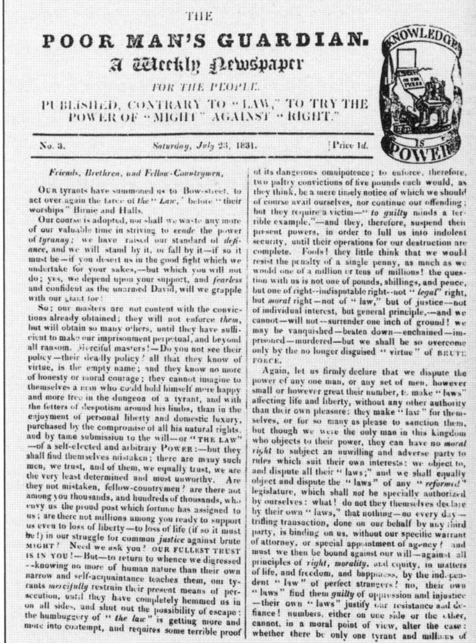

THE

POOR MAN'S GUARDIAN.

A Weekly Newspaper

FOR THE PEOPLE.

PUBLISHED, CONTRARY TO "LAW," TO TRY THE POWER OF "MIGHT" AGAINST "RIGHT."

No. 3. Saturday, July 23, 1831. Price 1d.

KNOWLEDGE IS POWER

Friends, Brethren, and Fellow-Countrymen,

OUR tyrants have summoned us to Bow-street, to act over again the farce of *the "Law,"* before "their worships" Birnie and Halls.

Our course is adopted, nor shall we waste any more of our valuable time in striving to *evade* the power of *tyranny;* we have raised our standard of *defiance*, and we will stand by it, or fall by it—if so it must be—if you desert us in the good fight which we undertake for your sakes,—but which you will not do; yes, we depend upon your support, and *fearless* and confident as the unarmed David, will we grapple with our giant foe!

So; our masters are not content with the convictions already obtained; they will not enforce *them*, but will obtain so many others, until they have sufficient to make our imprisonment perpetual, and beyond all ransom. Merciful masters!—Do you not see their policy—their deadly policy! all that they know of virtue, is the empty name; and they know no more of honesty or moral courage; they cannot imagine to themselves a man who could hold himself more happy and more free in the dungeon of a tyrant, and with the fetters of despotism around his limbs, than in the enjoyment of personal liberty and domestic luxury, purchased by the compromise of all his natural rights, and by tame submission to the will—or "THE LAW"—of a self-elected and arbitrary POWER:—but they shall find themselves mistaken; there are many such men, we trust, and of them, we equally trust, we are the very least determined and most unworthy. Are they not mistaken, fellow-countrymen? are there not among you thousands, and hundreds of thousands, who envy us the proud post which fortune has assigned to us; are there not millions among you ready to support us even to loss of liberty—to loss of life (if so it must be!) in our struggle for common *justice* against brute MIGHT? Need we ask you? OUR FULLEST TRUST IS IN YOU!—But—to return to whence we digressed—knowing no more of human nature than their own narrow and self-acquaintance teaches them, our tyrants *mercifully* restrain their present means of persecution, until they have completely hemmed us in on all sides, and shut out the possibility of escape; the humbuggery of "*the law*" is getting more and more into contempt, and requires some terrible proof of its dangerous omnipotence; to enforce, therefore, two paltry convictions of five pounds each would, as they think, be a mere timely notice of which we should of course avail ourselves, nor continue our offending; but they require a victim—"*to guilty* minds a terrible example,"—and they, therefore, suspend their present powers, in order to lull us into indolent security, until their operations for our destruction are complete. Fools! they little think that we would resist the penalty of a single penny, as much as we would one of a million or tens of millions! the question with us is not one of pounds, shillings, and pence, but one of right—indisputable right—not "*legal*" right, but *moral* right—not of "law," but of justice—not of individual interest, but general principle,—and we cannot—will not—surrender one inch of ground! we may be vanquished—beaten down—enchained—imprisoned—murdered—but we shall be so overcome only by the no longer disguised "virtue" of BRUTE FORCE.

Again, let us firmly declare that we dispute the power of any one man, or any set of men, however small or however great their number, to make "laws" affecting life and liberty, without any other authority than their own pleasure: they make "law" for themselves, or for so many as please to sanction them, but though we were the only man in this kingdom who objects to their power, they can have no *moral right* to subject an unwilling and adverse party to rules which suit their own interests: we object to, and dispute all their "laws;" and we shall equally object and dispute the "laws" of any "*reformed*" legislature, which shall *not* be specially authorized by ourselves: what! do not they themselves declare by their own "laws," that nothing—no every day—trifling transaction, done on our behalf by any third party, is binding on us, without our specific warrant of attorney, or special appointment of agency! and must we then be bound against our will—against all principles of *right, morality*, and equity, in matters of life, and freedom, and happiness, by the independent "law" of perfect strangers! no, their own "laws" find them *guilty* of oppression and injustice—their own "laws" justify our resistance and defiance! numbers, either on one side or the other, cannot, in a moral point of view, alter the case: whether there be only one tyrant and millions of

FIGURE 7.2
Source: Bodleian Library, Johnson, d. 383(3)

By the 1830s, the early reformist types of argument became overlaid with a more radical critique of capitalism as a whole. The focus of attack for many radical publications switched from political oppression to the new commercial system and the particular inequalities produced by the emergent economic and industrial order and the law. Increasingly, the papers called for mass agitation and the power of united

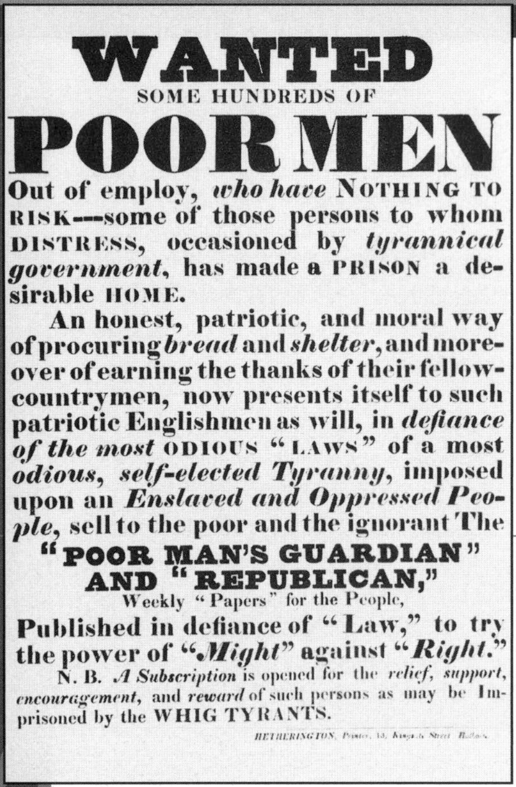

WANTED
SOME HUNDREDS OF
POOR MEN

Out of employ, *who have* NOTHING TO RISK---some of those persons to whom DISTRESS, occasioned by *tyrannical government*, has made a PRISON a desirable HOME.

An honest, patriotic, and moral way of procuring *bread* and *shelter*, and moreover of earning the thanks of their fellow-countrymen, now presents itself to such patriotic Englishmen as will, in *defiance of the most* ODIOUS "LAWS" *of a most odious, self-elected Tyranny*, imposed upon an *Enslaved and Oppressed People*, sell to the poor and the ignorant The

"POOR MAN'S GUARDIAN" AND "REPUBLICAN,"
Weekly "Papers" for the People,

Published in defiance of "Law," to try the power of "*Might*" against "*Right.*"

N. B. *A Subscription* is opened for the *relief, support, encouragement*, and *reward* of such persons as may be Imprisoned by the WHIG TYRANTS.

HETHERINGTON, Printer, 13, Kingsgate Street Holborn.

FIGURE 7.3
Source: Bodleian Library, John Johnson Collection

action of the working and labouring classes. Some of the most famous radical titles are associated with this period (Figures 7.2 and 7.3). The *Poor Man's Guardian* (1831), *Working Man's Friend* (1832), *Destructive* (1832), *Porcupine* (1833) and the *Gauntlet* (1833) all enjoyed high circulations by the standards of the day. In order to evade prosecution for not paying the stamp tax, some publications were printed either on cloth, like the *Political Handkerchief* (1831), or on a thin wooden veneer, like the *Political Touchwood* (1830).

Circulations for radical papers such as the *Poor Man's Guardian* are estimated to exceed 16 000 copies for some editions. This figure, high by comparison with other publications of the time, must be multiplied by the actual readership of each copy:

even if a cautious estimate of ten readers per copy is taken as the norm for radical papers such as the Northern Star and its successor, Reynolds News, each reached at their peak, before the repeal of the stamp duty, half a million readers when the population of England and Wales over the age of 14 was little over 10 million.
                          Curran and Seaton (1991), p.14

From the late 1840s onwards, however, the power of this type of newspaper began to decline. Some titles became affiliated to organised labour and union movements and, rather than advocating total change in society, they argued instead for practical reform. The decline in radical publications is also explained in a number of other ways.

From the 1830s onwards, the radical press had to compete for sales with new publications which were stamped and legal and aimed at a more popular, educational or entertainment market. These appeared as weekly, instructive periodicals or as popular Sunday newspapers: *Lloyd's Weekly News*, the *Illustrated London News* and the *News of the World* all developed large, popular circulations during this period (Figures 7.4 and 7.5). The opposition to the stamp tax, or the 'tax on knowledge' as it became known, increased, and it became recognised that, contrary to its intended functions, it depressed the sales of the legal and respectable papers rather than those which continued unstamped. The solution to this paradox, for those in authority, lay in the reduction and then removal of the tax, which was finally repealed in 1855. As prices dropped and new technologies of production made possible cheaper, faster, more efficient processes, advertising came to play a central role in determining profitability, establishing what Curran and Seaton (1991) have called a 'new licensing system'. Newspapers like the *Daily Telegraph* (1855) championed new forms of popular daily journalism that developed first in the Sunday press, often illustrated, and featuring crime, sports stories and fashion reports, for instance. Newspapers came to depend upon large-scale investment, and became businesses. The latter half of the nineteenth century saw the continued expansion of this popular market, in part assisted by growing levels of literacy.

FIGURE 7.4
Source: Bodleian Library, Johnson, d. 405–407

FIGURE 7.5
Source: Tim O'Sullivan

Activity 7.6

Choose one particular newspaper, local or national, and investigate its history. Research the key elements which have shaped its growth and development.

Using local library facilities, examine some of the different types of newspaper which were produced in your own locality or region during the nineteenth century. Visits to local newspaper archives can provide additional resources.

To what extent do radical publications exist today? In what ways do they differ from the earlier types of publication discussed above?

Choose some examples of popular papers from the late nineteenth century. How do they compare with the popular press of today?

More generally, research the history of tabloid and broadsheet newspapers and their forms of news in the last 20 years.

The Development of British Cinema from the 1890s to the 1920s

> An historical survey needs to begin with the problem of how the cinema came into existence and to consider the reasons why certain potentials were realised and others ignored.
>
> *Armes (1978), p. 7*

There is some debate over the first cinematic performance in Britain. The first projected moving photographic picture show to a paying audience in Britain is generally recognised to have taken place at the London Polytechnic, Regent Street, in February 1896. This was a screening organised by the British representative of the French Lumière brothers, Louis and Auguste, who had staged what is generally regarded as the very first cinematic showing in the world, involving projection and audience payment, in Paris, December 1895. While this event is regarded as the forerunner of cinema, it is important to note that many other inventors and entrepreneurs across Europe and in the USA were on the brink of claiming to be the first to exhibit moving pictures. In 1894, the first English Kinetoscope Parlour had opened. This offered customers the chance to try Thomas Edison's patent kinetoscope, which was a coin-in-the-slot machine for viewing animated photographs.

The cinema is generally regarded as a means of modern mass communication which was invented. The technical development of *film* and the apparatus to project moving images were the result of processes of invention; however, the *cinema*, as a social institution, was discovered and evolved to realise the potentials of the technologies in particular ways. It did not emerge 'naturally' or 'pre-given' from the technologies. The principles underlying visual projection had been known and operated for centuries before the 1890s. The camera obscura, for example – a darkened room into which light passed through a small hole or lens, producing an inverted but projected picture on the wall opposite – had been used in Italy in the sixteenth century. Many inventions, including those central to the early development of cinematography, are best viewed as parts of complex and interwoven relationships:

> Cinematography was unusually the by-product of such various developments as the search for new types of explosives, the industrialisation of agriculture, and the invention of a new material for printers' rollers.
>
> *Chanan (1980), p. 10*

Important influences on the emergence of moving picture technologies prior to this period include:

1 *Developments in photography* from the 1820s onwards. These include not only technical innovations but also consideration of the impact of photography on the visual arts and systems of representation.

2 *Developments in the 'science of perception'*. From the early nineteenth century some scientists had experimented with optical devices in the search for a more adequate understanding of how people 'saw' their environment and the world around them. Several experiments were conducted which examined optical illusions, and the machines produced to test scientific hypotheses were later exploited in the Victorian, middle-class fascination for parlour games and spectacles. The bioscope and early animation machines were developed partly with this scientific impetus and social/commercial application in mind.

3 *Developments in the 'scientific study of motion'.* These were greatly assisted by, and in turn perfected, cameras and other photographic technologies. The work of some physiologists and photographers in Europe and the United States became concerned with capturing motion on **film** as realistically as possible.

4 *Pre-existing forms of exhibition and spectacle*, which included a diverse number of influences. Puppet shows and peep shows were popular much earlier than the nineteenth century. Theatrical traditions and devices, often using sophisticated lighting techniques, were also an important consideration. Of these precursors of the modern cinematic experience, one of the most important was the Magic Lantern, with which the principle of visual projection, albeit of still images, was firmly established. Throughout the nineteenth century Magic Lanterns were developed to produce more and more sophisticated effects, some involving simple types of movement. The lantern and its applications developed, as Chanan has noted, somewhere 'between science and magic'. It was employed as a means of entertainment in music halls and fairgrounds, as a means of instruction, typically in the lecture hall, and as a domestic toy. Of these settings, the music hall and the travelling fairground became major exhibition centres for magic lantern shows, introducing the idea of frequent and reproducible visual performances: spectacles, often introduced by showmen, for which audiences paid money.

> *In the few years immediately before and after the Lumière brothers' invention in 1895, critics, journalists, and the pioneer cinematographers disagreed considerably among themselves as to the social function that they attributed to, or predicted, for the new machine; whether it was a means of preservation or of making archives, whether it was an auxiliary technology for research and teaching in sciences like botany or surgery; whether it was a new form of journalism, or an instrument of sentimental devotion, either private or public, which could perpetuate the living image of the dear departed one, and so on. That, over all these possibilities, the cinema could evolve into a machine for telling stories had never been considered.*
>
> *Metz (1974), p. 93*

It was, however, the ability to tell stories, recognised and developed by the traditions and expanding industries of popular entertainment, motivated principally by commercial gain and opportunity, which accounted for the very rapid take-off of cinema as a mass medium. By the end of 1896, only months after the initial public performance of film in Britain, moving pictures were part of many music hall shows up and down the country (Figures 7.6 and 7.7). The spectacle of moving pictures was augmented by music and often by live, spoken commentary or narrative to accompany the visual performance.

FIGURE 7.6
Source: D.J. Wendon, The Birth of the Movies, E.P. Dutton & Co., 1974

To-Night ! To-Night !

CALDER'S FAMOUS
CINEMATOGRAPH
AND
Popular Concert.

Don't miss seeing the Grand NEW PICTURES of

THE DREYFUS COURT MARTIAL.

The Prince of Wales in Edinburgh.
Sir Redvers Buller Embarking for Transvaal.
Scenes at the Highland Brigade Camp.
The Invercharron Gathering.
The Grand Fire Dance.
Barnum & Bailey's Procession.
The Mysterious Astrologer's Dream.
Spendid Train Scenes.
Grand Coloured Dances.
Comicalities and Burlesque Scenes, &c., &c.

Pictures of absorbing interest and Astounding Transformations.

SPLENDID • CONCERT
By First-Class Artistes.

DOORS OPEN AT 7.30.   CONCERT AT 8 P.M.
Popular Prices See Bills.

A BRIGHT UP TO DATE SPARKLING ENTERTAINMENT

FIGURE 7.7
A poster advertising a cinematographic show. The trial and imprisonment of Alfred Dreyfus was a cause célèbre in France in the 1890s *Source:* D.J. Wendon, The Birth of the Movies, E.P. Dutton & Co., 1974

This expansion in exhibition continued with accelerating speed and profitability into the 1900s. Renting and hiring circuits developed to supply and distribute films. Specialised premises and commercial interests pulled the exhibition of films out of music halls, first into vacant shops, known as 'shop shows' or 'penny gaffs', and after 1906 into custom-built premises – 'picture palaces', 'bijoux palaces' and 'majestics' (Figure 7.8). By 1909, largely to regulate the size of auditoria, but also to introduce safety regulations concerning cinema assemblies, the First Cinematographic Act was passed in Parliament. In this year, estimates suggest that British production amounted to only about 20 per cent of films shown in British cinemas, and that 40 per cent were French, 30 per cent American and 10 per cent Italian.

By 1910, some 1600 cinemas were in existence in Britain, and, by the outbreak of the First World War in 1914, this figure had jumped to 4 000. The Cinema Commission of 1917 estimates annual weekly attendances at cinemas as 7–8 million pre-1914. It reported attendances of 20 million per week in 1917. By the end of the war, British cinema exhibition had developed into a major industry, based on a cinematic form inconceivable in the 1890s – the extended fictional feature film. This was reliant upon an increasingly complex product: melodramas, comedies, westerns, travelogues and superspectaculars were some of the early genres of popular 'silent' film (Figure 7.9). By the outbreak of war in 1914, however, Hollywood-produced American films accounted for over half of the domestic market: 'Ever since 1913 British audiences have seen more American than British films. Hollywood imagery, values and myths have for over sixty years been part of the imaginative and fantasy furniture of British minds' (Tunstall 1983, p. 55). This trend – a domestic market dominated by overseas, mainly American

FIGURE 7.8
Source: D.J. Wendon, The Birth of the Movies, E.P. Dutton & Co., 1974

FIGURE 7.9
Source: D.J. Wendon, The Birth of the Movies, E.P. Dutton & Co., 1974

productions – continued into the 1920s and, arguably, to the present day. Government legislation in 1927, the year of the first 'talkie', attempted to guarantee and preserve a quota of the home market for domestic production. Cinema attendances grew rapidly in the 1920s and throughout the inter-war period, becoming 'the essential social habit of the age' (Taylor, 1965).

Activity 7.7

Conduct some independent research on the early history of cinema in Britain. Oral history and local library and historical archives can be useful sources.

Research and build up a history of cinema from the earliest years onwards in your own local town or area. Supplement this where possible with interviews and local newspaper archive research.

Investigate the reasons why the American Hollywood industry, and its films, have dominated British exhibition and production from the 1920s onwards.

Drawing on your own research and reading, complete the history of cinema in Britain from the 1920s to the present.

Public Service Broadcasting

The concept of Public Service Broadcasting has been central to the idea of broadcasting in Britain since its very earliest days in the 1920s. The notion was championed by the BBC's first Director General, John Reith, and has served as a model for radio and television broadcasting in Britain, and in many other parts of the world. Central to the concept of Public Service Broadcasting in Britain is the licence fee that everyone who owns a television set is required to pay.

The concept of Public Service Broadcasting, and the notion of the licence fee that underpins it, have been regularly called into question. Since the 1980s various governments have attempted to 'deregulate' and commercially open up broadcasting and this, coupled with the expansion of satellite, cable and digital systems, has meant that the concept of Public Service Broadcasting is in a perpetual state of crisis. In recent years governments and broadcasters, and particularly the BBC, have had to redefine the concept for the changing values of the twenty-first century.

As we live in an increasingly multi-media environment, broadcast audiences are becoming fragmented. Broadcasters can no longer address a single national or mass audience, but rather a diverse range of audience groups, many of whom have access to multichannel, digital radio, television and online services. They are increasingly seen as consumers, rather than citizens, who are able to choose and to pay for what they select as extra entertainment and information.

1920 – 1945: The BBC – the voice of the nation

From the beginning of broadcasting, governments have tried to control its application and forms. As early as 1904 the Postmaster General took responsibility for the allocation of broadcasting frequencies to avoid the 'chaos of the airwaves' that the introduction of commercial radio had created in America.

In 1922 a group of radio equipment manufacturers, called the British Broadcasting Company, were given a licence to run a monopoly broadcasting service in London, Manchester and Birmingham.

The general manager of this new company was John Reith. All radio or 'wireless' set owners were supposed to pay a fee of ten shillings (50p) which was collected by the Post Office, who then passed on half to the company. As Scannell and Cardiff (1991) note, without any real discussion or ideological rationale two key ideas that were to shape broadcasting had been established: the annual licence fee and the notion of a national monopoly.

In 1925 the government concluded that, although radio was too important to be left in the hands of a commercial company and that it was inappropriate in a democracy for broadcasting to be under direct state control, there was a need to maintain some kind of regulation on who provided what types of radio service. As a compromise, by Royal Charter, the British Broadcasting Company was changed from a commercial company into an independent and publically-funded organisation, the British Broadcasting Corporation, acting as a monopoly and 'as a trustee for the national interest' (HMSO, 1966).

The Royal Charter established the BBC's constitution: there would be twelve governors (chosen from the 'great and the good') appointed by the Privy Council for a five-year period. The governors would in turn appoint a Director General who would be responsible for the day-to-day management of the BBC. John Reith was appointed the first Director General of the Corporation and this structure has continued into the twenty-first century.

John Reith is an interesting character whose beliefs influenced the development of British broadcasting from the 1920s up to the present time. He argued for a particular purpose for broadcasting. In a book *Broadcasting over Britain* (1924) he said that to have used 'so great a scientific invention' as radio just for entertainment would have been 'an insult to the character and intelligence of the people' (Reith 1924, p. 17). This philosophy for public service broadcasting is often summed up as being 'to educate, to inform and to entertain'. Some commentators suggest that Reith saw the BBC 'as if it were a kind of national church, its producers a priesthood and himself as a kind of cardinal or pope, at times even perhaps a Messiah' (Smith 1986, p. 8).

Like many others in the 1920s and 1930s, Reith was concerned that the 'average' citizen was ill-equipped for the demands of democracy. He believed that the BBC, through the new medium of radio, presented a great opportunity for helping the less educated and the less informed, and for both 'bringing culture to the masses' and 'bringing the nation together'. The BBC bought national events to a wider, national, public. Sporting occasions like the Oxford and Cambridge Boat Race or the Derby were broadcast by the BBC and people throughout the country tuned in to listen. The BBC had broadcast live King George V's opening of the Wembley Exhibition in 1924 and started the annual Christmas Day speech by the monarch in 1936. It also routinely broadcast other grand state and civic occasions. These broadcasts meant that many people throughout Britain heard for the first time the voices of their kings and/or queen and leading politicians. In this way, according to Cardiff and Scannell, the BBC helped create a sense of a national community.

Reith's vision was that the BBC had a responsibility to unify the whole nation in a public service where everyone had access to a diversity of high-quality programmes and reliable, objective news. He believed that the new medium of radio should be used as an influence to develop the nation's citizens. It has been argued that Reith's vision for British broadcasting was based on an idealised image of a middle-class family sitting at home listening to the radio; a small part of the larger national family united through broadcasting (see Figure 7.10).

One of the ways in which Reith's vision of radio broadcasting was realised was through the idea of 'mixed programming' and his abhorrence of what was called 'tap listening'. This was a term used in the BBC during the pre-Second World War period to describe the way listeners might be tempted to turn on the radio, like a tap, and leave it running as 'background accompaniment to work or domestic activities' (O'Sullivan 1995, p. 178). The idea that the listeners might use the radio for indiscriminate background listening was strongly disapproved of. The BBC therefore used various strategies including long pauses, up to five minutes of silence, to 'interrupt' the broadcasts to make it difficult for the listener to do this.

FIGURE 7.10
First issue of The Radio Times, 28 September 1923
Source: Radio Times

The imagined ideal of the radio listener, 'his' needs and the function of the BBC were illustrated by this notion of mixed programming. The listener, like reading a broadsheet newspaper, would work through the evening's schedules going from news and current affairs to political articles, to sports reports and entertainment or perhaps to an arts feature or a learned talk equivalent to a newspaper's leader or editorial. It was envisaged that, having just listened to a programme that the listener had chosen to listen to, that 'he' might remain listening and discover something else that, although not chosen, was of interest and value; and so by chance the nation as a whole would slowly come to be familiar with, and appreciate, the great classical works of art and literature.

In retrospect Reith's attitude can seem to be paternalistic and elitist especially in his attitude to radio listeners. Reith did not trust the public to make their own cultural choices, instead he argued that they needed to be guided and that rather than give the public what they wanted Reith suggested that 'few know what they want, and very few what they need.' (Reith, 1924)

According to many commentators, one of the strongest criticisms that has been made of Reith was his apparent political naivety. Although he had a clear idea of what broadcasting should offer in cultural and moral terms, he never questioned its political role, perhaps assuming that 'independence' guaranteed impartiality. Partly because of the limits the charter placed upon the BBC's ability to deal with issues of 'controversy' and partly because of Reith's identification of a national culture that included the state, the church, the monarchy and his own 'elite' upper-middle-class Calvinist values, the BBC always seemed firmly to support the state, the establishment, and what was often identified as the 'national interest'. Reith believed that the BBC should be above political fighting and at the time of the General Strike in 1926 he stated that, 'Since the BBC was a national institution and since the Government in this crisis was acting for the people ... the BBC was for the Government in the crisis too' (quoted in Garnham 1980).

One of the main legacies of Reith's time as Director General is the acceptance of the system of financing the BBC through the licence fee. As Garnham points out, the BBC has never been financed independently by the licence fee but rather by the government deciding how much that licence fee should be. The BBC is therefore dependent upon the 'goodwill' of the government when its charter comes up for renewal and sometimes this goodwill has been absent. The BBC is also dependent upon the ideological imperatives of whatever political party is currently in power. During the 1980s, when the philosophy of 'deregulation' and 'market forces' was paramount, the licence fee's increases were severely limited and the BBC was put under considerable financial pressure to increase its income from commercial activities. Other aspects of the power that any government of the day has over the BBC include the appointment of governors, the right to veto the broadcast of any programme and to insist on the right to broadcast any message of its own.

The paradoxes associated with Reith are perhaps well illustrated by his attitude to *Children's Hour* which he introduced in 1922 (only eight days after the British Broadcasting Company was registered). *Children's Hour* was a 'miniature BBC'. Reith assumed that listening for children of 'well-to-do' families would take its place amongst the carefully supervised routines of lessons, recreation, pastimes and hobbies. For the children of the poor Reith saw *Children's Hour* as a 'kind of antidote' to the harm done to them by their living conditions, a 'happy alternative to the squalor of the streets and backyards' (Reith quoted in Oswell, 1998). This can be read as both patronising and elitist but in attempting to address children in working-class families in the 1930s, and to improve their domestic and cultural life, it can also perhaps be seen as both ambitious and admirable. However misguided Reith may have been it is undeniable that it is mainly through his vision back in the 1920s that the BBC is today so highly respected around the world.

Activity 7.8

Investigate the amount of children's broadcasting that exists on radio and television. Are there any significant differences between the types of programmes that are offered by the BBC, terrestial commercial television and the digital channels? What do you think are the reasons for these differences? To what extent can these programmes be described as offering a public service?

By the time John Reith retired from the BBC in 1938, nearly nine million radio licences were being issued annually (representing nearly three-quarters of all households in Britain). The BBC was established as 'the voice of the nation'.

There was, however, competition from commercial radio stations broadcasting from France and Ireland. In 1925 there had been a fifteen-minute fashion feature broadcast in English from the Eiffel Tower, sponsored by Selfridges. It was organised by Captain Leonard Plugge, who in 1932 established the International Broadcasting Company that broadcast regularly from Radio Normandie in Fecamp, France. In 1933 both Radio Luxembourg from Europe and Radio Athlone in the Irish Free-State started broadcasting across Britain.

All of these services, to some degree or another, were available in England, particularly in the South and West. Radio Luxembourg had pirated a long-wave signal and generally could be received throughout the country. It was by far the most popular of these commercial stations, both with advertisers and with the domestic audience. The commercial radio stations, perhaps because they were not burdened with ideas of defending or promoting cultural standards, seemed more able to address the listening needs of the mass of British listeners in a way that the BBC could, or would, not. Their presenters became well-known personalities, unlike the BBC announcers who remained anonymous, and they had a more conversational mode of address, talked over the music and spoke to listeners by name. The continental stations also offered 'American-style' programmes including soap operas and dance band music.

A particular attraction of these radio services for listeners in Britain was the alternative that it offered to the Reithian Sunday. Sunday was the one day of the week when the listening population had time to listen and they wanted 'relaxing fare' rather than 'wholesome brightness'. What was available to them on BBC radio was Reith's notion of what was suitable for the Sabbath, religious broadcasts, talks and classical music. Initially broadcasting did not start until 12.30pm (presumably on the assumption that the majority of the audience would have been at a Sunday morning church service) and had a break at 6.00pm, so as again not to be in competition with evening church services. The foreign commercial stations took advantage of this and soon, on Sundays, the number of listeners to these stations far outweighed the number of listeners for the BBC's services.

Second World War

With the crisis brought about by the outbreak of war in 1939, and particularly after Dunkirk in 1940, the BBC's role had to change. The audience could no longer be seen as the comfortable middle classes, actual or aspiring, but instead had to include workers in munitions factories, soldiers, sailors and airmen, as well as their wives, sisters and girlfriends, who were now being encouraged to move out of their domestic world and work in the factories or on the land. Instead of individual middle-class families sitting around the fireside, the audience had to be conceived of as a national, communal one in factory canteens or military camps. In an attempt to address this 'new' audience, the BBC's newly formed Listener Research Unit actually asked people what they wanted and reported back on the popularity or otherwise of particular programmes.

The idea of 'segmenting' the BBC's provision to meet different audience requirements meant that its National Service was split into two: the Home Service, which continued to follow the style of the old National Service closely with its talks, plays and classical music, and the new, lighter, more popular Forces Programme, which was aimed specifically at this new working-class audience. The Forces Programme took on many of the populist styles and personalities of Radios Luxembourg and Normandy, including American shows by Bob Hope and Jack Benny, in an attempt to please listeners as well as boosting their morale.

The style and content of the language became more popular and down-to-earth, with slang, humour, innuendo and occasionally some irreverence or vulgarity. Shows were often broadcast from factory canteens or barracks, and the 'live' audience was heard either through their laughter and applause or when 'ordinary' members of the public spoke directly into the microphone to make requests or to send messages. New programmes like *We Speak for Ourselves* allowed working-class people to be heard for the first time on radio, and fictional drama series like *The Plums* were based on a supposedly 'typical' working-class family and tried to reflect the realities of urban wartime life: bombings, rationing, shift work and members of the family fighting away from home. In order to maintain morale and the war effort at home and abroad, the BBC had to identify with popular, public regional culture, especially in music and comedy (see Figure 7.11).

FIGURE 7.11
People in a London pub listening to a broadcast by Winston Churchill in August 1941
Source: Hulton Getty Picture Collection Ltd

The need for news and information during the war resulted in the rapid growth of the BBC's own news-gathering service. Topicality became an important news value: 'on-the-spot' reports from journalists accompanying troops in France and Germany towards the end of the war had a freshness and immediacy that would have been impossible pre-1938.

1945–1990: Expansion and Competition

After the war this new 'popularist' philosophy remained: the Forces Programme was renamed the Light Programme and many of its shows carried on. The Home Service also continued and the Third Programme was introduced in 1946, most closely reflecting Reith's original aim of offering 'high cultural quality'. These three stations – the Light Programme, the Home Service and the Third Programme – continued the BBC's monopoly of national radio and remained unchanged until 1967 when Radios 1, 2, 3 and 4 were introduced.

The BBC had begun broadcasting television regularly in 1936, although the broadcasts were stopped in 1939 for the duration of the Second World War. After 1945 the BBC resumed its TV transmissions and until 1955 retained a monopoly over radio and television.

One of the events that brought people into contact with television for the first time was the live coverage of the Coronation of Elizabeth II in 1953. It was watched by 50 per cent of the population, about 25 million people – twice the radio audience. The coverage lasted all day and used 21 cameras spread around the centre of London and including, after some resistance, cameras in Westminster Abbey. The commentary was by Richard Dimbleby, who from that point on became a household name and the 'voice of the BBC'.

Activity 7.9

Research what BBC Television was like before the introduction of commercial television. Look in libraries to see what information is available: there may be old copies of the Radio Times, or old newspapers may have details of daily broadcasts. Interview someone who used to watch television in its early days.

Try to find out the types of programme being broadcast, the time slots or scheduling of these programmes (look particularly at Sundays), how people 'consumed' television in those days and how that is different to the way we use television today.

In 1954 the Conservative government introduced a Television Act which proposed the setting up of television broadcasting services 'additional to those of the BBC and of high quality ... which may include advertisements' (HMSO, 1966). The Television Act included the remit that commercial ITV companies too should offer a 'public service' and the new services were also required to 'inform, educate and entertain' the national audience with due regard for impartiality and balance. This was to be done by providing religious and educational programming as well as local and national news, including a half-hour national news bulletin during the evening peak viewing hours.

This was one of ITV's most important early contributions to the development of public service television, its current affairs and news broadcasts, presented by Independent Television News (ITN). They introduced probing interviews and on-the-spot reports, which were very different from the BBC's deferential attitude to politicians and the practice of allowing them to give their viewpoints unchallenged. Commentators like ITN's Robin Day were not so deferential in their questioning of politicians and the reporting of 'great' events like the state opening of Parliament. Through ITN, commercial television offered an alternative to the reverence of Richard Dimbleby's BBC commentaries.

The new television companies, however, were to be 'independent', that is, free of the licence fee. They received their income from the selling of advertising space and in return had to pay a levy to the government based on each company's advertising revenue. Any money left over would be profit paid to the company's shareholders. Income for commercial television was therefore dependent upon the number of viewers, the 'ratings', and how much advertisers could be charged for airtime. ITV's scheduling policy was therefore one of broadcasting popular programmes at peak times and those of a more minority interest on the periphery of the schedules. As a result one of the first genres of programmes to become established were American-style quiz-shows like *Double Your Money*, *Take Your Pick* and *Opportunity Knocks*.

Many writers have referred to the 1960s as the 'Golden Age' of television. BBC television in particular, under the Director General Sir Hugh Greene, could take risks because it was financially secure with its guaranteed funding. During this period the BBC can be seen to have played a major role in confronting viewers with the social changes that had taken place during the previous decades. Just as radio in the 1930s had brought its version of the realities of unemployment in the north of England or slum conditions in the cities to Home Counties audiences, so the television drama *Cathy Come Home* (1966) exposed the plight of the homeless in what prime minister Harold Macmillan had called, in 1959, a society where people had 'never had it so good' (Figure 7.12).

FIGURE 7.12
Cathy Come Home, 1966
Source: BBC Picture Archive

Television genres that are familiar today were becoming established. Satirical programmes like *That Was The Week That Was*, soap operas like *Coronation Street*, police series like *Z Cars* and situation comedies like *Steptoe and Son* all provided entertainment but at the same time allowed 'ordinary domestic life' to be shown – what Richard Hoggart (1957) and Raymond Williams (1965) called the 'lived experience', the 'popular' culture, the everyday life of everyday people. Television could be seen to be discovering and disclosing information and images about segments of society that had either been ignored or else portrayed only in the rather cosy images of *Dixon of Dock Green* or Ealing comedies, or as second-best imitations of 'high culture'.

This 'domestication' of television can be seen to reflect both the daily experiences of the majority of people and the method of their consumption of television: sitting at home watching other people, real or fictitious, sitting in their homes, keeping each other company, helping to cope with life, and the next day sharing the experience with others, talking about what they had watched the night before. Television and domestic life became interwoven; television also became part of national and personal identity and generational memory (for example, the way in which people are able to remember how they first heard the news of the assassination of President Kennedy in 1963, or in 1997, watched the funeral of Diana, Princess of Wales or, in 2001, saw the events of 11 September unfold live on television).

Although television appeared to be operating under two different systems, BBC and ITA, many analysts have noted that the people who managed these systems still appeared to be from the same social background: public-school educated, university-trained, and with similar ideas about 'public service' and 'public interest' (see Kumar, 1977). Both systems had similar boards of management drawn from the same small and restricted social elite. The programme makers often moved between the two organisations and having been trained by the BBC, shared a common professional 'ethos'. Both organisations were dependent upon the goodwill of the government for their finances, the BBC through the increases of the licence fee and the ITA through the advertising levy that the broadcasting companies had to pay to the government.

When, in 1962, the Pilkington Committee was charged with investigating the service offered by the ITV companies, it concluded that they equated 'quality with box-office success' and 'failed to live up to [their] responsibilities as a public service' (Garnham, 1978). Because of this, according to Goodwin and Whannel (1990), ITV was not allowed to extend its services and the next allocated television channel was given instead to the BBC. BBC2 started transmission in 1964 and pioneered colour transmission in 1967. ITV had to wait until the Annan Report on Broadcasting (1977) and almost twenty years before it was allowed a second commercial channel. The 1981 Broadcasting Act granted the new franchise to the ITV companies, and Channel 4 in England and Scotland (S4C in Wales) started broadcasting in 1982.

Both BBC2 and Channel 4 were also 'public service' channels, set up to provide an alternative to mainstream stations. BBC2 was intended to counter the popular mainstream. Channel 4 was specifically required to 'cater for tastes, interests and audiences not served by ITV (or other television channels), to innovate in the form and content of programmes and to devote a proportion of its airtime to educational programming' (Channel 4, 1991). In Wales, S4C has a remit to produce Welsh-language programmes. Channel 4 is a 'publisher broadcaster': the only programme it makes is *Right to Reply*, and all others are commissioned and produced by independent programme makers, or other television companies including those imported from abroad.

Activity 7.10

Both BBC2 and Channel 4 were introduced to cater for minority interests and special needs groups. Look through past and present schedules for both BBC2 and Channel 4 and try to assess to what extent these channels have fulfilled their remits.

Channel 4 was originally funded by a levy on all the ITV companies, who in return sold and shared the advertising space on the new channel. This guaranteed Channel 4 an income and released it from direct commercial pressures. However, under the 1990 Broadcasting Act, the channel became responsible for its own funding by selling its own airtime. Many commentators feel that this has resulted in Channel 4 being more commercial, less adventurous and failing to meet its public service remit. They point to the high price the channel was prepared to pay to keep the popular American shows like *ER* and *Friends*, as well as the launch of *E4* and increasing numbers of early-evening sitcoms and talk shows (such as *Richard and Judy* 'poached' from ITV), and recent shows like *Big Brother* and *Ibiza Uncovered*, as evidence of Channel 4's more populairst scheduling. In 2002 it was claimed that Channel 4, in an auction against the BBC, paid over £800 000 per episode for the latest series of *The Simpsons*. Channel 4, however, has continued to lose out against increasing competition and in 2002 decided to close down its film operation, Film Four, and has undertaken a radical restructuring of its schedules; most notably axing the soap opera *Brookside*.

The Conservative Governments in the 1980s were critical of the licence fee which they described as an 'indirect tax', especially unfair on those who did not use the BBC's radio and television services. In 1986 the Government set up an inquiry, the Peacock Committee, to investigate whether some of the

BBC's services could be sold off or whether the BBC could be financed by advertising. In 1988 the Conservative Government published a White Paper, 'Broadcasting in the 1990s', which highlighted three key Conservative concepts for broadcasting: competition, choice and quality. The free-market philosophy behind the White Paper suggested that if competition among broadcasters was increased then listeners and viewers would have more choice; this would in turn mean that only the successful stations would attract high enough ratings to survive and bring in the required advertising revenue. To attract the higher ratings broadcasters would have to be more responsive to audience demands, and so viewers would benefit from improved quality.

Activity 7.11

Try to assess the success or otherwise of the government's aim to increase competition, choice and quality. Look specifically at either television or radio and consider the following questions:

● In what ways can competition between services be considered to have increased since 1990? Are there any ways in which competition could be considered to have decreased?

● Do viewers or listeners feel that they now have more choice? Has there been any reduction in choice?

● Are viewers and listeners aware of an increase in quality on new or existing services? Is there any evidence to suggest that there may have been a decrease in quality in some services?

● Is there a difference between the ways the Broadcasting Acts have affected radio and the ways they have affected television?

● How have Channel 5, Sky and other satellite and digital services impacted on choice, competition and quality?

1990–Present: Public Service Broadcasting in the Digital Age

The period since the 1990 Broadcasting Act has seen both a substantial expansion of the broadcasting services available to audiences in Britain and a merging and concentration of media companies. Broadcasting in the twenty-first century is going through a radical change of emphasis that seems to finally mark the end of the 'Reithian' philosophy of public service that has underpinned British broadcasting since the 1920s. The ideal of 'free' quality broadcasting available to all irrespective of ability to pay more than the licence fee, has been increasingly challenged by an expanding range of specialist radio and television channels. These services tend to represent a niche view of broadcasting or are more concerned with 'narrowcasting', ratings and advertising-income rather than quality and expect their audiences to pay for what they want. Instead of being seen as a nation of citizens, viewers and listeners are increasingly being seen as consumers in a variety of particular niche markets.

British broadcasting organisations increasingly compete with large multinational companies like News International or Time Warner AOL from America, Bertelsmann from Germany and Matsushita from Japan. These companies have the financial reserves to be able to develop new media markets, particularly digital and Internet services and to buy up other smaller organisations. There is a drive towards 'convergence' where the various broadcasting, telecommunications and online services will combine with computer companies to provide a 'one box does it all' service.

Since its creation from the merger of BSB and SKY in 1990, BSkyB has become dominant in the British digital television market and has already switched off its analogue services. It has been successful, through its aggressive marketing, its 'free' set-top decoder boxes and cross-promotion in News International newspapers like *The Sun*, in winning digital subscribers. There have been many sports deals in cricket, boxing and football, where BSkyB has bought the exclusive rights to major events, effectively monopolising the young C2 males who will pay extra to see these events. In 1996 BSkyB paid £674 million, over a five-year period, for the exclusive right to show live Premier League football matches and in 2001 agreed to pay a further £1.1 billion for BSkyB's rights to the live broadcast of sixty six games of football per year for the next five years. BSkyB will hope to recoup these costs through advertising and additional subscribers who they hope will be prepared to pay an extra, one-off 'pay-per-view' premium to watch these matches.

This strategy of expanding the satellite subscription market by buying up more and more sporting events seems to have been very successful, and BSkyB aims to increase its numbers of digital subscribers from about 5.5 million in 2002 to 7 million by 2003. The main rival to BSkyB, ITV Digital, found that matching both the BSkyB offer of 'free' set-top decoder boxes and paying for exclusive coverage of league football matches was a strain on its financial reserves and in 2002 ITV Digital went bankrupt. It was then agreed with the government department responsible for media, the Department of Culture, Media and Sport, that the BBC would take over the ITV Digital infrastructure and, in conjunction with a few commercial channels (including, ironically, BSkyB), would offer a free, but limited, terrestrial digital television service, called Freeview.

BSkyB is estimated to be available, either by direct satellite or through cable services, in 10 million homes in Britain, and to account for about 5–6 per cent of total television viewing, although in households with satellite or cable the percentage of 'non-terrestrial' viewing is usually considerably higher, at around 40 per cent of total viewing. The Government has said that it will switch off analogue television when 95 per cent of the country has access to digital services. However, despite the apparent popularity of BBC's Freeview, many viewers seem resistant to the idea of digital television, and by the beginning of 2002 it was estimated that only 25 per cent of homes had digital services. It is unclear when the 95 per cent threshold is likely to be reached. In 2002 the annual cost of a colour television licence was £109 while the annual cost of subscribing to BSkyB Digital's full range of services was £384 per year, not including any additional pay-per-view charges. For a minority of viewers, despite the cost of these extra services, there does seem to be a perceived need for 'more choice' or something different to the terrestrial diet on offer.

Share of viewing in all UK homes						
	BBC1	BBC2	ITV	C4	C5	Total multi-channel*
1994	32.4	10.6	39.5	10.7		6.8
1995	32.2	11.2	37.2	10.9		8.5
1996	32.5	11.5	35.1	10.7		10.1
1997	30.8	11.6	32.9	10.6	3.1	11.8
1998	29.5	11.3	31.7	10.3	4.3	12.9
1999	28.4	10.8	31.2	10.3	5.4	14.0
2000	27.2	10.8	29.3	10.5	5.7	16.6
2001**	26.5	11.3	28.2	10.0	5.6	18.5

* Includes Sky, NTL, Telewest and Ondigital.
 **2001 figures are January to June

FIGURE 7.13
Source: Guardian

Activity 7.12

Investigate the costs of the various digital satellite and/or cable packages that are on offer. Analyse and compare digital and terrestrial schedules for one evening. What do subscribers pay for? Conduct some interviews to try to discover who watches digital television, why, how much they pay, and what they feel digital television services offer that analogue television does not.

The BBC does not have the same financial reserves that companies like BSkyB have and so faces difficulties in going into a 'bidding war' over particular prestigious sporting events, series or personalities (see Figure 7.14). In 2000 the BBC lost its *Match of the Day* programme when ITV won the right to broadcast Premier League matches by offering £61 million a year in comparison to BBC's bid of £40 million. As the broadcasting audience becomes increasingly segmented so the Reithian idea of one large homogenous national audience of 32 or 39 million people joining together watching the same programme becomes increasingly old-fashioned. The BBC may still regularly appear in the top five of the BARB charts with its audiences of 15 or 16 million viewers for episodes of *EastEnders,* but as Figure 7.13 demonstrates, both the BBC's and ITV's shares of the television audience as a whole are slowly decreasing. This means that it becomes increasingly difficult for the BBC to call itself the 'national' broadcaster when less than a third of the television audience is regularly watching its programmes and hence more difficult to justify a 'universal' licence fee.

The decline in audience share has also affected ITV's public service provision. As a decrease in ratings means a fall in income from advertising, the ITV companies are more concerned with making and broadcasting popular programmes rather than fulfilling any public service remit. This means that news, documentaries and current affairs programmes tend to become marginalised. ITN in particular has been criticised by the Independent Television Commission for its increasingly 'tabloid' approach to news on *News at Ten*. The ITC claims that there has been a decline in the reporting of 'hard' news such as business, politics and overseas news and a concentration instead on human interest, showbiz and sensationalist stories.

The BBC is, in theory, still very popular. The BBC attracts large audiences at times of 'national events', celebrations or crises such as the Golden Jubilee celebrations, the funeral of Princess Diana, general elections and when the English football team plays Germany. The BBC has also tried to maintain audience share through populist programming such as docusoaps and 'make-over' programmes. One advantage for the BBC is its large archive of high quality and popular programmes. As the number of television broadcasters expands so there is an increasing scarcity of good programmes. Commercial television companies are increasingly unwilling to spend large amounts of money making programmes and so rely on buying from other programme-makers. The BBC, despite 'wiping' much of its early programme archive, is in a strong position to re-run old favourites and 'classics' such as *Dad's Army, Only Fools and Horses* or *Blake's 7*.

The BBC also has a world-wide reputation and the brand name 'BBC' is a strong asset. BBC Worldwide, a commercial arm of the BBC set up to sell programmes such as *TeleTubbies* and *Walking With Dinosaurs* abroad, contributed £96 million to the BBC's income in 2001.

HOW THE BBC SPENT YOUR MONEY	
BBC1	£752m
BBC! And BBC Widescree	£30mn
BBC CHOICE	£34m
BBC NEWS 24	£50m
BBC PARLIAMENT	£2m
Digital radio	£6m
BBC ONLINE	£23m
Digital development costs	£9m
Restructuring	£31m
Corporate centre	£60m
Licence fee collection costs	£133m
BBC2	£406m
National and regional television	£185m
National, regional and local radio	£149m
BBC Radio 1	£37m
BBC Radio 2	£42m
BBC Radio 3	£62m
BBC Radio 4	£89m
BBC Radio 5 Live	£55m
Total	£2,155m

*1999 figures

FIGURE 7.14
BBC Spending Figures

The Future of Public Service Broadcasting

It is hard to predict what the future holds for public service broadcasting in Britain. In August 2000 Richard Eyre, the then chief executive of ITV, said that 'public service broadcasting will soon be dead'. However, according to Tessa Jowell, the then Minister for Culture, Media and Sport, speaking at the Radio Festival in 2001, Public Service Broadcasting is as important in the digital future as it is today: 'The BBC must be enabled to fulfil its remit in the future as it has in the past.' However, she also stated that 'Public Service Broadcasting needs to be restated and re-defined for the future that beckons.'

When broadcasting started in Britain in the 1920s the Government was keen to exercise strong control over who broadcast and to whom. Over eighty years later, however, governments are able to assert less and less direct control and are willing to leave broadcasting more open to market forces. This is particularly complicated and contradictory for the BBC, seen still as the national broadcaster and with considerable prestige and popularity both in Britain and around the world.

As part of its research for the 2002 Telecommunications Act, the Independent Television Commission asked the general public its views on public service broadcasting. Generally people spoke in favour of the concept and felt that it was a 'good thing' and should be maintained; however, the same public is also against raising the licence fee. It is also true that despite the growth in alternative digital services about 80 per cent of television viewers still watch BBC and ITV programmes, usually on analogue television sets. However, those programmes most associated with 'public service', documentaries, current affairs, religious and educational programming, are generally less popular with viewers. These programmes, both on BBC and ITV, are being increasingly marginalised in the schedules. This is part of the debate over the moving of ITV's *News at Ten*, and the moving of the BBC's *Panorama* from a weekday mid-evening slot on BBC1 to a Sunday evening slot on BBC2. The BBC is increasingly trying to make 'popular' public service programmes such as *Blue Planet*, *The Abyss*, *Walking With Dinosaurs* or *The Body* with John Cleese as well as broadcasting 'themed' nights on issues such as 'cracking crime' or the National Health Service.

Activity 7.13

Analyse the schedules of the current terrestrial television channels:

- Try to identify programmes and/or segments under the categories of entertainment/information/education.
- What is the balance between these three categories?
- Does it vary between different channels?
- Why?
- Try to identify the types of audiences aimed at by different programmes and/or segments.
- Are any particular groups predominant?
- What minority interests are excluded from the terrestrial television schedules?

The concept of public service broadcasting has been inextricably linked to the idea of a national broadcaster addressing the national audience within a national culture. However, as the cultural diversity that exists in British society develops, this idea of a unified national audience becomes less tenable. Commercial broadcasters are also less keen on the idea of a national audience as they want to maximise their viewing figures, target those sectors of the community most attractive to advertisers and address multinational consumers across a range of networks. Increasingly channels like the Discovery Channel design their programmes to be seen by, and be accessible to, audiences across the world. This is part of what drives the process known as *globalisation* (see Chapter 8).

As the terrestrial channels' share of the viewing and listening audience gets smaller it becomes increasingly harder for the BBC to justify a universal licence fee that has to be paid by everyone who watches television irrespective of what channels they are watching. Many people complain of having to pay £109 per year when they rarely watch BBC television or listen to BBC radio. Like other public services the licence fee is also a difficult one for politicians to justify and the defenders of the licence fee may be in decline. Without the licence fee, however, it is difficult to suggest other methods of financing public service broadcasting. Subscription or sponsorship are sometimes suggested as possible solutions but it is feared that only a well-off minority would pay subscription to BBC channels and it is unclear what would be left 'free' for those unwilling, or unable, to pay. Sponsorship has made considerable inroads into British broadcasting in recent years but, given the heritage of public service, remains constrained.

Activity 7.14

Consider alternative methods of financing the BBC:

What are their advantages and disadvantages?

Are there particular groups of people who might benefit from or be disadvantaged by any of these alternatives?

Are any of these alternatives a better solution than the licence fee? In what ways?

In dealing with its current situation the BBC is starting to identify particular niche markets where it may be able to maintain its public service ideal, for example in arts and cultural programming, children's television, targeting particular ethnic groups and in news. It also continues to compete aggressively on its popular terrestrial television channels. The BBC has introduced a range of new free digital radio and television services including *News 24* and *Parliament* channels, *BBC3* for 'young people' and *BBC4*, the new arts and current affairs channel, as well as two new digital television services for children, *CBBC* and *CBeebies*. New digital radio stations include *1Xtra* that specialises in new black music, *6Music*, the *Asian Network*, *BBC 7* and *Five Live Sports Extra*.

In view of Reith's endorsement of *Children's Hour* in the early days of radio, it is interesting to note the way in which the BBC is still today targeting children as part of the audience for these new digital services. *CBBC* is aimed at children between the ages of six and thirteen and offers a range of drama and documentary programmes and claims that over three-quarters of its output is produced in the UK. This is seen to be a contrast to much of children's programming on the satellite and cable channels that is primarily American cartoons. *CBeebies* is for the 'under-fives' and aims to help young children 'learn through play'. The radio station *BBC 7* also offers children's programmes, radio drama and readings and stories.

The BBC is still required to get approval from the Ministry of Culture, Media and Sport, for any changes it may wish to make to its services. When the BBC originally proposed its new youth-orientated digital television channel, *BBC3,* the Government, under pressure from the commercial television companies, objected on the grounds that the proposed schedule was too similar to existing channels such as *E4*, *MTV* and *Sky One*. The BBC had therefore to redraft its proposals to make *BBC3* more distinctive by agreeing that 80 per cent of the service's output would be material especially commissioned for *BBC3* and that it would feature new talent.

However, the BBC's attempts to move into the digital market have been criticised by commercial companies who say that it is unfair competition as the BBC is guaranteed its income from the licence fee. There has been considerable criticism of the current Director General Greg Dyke. Dyke has been accused of pursuing ratings at the expense of the BBC's public service remit by leading the BBC into an aggressive expansion of digital broadcasting, its online services, the popularist scheduling of *BBC1* and reportedly spending £10 million on a package of films including *Harry Potter and the Philosopher's Stone*.

According to Dyke, speaking at the 2001 Radio Festival, the BBC has a continued national role across the whole of Britain. He claimed that the BBC is 'part of the glue which brings the whole of the nation together' at a time when there are many pressures forcing it apart. Increasingly, however, Reith's vision of free quality broadcasting for all seems old-fashioned and obsolete. The main public service broadcaster, the BBC, still exists and most people, whether citizens or consumers, seem to want the BBC's public service broadcasting to continue. However, it is unclear what priorities will shape public service broadcasting and who its audiences will be and how it will be paid for beyond the next ten years.

Further activities

1   Read Chapter 5 and then design and conduct surveys into the viewing habits of broadcast audiences. Correlate types of service and programme with particular types of audience. Identify and explain any particular patterns or variations that occur.

2   Identify ways in which the analysis of the history of radio or television helps to explain the present organisation and output.

3   Read Chapter 5 and choose one media company to explore in more detail. Using sources of information such as *The Guardian Media Guide* try to establish the particular media interests the company may have. Suggest how this media integration benefits the company and consider to what extent it may also benefit the consumer.

4   How have changes in broadcasting organisation and legislation affected the forms and contents of programmes available today?

5   Define what is meant by 'public service broadcasting' and consider its future role in the provision of media information and entertainment services. Identify the parties involved in the debate about its future and list the arguments for and against the concept. Consider how commercial broadcasters should respond to the concept of Public Service Broadcasting.

6   Access www.bbc.co.uk/info where you will find the BBC's explanation of the licence fee and how it works. There are also copies of the latest BBC Annual Review. Summarise the debate surrounding the BBC's licence fee. Conduct research on attitudes to its continuation or replacement.

Further Reading

Barnard, S. 2000: Studying Radio. ARNOLD.

Cain, J. 1992: The BBC: 70 Years of Broadcasting. BBC.

Corner, J. 1991: Popular Television in Britain. BFI.

Crisell, A. 1997: An Introductory History of British Broadcasting. ROUTLEDGE.

Franklin B. (ed). 2001: British Television Policy: A Reader. ROUTLEDGE.

Goodwin, A. and Whannel, G. (eds). 1990: Understanding Television. ROUTLEDGE.

Hartley, I. 1983: Goodnight children…Everywhere. An Informal History of Children's Broadcasting. MIDAS BOOKS.

Hoggart, R. 1957: Uses of Literacy. PELICAN.

Jenkins, K. 1991: Re-thinking History. ROUTLEDGE.

Kumar, K. 1977: 'Holding the middle ground: the BBC, the public and the professional broadcaster' in Curran J., Gurevitch M., and Woollacott J. (eds). Mass Communication and Society. ARNOLD.

Naylor R., Driver S. and Cornford J. 2000: 'The BBC goes online: public service broadcasting in the new Media Age' in Gauntlett D. (ed). web.studies. Rewiring Media Studies for the Digital age. ARNOLD.

O'Sullivan, T. 2000: 'Media History' and 'Public Service Broadcasting' in Fleming, D. (ed): Formations: a 21st Century Media Studies Textbook. MANCHESTER UNIVERSITY PRESS.

Oswell, D. 1998: 'Early children's broadcasting in Britain: programming for a liberal democracy' in Historical Journal of Film, Radio and Television, Volume 18, Number 3. CARFAX.

Oswell D. 2002: Television, Childhood and the Home. OXFORD.

Scannell, P and Cardiff, D. 1991: A Social History of British Broadcasting Volume 1. BLACKWELL.

Scannell, P. 1996: Radio, Television and Modern Life. BLACKWELL.

Seymour-Ure, C. 1996: The British Press and Broadcasting since 1945. BLACKWELL.

Street, S. 1999: 'Radio for sale: sponsored programming in British radio during the 1930s' in Sound Journal. **www.speke.ukc.ac.uk/sais/sound-journal**

Tracey, M. 1998: The Decline and Fall of Public Service Broadcasting. OXFORD UNIVERSITY PRESS.

Williams, K. 1998: Get Me a Murder a Day! A History of Mass Communications in Britain. ARNOLD.

Williams, R. 1965: The Long Revolution. PELICAN.

General Media History

Briggs, A. and Burke, P. 2002: A Social History of the Media. POLITY.

Jenkins, K. 1991: Re-thinking History. ROUTLEDGE.

Ward, K. 1989: Mass Communications and the Modern World. MACMILLAN.

Williams, K. 1998: 'Get Me a Murder a Day': A History of Mass Communications in Britain. ARNOLD.

Winston, B. 1998: Media Technology and Society: A History from the Telegraph to the Internet. ROUTLEDGE.

Press History

Boyce, G. et al (eds). 1978: Newspaper History: From the 17th Century to the Present Day. CONSTABLE.

Bromley, M. and O'Malley, T. (eds). 1997: A Journalism Reader. ROUTLEDGE.

Cranfield, G. A. 1978: The Press and Society. LONGMAN.

Curran, J. and Seaton, J. 1997: Power Without Responsibility. ROUTLEDGE.

Franklin, B. 1997: Newszak and News Media. ARNOLD.

Harrison, S. 1974: Poor Men's Guardians. LAWRENCE & WISHART.

Lee, A.J. 1976: The Origins of the Popular Press 1855–1914. CROOM HELM.

McNair, B. 1999: News and Journalism in the UK. ROUTLEDGE.

Seymour-Ure, C. 1991: The British Press and Broadcasting Since 1945. BLACKWELL.

Thompson, E.P. 1968: The Making of the English Working Class. PENGUIN.

Tunstall, J. 1996: Newspaper Power: The New National Press in Britain. CLARENDON.

Cinema History

Abrams, N., Bell, I. and Udris, J. 2001: Studying Film, ARNOLD.

Armes, R. 1978: A Critical History of British Cinema. OXFORD UNIVERSITY PRESS.

Armes, R. 1988: On Video. ROUTLEDGE.

Barnes, J. 1976: The Beginnings of Cinema in Britain. DAVID & CHARLES.

Barr, C. 1986: All Our Yesterdays. BFI.

Chanan, M. 1980, 1995: The Dream that Kicks: The Pre-History and Early Years of Cinema in Britain. ROUTLEDGE.

Curran, J. and Porter, V. (eds). 1983: British Cinema History. WEIDENFELD & NICOLSON.

Geraghty, C. 2000: British Cinema in the Fifties. ROUTLEDGE.

Hill, J. 1986: Sex, Class and Realism: British Cinema 1956-63. BFI.

Monk, C. and Sargeant, A. (eds). 2002: British Historical Cinema. ROUTLEDGE.

Murphy, R. 1989: Realism and Tinsel: Cinema and Society in Britain 1939-48. ROUTLEDGE.

Nelmes, J. (ed). 1999: An Introduction to Film Studies. ROUTLEDGE.

Robertson, J. C. 1989: The Hidden Cinema: British Film Censorship 1913-1972. ROUTLEDGE.

Richards, J. 1984: The Age of the Dream Palace: Cinema and Society in Britain 1930-39 ROUTLEDGE.

Stead, P. 1989: Film and the Working Class. ROUTLEDGE.

Walker, A. 1986: Hollywood England. HARRAP.

Broadcasting History

Abercrombie, N. 1996: Television and Society. POLITY PRESS.

Barnard, S. 1989: On the Radio. OPEN UNIVERSITY PRESS.

Barnard, S. 2000: Studying Radio. ARNOLD.

Briggs, A. 1995: The History of Broadcasting in the UK, Volumes 1-5. OXFORD UNIVERSITY PRESS.

Clarke, S. and Horrie, C. 1994: Fuzzy Monsters: Fear and Loathing at the BBC. HEINEMANN.

Corner, J. (ed). 1991: Popular Television in Britain. BFI.

Corner, J. and Harvey, S. (eds). 1996: Television Times: A Reader. ARNOLD.

Crisell, A. 1994: Understanding Radio. Routledge.

Crisell, A. 1997: An Introduction to the History of British Broadcasting. ROUTLEDGE.

Goodwin, A. and Whannel, G. (eds). 1990: Understanding Television. ROUTLEDGE.

Hood, S. (ed). 1994: Behind the Screens. LAWRENCE & WISHART.

Kumar, K. 1977: 'Holding the middle ground: the BBC, the public and the professional broadcaster' in Curran J., Gurevitch M., and Woollacott J. (eds). Mass Communication and Society. ARNOLD.

Lewis, P. and Booth, J. 1989: The Invisible Medium: Public, Commercial and Community Radio. MACMILLAN.

O'Malley, T. 1994: Closedown? The BBC and Government Broadcasting Policy, 1979-92. PLUTO.

Scannell, P. 1996: Radio, Television and Modern Life. BLACKWELL.

Scannell, P. and Cardiff, D. 1991: A Social History of Broadcasting. BLACKWELL.

Street, S. 2002: A Concise History of British Radio. KELLY PUBLICATIONS.

Svennevig, M. 1998: Television across the Years: The British Public's View. ITC/UNIVERSITY OF LUTON PRESS.

CHAPTER EIGHT CHANGING MEDIA WORLDS

The key theme in this chapter is change, and two main areas of study dominate the agenda. Each in turn deals with a specific series of questions about the changing nature of the media, in a twenty-first century world that is changing and often unstable. The first focus for study encourages you to assess some of the issues involved in the ways in which *new media technologies* and networks are being harnessed and developed in the current phase. The central questions here concern how they are 'displacing' or impacting on older and established forms of media production and consumption, and the extent to which, as is often claimed, they offer the potential for new and diverse kinds of cultural communities and relations to emerge, locally and globally.

The second, and linked focus of the chapter entails the analysis of world-wide media networks and the continuing development of international or *global culture*. This is a process which has deep historical roots but which many commentators have suggested has accelerated rapidly from the 1960s onwards. In part, this can be accounted for in terms of the development and potentials of certain 'new' media channels and communication technologies – notably satellite and digital forms of broadcasting and the Internet – and their abilities to cross national and international boundaries. However, it is not only at the global level that new media technologies and networks are credited with the power to effect radical forms of change in our social and cultural environments. The two areas contain some of the key dilemmas and debates involved in national media policy in the current phase. Changes in media policy in the UK in the last ten years have in part been stimulated by the dynamics of new media technologies – cable, satellite and digital systems – but, as we shall suggest, there are other commercial and cultural issues at stake here too.

New Technologies for New Times?

Since the 1950s we have lived through a period which has often been characterised as a 'communications revolution', a cycle of profound and accelerating social and cultural change often attributed to the impact of new media technologies and computer networks. Developments in these technologies continue to play a key part in restructuring and changing certain aspects of the production, distribution and reception of 'old' media. Cable and satellite forms of broadcasting, video, CD and DVD recorders, computer networks, word processors and digital technologies have all in recent years been developed and marketed, adding new intensity to the media saturation of modern life. Collectively, they have contributed to an important series of changes in many households and domestic environments. These private spaces are increasingly 'multi-screen', 'multi-channel', multi-media, 'wired' or 'cabled' households, connected to what used to be referred to as the 'information super-highway', where the computer terminal, email, mobile phone and Internet operate alongside more established media. For some writers the development of these new communication systems marks a significant historical break with the past. Mark Poster (1995), for instance, has suggested that we have now entered the 'second media age', and David Gauntlett (2000) has argued that as a result, Media Studies now needs to be fundamentally overhauled, 're-wired' for the digital era of the web.

FIGURE 8.1
Source: Paul Hickinbotham

FIGURE 8.2
Source: Paul Hickinbotham

Activity 8.1

Map the changes in media technologies and forms in your own household in recent years. Start with the most recent or current changes that you can think of and work back. It may be useful to involve other, older members of your family or household in this activity and to develop a generational map. Do you know older people who can remember what home life was like before or in the early years of television, for instance? How have new media networks changed your social and cultural life? (Figures 8.1 and 8.2)

As well as having important consequences for private, leisure or 'non-work' time, the development and expansion of these new technologies have also had important implications for public institutions and affairs – in the workplace, the college or the supermarket, for instance (see Figure 8.3). In the face of these changes, it is important to bear in mind that all media – including the press, cinema, radio and television broadcasting – have relied on the development and regulation of 'new' media technologies. The printing press, the film projector, gramophone, 'wireless' and television have all, at one time, been regarded as rather marvellous, new, unfamiliar, 'one-way' machines

FIGURE 8.3
Source: Jarrod Cripps

for social and political communication. For many, they have been defined as key historical agents, capable of bringing about 'revolutionary' forms of social and political change. In the first chapter of this book, we suggested that the media, because of their public and private visibility and presence, have often operated to condense anxieties, debates and aspirations about more general forms and directions of change in the modern period.

As suggested in Chapter 7, however, the history of the various media concerns the ways in which these 'machines' have been socially and commercially organised for the provision of information, entertainment and culture. This emphasis on the commercial or political forces that constrain or condition the social realisation of the technologies is an important counter to pure *technological determinism* (see Chapter 7, p. 195). Such determinism is an oversimplified view that isolates and exaggerates the power of technologies themselves to cause effects directly, without sufficient understanding of the variety of factors which may govern the technologies' social applications and use (see Williams, 1990, and Heap *et al*, 1995).

From satellite and digital TV, to mobile telephones and the Internet, recent debates about changing media technologies have focused on a series of general themes. These have often been subject to optimistic or pessimistic forms of assessment and interpretation.

FIGURE 8.4
Source: Tim O'Sullivan

Computerisation and the consequent shifts from analogue to digital systems are at the heart of many recent developments. Computers and the telecommunications networks that also carry telephone calls, e-mails, faxes or website access provide the technical basis for a massive growth in computer-mediated communications. These have given rise to increasingly sophisticated systems for information storage, management, access and distribution and have transformed many of the processes and practices involved in older generations of media production and consumption. Developments in new information technologies have, for instance, been central in the total redesign of newsrooms – for both press and broadcast production in the last twenty years. At a general level, it is the *convergence* of these technologies within modern telecommunications' industries and their networks that is responsible for a greatly increased speed and scale of information interchange. This shift in scale concerns not only the amount of information but also its reach and destination, via satellite links and world-wide computer networks. Cable systems, based on digital broadband technologies, provide additional extensions to networks at local, regional or national levels. Furthermore, the goals of these kinds of development are ever more integrated digital systems which are capable of handling and linking up many types of information: written and spoken languages, music, still and moving visual images, data of all kinds. Previously discrete media are merging into new and hybrid, *multimedia* forms, most obviously, for example, in the cyberspace worlds of the Internet and its virtual communities. For instance, the modern networked

FIGURE 8.5
Source: Paul Hickinbotham

personal computer at home, school or work (Figure 8.4) allows the user access to a whole range of previously discrete and separate sources of information and mediated culture. This integrates books, radio, music, film/DVD/CD and television as well as online newspapers, websites, advertising and many related and expanding communication services (see Figure 8.5).

Within these developments, much has been made of the *interactive* qualities of new media technologies. If older systems tended to the 'one-way' form of communication (see Chapter 1), new media, it is claimed, allow for greatly increased diversity and interactivity, to the point that they fundamentally challenge the old ideas of '*broadcasting*' or '*mass*' communication. In the context of television, interactivity has been developed in a number of ways. Satellite and digital TV stations require the viewer to choose from greatly expanded repertoires or menus, thus 'liberating' them from the older, and restricted, mass scheduled system. VCTV (viewer-controlled television) in the United States, for instance, has allowed viewers to create their own schedules. New personal video recorder systems are under development. Digital television viewers in Britain now regularly have access to sports programmes and coverage where they can choose channels with different camera angles, replays, commentaries or computer-generated information as interactive accompaniments to their viewing of live coverage. The red interactive button is increasingly on our TV screens.

Since the early 1990s, satellite and digital TV channels have pioneered the round-the-clock selling of a wide range of domestic, consumer, lifestyle and electrical goods to consumers 'at home', interactively linked by phone or Internet and with the goods paid for by credit card. From the mid-1990s, supermarket chains and many other retail outlets in Britain have also developed Internet-based shopping services. Interactive home shopping, banking, holidays, cars, and other on-screen computer and digital services and games are further examples of the ways in which the interactive potentials of new technologies are being developed and mobilised. Trials of the potentials of interactive television systems are being developed all over the world as technology companies and their investors attempt to realise the commercial viability and potential of different services and their systems. In addition, interactivity allows for rapid viewer response: the computer terminal linked to the screen or mobile telephone enables viewers to 'answer back', whether this is in the form of votes in a televised talent contest like *Pop Idol* or in registering opinions on matters of political or current affairs.

Activity 8.2

What kinds of *interactivity* do new digital and Internet media systems make available? How do these represent advances over previous systems?

Assess the popularity of *computer games*. How have they changed patterns of leisure inside and outside the home? Who do they appeal to and why? How are computer games changing? What factors 'drive' these changes?

Interactivity, combined with greatly increased numbers of channels for new information, entertainment and communication services, has given rise to one of the most hotly debated issues, the implications of greater or expanded forms of *consumer choice*. For many writers, new media technologies have brought about the possibilities for much greater, more complex forms of choice and 'menu' (compare, for example, the terrestrial TV schedules from 1990 with the full terrestrial, satellite and digital formats available now). New media technologies have had important consequences for the costs involved in

FIGURE 8.6
Source: Tim O'Sullivan

many forms of contemporary media production and have allowed expansion and segmentation to take place in new media markets. In some cases the costs of investment in these new sectors are extremely high, as BBC and ITV ventures into digital television and related services illustrate in dramatic terms. In other cases, cheap, new technologies have enabled new forms of independent media production, as for example in digital film production, computerised music samplers and mixers or E-zines on the Internet. Viewers, listeners and readers may now exercise choice across new, increasingly segmentalised, fragmented or specialised, 'narrowcast' channels and services, as for example in the case of sports, movie, home 'lifestyle' or children's channels, and so on. Websites and the Internet have added their own, often linked multiple expansion to this proliferation and fragmentation.

There are two issues that need to be considered in this context. First, to what extent have video, DVD, satellite, cable and digital forms provided genuine *diversity* as opposed to a repackaging of old formats – 'more of the same'? This issue has been uppermost in most recent discussions about the changing nature of television in Britain (see Figure 8.6). Second, there are important and related arguments concerning access to these new forms and services. Rather than operating as public services, open to all, the great majority of new information and entertainment channels require private investment or subscription. You have to pay to view them. Individual spending power has increasingly become a key factor in determining whether one can or cannot afford to participate in the new media services and the new information/network society. Consumer 'choice' and communication can be exercised, but at a price. This tension between commercial and democratic interests has often been linked in the concerns for broadcasting quality in the 1990s. This has been one of the key issues in recent debates surrounding the future of public service broadcasting in Britain, outlined in the final case study in Chapter 7.

In summary, the debates about the development and impacts of new media and communication technologies in the current, early twenty-first century phase are extensive, and more complicated and interwoven than they might appear at first sight. Advertisements for new media and their services tend to stress the ways in which they 'liberate' viewers and consumers and offer whole ranges of new and effortlessly exciting possibilities. The theme of consumer freedom or sovereignty has also been central in the policies promoting deregulation which have accompanied and fuelled their growth. All the 'old' media – press, cinema, radio and television, and their traditional forms – now face considerable challenges as they compete in changing markets and circumstances. Changes in media production – for instance, in electronic or web-based publishing, 'webcasting' or the increasingly sophisticated portable digital video camera – as well as in the forms of what is produced and consumed are of considerable significance in any current analysis. Curran and Seaton (1997) have argued that the major debates here have often been posed between the '*neophiliacs*', who welcome the new media technologies and networks in optimistic terms, and the '*cultural pessimists*', who view these developments with considerable disquiet and scepticism. The two, contrasting positions can be summarised as follows:

Screen-based: video, cable, satellite, digital TV, High Definition TV, animation & effects, etc.
Screen-based print: DTP, digital printing, design & distribution, CD text systems, e-mail,
    Internet, electronic publishing, mobile phobe texts, broadband.
Music: digital synthesisers, samplers, video, CD, DAT, etc.

Neophiliacs:	**Cultural pessimists:**
Questions of choice	**Questions of choice**
1 Many more channels – 'Communacopia'.	1 Market forces, especially when deregulated, squeeze out minority tastes, unless rich consumers. Competition for popular market ('wall-to-wall Dallas') restricts actual choice.
2 Segmentation and narrowcasting.	2 Rental and purchase costs lead to exclusion of poor and powerless.
3 Experimentation, growth and innovation.	3 Costs of production lead to more imports and cheaper forms of output.
Democracy	**Democracy**
1 More information and services available to consumers.	1 Increased control by media barons and multinational companies.
2 Interactive uses (voting, WWW sites, etc.).	2 Loss of public-service principles and public sphere, issues of regulations.
3 DIY and community production leads to autonomy.	3 Increasingly privatised culture, reliance on advertising revenue.
Demand	**Demand**
1 Technological determinism?	1 Failure or low take-up of some new technologies, cost exclusion.
2 IT 'revolution', the 'wired' society.	2 Video growth and decline of terrestrial, public-service TV viewing (displacement).
3 Growth of private commercial culture.	3 Quality of existing services eroded.

FIGURE 8.7
New media technologies: debates

The Internet

The Internet brings together satellite and telephone communication with multimedia – sound, text and video. It has revolutionised the way we shop, and the nature of our leisure time. These changes have happened with extraordinary speed. By the end of 2000 the number of people online around the world was between 360 million and 380 million.

The distribution of the world's online population is uneven. More than 97 per cent of all Internet hosts are in developed countries that are home to only 16 per cent of the world's population. Iceland, for example, with a population of only 250 000, has 20 times as many Internet hosts as the world's 100 poorest countries combined.

Global Media Atlas (2001), p. 84

In the early stages of the twenty-first century, any discussion of changing and emergent media technologies and their cultural forms and implications would not be complete without special consideration of the Internet – 'the Net' or 'world-wide web', as it has become known (see Figure 8.8). This is the label that since the late 1980s has been applied to the developing interconnected telecommunication computer networks that enable computer-mediated communications, 'Nets' to link people from around the world into public forms of discussion and interchange. As Frank Webster has noted:

> The scenario of networked computers is often compared to the provision of electricity: the 'information grid' is seen as analogous to the electrical supply. As the electricity grid links every home, office, factory and shop to provide energy, so the information grid offers information wherever it is needed. This is, of course, an evolutionary process, but with the spread of an ISDN (Integrated Services Digital Network) we have the foundational elements of an 'information society'.
>
> Webster (1995), p. 7

The web has enabled the rise of what have been referred to as *virtual communities*, the diverse collectivities and groups of dispersed users which emerge as a result of computer-mediated communication. These differ from both older 'face-to-face' communities and those established under traditional systems of 'mass' communication. The origins of the Internet lie in American military research in the 1970s, and electronic mail and computer conferencing systems grew out of these early developments. The networks have grown dramatically, stimulated in part by the need for faster, global communication systems for financial or official forms of communication and data, and also by the growth of other diverse and sometimes unofficial groups of users. Howard Rheingold has outlined the basic principles involved in this growth, which has centrally involved the proliferation of Bulletin Board Systems (BBSs) and websites:

> The population of the grassroots part of the Net, citizen-operated BBSs, has been growing explosively as a self-financed movement of enthusiasts, without the benefit of Department of Defense funding. A BBS is the simplest, cheapest infrastructure for computer-mediated communication: you run special software, often available inexpensively, on a personal computer, and use a device known as a modem to plug the computer into your regular telephone line. The modem converts computer-readable information into audible beeps and boops that can travel over the same telephone wires that carry your voice; another modem at the other end decodes the beeps and boops into computer-readable

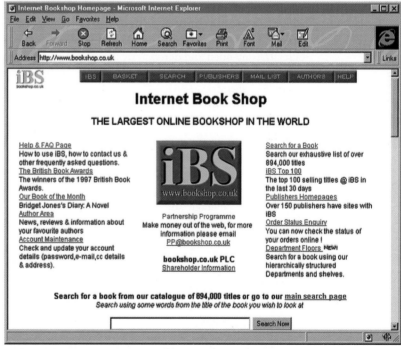

FIGURE 8.8
Source: Tim O'Sullivan/Internet Book Shop

bits and bytes. The BBS turns the bits and bytes into human-readable text. Other people use their computers to call your BBS, leave and retrieve messages stored in your personal computer, and you have a virtual community growing in your bedroom.

Rheingold (1994), pp. 8–9

It is difficult to assess the full implications of the Internet for contemporary culture and social relations. It is still, as Rheingold and others have remarked, unpredictable and volatile and the ups and downs of the e-commerce sectors in recent years have illustrated this effectively. What can be noted, however, are the actual and likely impacts on existing media, short-circuiting, fragmenting and threatening to displace or make obsolete in a variety of ways their previous formations, communities and networks. It is, however, important to counter the rather apocalyptic or utopian claims that have often accompanied the current stage of development (see Gauntlet, 2000, especially Chapter 1). Celebrations of the expanding potentials of the Internet or web are currently countered by anxieties over its regulation, 'piracy' and illicit use. A major factor in website development in the UK, like many other locations, has been the provision of pornography, for instance, and developments in radio and television streaming and music provision have been problematic with regard to questions of copyright and ownership (see Chapter 6, p. 168). Perhaps one of the key debates or claims to consider in this context concerns notions of a new 'electronic democracy', ushered in by the Internet. For writers like Rheingold, there are four key social criticisms or issues that need to be borne in mind when assessing the claimed democratic potentials of computer-mediated communication networks like the Internet.

1 The first issue concerns the degree to which electronic communications networks are simply continuing a process of 'commodification'. That is, turning political and other processes into advertised, sponsored or pay-per-view consumer products. Think of the pop-up ads and 'spam' which characterise most websites or e-mail systems, for instance. These processes could act against the aspirations and hopes of many online activists, who see the Internet, in part, as a way of revitalising open and democratic discussion and access to a renewed, modernised public sphere, in tune with the changing demands of modern times (see Jordan, 1999 and Street, 2001).

2 Secondly, a number of writers have pointed to the ways in which new interactive networks have a darker side, in terms of their involvement in processes of surveillance, control and disinformation. This theme sees an increase in the monitoring of network information comprising part of a modern assault on the personal and private liberties of citizens. From this perspective, the web or Internet becomes a more ominous kind of modern entrapment – not liberation.

3 A number of writers – especially those who believe that we have entered the postmodern condition (refer back to discussion in Chapter 1) - argue that new information technologies have now reached a stage in their development whereby they have changed what used to be understood as reality, into 'a slicked up electronic simulation' (Rheingold). This, ever more 'hyper-real', 'cyberspace' world is the product of the new technologies, which in fact produce a web of *simulated illusion* and identity that grows more 'real' and 'lifelike' as more people invest in it and as the technologies, and the corporations which own them, become more powerful by reaping the benefits. Identity is yet again at stake in the current period, in debates over computer games, and computer mediated forms of the 'old' and 'new' in Media Studies (see Gauntlett, D. 2000).

4 A final issue concerns the reliability of what appears on the net. How can we trust the sources of information, their accuracy and truthfulness?

The Internet is currently used most extensively for e-mail services, followed by – in descending order – information searches, news updates, job related or educational tasks, shopping and paying bills, searching for jobs, games or entertainment (see Figures 8.9 and 8.10). The convergence and interactivity between television and personal computer screen has yet, however, to fully take place, as the relations between '*lean forward*' (attentive, solo computer keyboard activity – 'at work') orientations increasingly co-exist and negotiate with '*lean back*' (at leisure, family or group TV viewing – 'at home'), in a mix of public and private circumstances and settings. In the short term, profitability is likely to continue to be a key factor in the development of the Internet as a medium.

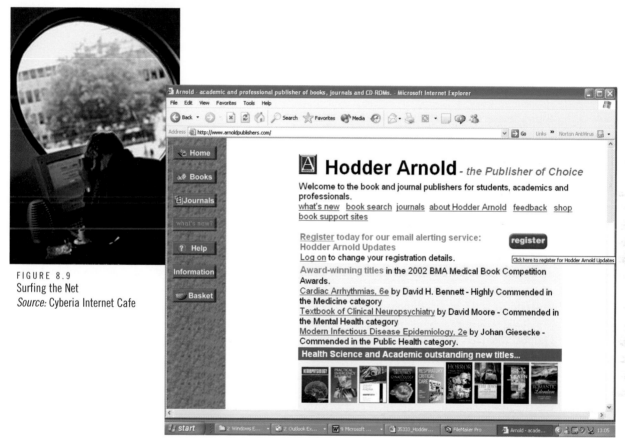

FIGURE 8.9
Surfing the Net
Source: Cyberia Internet Cafe

FIGURE 8.10
Website of publishers Arnold
Source: Arnold

Activity 8.3

Study the data concerning Internet use in Figure 8.11. Write initial notes or questions about the patterns they reveal. What, in your view, are the key conclusions and issues that might be based on this evidence? Make notes about further research that might follow from your analysis.

INTERNET USER PROFILE
Percentage of GB adults using Internet in last 12 months

Sex	%	TV area	%	Age	%	Social Grade	%
Male	49	Scotland	35	15–17	77	AB	66
Female	34	North east	37	18–24	68	C1	54
		Lancashire	40	25–34	56	C2	36
		Yorkshire	35	45–54	44	DE	20
		Midlands	40	55–64	25		
		Wales/West	37	65+	8		
		East Anglia	44				
		London	49				
		Southern	46				
		South West	36				

Note(e): 'Internet usage' includes the world-wide web, e-mail and associated services.

FIGURE 8.11
Source: The Lifestyle Pocket Book 2001: p. 124

Everywhere and Nowhere: Global Culture

From the National to the Global

One recurrent theme in recent writing about the media, notably about television, has concerned the need for students and researchers to recognise the importance and growth of *world-wide* media networks. No longer can, or should, the study of the media be locked into an inward-looking, ethnocentric focus, fixed solely on the characteristics and dynamics of the domestic, particular, national situation. It is the global dimensions of media networks that now demand attention.

Despite the fact that media institutions in Britain continue to be guided in decisive ways by a framework of ideas, values and organisational considerations in which the 'imagined community' of the British nation – 'British' identity, history, heritage and so on – continues to occupy a central place, changes in the last thirty years or so have altered things considerably. The British cultural economy in the twenty-first century, more than ever before, is part of a wider set of global cultural relations. This encompasses both economic and cultural flows of international import and export, in businesses and cultural commodities, in media hardware and software.

Some evidence for this changing state of affairs can be found very readily in everyday forms of media consumption. British terrestrial forms of television, for example, regularly feature a mix of films and programmes that have been produced in other national locations around the world, originally for other audiences. Films from America, India, France and Canada are scheduled side-by-side with TV series and co-productions from the USA and Australia, and live or recorded sports coverage from Japan, New Zealand and Germany. The amount and typical content of imported programming has varied historically. Developments in satellite, digital and cable TV channels have added to the amounts of imported material, and continue this growth.

Activity 8.4

Analyse the terrestrial TV schedules for one week according to the percentages of 'home' and imported programmes shown. Break down imports into their national origins. Compare the patterns which emerge with a similar analysis of satellite or cable TV schedules for the same week. What kinds of programme are imported and from where? What conclusions might be drawn from this analysis overall?

A

In British cinemas, the pattern of American dominance over the production of films appearing on British screens was established well before the Second World War. This pattern is still repeated (see Figure 8.12), with some variations, and not just in current multi-screen cinemas; it also reappears in the video/DVD rental store and on satellite movie channels. In the case of music, MTV has been an interesting case. Film stars and television personalities, stars of music and sport, are mediated and merchandised to world-wide audiences, often in media spectaculars that involve simultaneous, live, global link-ups, performances or appeals. In terms of music, British charts and music radio also give access to many international forms, styles and crossovers. The emergence of the category of 'world music' in the 1980s, with its mission to introduce western ears to non-western styles of music, to provide a platform for many voices allowing instruments and traditions to communicate together irrespective of national boundaries and the commercial dictates of the mainstream music industry, has been one development here worthy of discussion (see Burnett, 1996 and Negus, 1996).

FIGURE 8.12
Source: Jarrod Cripps

FIGURE 8.13
Piccadilly Circus
Source: Jarrod Cripps

Advertising campaigns and imagery have accompanied their products across national boundaries to the extent that the icons of Coca-Cola, Benetton, Del Monte, AOL and many others have become truly world-wide signs, part of the 'global language' of the twenty-first century (see Figure 8.13). 'Personalities' from Madonna to Mel Gibson, the Beckhams to Britney Spears are mediated to audiences on a world-wide basis. Newspapers, magazines and other print media are also tuned into these processes. In addition to relaying news and information from around the world, they may be co-ordinated for a number of national editions (*Cosmopolitan, Reader's Digest, National Geographic*) or aimed at international or pan-

national markets (*Time, Newsweek,* the *Financial Times*). Increasingly they are available in online electronic formats for world-wide computer access.

The processes and duties associated with mediating accounts of the 'world out there' into British public and private life have been a long-established function of the British media, particularly in fulfilling their public service remit (see Chapter 7) and their consequent relations with domestic audiences. In broadcast news segments on radio and TV, in holiday feature or travel documentary programmes, we are effortlessly transported or moved around the world in live, recorded or 'virtual' time (see Couldry, 2000).

Activity 8.5

Monitor or map this process in one evening's television viewing. Where in the world does television take you? How do the available channels compare?

Living in the Global Village

For many recent commentators, these and other aspects of modern culture are understood as part and parcel of the shift into *postmodern* conditions, whereby older forms of national identity and their historical 'securities' and divisions are being replaced, challenged and dislocated by new, multiple, cross-cutting allegiances derived from a diversity of local and global movements and imagery. As we noted in Chapter 1, this is a version of ideas popularised by Marshall McLuhan in the 1960s, concerning the effects on the world of television and computerised media technologies and communication networks, and their potential to establish a 'global village'. In the 'global village', differences of time and space or geographical or national location are eroded as a result of the instantaneous nature of modern media and world communications. In this vision, as the speed, extent and complexity of communication systems accelerate, the world 'shrinks' and the media synchronise us into a random, virtual, 'world time'. They also enable us to tune into a globally derived 'cocktail' or mix of places, events, personalities and locations.

The mediation of these two dimensions – of time and of space – is crucial in the construction of social identity at both public and private levels. A great deal of postmodern analysis has echoed and extended McLuhan's arguments on these themes. We have become, it is argued, dislocated and resynchronised into a new kind of simulated and decentralised world. There are now few limits or boundaries, it is suggested, in the new 'cyberspace' worlds of 'hyperculture', with their excess of information and entertainment (see Morley, 1991, Stevenson, 2002, and Jordan, 1999, for useful discussion).

Multinational Conglomerates

In the face of these and many other arguments and claims, it is important to recognise that *globalisation* is a process which encompasses two linked levels of relationship. First of all, a great deal of this process lies behind the growth in channels and technologies of images and information, whether online, on screen or on the page. Several writers have argued that internationalisation began, in fact, as a normal part of the commercial development of media markets in the early part of the twentieth century. The logic of this process has seen the emergence of multinational conglomerates, media companies with extensive networks of interests operating across national boundaries. One example is Rupert Murdoch's News International Corporation (see also Chapter 6):

it provides the archetype for the twenty-first century global media firm in many respects ... Murdoch's goal is for News Corporation to own every form of programming – news, sports, films and children's shows – and beam them via satellite or TV stations to homes in the United States, Europe, Asia and South America ... News Corporation operates in nine different media on six continents.

Herman and McChesney (1997), p. 71

In the British context, internationalisation encompasses both the ways in which British companies have invested in operations outside the UK (EMI, for example), and the ways in which American, European, or Japanese companies have bought into British media sectors in the domestic market (USA or Canadian interests in UK cable TV, for example). Multinational conglomerates are geared to operate in and to develop world-wide cultural markets for information and entertainment facilities. Their activities concern the technical production and distribution of cultural commodities, not just for particular domestic national consumption, but for readers, listeners and viewers who inhabit a range of diverse national and international territories (see Hannerz, 1996 and Barker, 1997, 1999).

If the first level of analysis here concerns the growth and development of world-wide multimedia conglomerates and their structures, networks and transnational operations, the second linked level concerns the consequences of their growth and operation, the cultural flows of commodities – packaged programmes, films, images, websites, etc – and their reception by audiences in diverse situations world-wide. At the heart of current debates about globalisation are a number of key issues that concern contested interpretations of the increase in international forms and patterns of media operation.

Convergence or Diversity?

For many writers, globalisation is a process that ultimately results in '*sameness*' or *homogeneity* on an increasingly world-wide basis. As Hebdige once suggested in this context: 'The implication here is that we'll soon be able to watch *Dallas* or eat a Big Mac in any part of the inhabited world' (1989, p. 51). Put crudely, world culture and media have become relay stations for the most powerful multinational corporations and their forms of popular, profitable culture.

For others, these considerations of similarity or convergence have to confront the *diversity*, dynamism and unpredictability of world culture and the fragmentation of audiences, both within and across national boundaries. Emphasis on the power of the multinational media conglomerates and their products is therefore counter-balanced by an emphasis on the potential and actual diversities of their creative origins and reception, the unpredictabilities of their use and cultural impact. In order to develop these issues further, we need to step back from discussions of globalisation, and set them in the context of related studies of media or cultural imperialism. 'We' also need to remember the particular national point of view and part of the globe from which these issues are addressed.

Points of View

Differing nation states and parts of the world organise access to systems of media production in widely different ways. Access to the means of reception also varies very widely from country to country. For example, to look at two extreme cases, in Mali, West Africa, it has been calculated that there are seven radio sets and two TV sets per hundred population. This stands in stark contrast to the United Kingdom, where there are 148 radio sets and 72 TV sets per hundred population. Furthermore, although the world-wide patterns of ownership of television sets, video or DVD recorders, radios, personal computers, Internet connections and so on, may be a significant indicator of the conditions of access and the relative availability of the hardware necessary for media reception, they tell us little about the ways in which these media may be used in context. Equally they reveal little about the related questions of content – what is broadcast or available to watch or listen to within different international or national territories.

It is important to bear in mind the broad historical perspective, and recognise that the international growth and spread of organised systems of mass communication and broadcasting in the modern period has been part of broader political and economic processes of industrialisation and commercialisation.

Activity 8.6

Compare the structure and range of media sectors in Britain with those in any other countries that you can get access to. Refer to the *Further reading* list at the end of the chapter for some useful sources.

Modernisation and Development

Some historians and other writers have suggested that the growth and diffusion of mass media did not just follow more general patterns of industrialisation and trade, but played the essential role in what was viewed as an overall process of 'modernisation'. Early studies often emphasised this function and the impact of media in what was perceived as an inevitable and world-wide development process. The media – particularly newspapers, films, radio and TV – were identified as key agencies for changing, 'modernising', the attitudes and values of populations experiencing world-wide industrialisation. In particular, 'developing nations' – often newly independent from colonial rule – were the basis for studies in the 1950s and 1960s which sought to assess the ways in which the media might be used to manage and change traditional ways and beliefs: for example, by means of educational or advertising campaigns and programmes. From this point of view, the media were regarded as neutral agencies capable of engineering positive social and cultural change, and assisting in the pursuit of greater industrial, technical, economic or social 'development'. Two key factors tended to be absent from this view: first, the power of the 'developed' nations, and second, the increasing dependency of 'developing' economies and nation states. These ideas have, however, formed the basis for more recent studies of international media relationships, and a series of debates concerning media or cultural imperialism.

Media Imperialism

Fundamental to this view of international media relations is the general argument that capitalist, western media have dominated and controlled the cultures of the Third World and developing nations. Far from any benign or neutral process of 'modernisation' taking place, Western, especially American, communication systems and the values they carry and promote, have 'invaded' and have established forms of world-wide control and influence in the production and supply of information and entertainment. This process is seen as historically systematic and linked to the more general economic and political processes of first colonial, and then imperial, developments in the twentieth century. 'Imperialism' in this sense refers to the ways in which certain industrialised nation states have emerged as 'world powers' and established empires, by extending their forms of control and rule over other political, economic and cultural communities and nations for the purposes of commercial advantage, military security and political or ideological 'mission'. Whereas colonialism is viewed as an early stage in this process, predominantly concerned with economic advantage and exploitation, imperialism results from wider and more complex forms of dominance, directed towards empire building on the global level. Imperialism is the systematic production of massive disparities in wealth, power and influence, on a world-wide scale. Dominant, 'First World' (a term usually referring to North America, Western Europe, Japan and Australia) economies are able to control supply and demand on world markets, and poorer countries are encouraged to import First World goods and commodities in exchange for raw materials or cheap labour.

Our concern here lies with the related but cultural aspects of these processes. From the early 1970s onwards, studies of international media flows and relations have consistently pointed to what Varis (1974), in the context of TV, called 'one-way traffic', *from* the relatively restricted centres of advanced commercial states, via multinational corporations, *to* world markets, especially the 'developing' markets of the 'Third World' (nation states in South America, Asia, Africa) and 'Second World' (the now ex-Soviet bloc and China). This traffic, it is argued, introduces and cultivates the values and commodity cultures of consumer capitalism. Media networks become vehicles for the world-wide dissemination of language, identity and aspirations, for cultivating values congruent with the dominant ideologies of Western capitalism (see Herman and McChesney, 1997 and Barker, 1997).

An early focus for work of this type was the Hollywood dominance of world film industries, although more recent studies have focused on later 'waves' of television, video (Alvarado, 1988), satellite, advertising, news and music (Malm and Wallis, 1984). In a study first published in 1969, entitled *Mass Communication and American Empire*, Schiller argued that American TV exports represented part of an imperialist policy to subjugate the world – world domination is the aim. Importantly, this type of analysis noted that the process did not solely concern the programmes, films, adverts and so on. It also embraced the changing technologies of production and reception, the practices of production, and the patterns of tastes, aspirations, fashions and lifestyles which are cultivated or 'transmitted' by these commodities. For writers like Schiller (see also his more recent writing, for example 1991), the media play an important part in a general process of cultural imperialism. In this view, traditional and indigenous cultures world-wide are 'penetrated' and transformed by American cultural influences, which act to 'spearhead' forms of global American consumerism. For developing nations, a major problem is to try to retain or preserve cultural autonomy in the face of external, often American, influence. From such a point of view, satellite and digital broadcasting systems and the Internet, with their abilities to cross national boundaries, have simply enabled this process to occur more rapidly and completely. These forms of delivery threaten what has been referred to as the 'audiovisual space' (Mattelart *et al*, 1984) or cultural autonomy of many nations, with significant consequences for cultural identities (see Barker, 1999 and Tomlinson, 1999).

FIGURE 8.14
Source: Paul Hickinbotham

From the mid-1970s, these themes of cultural dependency and the global communications power of developed nations have formed a regular focus for debate and criticism at meetings of UNESCO (United Nations Educational, Scientific and Cultural Organisation). UNESCO has had to deal with a series of demands for a New World Information Order, which would seek to redress the imbalance between information-rich and information-poor countries and nation states. Such proclamations, however, appear to have had limited material impact on subsequent global developments.

Assessing Imperialism

Imports and Exports

In recent years, the debate about media imperialism has developed in a number of ways (see the *Further reading* list at the end of the chapter). At the heart of these developments has been a reassessment of some of the evidence cited in favour of its operation. This has largely concerned television. The patterns indicated here based on research undertaken in the last twenty years (see Barker, 1997 for useful summary), suggest that, world-wide, imported programmes average about one third or more of total programming. The USA imports relatively little – between 2 and 5 per cent. Canada is a major importer of American-originated programmes (up to 40 per cent), and Western European systems also import about this amount. Many Latin American stations have 60 per cent or more of their schedules filled by American output, and this pattern is repeated in many African, Asian, Pacific and other Third World sectors. Some 40 per cent of programming in the former Soviet Union nation states is imported. At a global level, most of the programme material imported originates from the USA, and to a lesser extent from Western Europe, Japan and Australia. It is important to note that these flows are mainly of a recreational kind: light entertainment, movies and sports programmes. These programmes can be bought in packages at a fraction of the price it would cost to produce 'home-grown' versions, and therefore the economic logic for purchasing them to fill schedules worldwide is clear and compelling. For example, a study of Zimbabwe TV notes:

> *ZTV can only afford to produce about twelve hours of indigenous drama a year, albeit incredibly cheaply with the actors also doing day jobs and providing their own costumes. Drama series like Ziva Kawakaba (Know Your Roots) are very popular with the majority black audience, but the advertisers know that they are going to get better value for money from imported programmes that appeal to the more affluent white or middle-class black audiences. And ZTV know that they can acquire an episode of Miami Vice, say, for the special 'Third World' rate of $500 – a fraction of the already minimal budget of an episode of Ziva Kawakaba.*
>
> Dowmunt (1993), pp. 6–7

Activity 8.7

Carry out some research on television schedules around the world. Using the Internet, search for television stations and their daily schedules in a number of developing nations like Fiji, Papua New Guinea, Peru, Mali or Tanzania. How much imported programming is there? What types of programmes are imported? What kinds and how much programming is 'home-grown' – originates from local facilities?

More work is needed on these patterns in the age of expanding video, satellite and digital, multi-channel forms of delivery and their interchange with the Internet and the web. We should also note that a significant dimension to this debate concerns not just popular programme formats like the 1980s American soap opera *Dallas* but also the mediation of news and other forms of information; for example, with the multinational operation of the Cable News Network (CNN) or MTV. A series of studies has criticised the international operations of major Western news agencies, and their abilities to set the global news agenda in this context (see Gurevitch, 1991). This has been especially pronounced in the context of the Gulf War or the reporting of other USA interventions, in Afghanistan, for instance.

For some writers, the model of 'one-way flow' vastly oversimplifies what is in fact a much more complex set of interrelationships occurring within different continental, linguistic and geographical regions. Examples of regional flows would include Latin American telenovelas (soap operas) which circulate from Brazil to other Latin American locations and to Spain, Portugal and the USA. In recent years, MTV has moved away from a global policy to create particular national or continental forms of music programming. However, the main challenge to the media imperialism thesis in recent years has focused on questions about the limits to the evidence provided. In short, does the evidence concerning amounts of imported programming add up to the 'imperialist effect'? As one writer observed, nearly twenty years ago:

> *There is an assumption that American TV imports do have an impact whenever and wherever they are shown, but actual investigation of this seldom occurs. Much of the evidence that is offered is merely anecdotal or circumstantial. Observations of New Guinean tribesmen clustered around a set in the sweltering jungle watching* Bonanza *or of Algerian nomads watching* Dallas *in the heat of the desert are often offered as sufficient proof.*
>
> *Lealand (1984), pp. 6–7*

What is centrally at stake here is the way in which increasingly mobile media audiences, in a diversity of national and other cultural locations, may make sense of and relate to imported programming (see Figure 8.15). Those who support the ideas of media imperialism assume that American films and programmes 'blot out' authentic and original forms of indigenous culture, and replace them with the ideologies and values of American consumer capitalism. However, little actual evidence has been presented about the precise nature of the forms of reception or decoding which are in play in the world-wide situations confronted with such imported material. Some recent developments in this context are worth noting.

FIGURE 8.15
Traditional semi-nomadic ger dwelling in Arhangai, Outer Mongolia, complete with satellite dish
Source: Barbara Hind

Watching 'Dallas'

By the mid-1980s, many cultural critics and writers agreed with the then French Minister for Culture, Jack Lang, when he attacked the American soap opera *Dallas* as 'the symbol of American cultural imperialism'. Set in a world of Texan oil families and their private and public feuds and conflicts, the soap opera had enjoyed massive international popularity in over a hundred countries world-wide (see Ang, 1985, Silj, 1988). One study which set out to explore how *Dallas* was made sense of in a diversity of cultural and global locations, was carried out by Katz and Liebes (1990). They studied a large number of groups, including, for example, newcomers to Israeli society from a diversity of ethnic and cultural contexts. They viewed the dispersed and different audience groups that formed the basis for their study as active, and as capable of negotiating a range of diverse positions with regard to the serial, its stories and characters, and its relevance to their own lives. The study offers some evidence for the need to reassess this aspect of the imperialism thesis. Audiences on the 'receiving end' of American cultural products like *Dallas* emerge as active agents, more complex, critical or resistant and certainly less predictable in their cultural responses than has been assumed. Certainly, as Tomlinson in his assessment points out, 'We clearly cannot assume that simply watching *Dallas* makes people want to be rich' (1991, p. 49). The detailed study of the uses made of television in diverse national and ethnic locations has recently been developed in a series of studies by Lull (1988, 2000). For relevant discussion of some of these themes, refer back to Chapter 5.

Activity 8.8

Choose some recent examples of films or television programmes that have followed *Dallas* around the world. How and why do *Monsters Inc*, *Chicken Run*, *Gladiator* or *Dawsons Creek* and *Buffy* achieve global success with audiences in many different cultural locations? To what extent do they act as vehicles for particular values?

Perspectives and Problems

One important and related question has been posed in recent work. This first emerged in an account given by Pennachioni (1984) of some observations of television viewing she made in north-east Brazil. One of the situations she describes concerns a group of poor country people in this area who were laughing at a communally watched, televised Charlie Chaplin film. Pennachioni noted that she and they appeared to be laughing at the same things, but that this was by no means necessarily the case. On the basis of this encounter, she suggested that Western media researchers face formidable problems of understanding and interpretation. They and their research subjects, people in Third World settings, may appear to 'laugh at the same things' – the tramp character in Chaplin's films – but within very different, even irreconcilable frames of reference. Ultimately, her study poses some important questions about the assumptions often made about Third World audiences by Western researchers and their methods.

The study also highlights some important issues about the 'universal' nature of the appeal and meanings of images like Chaplin or even more recently J.R. Ewing in *Dallas* or characters in the Australian soap opera *Neighbours*. Tracey (1985) has posed a number of provocative questions in this context by suggesting that the world-wide appeal of American popular culture must, in part, be explained not just

FIGURE 8.16
Bollywood, Leicester
Source: Tim O'Sullivan

by its imposition, but by understanding how it taps into certain *universal* feelings and 'common chords', which transcend national cultures and differences of lived, situated identity. As Tomlinson notes, however, this kind of argument comes dangerously close to ignoring the historical power of Western media systems to saturate developing cultural economies with their types of material: 'One reason why Chaplin's humour can be plausibly seen as universal is that it is universally present' (1991, p. 53). Tufte (2000) has recently written a fascinating study of telenovelas (TV soap operas) and their reception in Brazil. His account crystallises and develops many of these issues.

In summary, this section has suggested that there is considerable evidence available which points to the global concentration of power over media production and distribution. This has tended to be concentrated in Western nations, states and corporations. Debates about the dynamics of media imperialism may need to address more directly questions of how international audiences for the films, channels, programmes, music, videos and so on make use of and interpret these cultural products in their daily lives (see Figure 8.16). In so doing, they also need to deal with the arguments and ideas contained in recent accounts of 'globalisation'. Both of these issues are centrally linked with the emergence of more complex, new, multi-channel, multi-media technologies, satellite, cable, digital DVD and the Internet being perhaps the prime examples of the moment. Media Studies has to move with these convergent, global and interactive times and changes if indeed it is to remain relevant and viable as a means of systematically participating in, challenging or changing the mediated environments of the twenty-first century.

Further Reading

Ang, I. 1996: Living Room Wars: Rethinking Media Audiences for a Postmodern World. ROUTLEDGE.

Barker, C. 1997: Global Television: An Introduction. BLACKWELL.

Barker, C. 1999: Television, Globalization and Cultural Identities. OPEN UNIVERSITY PRESS.

Bauman, Z. 1998: Globalization: The Human Consequences. POLITY.

Briggs, A. and Burke, P. 2002: A Social History of the Media. POLITY.

Couldry, N. 2000: The Place of Media Power: Pilgrims and Witnesses of the Media Age. ROUTLEDGE.

Curran, J. and Seaton, J. 1997: Power without Responsibility: The Press and Broadcasting in Britain. ROUTLEDGE.

Dowmunt, T. (ed). 1993: Channels of Resistance. BFI/CHANNEL 4.

Doyle, G. 2002: Media Ownership. SAGE.

Doyle, G. 2002: Understanding Media Economics. SAGE.

Gauntlett, D. (ed). 2000: web.studies rewiring media studies for the digital age. ARNOLD.

Golding, P. and Harris, P. (eds). 1997: Beyond Cultural Imperialism: Globalization, Communication and the New International Order. SAGE.

Hannerz, U. 1996: Transnational Connections: Culture, People, Places. ROUTLEDGE.

Hayward, P. and Wollen, T. (eds). 1993: Future Visions: New Technologies of the Screen. BFI.

Herman, E. and McChesney, R. 1997: The Global Media: The New Missionaries of Corporate Capitalism. CASSELL.

Herman, A. and Swiss, T. (eds). 2000: The World Wide Web and Contemporary Cultural Theory. ROUTLEDGE.

Howes, D. (ed). 1996: Cross-Cultural Consumption: Global Markets, Local Realities. ROUTLEDGE.

Jordan, T. 1999: Cyberpower: The Culture and Politics of Cyberspace and the Internet. ROUTLEDGE.

Kennedy, A.J. 1999: The Internet: The Rough Guide. ROUGH GUIDES LTD.

Lull, J. 1988: World Families Watch Television. SAGE.

Lull, J. 2000: Media, Communication, Culture: A Global Approach. POLITY.

Mackay, H. and O'Sullivan, T. (eds). 1999: The Media Reader: Continuity and Transformation. OPEN UNIVERSITY/SAGE.

Mackay, H, with Maples, W. and Reynolds, P. 2001: Investigating the Information Society. OPEN UNIVERSITY PRESS.

Mayer. P.A. (ed). 1999: Computer Media and Communication: A Reader. OXFORD UNIVERSITY PRESS.

Morley, D. and Robins, K. 1995: Spaces of Identity: Global Media, Electronic Landscapes and Cultural Boundaries. ROUTLEDGE.

Murdock, G. and Golding, P. 1991: 'Culture, Communications and Political Economy' in J. Curran and M. Gurevitch (eds). Mass Media and Society. ARNOLD.

Ostergaard, B. (ed). 1997: The Media in Western Europe. SAGE.

O'Sullivan, T. and Jewkes, Y. (eds). 1997: The Media Studies Reader. ARNOLD.

Poster, M. 1995: The Second Media Age. POLITY.

Reeves, G. 1993: Communications and the 'Third World'. ROUTLEDGE.

Rheingold, H. 1994: The Virtual Community: Finding Connection in a Computerised World. MINERVA.

Slevin, J. 2000: The Internet and Society. POLITY.

Smith, A. 1993: Books to Bytes. Knowledge and Information in the Postmodern Era. BFI.

Sreberny-Mohammadi, A. 1991: 'The Global and the Local in International Communications' in J. Curran and M. Gurevitch (eds). Mass Media and Society. ARNOLD.

Street, J. 2001: Mass Media, Politics and Democracy. PALGRAVE.

Thussu, D.K. (ed). 1998: Electronic Empires: Global Media and Local Resistance. ARNOLD.

Tomlinson, J. 1991: Cultural Imperialism. PINTER.

Tomlinson, J. 1999: Globalization and Culture. POLITY.

Tufte, T. 2000: Living with the Rubbish Queen: Telenovelas, Culture and Modernity in Brazil. UNIVERSITY OF LUTON PRESS.

Van Dijk, J. 1999: The Network Society. SAGE.

Webster, F. 1995: Theories of the Information Society. ROUTLEDGE.

Williams, R. 1974, 1990: Television: Technology and Cultural Form. ROUTLEDGE.

Winship, I. and McNab, A. 1996: The Student's Guide to the Internet. LIBRARY ASSOCIATION.

Winston, B. 1998: Media Technology and Society: A History from the Telegraph to the Internet. ROUTLEDGE.

Journals: Convergence, New Media and Society, Television and New Media.

CHAPTER NINE
MEDIA PRACTICE

Practice and theory in Media Studies cannot and should not be separated. Their relationship is both complementary and integral to a full understanding of the subject. Practical work plays an important part in many subject areas: for instance, it is an established and well respected part of the science curriculum where students carry out 'practicals', often to 'test theory'. In English or Art and Design, doing one's own work is both an opportunity to reinforce what has been taught but is also, perhaps more importantly, to develop one's own analytical or creative skills and abilities. Media Studies requires both the traditional skills of critical reflection and analysis but this tends to be combined with some technical experience or production appreciation or competence. Active involvement in media practice, producing short pieces for radio, video or magazines, developing marketing packages, designing websites and so on, can help not only to reinforce and develop some of the ideas and issues in this and other books but also to highlight and lead to a greater awareness of the difficulties and dilemmas associated with professional media production.

This chapter looks at the three main stages involved in undertaking a practical project involving media production:

- *pre-production*, **including purpose, audience and considering the technology and resources required and available;**
- *production*, **including style, content, interviews and vox pops;**
- *post-production*, **which includes review and evaluation. We will discuss how practical work can offer the opportunity to apply and investigate many of the key areas of knowledge and ideas that are discussed in this book, looking in particular at such areas as audiences, institutions and representations.**

Media courses at every level usually try to integrate critical study with practical production and therefore expect students to carry out some kind of practical production work. At its best this should enable students to gain valuable, even vocationally relevant experience and to develop technical, conceptual and working skills as well as building up a portfolio of work to show to those who 'gatekeep' – control access to – the next career stage, whether it be Higher Education or employment. Practical exercises are also important because they show that the output of different media are the result of clear social, technical and economic contexts, the products of organisational requirements as well as women's and men's own individual actions. However, there is a danger that sometimes this emphasis on 'doing'

241

can be rather crude and simplistic, merely providing students with a set of 'testable skills' that lack any reflective, critical or flexible conceptual frameworks.

FIGURE 9.1
Source: Tim O'Sullivan

Playing a part in the production of particular media texts can focus questions about the criteria by which professional media producers interpret 'reality' and how it is represented back to us and other audiences. These are rarely just technical questions, for example, production work can help to illustrate the importance that the notion of a given 'audience' can have in determining both the shape and content of a production. It also provides you with an opportunity to experience directly a version of the constraints, decisions and structures involved in media production and to understand the impact that these can have on the shape and outcome of the process and the final product itself.

As most media production involves working with others, there is also the value of working and negotiating with groups of people who may have different ideas, perspectives, ideologies and motives and finding out how you work as a member of a group. The development of these skills can help prepare you for the life of an extended professional, a self-critical, flexible problem-solver, multi-skilled and working in whatever industry or business you choose to make your career. Most importantly, this chapter considers the process of evaluation and self-reflection that should accompany any practical or production exercise and helps to identify the social and other organisational skills that can be 'transferred' across to a variety of different occupations and professions.

Activity 9.1

Find out what practical work you are required to produce for your course and what facilities (such as equipment, technical help, time, etc) are available to you. What percentage of your final marks does this work represent? Spend some time reading through the assessment criteria for this practical work to ensure that you understand clearly what it is you have to do; for example, what, if any, marks are for 'technical competence' or your use of media language and the codes and conventions of your chosen medium and genre? Are you assessed for your research or how clearly you identify your target audience? Are you required to write an evaluation afterwards? If so what should it contain, probably not a day-by-day account of what happened but rather some kind of analysis of the strengths and weaknesses of your practical production plus evidence that you are able to link the practical work with the key themes and issues of your course.

Pre-Production

Purpose

The period of planning and designing a media production known as pre-production is perhaps the most time-consuming of the stages involved in media practice. Most productions start with an idea, an interest, a point of view or a topic that someone wants to explore. This may be in response to a given brief, where the producers have to work to a specification given to them by others, for instance the 'client'; or the producers may have a free hand to work on an expressive or more creative piece of their own choice. Most practical work encountered in educational settings will usually be part of the assessment for your course and so will have particular aims and constraints. As a student you will most probably begin with exercises that aim to help you to understand and develop confidence with certain techniques, equipment and procedures. At later stages, you may be given greater autonomy to negotiate what you want to produce, and how you would like to go about it.

Activity 9.2

An effective way in which to practise video skills is by producing a short trailer for a film. You could create four or five key shots and edit them together in a way that creates a sense of excitement or enigma. You might perhaps record a short voice-over giving the title of the film and its release date and also include a short extract of appropriate music. A caption shot at the end with the title of the film allows you to try out IT skills. This might be further developed by extending the piece into a 'proper' trailer or creating a web page that contains video material as well as other information.

You could also carry out similar exercises for other media forms such as the introductory sequence for a soap opera or situation comedy – perhaps set in your school, college or neighbourhood. This could either be radio or television-based. In their eagerness to get their hands on cameras many students tend to overlook radio although it can be a challenging and creative medium to work in.

As the ideas develop and the brief is interpreted, both the specific aims of the production and the sense of target audience should be defined and clarified. This is especially important if the production draws on group work. Whatever the medium and the technologies being used, however long or short the production, all successful productions should be clearly thought out and have a thoroughly researched and planned structure. Depending upon the medium used, and how ambitious the finished production is, this planning and preparation can take up to 50 per cent of the available time and effort. Start early and plan ahead in as much detail as possible.

Some assessment criteria require students to produce a Production Log or portfolio. This is like a diary or working record detailing the production process from the very beginning. It should contain references to all the sources of information that have been used, details of all the decisions that have been taken as well as a reminder of all the things that went wrong. The log does not have to be reflective as that occurs in the evaluation stage, but it is useful to jot down thoughts and ideas as they occur to you. This will be useful when you come to write an evaluation as you may well have forgotten some of your earlier ideas and actions. For group projects the log provides evidence of the involvement of all team members and their input to the project.

As part of a team producing a media text and product, some of the questions that you will all need to consider at this initial stage are:

- What are the key aims of the production? How are these established? Who by?
- Which medium is most appropriate or available for it?

- What resources are available to fund and execute it? What resources might be developed and how?
- How can it be managed most effectively to meet the deadline?
- Who is in the group and how well will we work together?

All media texts aim to produce some kind of meaning and impression, whether it be explicitly informative or educational, or more open or entertaining. There may be a clear and unambiguous message to be presented, for instance in a website designed to promote to maximum advantage a college or local sports club, or there may be a more abstract and open-ended goal, trying perhaps through the use of visual images to convey an emotion or feeling prompted by a particular piece of music, or simply a journalistic piece hoping to elicit a variety of responses perhaps in relation to a controversial local issue. As we have argued in this book, the links between media texts and their meanings can sometimes be less than straightforward and many different criteria can be used in evaluating them.

Most productions should start by developing a sense of purpose and a clear set of aims (usually written down) that have to be defined and understood by all those involved in the production. If your practical work is part of an assessment then it should be easy to identify what it is you have to do to satisfactorily complete the task. Most assessments will have a set of criteria that will be used to award marks to your work, for example you may be awarded marks for length and content as well as the number of people you can work with. You may need at this early stage to consider how your group will work, who will do what and take particular responsibility for aspects of the project. Often team working and organisation will be part of the assessment criteria as well as your own individual post-production reflection and evaluation of the success, or otherwise, of the production process.

Perhaps the most common danger involves being *too ambitious* in deciding upon the aims of a production, particularly when there are limited resources of time, money and equipment. It is probably unrealistic, for example, if using video for the first time, to try to produce a thirty-minute programme for a general audience about the role and influence of the car in industrialised society. It might be a very interesting programme, or more probably a series of programmes, but are the resources required to make it really available? There is also a law of diminishing returns that means that if a production is over-long it has less chance of being successful. Be realistic as well as imaginative in defining the scope and scale of your project within the terms of your brief. Inevitably what you would ideally like to do should and will be tempered by the resources available.

A clearly defined set of aims provides one of the measures of the success or otherwise of a production and is an important part of the later review and evaluation process. It is therefore often useful to ask the question, 'At the end of watching, reading or listening to my piece of work, what should the target audience do, think, feel?' Pinpoint precisely what it is you or the production brief want to get across to the audience. For example, in the context of a short three-minute radio news package on a proposed local road bypass, should they:

- Understand the seriousness of the local traffic problem?
- Know what the local council's plans are?
- Understand the objections being raised by local conservation and other groups?
- Know how to get more involved and make their own opinions heard?

Audience

For most productions, whether student or 'professional', audiences should be considered: the types of readers, listeners or viewers you want to communicate with. This helps focus the style and content of the work. For *Time* magazine the audience may be millions of readers throughout the world, for Classic FM it may be five or six million listeners in Britain who enjoy particular types and packages of classical music, whereas for the *Newbury Weekly News* (see Chapter 6) it may only be a few thousand readers living in West Berkshire who share a more or less common interest in local events, news and personalities.

When thinking about your target audience it is important to try to be as specific as possible. Is the audience a defined group of people? If so, how would you categorise them? Are you trying to appeal to any particular subcultures, age groups, ethnic or gender groups, or other types of constituency? Are they local or dispersed? What else do they have in common – perhaps in terms of their interest in the media or a particular place or pursuit? What common levels of knowledge or experience in relation to your chosen topic can you assume? Perhaps the same locality and knowledge of the local community? Do they have similar hobbies and interests?

Often students target fellow students because they are easily accessible and share many common interests and values. However, it is often more rewarding to try to target different groups: this may be in terms of age and generation (a television programme for young children between the ages of eight and ten, for example, or a radio programme for people over forty) or gender (asking females to produce magazine articles, features and advertisements aimed at teenage boys or vice-versa). It is, however, essential to be realistic when defining your audience. Unmarried males over the age of fifty who live beside the sea and are interested in volleyball do exist, but it could be very difficult to reach a significant number of them or to effectively target their general attention, needs or attitudes.

It is important to spend time thinking through how the audience is identified: for instance, is it an established and recognisable community or is it a new configuration created specifically for your project? There can be some difficulty in assessing what a new audience might want, particularly if the text is aimed not at meeting an existing need in competition with other products but at creating a new one. This is why many mainstream producers work within notions of budget and genre: because it provides some of the key rules and conventions which guide success and can help show producers what audiences like, based on the 'formula' that has worked in the past (see Chapters 3 and 5).

Activity 9.3

Compare and contrast programmes from different genres, for instance a police drama with a soap opera, to see how specific visual conventions and codes are associated with these different genres.

Modify the focus and scope of this activity to suit your particular interests or production project.

In planning your production, it is helpful to consider how the target audience and their perceptions, needs and patterns of media consumption might affect the shape and content of your production and the audience's response to it. What assumptions have to be made about the audience's feelings, prejudices, and levels of prior knowledge and understanding, and how might this affect the way your production is presented or received – encoded and decoded? Think carefully, for example, about the medium you might employ and the scheduling of your production.

Activity 9.4

Using a production idea of your own, outline a profile of the people you aim to communicate with. Refer to Chapter 4 on Audiences and Reception and consider the following categories: age; gender; social class; ethnicity; location; lifestyle. Is there any other information or category that could be useful?

The Medium

The medium that will be used for some student productions is predetermined by the syllabus that they are studying; others who can choose which medium to use often start with the vague idea of 'designing a website', 'doing something on video' or 'producing a piece for radio'. However, it should only be after clarifying questions about aims, target audience, format and resources that the most appropriate medium can be decided upon, if circumstances allow such choice. The aims of a production will influence the medium used because some topics are more suited to certain media than others. For example, if the topic is very visual, for instance the recording of a piece of student drama, then a medium which can encompass the visual would seem to be most appropriate. If the aim is to transmit a lot of facts and data (for example, the viewing or readership profiles for particular media texts) then a printed medium or a website may be more successful than an audio one. If the production focuses on music, perhaps a profile of a particular group, singer or type of music, then video or radio may work better than printed material. If the aim is to inform through the use of different points of view or experts, then radio or a printed medium may be more suitable than a visual one which might consist mainly of 'talking heads'.

The target audience may be a significant influence on the decision about the most appropriate medium, as groups of people have different preferences and patterns of media use – how they receive information, and are engaged, persuaded or entertained by it. This theme was discussed in Chapter 5. Different audiences consume the media in different ways and in different social contexts; whereas some groups are more disposed to sit and read privately, others prefer a visual or more interactive medium that they can share.

Activity 9.5

There are several ways of investigating how existing conventions and patterns of consumption are affected by ideas of particular 'groups' of target audiences:

1   Take the front-page of either a broadsheet newspaper or tabloid newspaper and 'reverse' it, rewriting the stories for a set of particular, different readers. Reselect and prioritise the stories, and redesign the page layout accordingly.
2   Compare and contrast the way advertisements on radio stations such as Classic FM and a local independent chart station are shaped and presented for their different audiences. Select one advert from each station for detailed analysis.
3   Choose a production in one particular medium, say, radio, and then consider how it would be modified if produced for another medium, say, print, television or online consumption.

Technology and Resources

One theme explored in Chapters 6 and 7 was how media texts and output are produced under certain conditions: technical, organisational and other factors such as finance are important determinants which shape production. Your production will have to work to a budget, often very small (or even non-existent!) and perhaps with a group of others. Often the budget will limit the time, the equipment and the personnel available, and this may significantly affect the production values. This can include the technologies and expertise that you might use. If hi-tech equipment with lots of special effects is available there is often a strong temptation to use it irrespective of the time, cost or purpose of the production. The temptation to use special effects as a substitute for content carries the danger that *what* is being said becomes less important than *how* it is said and communicated. With most media becoming increasingly dependent upon new convergent, computer-based technologies, it is easy to become fascinated by new pieces of equipment that seem to do the same tasks faster and more easily as well as offering many additional gimmicks. Although technical competence may be part of the assessment you are working towards, it will not be the sole criterion for success, and often older, tried and tested methods can be more successful in producing the desired end result without the necessity of having to master new or unfamiliar technology in a short space of time. You and your production team therefore need to take careful stock of budget and technical possibilities before proceeding too far with your production. You need to consider what you can afford to do and what technical limitations you have to work within.

Increasingly the gap between the technology available in schools and colleges and that used by professional media producers is closing, as PC-based, electronic equipment becomes smaller, more sophisticated and cheaper. In video, for instance, the digital editing processes such as Apple's iMovie or Final Cut Pro used in a student production may be very similar to that used by mainstream production companies. In both journalism and radio the production process is converging around multimedia PC packages such as QuarkXpress, Pagemaker, Photoshop and Cool Edit Pro and these have all stimulated a range of affordable imitations. For designing web pages there are now software packages like Dreamweaver that will implement many of the tasks for you.

Guidelines for writing a script

- Decide what is to be said.
- List the points in a logical or agreed order.
- Make sure that the opening is both interesting and informative.
- Try to visualise the individual listener or viewer. Remember that often we watch/listen or read alone or in small, intimate gatherings (often with our close family), so the production should have that same intimate feeling.
- Try out what is to be said by speaking the text aloud, then write it down if it sounds 'natural'. Some people have better speaking voices than others and it is important to make sure that the best voices are used.
- Try to write in short sentences or phrases but keep the language 'natural'. Some people immediately start to talk in an artificial, convoluted and rather pompous way when being recorded. This will usually detract from what is actually being said.
- If someone else is going to speak the text, make sure that they can understand it. Use clear punctuation and paragraphs and have the script typed with double spacing.
- Allow for rehearsals.

The time and technologies that are available for your production will determine to a large extent the actual process of putting together the text. Despite what you, as a producer, may wish to do, it is quite likely that you will have to adjust your ideas to the equipment, budget and time available. It is easier to disguise a poor or inappropriate location if close-ups are used; perhaps an 'exotic' location can be suggested by music and a few simple close-ups rather than travelling to a location and taking long, panning shots. Television pictures are based upon a 'language' or 'grammar', where every type of shot carries a certain meaning and, when placed into a sequence, this builds up a story or message that can potentially be understood by people from many different cultures – a kind of visual Esperanto or cartoon. As audiences become more tele-literate and increasingly share the same, often American derived production values, these styles and languages become more and more global, so that we all come to share an understanding of what a close-up or an establishing shot means and when it is appropriate to use them. Cost and time, however, can often determine the type of shots used, and how the grammar is put together and encoded.

Activitiy 9.6

Record an extract from a television programme, list all the different shots and note how the 'grammar' is used, for instance by cutting from the outside of a building to a group of people talking indoors so that we assume that it is the same building. Try to find other examples.

Research how developments in television technology have influenced the 'look' of programmes. Compare some current examples of television output with the output of the 1950s and early 1960s, looking in particular at the use of graphics and computer-generated special effects, and the number of angles of cameras being used. Sports programmes are a particularly interesting genre to look at, especially high-profile events like the Olympic Games or world championships. What changes are occurring now and under way for the near future? (You may wish to modify this activity to suit your own production project).

For video productions and projects, it is useful to prepare a storyboard as early as possible and to refine this with as much detail as possible as the project develops. When designing a website a storyboard is also useful as a means of demonstrating the relationships between the different pages and how visitors will navigate the site.

If you are working to someone else's brief, perhaps a teacher or tutor, it is useful at this stage to have a meeting, outlining your ideas and making sure that they are appropriate to the task you have been set.

Guidelines for preparing a storyboard

- Decide what is to be shown.
- List the visuals in a logical order.
- Sketch the main elements and what will be in each shot.
- Describe the type of shot, e.g. long shot, close-up, etc.
- If possible give a rough idea of the length of each shot.
- Explain what sound or dialogue is going on at the same time, e.g. music, speech, etc.
- If someone else is involved in the shooting then make sure that they too can understand the storyboard.

Activitiy 9.7

1   Plan and produce a storyboard for a video lasting no longer than three minutes. The video should aim to tell a story or create an atmosphere using only pictures – no sound or dialogue.
2   Create a storyboard that shows the way 'real time' is condensed, for example for a very short sequence of video film of a journey or depicting a simple household task like making a cup of coffee. What stages can be left out or shortened (the kettle coming to the boil?) How is this shortening of time indicated? How is one shot bridged with the next?

Checklist for planning a production

- Estimate how much time is available and how it is going to be allocated. A timescale for all the different jobs, working back from the final deadline, is very useful.
- Make an action plan, listing all the research to be done, letters to be written, telephone calls to be made, interviews to be arranged, etc, and put beside each activity the name of the person who will be responsible for making sure that it is completed on time.
- Be realistic. How much money is there to spend? A rough costing needs to be worked out. Include the expenses incurred while undertaking research, any travelling expenses or photocopying, as well as the cost of any extra materials that may have to be purchased. Copyright is often overlooked, but it may also have to be paid for and can be very expensive, particularly for well-known pieces of music or film images and clips.

Production

Style

Although, as Chapter 5 suggested, we often consume the media while paying very little direct attention, any successful production should aim to engage the audience so that, at the least, they will want to carry on watching, listening or reading. This can often mean compromising length and detail in favour of something that is short, sharp and to the point in content, rather than a production that is long, worthy but inappropriate. If your production is aimed at fellow students it is worth thinking about what attracts you and your peers to particular texts, to think about the techniques that might be successful and those that will not.

If a production is aimed at a youth audience, a short documentary about a local band or music scene, then the style usually borrows from current musical trends and includes fairly rapid editing, fast-moving visuals, graphics, loud soundtrack, special effects and a variety of messages all being broadcast simultaneously. This style has become well known and is often copied. However, what looks easy and 'rough' is often difficult to do successfully with limited resources. It can be more worthwhile and satisfying to try for a more original style or topic that is within both your means and resources. For example, young people are increasingly surfing the web in the privacy of their bedrooms and it may be that a website is a more appropriate way of promoting a band. A website could include video and audio files as well as biographical and merchandising details.

Activity 9.8

Explore how editing sound and images can affect the 'meaning' of a sequence. Experiment with various styles of visual presentation by playing around with a series of images, putting them in different sequences, varying the lengths of time they are on the screen, using different editing effects such as fades and/or wipes and by using different types of soundtracks, for example classical and/or pop music.

If the production has an older audience as its target, perhaps a publicity campaign about a local primary school aimed at the parents of young children, then a more sedate style would probably be more appropriate; a loud rock-music background is not likely to work effectively with this type of audience or topic. Some productions make a claim to be spontaneous, and some, like *The Big Breakfast* on Channel 4, or Chris Evans' shows on radio and television and the *Chris Tarrant Breakfast Show* on Capital Radio, have aimed to be whacky and anarchic in their apparent lack of planning and rehearsal; what has often been called 'zoo radio'. Almost all radio and television shows, however, have a well-prepared script and managed sequence, and as part of 'mainstream' broadcasting, will have well-prepared playlists and fairly tightly controlled time schedules especially if they have to fit in advertisements and work to set points in the schedules such as the news 'on the hour'.

Content

All media texts have some kind of *narrative* – a story to tell – and should have a structure that is appropriate and, hopefully, effective for the purpose (see Chapter 2). Producers (and audiences) both have ideas and expectations, sometimes articulated, often just assumed, as to what a particular production is about, where it should start from and how it should develop and finish. This will depend on such factors as whether or not the programme is part of a series, whether the characters or narrative are already familiar, or whether it is a one-off that has to create its characters' identities quickly and have a self-contained narrative within a given time-slot.

Chapter 2 also discussed the significance of *title sequences* (p. 47). Most radio and television programmes are 'top-and-tailed', usually through the use of theme tunes, text or graphics. An effective start and introduction is sometimes made by using a sound or visual montage that not only introduces some of the main issues of the production but also hopefully attracts the audience's attention. For example, in the film *William Shakespeare's Romeo and Juliet* (1996) the introductory sequence, before the title is shown, is a fast-edited montage of images that both introduces the main characters in the story but also shows how the story has been updated to modern Los Angeles. It also creates a sense of urgency and tension that very effectively captures viewers' interest and creates a desire to continue watching the film.

Most successful productions *vary their pace and content*, perhaps by following a 'talking head' segment with some action shots, or a piece of music with some speech. Each segment should lead naturally into the next. The American soap opera *Dallas*, which was exported world-wide in the 1980s (see Chapter 8), was particularly successful in working to a pattern where each scene started with an establishing shot (the Southfork Ranch or the front of the Ewing Oil office), moving through a series of mid to head-and-shoulder shots and ending with a close-up of someone's face to emphasise the emotion and drama. Each scene usually lasted for no more than two or three minutes and the pattern was repeated again and again throughout the programme. Each visual change of scene was 'bridged' by soft music that rose in volume as the camera closed in on someone's face for that scene's particular climax.

Whatever the format of your production you may wish to use or manipulate existing material, i.e. material taken from other sources rather than produced by you or other students. If you do you should bear in mind copyright issues, and in this respect, any assessment criteria that may be relevant for your production.

For video productions when both sound and vision have been planned and detailed on scripts and storyboard, they should be married together into a *shooting script*. Although this is a long and complex process, it is important for everyone involved in the project to understand and agree exactly what is required of them and how their part fits into the overall production schedule. If you are making a documentary, perhaps about some aspect of your local community, then two or three different voices can be used for voice-overs, perhaps varying between male and female, as one person's voice can quickly become monotonous. A commentary is often made to sound more realistic by using background noise, or 'actuality', such as traffic noises or birdsong, to give a sense of realism, involvement and of being 'on the spot'.

Activitiy 9.9

- Choose a radio or television programme and study its main segments. How many are there? How long are they? How are they linked? Is there a pattern? Carry out a small practical exercise where you attempt to replicate one or two of these segments. This activity can be tried for several different genres of programmes.
- Plan and produce a seven-minute radio feature for a 6.30pm magazine programme to be broadcast in your locality. Each segment should be no longer than 90 seconds and should include both an introduction and an 'outro', as well as a variety of different presenters.
- Look at a recorded television programme and analyse one particular segment. Watch it to see how it has been constructed. Try to note every shot, giving its type and duration. Note also the use of any graphics or 'cutaways' – where the camera 'cuts' to a shot other than the main subject, often the interviewer. Look particularly for the ways that sound and pictures are linked. Working back, now transcribe the commentary and reconstruct the script, giving commentary, camera shots and other relevant information. Again this activity can be tried across several different genres.

In an attempt to create a heightened sense of realism, modern documentaries often require the filming process to be as discreet as possible, frequently using the 'fly-on-the-wall' approach discussed in Chapter 4. One method that has become increasingly popular in investigative television programmes is to use a participant observer – someone who becomes one of the group or social situation under observation (see Chapter 10). These methods have been criticised and have important ethical implications, particularly for individual privacy, and they prompt questions about the role and boundaries of investigative journalism, particularly as technology improves and recording equipment becomes smaller and more sophisticated.

If you are working in printed material such as producing a feature for a local newspaper or magazine, the copy frequently has an 'inverted pyramid' structure, setting out a story with the five Ws (who, what, when, where and why) in the first paragraph, subsequent paragraphs being a mixture of additional

FIGURE 9.2
Inverted pyramid structure of
newspaper/magazine story
Source: R. McRoberts, Media
Workshops: Vol. 1, Words,
Macmillan, 1987

activity 7.4

Choose a radio or television programme and deconstruct its
different segments. How many are there? How long are they?
How are they linked? Is there a pattern?

7.3 McRoberts, Macmillan, 1987

KATOOMBA, 4 April. – Local police and volunteer searchers
this morning rescued four school boys trapped overnight on a
mountain ledge. One of the boys fell late Tuesday afternoon.
FACTS A friend climbed down to him, while another went
for help. Darkness, however, fell before police were told.

**BACK-
GROUND** The boys were taking part in a survival course
run as part of their school Physical Education programme.

FACTS When lifted to safety the boys were examined by a police doctor. They were
unharmed apart from minor ab-
rasions.

QUOTE 'I feel fine,' said one of the
boys. 'I wasn't scared just
cold.'

FACTS The boys' parents were
informed of the acc-
ident late last
night.

**BACK-
GROUND** The school has
only just start-
ed this
course

Printed material frequently has an 'inverted pyramid' structure
(Figure 7.3), setting out a story with the five Ws (who, what,
when, where and why) in the first paragraph, subsequent
paragraphs being a mixture of additional information and
background. Paragraph three or four usually contains a quotation. One advantage of writing a feature this way is that the
end of the article should contain the least useful information
and can therefore be most easily cut if there is a shortage of
space.

information and background. Paragraph 3 or 4 usually contains a quotation. One advantage of writing
a feature this way is that the last paragraph, at the end of the article, should contain the least useful
information and can therefore be most easily cut if there is a shortage of space (see Figure 9.2).

Activity 9.10

Read the following information and write and design a newspaper story, following the 'pyramid' guidelines:

Fire brigade: Fire began at 7.05am today in Laing's Hotel, The Parade, Seamouth. Believed started in kitchen
storeroom and spread rapidly by adjacent lift shaft to all three floors. Woman and man badly burned. Brought
out by firemen.

Police: Four people taken to Axebridge Royal Infirmary by ambulances. Flames began to break through roof.
Ambulance 1 took chef Alan Edwards, of 6, Langsett Road, Seamouth. Second contained hotel owner Alan
Laing and wife, and a guest, Miss Irene Smollett of Exton.

Hospital: Miss Smollett and Mr Laing dead on arrival. Chef badly burned on face and hands: admitted. Wife
treated for shock.

Hotel receptionist, Karen Broughton, said:

'Alan was preparing breakfast when he discovered the fire. He was burned trying to fight it. He told me, and I roused the Laings and we ran round the hotel warning the other staff and 17 guests. Everyone seemed to get out safely but when Mr Laing held a roll-call Miss Smollett was missing. He ran into the hotel. It was well alight by then. Then the fire brigade arrived.'

Chief fire officer, David Granville, said:

'My men found Mr Laing and a woman huddled at one of the top floor corridors. We got them out just before the roof collapsed. There was no hope of saving the building. Its age and the draught from the lift shaft meant it was certain to be destroyed once the fire had a good hold.'

Hotel built 1842. The Laing family have owned it for 53 years. Lived with wife, Anne, in hotel. Aged 63, wife 58. No children.

Media Techniques. Newspaper and Radio Journalism.
© London Institute.

You can also produce various different versions of this news item by writing for a tabloid and/or broadsheet newspaper, online, or producing a variety of different radio news bulletins perhaps for R.1's Newsbeat and /or R.4's Six O'clock News.

Interviews

Interviews can play a large part in both the research and the production stages, particularly if the aim of your production is to inform or persuade. As edited parts of interviews are often included in the final programme, interviews are important not only as a means of acquiring information but also because they may affect the shape, content and style of a production as well as raise questions of 'balance' and impartiality. It is also very frustrating if you have an interview where the person being interviewed is saying something important but the quality of the recording is too poor to use in the final production (see the section on interviews in Chapter 10).

If a production is investigating a sensitive or controversial issue of law and order, for example, drinking and driving or drug abuse, then the people most often interviewed are representatives of the police or related judicial, legal or medical professions. This is because they are relatively easy to contact, and usually have someone whose job it is to deal with the public and answer questions. They are often considered the 'experts' in matters of law and order, who mediate between 'us', society, and 'them', the criminals. It may well be in their own interest to gain media exposure, as they often have a point of view, some information or an appeal for information that they want to publicise. This dependence upon a quick and easy soundbite is often much more convenient than trying to obtain an interview with someone who represents the opposite – or an 'anti-establishment' – view. Not many people are willing to admit publicly that they drink and drive or take illegal drugs, although you may be able to get an interview with someone who has 'reformed'. This unwillingness to 'confess' in public may be circumvented by offering someone anonymity, perhaps by appearing with the face blacked out or the voice distorted, but this is increasingly difficult to achieve without looking either clichéd, performed and humorous.

Guidelines for an interview

- Check equipment, particularly the sound levels, as there may be only one opportunity to carry out a particular interview.
- Be prepared. Think about the type of interview and have a clear idea of its purpose. Will the person being interviewed be sympathetic and co-operative, or reticent and unwilling to impart the relevant information?
- Introduce yourself, say who you are, and state the purpose of the interview and its context.
- Ask 'open' questions and cover the 'What', 'Where', 'Why', 'When', 'How' or 'Who'.
- Think about the 'shape' of the interview. Structure the questions, possibly around the past, the present and the future. 'What did you do before…?' 'What are you doing now…?' 'What are your plans for the future…?'
- Recap the main points and check dates and the spellings of names of people and places.
- Ask a 'bucket' question along the lines of 'Is there anything else you would like to say?' This allows the interviewee to drop in anything not covered so far.
- Close the gate. There was a famous reporter who during his career got a number of exclusives, and one of them concerned a vital witness in a notorious case. This witness, a woman, would not talk to any reporters, although hordes of them laid siege to her in her house. This reporter, like everyone else, got no reply when he called. However, he left a visiting card with a note saying that he would very much appreciate a chance to talk to the woman, and he promised that the interview would be on her terms. Later that day the woman rang him, saying that she did not want to talk to the entire press, so would he come that afternoon for an exclusive interview. Years later when they met again the woman asked the reporter if he knew why she had picked him rather than any of the others. 'Was it my little note on the back of the visiting card?' he asked. 'No,' she replied, 'lots of them tried that one… but you were the only one who closed my garden gate properly on the way out.' The lesson is that a little care and consideration as well as perseverance and initiative can sometimes pay big dividends.

If you are planning to incorporate interviews in your finished production, you will need to arrange the interviews well in advance, as most people are unwilling or unable to stop what they are doing and immediately answer questions in any meaningful or useful way. They will probably want to know what the production is about and why they are being asked to appear in it. Interviewees may ask to see your questions in advance if they want time to prepare their answers. Some interviewers feel that this loses the spontaneity and excitement of an interview, but, although it may be considered unprofessional, it is common practice, especially if the interviewee is important to the content or style of the programme. Increasingly some people, particularly politicians and those in authority, also ask to see the finished, edited product, and can even ask for a right of veto in case they feel that they have been misrepresented. Most professionals would regard this as unacceptable, although in some cases producers do agree and then state in the programme that this has occurred. It is usual, however, to send a copy of the finished product to anyone who has helped in its construction.

When drafting your questions for an interview, it is helpful first to make a list of the key points that you need to cover and their sequence. Good questions are simple and direct and you should be prepared to deviate from the prepared sequence if other relevant issues come up. Listen carefully to the answers as they often provide you with your next question. Wherever an interview takes place it should allow both the interviewer and the person being interviewed to relax, as it is usually when people are relaxed that they start to talk more naturally. Body language is a good indication of how people are feeling. People being interviewed often prefer to conduct the interview on familiar territory, frequently in their own homes, offices or where they feel in control. If your interview is being recorded for use in a production, it is important to have an environment that does not have any disturbing background noises, such as roadworks or police car sirens. These may not be noticeable in the excitement of carrying out the actual interview, but can be very obvious and distracting when reviewing the material, and although sometimes they can be removed at the editing stage there can be difficult problems with continuity.

Activity 9.11

There are several exercises that you can do to improve your interviewing techniques:

- Try out some of the interviewing exercises that illustrate the effect of body language: for instance, conducting an interview sitting back to back where there is no eye contact, or across a desk with a physical barrier between the two people, or in unfamiliar surroundings.

- Think up a scenario and topic for an interview and ask someone to play the part of the interviewee and to nominate a topic. Try to conduct the interview as realistically as possible, with either pen and notebook, or audio or video equipment. Swap notes and discuss the interview afterwards and assess to what extent the interviewee was reassured and put at his or her ease. Are there any ways in which your interview could have been improved?

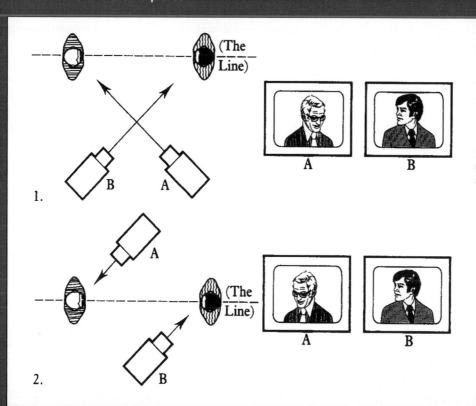

FIGURE 9.3
The positioning of cameras so as not to 'cross the line'

'Crossing the Line'

Most interviews on television are carried out with one camera, filming the interviewee, and the 'cutaways' (where the interviewer is asking the questions) and 'noddies' (where the interviewer nods in agreement) are filmed later. A more complicated way of conducting interviews on video without having to use cutaways is to use two cameras.

When you are recording an interview, whether with one or two cameras, it is an important convention that the impression of two people talking to each other is achieved. This is done by setting up the cameras in such a way that they do not cross an invisible line but both stay on the same side of this line. The effect is that of one person looking to the left talking to the other who is looking to the right. In Figure 9.3, cutting between cameras A and B on the same side of the line would be acceptable and give the impression of the two speakers facing each other as in a conversation. If, however, one camera crosses the line, the speakers no longer look as if they are talking to each other and this might confuse the audience, or at least be unsettling.

Vox Pops

Vox pops, from *vox populi*, Latin for 'the voice of the people', are a common and widely used convention in much media output. Producers appreciate them because they are fairly easy and cheap to produce and are popular with audiences, who appreciate them because they are usually humorous as well as appearing to let 'the man or woman in the street' air his or her point of view. In television or radio the vox pop is usually a series of short reactions or comments from members of the public about a given topic, for instance a local traffic problem, often recorded in the local high street or shopping centre to give a sense of immediacy and context.

The reporter is rarely heard asking the question, except perhaps at the very beginning. On the finished package the public's answers are strung together to give a variety of voices and opinions or perhaps a common point of view. On television this device is frequently used to add some humour or as a more light-hearted alternative to 'talking heads'. In print, for instance in a local newspaper, it is presented as a series of interviews carried out 'on the streets' often under the banner of 'What our readers say'.

Post-Production

Post-production, although the final stage of a media production, is possibly the most vital and valuable, because it contains two important operations: the editing or putting together of all the work, and an evaluation of how successful the whole exercise has been. This should include a review of what has been learned about the process of creating media products plus, wherever possible, feedback from listeners, readers or viewers.

Editing

Audio and video editing is necessary because, although some programmes may broadcast events or interviews 'live', generally very little of the raw material that has been filmed or recorded is tidy enough to be seen or read by audiences without going through some sort of editing process. Editing can be time-consuming, taking longer than the actual production stage, but for many people it is also the most enjoyable and creative part, as it is often at this stage that you, as a producer, can have the greatest impact.

Editing has four main functions: to make sure that the production is the required length or time; to remove unwanted material or mistakes; to alter, if necessary, the way or the sequence in which events will be portrayed; and finally, and perhaps most importantly, to establish the particular style and character of a production. There is still time to change ideas, and the editing stage offers you the opportunity to experiment with different combinations of media or sequences. Each combination will work in a slightly different way and each version may create distinctively different meanings.

As the producer, you will often have an ideal vision of the final production that may be carefully planned and written down in detail on paper or may just exist in your mind's eye. Sometimes this ideal works, sometimes it is unachievable, and the editing stage is often a process of experimentation and trial and error to see what works. Frequently, because of time and money constraints, the editing stage will often end in some sort of compromise between what is desirable and what is actually achievable.

Review and Evaluation

There are many criteria for assessing the success or effectiveness of media productions. For mainstream professional media producers these are often external or institutional and can be related to commercial or critical acclaim, ratings, sales and finishing within time and budget. For those working on media projects within educational settings, the criteria for success also concerns gaining a good mark or grade. For many producers success may be more subjective, reflective and often largely personal, although still dependent to some extent on the opinion of others, such as peer groups, tutors or the target audience.

The process of review and evaluation is important as it should allow you the opportunity to stand back, reflect, and ask critical questions of the product and the processes involved in the production. The review also presents an opportunity for you to re-examine decisions you made earlier about the audience, the aims, style and content of the production, and to see if, in retrospect, these were appropriate and fruitful. Your Production Log will be particularly useful in reminding you of your earlier plans, thoughts and actions. The evaluation is also an opportunity for you to assess how well the existing codes and conventions of mainstream media may have been assimilated, copied or challenged and what has been learned about them. This may also be an important stage in your study of the media because it is where you bring theory and practice together and consider how they have informed and reflected on each other.

For many productions, one of the most direct criteria for success is whether the audience liked it or not. Although not all productions are aimed at a specific audience, most productions, whatever their size or length, have some kind of target audience in mind. The review is an opportunity for you to consider whether your production has succeeded in engaging with the intended audience – the listener, viewer or reader – and whether the aims and objectives of the production overall have been realised. There are a variety of ways in which you can gather these responses, from formal questionnaires (see Chapter 10) to less formally talking to people about their reactions. If you have produced a website you can ask visitors to email their responses back to you. If you are producing your work for an assessment it is likely that you will be expected to undertake some kind of measurement of audience feedback and that this will be part of the assessment criteria.

Remember that a finished product is an achievement and that it is very much in the processes of producing it that the most valuable learning often takes place. If you complete a finished product it should be shown or played to a sample of the target audience. Consider whether your audience had any preconceived ideas about how the production would (or should) look (or not look) like the 'real thing' and how this might have affected their expectations and responses.

You should use your notes or Production Log to produce a written evaluation that should show how you have reflected on the production process and how it has informed your understanding of the theoretical concepts studied in other parts of your course. You should also consider to what extent, in your view, your production achieved its aims and whether anything else, perhaps unanticipated, happened as a bonus. Although not the only concern, it will be useful for you to consider the technical quality of the finished product. Did it affect the audience's responses? You should also consider your own reactions, as not all productions are necessarily purely audience-led.

The whole interwoven process of planning, preparation and production can be reviewed to see what particular aspects, in both the audience's and your opinion, were successful or unsuccessful. What seemed to work or did not work, what could be changed or kept in for any future work? Did the production attract, entertain and hold the audience's attention? If you were working in news, feature or documentary forms, was balance one of your objectives, and if so how far was it achieved? Did your own social or political standpoint or values affect the content? Were there any particular problems in carrying out interviews, perhaps technical issues or problems in gaining access to particular people? If you were to do it again, what would you change and why?

Activity 9.12

Revisit Chapters 4 and 5 and consider what assumptions were made during your production process about the way certain groups or ideas should be handled; were any stereotypes used or how were they avoided? How were the decisions made in your group? Did you reach a consensus or was one opinion more dominant than the others? Was there any significant difference in the roles undertaken by different people in the group?

Most productions develop organically and their shape and emphasis changes during the production process, and adjustments are often made to the notional target audience, available material and to overall aims. What were the major problems in your production and how were they overcome? How did decisions about the conditions of production, the budget and the use of technologies affect the final form and content of the production?

Most productions are collective and collaborative enterprises, involving groups and team work. It is useful therefore to consider how well everyone worked together and how tasks and roles were negotiated and allocated. If there was any conflict, what were the main causes and was it resolved? Was there, for instance, a gender bias that allowed males to dominate the hardware and technical tasks, while the females tended to be left with other roles, such as presenting or researching?

The process of creating media texts, whether large or small, individually or as part of a team, is usually an exciting, worthwhile and challenging experience. It should offer you insight into how individuals work as well as how 'professionals' and media institutions operate. The experience should provide you with a greater and more grounded understanding of some of the choices, decisions and constraints that shape the form and content of media texts and output.

Professionalism

Producing a practical piece of work not only helps to illustrate in a very direct way the material and ideological implications of many of the dilemmas and constraints that 'professional' producers experience, but media practice can also provide some direct experience of the problems and standards that 'professional' producers work with and to, and that audiences respond to.

There are some dangers associated with practical work, and often people think that what is produced in the 'professional' mainstream media is the one and only way of constructing media images and the standard by which all other work should be judged or measured. This view can often imply that what is produced outside of the mainstream can be dismissed as amateur and inferior. Although the level of technology may be different, usually below that of professional industry equipment, many of the processes and problems may nevertheless be similar.

Many first-time producers expect that their finished product will look like the 'real thing' and be of the same standard as those produced by mainstream media. A realistic 'product' is often emphasised by professionals and others, who are often keen to talk about ideas of 'standards' and 'expertise'. These can, however, lead to an exclusivity and a mystique associated with the professionals' status. There are in fact many instances where the opposite is the case and the 'professional' is keen to use new ideas or emulate the success of the 'amateur', particularly in the area of youth programmes, or in magazines, where the 'off-the-street' style of scratch videos or fanzines has an immediacy that the mainstream can only copy and try to incorporate into its own output.

The value of individual practical work carried out as part of a Media Studies course is that it is not always necessary to replicate the professional or institutional patterns or constraints but that it may instead allow for the exploration of different, or alternative, experimental ways of presenting ideas and images. Like the *Adbusters* illustration in Chapter 2 you can attempt to parody or challenge the existing codes and conventions.

Activity 9.13

Produce your own 'anti-advertisements', perhaps showing the dangers of drinking or smoking too much. You could also refer to the section in Chapter 4 on gender stereotyping and then produce your own advertisement that challenges the dominant gender stereotypes that continue to feature in most advertising.

Working on practical exercises can involve 'deconstructing' what others have put together and learning to present alternatives – but first learn the rules, then how to break or bend them. Undertaking practical work is also likely to lead to a greater appreciation of some of the difficulties that professional media producers face in their everyday working lives, as well as developing an increased understanding of how social, political and economic constraints influence that work.

FIGURE 9.4
Source: Jarrod Cripps

259

Conclusion

Practical work in Media Studies is not just about being trained in existing media practices nor merely replicating the production skills and standards of the current media industries, rather it is concerned with developing vocationally competent students who are self-critical, reflective and analytical but who also have the social and organisational skills and understanding that are relevant in many different occupations, of which media may be only one option.

It is no longer the case that the only way into the media industries is by completing an Oxbridge degree and then moving to the BBC or a Fleet Street (or rather today, Canary Wharf) broadsheet. Today, Media Studies courses have established an important presence in schools, colleges and universities, and many of these courses are highly competitive. The media, information and cultural industries are now one of the largest employment sectors in Britain (see, for example, the reports by Skillset/DCMS (2001) and the DfES (2002)) and graduates from Media Studies University courses currently have a better chance than graduates of other subjects in gaining relevant employment. Studying the media – integrating applied practical experience with knowledge and analytical and organisational skills – can make a prospective employee more desirable to an employer, not only in the 'glamorous' media industries, but also in other related areas such as management, marketing and public relations. It is these and other related organisations that represent some of the key growth industries for the early part of the twenty-first century.

As the study of public service broadcasting in Chapter 7 illustrates, British radio and television industries are becoming increasingly fragmented, offering much broader ranges of choice for audiences. This choice is provided by an increasing range of channels and specialist services, served by a large and expanding number of independent production companies. Both the ITV companies and the BBC are required to have at least 25 per cent of their output produced by independent companies. This means that there is an increasing demand for people to work, albeit on a freelance, short-term or casual basis, in independent production houses or low-cost satellite and cable companies.

In magazine publishing there is an expanding range of publications aimed at specific, specialist markets and as media companies increasingly diversify into other areas, in both broadcasting online and e-publishing, traditional boundaries and separate career paths are less rigid. Economic pressures also mean that some smaller organisations like local radio stations try to employ as few people as possible and that those who are employed are 'multi-skilled' and flexible so that the person who presented the drive-time show in the morning will put together advertising packages for a client in the afternoon and may also have to fit in some administrative tasks.

This multi-skilling and flexibility is important as audiences fragment towards increasingly specialist 'narrowcast' and niche markets. There are also more opportunities for those who have not traditionally been dominant in the decision-making and production side of the media industries. More people from under-represented groups continue to be recruited into the industries to meet particular market or regulatory needs – new 'youth' and other markets or a local 'community' presence for some radio franchises. There is also considerable media production activity in local situations, at the local level through, for instance, the new access radio stations being awarded licences by the Radio Authority and OFCOM.

One of the most useful ways of understanding the artificiality of the production process is to see a live television programme being recorded. Most major television studios have shows where a live audience is required and if you contact their ticket office you will most probably be able to get free tickets. You may not be able to choose the show you see but seeing any show being produced in the studio and then comparing it with the edited, broadcast version is both entertaining and educational.

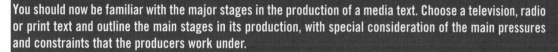

Activity 9.14

You should now be familiar with the major stages in the production of a media text. Choose a television, radio or print text and outline the main stages in its production, with special consideration of the main pressures and constraints that the producers work under.

Further Reading

BBC Centre for Broadcast Skills Training Wood Norton, Evesham, Worcestershire WR11 4TB. **www.bbctraining.co.uk** Publishes *'Putting You in the Picture'*.

BKSTS – British Kinematograph, Sound and TV Society Walpole Court, Ealing Studios, London W5 5ED. **www.bksts.com** Publishes *'Education, Training and Working in Film, Television and Broadcasting'* as well as running its own courses.

British Film Institute 21 Stephen Street, London W1P 2LN. **www.bfi.org.uk** Has a reference library and publishes books on courses and careers.

Broadcast Journalism Training Council www.bjtc.org.uk Validates broadcast journalist training courses.

Bectu – Broadcasting, Entertainment Cinematograph and Theatre Union www.bectu.org.uk Publishes *'Stage, Screen and Radio'* and runs a student link-up scheme.

Cyfle Gronant, Penrallt Isaf, Caernarfon, Gwynedd. **www.cyfle.co.uk** Runs training for the Welsh television and film industries.

FT – Film and Television Freelance Training www.ft2.org.uk Runs training schemes for freelancers and technical assistants.

ITV Network Centre 200 Grays Inn Road, London WC1X 8HF. **www.itv.co.uk** Publishes *The Official ITV Careers Handbook*.

National Council for the Training of Journalists Latton Bush Centre, Southern Way, Harlow, Essex CM18 7BL **www.nctj.com** Offers advice for potential entrants and is involved in the running and validation of courses.

National Union of Journalists 314 Grays Inn Road, London WC1X 8DP. **www.nujtraining.org.uk** Publishes the booklet *Careers in Journalism*.

Newspaper Society 74 Great Russell Street, London WC1B 3DA. **www.newspapersoc.org.uk** Runs the *Newspaper in Education* scheme and publishes the booklet *Making the Decision*.

Periodicals Training Council Queens House, 28 Kingsway, London WC2B. **www.ppa.co.uk/ptc** Publishes the annual *Directory of Magazine Training*.

The Publishing NTO 55-56 Lincoln's Inn Fields, London WC2A 3LJ. **www.publishingnto.co.uk** The national training agency for the Press.

Scottish Daily Newspaper Society 48 Palmerston Place, Edinburgh EH12 5DE. **www.snpa.org.uk** The major press training provider in Scotland.

Skillset 103 Dean Street, London W1V 5RA. **www.skillset.org** The industry training organisation for broadcasting, film, and video. Provides a substantial amount of information on training and careers and publishes *A Career Handbook for TV, Radio, Film, Video and Interactive media.*

Women's Radio Group Unit 13, 111 Power Road, London W4 5PY. **www.twiza.demon.co.uk/wrg** A training and networking charity for women interested in radio.

Allen, J. 1990: Careers in TV and Radio. KOGAN PAGE.

Boyd, A. 1998: Broadcast Journalism. Techniques of Radio and TV News. HEINEMANN (1ST EDN); FOCAL PRESS (3RD EDN).

Brierley, S. 2001: The Advertising Handbook. ROUTLEDGE.

Conroy, A. and Wilby, P. 1994: The Radio Handbook. ROUTLEDGE.

Davis D. 1969: The Grammar of Television Production. Revised by Elliot; further revised by Wooller. Published under the auspices of the Society of Film and Television Arts. BARRIE AND JENKINS.

Department for Education and Skills, 2002: An Assessment of Skill Needs in the Media and Creative Industries. DFES.

Evans, H. 1986: Pictures on a Page. HEINEMANN.

Fraser, P. 2002: '50 ways to improve your practical work' in MEDIA MAGAZINE Issue 1, September 2002, English and Media Centre, LONDON.

Hedgecoe, J. 1991: On Video. HAMLYN.

Hodgson, F. 1987: Modern Newspaper Editing and Production. HEINEMANN.

Kaye, M. and Popperwell, A. 1992: Making Radio. BROADSIDE BOOKS.

Keeble, R. 1994: The Newspapers Handbook. ROUTLEDGE.

Langham, J. 1996: Lights, Camera, Action! BFI.

Llewellyn, S. 2001: A Career Handbook for TV, Radio, Film, Video and Interactive Media. SKILLSET.

Medina, P. and Donald, V. 1992: Careers in Journalism. KOGAN PAGE.

Miller, J. 1990: Broadcasting: Getting In and Getting On. BUTTERWORTH.

Millersen, G. 1989: Video Production Handbook. FOCAL PRESS.

Niblock, S. 1996: Inside Journalism. BLUEPRINT.

Orlebar, J. 2002: Digital Television Production, ARNOLD.

Orton, L. 2001: Media Courses UK 2001. BFI.

Quilliam, S. and Grove-Stephanson, I. 1990: Into Print. BBC.

The Report of the Skillset/DCMS Audio Visual Industries Training Group, 2001: Skills for Tomorrow's Media, SKILLSET/DCMS

Stafford, R. 1993: Hands On. BFI.

Tunstall, J. 2001: Media Occupations and Professions. A Reader. OXFORD UNIVERSITY PRESS.

Watts, H. 1984: On Camera. BBC.

Watts, H. 1992: Directing on Camera. AAVO.

CHAPTER TEN

MEDIA INVESTIGATION AND RESEARCH

The purpose of this final chapter is twofold. First it aims to provide you with some key ideas, arguments and references to assist in your *evaluation* of the many different kinds of research evidence and data which you will encounter in a variety of published, online and other electronic formats. Second, we hope that the notes which follow will also help you to think critically about *doing* some media research. It is unlikely, at this stage of your studies, that you will be required to complete a major, primary research project. The emphasis in most syllabuses at this stage tends to be on forms of *textual* or *genre* analysis (see Chapters 2, 3, 4), with some *contextual* investigation of related production determinants and audience reception possibilities (see Chapters 5 and 6). However, it is very useful to be aware of some of the key processes, dilemmas and sources involved in media research as this can help you develop a more critical and analytical approach to your studies – and this should result in better grades or marks for assignments. No one can cover everything – especially in the age of the Internet and world-wide web…(about which more later!). But you will generally receive credit for an approach that demonstrates the ability to find and sift between sometimes competing forms of research and to select and marshal evidence in support of your overall views and considered responses to the questions you have been set or have set yourself. You will also be assessed on your ability to *communicate* your interpretations and evidence, in written or other formats.

Primary research is that which you design and carry out yourself, either on your own or as a member of a team. The data or information that this generates is a *primary* research source. *Secondary research* is where you draw upon the published research of others in investigating a particular and defined problem or question. Both may be used in response to a set essay or coursework assignment or a more extensive research project. In their published or now extensive and expanding online formats, secondary sources should always be carefully acknowledged and noted in full detail – especially if you quote from them – and always in end notes or in the bibliography which should accompany your final write-up, essay or report.

The Social Production of Research

More than ever before, research into the media and forms of mass communication does not take place in a vacuum, it is carried out for particular purposes. Since the early twentieth century, which is when formal research into the media began, research has been shaped and sponsored by a range of different forces and agencies. These include the media industries themselves and their related networks, government departments, political and policy groups, military organisations, advertisers, public opinion analysts, academic and educational bodies, as well as a range of pressure groups and 'moral entrepreneurs'. These have had important implications for the types of questions that researchers have set out to ask, and how they have been able to answer them. They have motivated the funding and direction of research in particular ways, towards answering some questions rather than others.

Activity 10.1

Make a list of all the different types of organisations that you can think of that have carried out research into the media from the beginning of the twentieth century to the present day. What typical questions have they asked or sought answers to? Why?

Types of Research and Investigation

Academic research into the various media has been developed and contested by a number of theories and their disciplines or hybrid, subject areas. These include Sociology, Psychology, Economics, History, Literature, Theatre and Politics as well as Media, Film, Cultural and Communications Studies. In broad terms, two particular styles and traditions of research have emerged. These are often referred to as the *quantitative* and the *qualitative* approaches.

Quantitative research seeks to measure systematically and hence to 'quantify' the phenomenon being studied, and to express the results in terms of statistical data or tables. The focus is generally on the large-scale patterns or frequencies that make up a particular population, generic form or media related activity, and its aims are to produce hard, numerical evidence about the world and the way it works. The typical methods used reflect this and include large-scale surveys and questionnaires, opinion polls and interviews, and content analysis. Examples would include: large scale, statistical studies of trends in TV viewing in the UK (1952–2002) or analysis of trends in popular press content (1983–2003), for instance (see also Figures 10.1–10.7).

Qualitative research, on the other hand, aims less at measuring and more at understanding, often from 'the inside', the subjects under investigation. It tends to work on a much *smaller scale*, for instance with specific groups in particular contexts, with a focus on gaining insight into their meanings and values and how these may relate to aspects of social and cultural experience and dynamics. These cannot, it is argued, simply be 'measured' and are not appropriate to statistical expression. As a result, the typical methods used include informal interviews and discussions, oral histories and forms of textual analysis. Examples would include detailed study of three families and how they negotiate an evening's television viewing or a study of one week's TV drama.

The two approaches and their different emphases have often been thought of as polar opposites and characterised as mutually antagonistic traditions. In fact, as Hansen *et al* (1998), Deacon *et al* (1999), Jensen (2002), and Berger (2000) have noted, while there are important differences between them, there are also some common issues which bring them together in the interests of more adequate, critical forms of understanding. What is termed research *triangulation* – drawing upon different kinds of research evidence and method and hence increasing the credibility and weight of the case and argument – is an important consideration here.

Activity 10.2

Look at the data presented in Figures 10.1 and 10.2 concerning cinema attendance in Britain in the post-war period and refer back to Figure 5.8. These are all examples of quantitative data and research. Write a short analysis of each table indicating what you think they tell us about the changing nature of cinema in Britain. What kinds of data, from what kinds of sources, have been used to construct them? How reliable and valid are they, in your view? Are there any further questions which you feel are implied or posed by these statistics? How might some qualitative research complement or develop the 'hard' evidence provided here? How might you update the information to encompass the years since 1994?

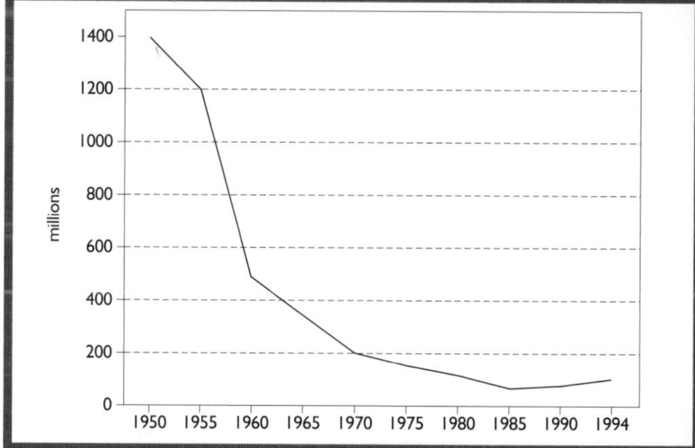

A

	Number of screens	Average number of admissions per screen (thousands)
1955	4 483	264
1960	3 034	165
1965	1 993	167
1970	1 553	128
1971	1 510	121
1972	1 531	106
1973	1 600	89
1974	1 590	90
1975	1 576	80
1976	1 562	68
1977	1 547	70
1978	1 563	81
1979	1 582	71
1980	1 576	65
1981	1 528	58
1982	1 439	45
1983	1 303	49
1984	1 246	43
1985	1 251	56
1986	1 229	59
1987	1 215	62
1988	1 250	62
1989	1 424	62
1990	1 552	57
1991	1 642	57
1992	1 805	54
1993	1 848	61
1994	1 919	64

FIGURE 10.1
UK cinema admissions 1950–94
Source: Cultural Trends 1994:23 © Policy Studies Institute

FIGURE 10.2
Note: Data only related to those cinemas which take advertising, covered by the Cinema Advertising Association. It is estimated that by 1992 this included all but between 30 and 40 cinemas in the UK

FIGURE 10.2
UK cinemas: number of screens and average admissions, 1955–94
Source: Cinema Advertising Association

In the first chapter of this book, we suggested that Media Studies in general is concerned with a number of linked stages in a cycle which encompasses media production, media texts and media consumption. You may find it useful to return to and review the discussion on p. 15 and Figure 1.5. Media research has not only addressed large-scale questions and issues concerning the *overall* role, use and presence of the various media in society. It has also focused on the particular conditions and contexts of *media producers* and production; the shape and forms of *media output and texts* which result from these contexts and activities; the programmes, images, front-page headlines, and so on; and their circulation; and finally their reception and use by *media audiences* and consumers. All three, the inter-relationships between them, and the media's relationship with the wider social and economic environment have formed the basis for some very different kinds of media research. Some of this has been *pragmatic*, largely industry-led, designed to provide definite answers to the problems of competition, marketing, sales, ratings, trends, forecasting, and so on. Ien Ang (1991) has written a valuable account of the history and dilemmas of television companies and their attempts to measure and 'know' their audiences, in the pre-digital era. Other research has been less pragmatic and more *critical* in design, carried out to make interventions into theoretical or policy debates (see for example, research summarised in Van Zoonen, 1994; Barnett, 2000; Cumberbatch, 1990; Jones, 1999, and Slevin, 2000).

In what follows, we offer some tips on approaching research in the areas of media production, media texts and media audiences, and the social, economic and political contexts within which they operate and occur. You will find it useful to extend and supplement this discussion by consulting some of the general references on research and research methods presented in the *Further reading* section for this chapter. Some useful website references are given in the list at the end of Chapter 1.

Stages in the Research Process :

- Define your topic and questions carefully and in detail. Identify what you are required to produce and by when. Organise your approach to the topic and make sure that what you are proposing is manageable in terms of time and available resources.
- Develop and write a plan for your research outlining the aims and methods you will use and why you will use them.
- Research and locate the information you need from various sources.
- Evaluate the information and evidence: what are the strengths and weaknesses?
- Organise and produce a first draft of your research findings and principal conclusions.
- Finalise your write up, checking that the length and focus are appropriate. Check that you have cited all sources correctly. Include an evaluation of your project as a whole, identifying any areas that might be strengthened or directions for future work.

Investigating Media Production

An interest in the activities and practices of media producers and their working environments is an inescapable part of Media Studies. As we have suggested, however, this level and stage of your studies is unlikely to require you to conduct first-hand, primary research on media producers and production processes. It is much more likely that you will need to know about and investigate the typical *production determinants* of a particular type of media text, the production processes and contexts and constraints that shape and account for its form. These would include things like budget, target audience, ownership and so on.

Activity 10.3

Choose a contemporary item of media output that you are familiar with and make notes about its production determinants – the factors which have shaped its production in certain ways. This might start by listing who was involved in the production, their roles and motivations and go on to consider their commercial or technical conditions as well as wider social and cultural contexts.

If you choose to go beyond this, one immediate research problem that you will encounter is *access*. Media organisations and institutions, like many others, are not easily open to researchers or students, especially in terms of the very many numbers of applications and requests for work experience or observation they often receive. They are more likely to respond positively, however, if you know what they do and are able to clarify what it is that you are interested in. In this sense, direct approaches to media organisations, locally, as well as nationally (unless you have good contacts!), are likely to be unsuccessful if you have not done some prior research on your topic – on the structure and characteristics of the wider media sector as a whole. A number of trade or industry publications and their websites, often reporting quantitative data, can be useful sources here. (These are summarised at the end of Chapter 1). Consulting sources like these should enable you to contextualise your research effectively and to refine and clarify your research questions. Not all questions, however, can be answered from the 'outside' and some will ideally require access to the 'inside' worlds of media producers, managers or performers themselves. This cannot be guaranteed, and when it is, may be variable in its terms and conditions. Rather than face-to-face interviews, you might try approaches by telephone or e-mail.

An interesting study to read in this context is Philip Schlesinger's (1987) account of news production in the BBC in the 1970s. The research was designed to explore how BBC news programmes were put together and in particular how the constraints of time, impartiality and professionalism had consequences for what was reported and broadcast. Schlesinger used two principal methods in his research: direct observation, inside BBC radio and TV newsrooms (some 90 days of observation over a four-year period), and a combination of formal and less formal interviews and discussions (over 120 in all) with news staff. Some production studies and related issues are summarised in Curran, J. (ed). 2000 and Tunstall, J. (ed). 2001. These studies provide useful models and pose some very interesting questions, but their scope and scale lie beyond the types of research and investigation that you are likely to be asked to undertake as part of your current course and level of study.

Investigating Media Texts, Genres and Forms

It is much more likely that you will be required to analyse some media texts or genres. In some cases you will be asked to produce an analysis of a particular text – a newspaper front-page, a film, a TV programme, etc and the contexts within which they are produced and consumed. A variety of approaches have been developed to study media texts and output, to try to investigate how they 'work' and how they 'carry' or mobilise certain ideas, values and meanings. In broad terms, these approaches tend to be either quantitative or qualitative in their design. For those that set out to measure media texts and output such as *content analysis*, the investigation tends to be focused at the *manifest* or surface levels and features of media texts. For those which adopt a more qualitative or interpretative emphasis, as for example in *semiotic* approaches (see discussion and examples in Chapters 2 and 3), or *discourse* analysis (see Fairclough, 1995) the analysis proceeds from these surface features to encompass the latent or underlying meanings which the texts draw upon. In some important ways, this analysis of textual meanings poses some related issues concerning audience reception (see Chapter 5).

Independent Critical Research

Many Media Studies courses require you to carry out and submit a piece of independent research. In the context of 'A' Level syllabuses, for instance, this is an element of the A2 section of the course. You will either be given a fairly free hand to choose a relevant topic which interests you or you will be required to choose one option, theme or topic from a prescribed list. Your research is likely to combine some primary and some secondary analysis and sources usually focused on aspects of media texts, genres or output.

Primary analysis:

This is analysis which you carry out yourself. A useful strategy is comparative textual analysis to highlight the distinctive features of texts and possibly how they have developed over time (in terms of genre, representation, etc).

Framework for such analysis: (for use with film or TV; you may need to adapt this for other media forms)

- Settings
- Narrative form and character roles
- Representations /audience identification
- Narrative themes/resolution and ideological 'messages'
- Audio-visual codes (technical)

The approach must be *analytical and not descriptive*, referring to key sequences or 'moments' from the text, e.g. the opening sequence from a film.

Secondary Sources:

Why use secondary sources?

a) In order to place the selected texts or items of media output in **context** and to understand more about:
- Their production determinants: who was involved (company, key individuals), their motivations (commercial, political, artistic, etc), the costs of production and so on.
- The wider social, political and cultural influences which are at work.

b) In order to develop **analysis and interpretation** drawing upon:
- Academic sources and references.
- 'Popular' sources - journalism, criticism or punditry.

These will offer interpretations which should be discussed but *not* used in place of first-hand personal, primary analysis.

Which secondary sources can I use?

- Academic journals: for instance *Screen*, *Media Culture & Society*, *Television and New Media* or *The European Journal of Communication*.
- Specialist magazines: e.g. *Sight and Sound*, *Broadcast*, *Campaign* and other relevant trade journals.
- Newspapers and popular magazines: for reviews or relevant articles and discussions.
- Websites: where it is very important to distinguish between those that are from a reputable source and those that are fan-based and mostly pure opinion. For examples see suggestions on p. 21.

A number of quite difficult issues are posed in the study of media texts, and in undertaking your own work and in evaluating the work of others, you will find it useful to think through the following general questions.

1   We are all used to watching, listening to, reading and generally consuming media texts and media output as part of our everyday lives. Interpreting media texts is something we all do as a matter of routine. How does analysis and research differ from these everyday activities? What about the researcher's own position and values? Don't we all have views and opinions about the

meanings or significance of media images and output? Can we generalise about these? Are there difficulties in carrying out analysis of media products that we are very familiar with?

2   Often, studies of media texts make distinctions between different 'layers' or levels of meaning which make them up. The 'manifest' or surface features are contrasted with the 'latent' or deeper-structure meanings. One of the suggestions here is that while most people will understand surface meanings, relatively few may be aware of the underlying codes at work in them. Also, the further one goes beneath the surface of any given media text, the more possibilities there may be for multiple meanings and readings.

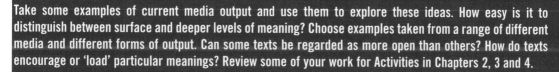

Activity 10.4

Take some examples of current media output and use them to explore these ideas. How easy is it to distinguish between surface and deeper levels of meaning? Choose examples taken from a range of different media and different forms of output. Can some texts be regarded as more open than others? How do texts encourage or 'load' particular meanings? Review some of your work for Activities in Chapters 2, 3 and 4.

3   How far can it be argued, and demonstrated, that media texts carry, 'prefer' or determine meanings? Recent work on media texts has tended to emphasise the 'polysemic' nature of much output – that it is, in principle, capable of mobilising many, many meanings and readings. Studies of audiences and their use of media texts in the last twenty years have also stressed the need to recognise the active, diverse and unpredictable ways in which people appropriate and make sense of media output. They also emphasise the need to take into account the diverse contexts of reception and backgrounds which have a bearing on how meanings are made (review discussion in Chapter 5). This emphasis has challenged the idea of the text as the sole bearer or carrier of meaning.

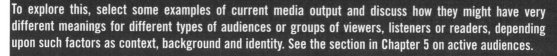

Activity 10.5

To explore this, select some examples of current media output and discuss how they might have very different meanings for different types of audiences or groups of viewers, listeners or readers, depending upon such factors as context, background and identity. See the section in Chapter 5 on active audiences.

Content Analysis

In the remainder of this section, we focus on content analysis. You should make a point of comparing this approach with that of semiotics, which is discussed in Chapter 2.

Content analysis is a method that has been developed to investigate the patterns that characterise the manifest or surface features of large quantities of media output. It can be carried out on a small scale, but given that its aims are to produce reliable, valid and representative information, the results of small-scale content analysis need to be treated with caution. It has been more typically employed on research projects investigating large-scale, historical trends, changes or patterns, including for example the representation of women and men in a variety of media genres and forms – from country music to advertising, television news, television series and films. Other applications have included mapping the incidence and types of violence in TV programming, as well as studies focused on other social themes, such as media coverage of industrial relations, ethnic groups, crime or environmental matters as Lisbet Van Zoonen has suggested.

> *In general its aim is to compare features of media output with concomitant features in reality. Thus, a typical conclusion of a content analysis study would be that the occurrence of violence on television grotesquely exaggerates the amount and type of violence one is likely to encounter in real life. In feminist research, the exemplary conclusion is that media output fails to represent the actual numbers of women in the world (51 per cent) and their contribution to the labour force.*
>
> *Van Zoonen (1994), p. 69*

So, content analysis, in general, is a method that aims to provide a *systematic* and *objective* description of the surface features of media texts. It may be used to investigate the broad contours of media output – for instance, in exploring the coverage of a given topic or theme: for example, how do the homeless, the disabled or the French, for instance, appear in British TV news programmes? Refer back to the research referred to in Chapter 6, Figure 6.9 as an additional example.

Activity 10.6

Figures 10.3, 10.4, 10.5, 10.6, 10.7 and 10.8 summarise the results of content analysis studies carried out in the early 1980s by the Commission for Racial equality and in 2000 by the Broadcast Standards Commission. Although conducted almost twenty years apart, both studies monitored the frequency and form of appearances on television by actors or participants according to their ethnicity. Examine the data and note down the principal conclusions that you would draw from them. In comparing the two sets of data, do the studies suggest any trends or changes in the visibility and representation of ethnic groups on British TV in the last twenty years? You should also note down any questions or issues that you feel the tables do not answer or any shortcomings you identify in their design. In the light of these studies, you may wish to design and carry out a small-scale content analysis of your own, to test out and explore these matters. In developing this activity you will find it helpful to refer to some recent and related work. See Cottle, S. 2000, Ferguson, R. 1998, Ross, K. 1996.

Ethnic origin	BBC1					BBC2			
	Week 1	Week 2	Week 3	Total no. of actors	% of total no. of actors	Week 1	Week 2	Total no. of actors	% of total no. of actors
White* (British)	176	133	157	466	92.6	18	32	50	100
West Indian	1	–	1	2	0.4	–	–	–	–
Black (African)	–	1	1	2	0.4	–	–	–	–
Indian	1	1	5	7	1.4	–	–	–	–
White (except British)	8	2	5	15	3.0	–	–	–	–
Middle Eastern	–	–	5	5	1.0	–	–	–	–
Chinese	1	1	2	4	0.8	–	–	–	–
Japanese	1	1	–	2	0.4	–	–	–	–
Black (USA)	–	–	–	–	–	–	–	–	–
TOTAL	188	139	176	503	100	18	32	50	100

* Includes Eire/N. Ireland

FIGURE 10.3
Total number of appearances of actors in BBC TV programmes monitored by ethnic origin
Source: Commission for Racial Equality, Television in a Multi-racial Society, 1982

Ethnic origin	London					Granada			
	Week 1	Week 2	Week 3	Total no. of actors	% of total no. of actors	Week 1	Week 2	Total no. of actors	% of total no. of actors
White* (British)	273	314	337	924	95.8	298	300	598	96.0
West Indian	6	4	10	20	2.1	6	4	10	1.6
Black (African)	1	1	–	2	0.2	1	1	2	0.3
Indian	1	–	–	1	0.1	1	1	2	0.3
White (except British)	4	6	2	12	1.2	4	6	10	1.6
Middle Eastern	–	–	–	–	–	–	–	–	–
Chinese	–	–	–	–	–	–	–	–	–
Japanese	–	1	–	1	0.1	–	1	1	0.2
Black (USA)	–	–	5	5	0.5	–	–	–	–
TOTAL	285	326	354	965	100	310	313	623	100

* Includes Eire/N. Ireland

FIGURE 10.4
Total number of appearances of actors in ITV programmes monitored by ethnic origin
Source: Commission for Racial Equality, Television in a Multi-racial Society, 1982

People from minority ethnic groups by programme type								
	1997		1998		1999		2000	
	N	%	N	%	N	%	N	%
National and Regional News	138	16	186	21	181	22	255	25
Factual	172	20	229	26	131	16	174	17
Light Entertainment	147	17	127	14	136	16	145	14
Sport	5	1	9	1	9	1	13	1
Religion	2	*	1	*	2	*	3	*
Children's programmes	3	*	9	1	22	3	17	2
Fiction	292	33	194	22	229	27	243	24
Film	114	13	134	15	125	15	180	17
TOTAL	873	100	889	100	835	100	1030	100
Base: All participants								

FIGURE 10.5
Source: Reproduced with kind permission from The Broadcasting Standards Commission

Level of appearance of ethnicity						
	Black		Asian		Other	
	N	%	N	%	N	%
1997						
Major	128	22	21	11	45	41
Minor	109	19	37	20	16	14
Interviewee/Incidental	336	59	131	69	50	45
TOTAL	573	100	189	100	111	100
1998						
Major	105	20	38	17	34	24
Minor	61	12	33	15	18	13
Interviewee/Incidental	358	68	154	68	88	63
TOTAL	524	100	225	100	140	100
1999						
Major	88	18	51	26	33	20
Minor	97	20	34	18	34	21
Interviewee/Incidental	295	61	108	56	95	59
TOTAL	480	99	193	100	162	100
2000						
Major	112	17	49	25	30	18
Minor	101	15	40	20	30	18
Interviewee/Incidental	452	68	111	56	105	64
TOTAL	665	100	200	101	165	100
Base: All participants						

FIGURE 10.6
Source: Reproduced with kind permission from The Broadcasting Standards Commission

Gender and age of participants: 2000										
	Black		Asian		Other		Total minority ethnic representation		Base	
	Male	Female	Male	Female	Male	Female	Male	Female	Male	Female
Age (years)	%	%	%	%	%	%	%	%	%	%
0-15	7	11	5	9	7	9	7	10	2	3
16-21	8	14	6	6	7	18	8	13	3	6
22-29	28	36	29	29	24	39	28	35	19	29
30-39	30	23	31	46	28	16	30	28	27	30
40-49	15	9	18	8	21	14	17	10	25	17
50-59	8	4	4	1	6	2	7	3	16	8
60+	3	2	7	-	6	2	4	2	8	6
TOTAL	99	99	100	99	99	100	101	101	100	99
Base: All participants										

FIGURE 10.7
Source: Reproduced with kind permission from The Broadcasting Standards Commission

Content analysis can also be used to make comparisons between different media – for instance, in analysing the different types of content regularly featured in tabloid and broadsheet newspapers in Britain. It has also been employed to monitor or to map historical changes and trends, as, for example, in Ferguson's (1983) study of the key themes in large circulation women's magazines in the post-war period (see Figure 10.8).

Activity 10.7

Study the data presented in Figure 10.8. Note the key conclusions you might advance on the basis of this analysis. Compare and contrast Ferguson's work with more recent types of analysis. See, for example, Chapter 14 in Stokes and Reading (ed). 1999.

Dominant themes	W	WO	WW	Total
Self-help: overcoming misfortune	35	32	40	36
Getting and keeping your man	11	10	15	12
Self-help: achieving perfection	13	14	6	11
The happy family	9	12	12	11
Heart versus head	12	8	12	10
The working wife is a good wife	9	13	7	10
Success equals happiness	11	8	8	9
Female state mysterious	–	–	–	–
Gilded youth	–	–	–	–
Other	–	3	–	1
n1	24	24	24	72

Sub-themes	W	WO	WW	Total
Getting and keeping your man	35	24	31	30
Self-help: overcoming misfortune	7	24	17	16
Heart versus head	26	8	14	16
The working wife is a good wife	18	15	15	16
The happy family	–	11	23	12
Self-help: achieving perfection	14	18	–	11
Female state mysterious	–	–	–	–
Gilded youth	–	–	–	–
Success equals happiness	–	–	–	–
Other	–	–	–	–
n2	14	17	12	43

Figure 10.8
Dominant themes and sub-themes in women's magazines, all subjects, * all titles, 1979–80 (%)
Source: M. Ferguson, Forever Feminine: Women's Magazines and the Cult of Femininity, Heinemann, 1983
* Excluding beauty
n1 = 1 per item, 3 items per issue, 4 issues per year; n2 = open-ended
W = Woman; WO = Woman's Own; WW = Woman's Weekly

Stages in Content Analysis

Content analysis can be applied to written, audio and visual forms of media texts and their contents, although these different characteristics have implications for the basic mechanics of the analysis itself. Content analysis is also a method that has been developed to deal with large-scale amounts of media content and this has usually necessitated the use of trained teams of researchers, using computers to compile and to analyse results.

The *first stage* of any content analysis should involve defining and 'pinning down' the research problem or question as clearly as possible. At this initial stage, you should be able to explain what it is that you are interested in and which basic patterns or frequencies of media content you are aiming to measure and why. You may even find it useful to think at this stage about how the results of your analysis might be interpreted. Make sure that your research question is appropriate to content analysis. Bear in mind, even at this early stage, the practicalities of what you are embarking on: for instance, do you have the necessary time, resources and access to media content to manage the analysis you are proposing to carry out? If you do not have all these, you will need to rethink or redesign your proposals.

This leads on to a *second stage* that involves more detailed planning and preparation. In spite of the fact that content analysis works most effectively when applied to large-scale or total amounts of media output, it is not always possible to cover everything. In fact, it is highly likely that you will need to construct a sample – a systematic selection from total output. If, for instance, you were interested in changes in content of *The Times* newspaper since 1800, it would prove too great a job to analyse every single edition. You would need to select a sample that was manageable but that was also representative, that is, an adequate reflection of the overall picture of trends in content since that time. For example, if you decided to select every edition of *The Times* published on Saturdays, your sample may be biased as a result and this will compromise the subsequent analysis. A number of methods are used to try to overcome this problem including random sampling or quota sampling. In these ways the researcher tries to ensure more precisely that the sample will accurately reflect the whole. If you want to study more than one medium, channel, or range of output, you will need to consider, in detail, precisely which combination of sources your analysis will be based upon.

Having defined your sample, the range of texts to be included in your analysis, you can then proceed to the *third stage*, measurement. The main point behind content analysis is to place parts of the text – the films, programmes, magazines, newspapers, adverts and so on – into certain categories. Think of an old post office sorting room. Each piece of the text – measured in predefined units – is like a letter being placed or 'posted' into a pigeon-hole or category. The idea is to see what kind of pattern is formed when all of the selected content has been divided into the available categories. Units will vary according to the medium, form and scale of the analysis. Words may be used, or pages, or other measures of printed text, for instance column centimetres. Photographs and components of images can equally form the basis for analysis. In broadcast or film forms, units of time are often employed as well as visual units of appearance or setting. Breaking the text down into units allows you to place it into categories, and these will vary depending on your focus and research question. Defining the range of categories – the 'pigeon-holes' in the sorting process – is of central importance to the analysis. Categories should be very clearly defined and avoid ambiguity. How they are defined will directly affect final results. For example, a study of the typical contents of tabloid newspapers might use a range of categories including 'sports news' and 'news about celebrities' to measure the contents of an agreed sample of current tabloid papers. These categories must be clearly understood. How the analysis would deal with a report of a sports star's deviant behaviour at a celebrity event would be a key test. As with a great deal of research, before carrying out the full-scale analysis, it is a good idea to try out or 'pilot' your study, testing out the units and categories you have adopted, refining or amending them as necessary in the light of this rehearsal. You are then in a position to carry out your analysis.

The *fourth and final stage* takes place after you have completed your measurements and you are able to examine your results and review the analysis as a whole. You will find it useful to ask the following questions:

- What kinds of patterns does your analysis reveal?
- Do your results provide evidence for, or answers to, your original research question?
- Are there any unexpected features?
- What problems did you encounter in carrying out the analysis?
- Are your results valid – do they reflect the real situation?
- What conclusions can be drawn from your data?
- If you were to repeat your analysis what changes would you make?
- What are the limitations to content analysis?

Activity 10.8

1   Refer back to your discussions of content analysis based on the data and figures used in the last two activities. Discuss those studies in the light of the four stages outlined above. What key issues do they raise for you about content analysis as a research method?
2   Choose a question that interests you about an aspect of current media output or content. Using the four stages above, design and complete, to pilot stage only, a content analysis relevant to your question. Discuss, or give a short presentation on, your outline. After this, you may choose to extend this activity into a more developed or completed analysis if you wish.

Investigating Media Audiences

How can information about audiences be discovered? Much depends on the type of information collected and why it is required. There is a constant production of audience data gathered by market research organisations primarily for commercial purposes. These data are essentially quantitative in nature.

Data discussed and presented in Chapters 1 and 5 reveal some of the broad patterns of media consumption. National totals for television programmes watched (the 'ratings'), newspaper circulation figures, etc, help to inform those working in the various media industries about the relative success of their products in competitive markets. Although these figures are quite crude in nature, they are still important indicators of cultural consumption. The fact that one in five people in Britain reads *The Sun* each day means it merits much more attention as a media text than, say, *The Times* with an average circulation of about 650 000.

One of the media industries' key motivations to research audiences is to supply data to potential advertisers who are looking to reach their target consumers in the most effective way. There has been an increasing trend towards monitoring the social profiles of media audiences. Such demographic data reveal how audiences are composed in terms of variables like social class, age and gender. This is valuable as a preliminary point of reference for audience research that seeks to investigate patterns of use, and it then may go on to ask how and why social groups respond differently to the media.

Some audience research has relied almost exclusively on quantitative data. The correlation of television viewing figures and attitudinal surveys according to socio-demographic variables like age and family membership has been used in *cultivation analysis*. This is designed to test whether television viewing could be said to influence general attitudes to the world. For example, Gerbner and Gross (1976) argued that the more television you watch, the more likely you are to have a fearful or distrustful attitude to the world outside.

However, quantitative statistics do have some serious limitations. They may reveal little about the meanings audiences produce from media texts and the context in which such texts are received. Illustrating this point are the television ratings figures compiled by the Broadcasters Audience Research Board (BARB – website provided at end of Chapter 1). These measure the audience size via a sample of computer-linked homes in which meters are installed. When members of the household select a programme to view, the meter records their presence and which channel is chosen. What is not measured, though, is whether the set is actually being watched, how it is watched or the motivation for watching, how much social interaction is happening within the room, or the kind of meaningful response produced by the programme. Currently, the only supplementary information systematically gathered is in the form of audience appreciation statistics – an index of how interesting and/or enjoyable viewers found a particular programme, sometimes gathered by means of a diary report.

Research Questionnaires

Questionnaires are survey methods routinely used in the investigation of media consumption, although they can also be deployed to find out about aspects of media production or organisational policy and practice. They come through the letterbox, in newspapers, magazines and online formats, and they often form the basis for structured interviews in the street, shopping centre or by telephone. Among the advantages claimed for them as research methods are their accuracy, their access to a wide range of respondents and their flexibility. Disadvantages might include their expense, problems of no return or delayed response, and ambiguities in design and response. Questionnaires are frequently employed to gather quantitative data and information about large-scale, representative populations, offering a choice of predetermined responses (the simplest being YES/NO tick boxes), although most will allow some space for more qualitative or open-ended forms of response.

Activity 10.9

Gather together a number of questionnaires from magazines, newspapers or other media-related sources. Analyse and discuss their design and respective distribution methods. What kinds of information have they been constructed to collect and why? How might they be improved?

Developing a Questionnaire

There are a series of stages involved in developing and carrying out a research project based around the use of a questionnaire. This may be the sole method to be used, or it may be used to explore a particular part or phase of an overall research problem. Initially, it is useful to clarify, discuss and define which responses you are interested in, and why. There should be a clear point to your questionnaire and you should be able to make out a convincing case for using a questionnaire in your study.

In developing a questionnaire, you will need initially to identify your topic area carefully and develop a sequence of appropriate questions. The sequence or order of questions may be an important factor, what you ask first and so on, and you will need to plan the length of the questionnaire overall. You will also need to consider the *sample size*, in other words, how many respondents you are aiming for and why. You will also need to think carefully about the *type of respondents* you are hoping to contact and elicit responses from. For instance, if your study is one which explores general patterns of radio use, your questionnaire will be different to one which seeks to investigate the use of radio by young women in the home.

As Rothwell (1996) has suggested, most questionnaires are made up of a number of standard components, although these will vary depending on the purpose and scale of your project. The typical components include:

- A **title**.
- An **identifying number**. This may be especially important where you wish to preserve the confidentiality of information collected. The number allows you to identify each individual respondent without necessarily revealing their name, status, etc.
- **Introductory remarks**. These may take the form of a covering letter supplied with the questionnaire or may be integrated into the opening section. This should explain the purpose of the survey, who is conducting it and why, and it is usual to provide assurances concerning the anonymity or confidentiality of data to be collected.
- **Instructions** for completing the questionnaire. Unless these are self-evident, they are usually provided just before the particular sections or questions to be answered. Typically they will explain the mode of response required – ticking boxes, circling numbers, etc. You may also need to indicate how the questionnaire should be returned for analysis.
- **Respondent details**. These may cover such matters as name, address, age, gender, occupation, etc. These details are often collected in an opening or closing section of the questionnaire. Remember to indicate that confidentiality will be preserved with regard to these and other details, as this may have a bearing on how your respondents answer your questions.
- **Focal data and questions**. These are questions or items which you will use to gather data on the attitudes, opinions or practices which lie at the heart of your investigation. These may take the form of what are known as *closed questions*, where the response is predetermined, typically the kinds which ask the respondent to tick boxes or circle numbers. For instance:

Do you own a compact disc player?   YES[ ]   NO[ ]
You can *list* a set of response *options*:
How long have you owned a personal stereo?
Less than 6 months [ ]
1 to 2 years [ ]
3 to 5 years [ ]
More than 5 years [ ]

You can also make use of questions which involve *scaling* or *ranking* where the respondent either chooses a point on a scale which you have predetermined, or is required to rank a number of given items or possibilities in order of preference, importance or significance. Examples of *scaled questions*:

How often do you listen to radio programmes in the evening?

Nearly always	Often	Seldom	Hardly ever
1	2	3	4

Sometimes a statement may be used to stimulate a scaled response:
Television soap opera serials deal effectively with important social issues.

Agree strongly	Tend to agree	Tend to disagree	Disagree strongly
1	2	3	4

In some cases, questionnaires may make use of the *semantic differential*, where words are used to establish the ends of a scaled dimension. For example:

Describe your favourite female film star by circling the numbers on the scales below which most closely correspond to your choice:

Strong	1 2 3 4 5 6 7	Weak
Active	1 2 3 4 5 6 7	Passive
Glamorous	1 2 3 4 5 6 7	Ordinary
Always the same	1 2 3 4 5 6 7	Varied performance
Like me	1 2 3 4 5 6 7	Not like me

Questions may also use *ranked responses* to show preference, for instance:
Place a number from 1 to 7 in the left-hand column adjacent to each item to indicate your preferences for weekend television viewing.

[ ] Comedy programmes
[ ] Feature films
[ ] Cartoons
[ ] Sports programmes
[ ] Music programmes
[ ] Game shows
[ ] News and Documentary programmes

- **Open questions**. In contrast to closed questions, open-ended questions do not have predetermined options for the respondent and allow for a much greater range of unpredictable responses or answers. The main purpose of open questions is to allow the respondent to express their own views or ideas on the given topic. An example would be:

  What do you think about the coverage of sport on television?

Responses to open questions like this one are more difficult to analyse because of their unpredictability. Usually, they will allow a space for the respondent to write their answer, and open questions are conventionally situated at the end, either of a given section or of the questionnaire as a whole.

- **Closing remarks**. You should always make a point of thanking your respondents and indicating how the questionnaire will be collected or should be returned to you.

As well as designing your questions and laying out your questionnaire to take account of these components, you should try to follow the following schedule and sequence in managing the overall project (adapted from Rothwell, 1996). Obviously, the sequence and times indicated may vary considerably, depending on the time available and the specific form and range of investigation aimed for.

- Identify topic areas and develop initial questions and format	1 week
- Discuss with tutor and revise	1 week
- Try out or pilot questionnaire and revise	1 week
- Print questionnaire and distribute	1 week
- Wait for responses, possible follow-up	2 weeks
- Collate, analyse and write up data	2 weeks
- Review effectiveness of questionnaire and complete final report	1 week
Total:	*9 weeks*

Activity 10.10

Choose a topic or an issue which you have encountered on your course in Media Studies which particularly interests you. Write some notes on how it might be researched using a questionnaire. Outline key questions and think about how you would interpret possible responses. If possible, discuss your outline notes with a tutor and other students.

If it is appropriate, design, pilot and carry out a small-scale questionnaire survey. You might choose, for instance, to compare aspects of large-scale, national or other patterns of media consumption with those which you research in particular, local circumstances.

Qualitative Approaches: Ethnographies and Interviews

Qualitative research seeks to uncover audience interpretations and observations via in-depth personal interviews and discussions with individuals or small groups. At its best, it should allow subjects to express their responses freely in as natural a setting as possible. Such an approach is sometimes called 'ethnographic' to refer to an emphasis derived from anthropological studies where the researcher sometimes tries to fit in with, and be accepted by, the people, group or subculture being studied. It has been influential in much recent audience research, especially with respect to studies of television viewing. Nevertheless, ethnographic and other qualitative approaches in general are not without their problems. Reliance on subjects' own perceptions and accounts, for instance, assumes that they are fully conscious of how they are responding to a media text. Thus, there is a need for skilful interviewing to probe beyond surface comments, while avoiding the temptation to put words in people's mouths:

> *Eighteen families were interviewed in their own homes during the spring of 1985. Initially the two parents were interviewed, then later in each interview their children were invited to take part in the discussion along with their parents. The interviews, which lasted between one and two hours, were tape-recorded and then transcribed in full for analysis.*
>
> *The fact that the interviews were conducted 'en famille' doubtless means that respondents felt a certain need to play out accepted roles, and doubtless interviews with family members separately would bring out other responses. However, I was precisely interested in how they functioned as 'families', within (and against) their roles.*
>
> *Moreover, the interviewing method (unstructured discussion for a period between one and two hours) was designed to allow a fair degree of probing. Thus on points of significance I returned the discussion to the same theme at different stages in the interview, from different angles. This means that anyone 'putting me on' (consciously or unconsciously) by representing themselves through an artificial/stereotyped 'persona' which has no bearing on their 'real' activities would have to be able to sustain their adopted 'persona' through what could be seen as quite a complex form of interrogation!*
>
> *Morley (1986)*

Research Interviews: Questions and Answers

Interviews are a research method that can be employed to investigate a wide variety of research problems and projects. We may commonly encounter them in the street, supermarket, at the door or on the telephone. They have become a major part of market research, public-opinion polling and other forms of social and commercial enquiry. In this section, we have assumed that you are interested in carrying out a study rather like Morley's, that is, small-scale and informal, aiming at insights into people's values and attitudes, *their* reasons and explanations for their media-related activities and forms of consumption or reception.

A consistent theme in discussions of interviewing as a research practice emphasises the basic point that if you want to find out something about people's activities, then the best way is to ask them. Research interviews, it is claimed, can give direct access to unique forms of experience and expression often denied by other methods. The strengths of interviews often include: their freedom (both the interviewer and interviewee are allowed to explore and negotiate the particular topic); their directness of contact, feedback and response; and *their* in-depth detail. Criticisms of projects which rely on interviews tend to include: questions of bias or distortion; their narrow and non-representative nature; and issues of interpretation and (mis)understanding.

The Informal Interview

If you opt for a project based on informal interviews, then you are probably interested in gaining qualitative insights or understanding of the meanings, interpretations, values and experiences of a small group of people. This may be the sole aim of the study, or you may choose to combine this approach with other methods, for example in linking textual analysis of a given item of media output to the study of its actual reception – how people respond to an advertising campaign, for instance. The task of the interviewer is to create and adapt to the conditions under which the interviewee will disclose or 'open up' their particular version or unique 'inside story' relevant to the topic under investigation. As a result, you will need to be alive to the multiple, often divergent perspectives, values and views held by people, and assume that you will encounter these. Informal interviews, in contrast to the more formal survey, adopt a conversational, flexible and more open-ended format, where the strict roles of interviewer and interviewee do not, ideally, intervene in the discussion. Rather than asking closed questions, researchers using this approach will employ open-ended, non-directed questions (see above under *Developing a Questionnaire*). The interviewer will not work with a fixed schedule of questions, often preferring a loose sequence of themes or points to be covered in discussion. Informal interviews will also tend to be carried out in 'natural' settings – the home, household, workplace, club, or other social setting, on 'territory' familiar to the interviewee rather than to the interviewer.

In general terms, researchers using informal interviews often also draw on observation, in some cases participant observation. They should also pay more attention to the process of each interview – including their own part in it – and how this might have implications for the insights gathered as a result; this is termed 'reflexivity'. The aim is to act less as an 'interrogator' and more as a 'guide' in the conduct of the interview and in the mutual process of 'finding out about' the topics being researched.

Stages in the Informal Interview

There is no one correct way to conduct an informal interview, and the process will generally require more skill, patience and insight on the part of the interviewer than are involved in the survey situation. The steps in the research procedure can be summarised as follows (adapted from O'Sullivan, 1996):

1 **Specification**. This initial, preparatory, stage has much in common with the first stages of any research procedure. It should involve, as a result, the precise definition of the aims of the study, of research on any other sources of relevant information, and a general clarification of goals. You will need to think through, and be able to defend, your choice of informal interviewing in terms of your chosen subject matter or topic selected for study. You should make a point of clearly establishing the limits to the study and clarifying your themes and questions for the interviews. How you will record the interviews is an issue which should be considered at this stage. Some piloting of your proposed sequence is also invaluable now, and you should discuss your research ideas with tutors and other students.

2 **Contact**. You will need to select and contact your potential interviewees. You may know them or not, they may be involved in a particular group or location. Think carefully about who and how you select for your interviews. When you make contact with them you should be able to briefly outline the nature of your research and the subjects you will want to cover in the interview. In general the interviewer will make her/himself available to suit the convenience of the interviewee, and it is the interviewee who

usually nominates the meeting place. You, in turn, should be able to let them know approximately how long the interview will take and reassure them about the confidentiality of the proceedings.

3 **Interviewing**. There is considerable debate about the best ways to record informal types of interview. The attempt to put people at their ease, or to 'fit in' with social circumstances, is often undermined by the practice of recording what is said. Many people are put off by, or at least wary of, large microphones being waved under their noses, even when (or especially when) they have been told to 'relax'. Researchers can use either one or a combination of the following techniques:

- Notes written by the interviewer during the interview.
- Memory, with notes written up after the interview.
- Audio recording, from which transcripts – written records – may be made.
- Video recording, from which transcripts may also sometimes be made.

All these have their relative merits and drawbacks. Note-taking or audio recording are perhaps the two commonest methods, although the issue of how the act and means of recording may 'distort' the outcomes and conduct of the interview deserves important consideration. It is always useful to make a careful note of the date and circumstances of the interview, the name of the interviewee and any other details relevant to the project. It may be important to reiterate your reassurance to the interviewee about the confidential nature of the interview. In some circumstances it is also useful to ascertain, before beginning the interview, how much time is available so that you can pace the interview accordingly. About one hour is usually regarded as a rough guide for the minimum time needed to conduct a productive interview, although flexibility is needed here. The main questions and sequence of key themes may have been decided in advance, but discussion and follow-up questions cannot always be anticipated. Most interviewers have to 'think on their feet', and the use of prompt questions – to draw out or to follow up a particular response – can be very valuable in keeping the interview flowing along the right lines.

4 **Analysis**. Having completed as many interviews as possible or appropriate to your project, and depending on the method of recording, you will now have a mass of 'raw' information. Once a collection of interviews has been gathered, how can the material be analysed and organised? In general, analysis requires that you first thoroughly familiarise yourself with your information, 'immersing' yourself in the different interviewees' accounts. Wherever possible, common themes and patterns should be identified, for instance in classifying discourses or recurrent points of reference. You may also need to be alive to key similarities or differences of interpretation or response and deal with the problem of explaining the wider origins of these similarities or differences. In our media-saturated society (see Chapter 1), responses to any single media text are bound to be influenced by exposure to previous related texts – what has been called intertextuality. For example, filmgoers viewing *Batman* may be influenced by having read the comics as children, seen the television series, been exposed to the publicity, had preconceptions about star performers like Jack Nicholson, and so on. Furthermore, individuals' frameworks of interpretation can always be seen as being partly a product of negotiating social determinants and identities such as class, gender, ages, nationality and ethnicity. This has formed a key theme and problem for much ethnographic audience research.

In the final stage of analysis, you will often have to write up your research report, and this will be supported by quotations or extracts from your interviews. In the context of the research problem that you began with, what have your interviewees told you about the topic under investigation?

As a basis for particular research projects, researchers have used interviews not only with individuals but also with groups of people. The benefits of this approach stem from the potential for discussion to develop among the group members and the value of this as a research resource. Market researchers, for instance, regularly employ 'focus groups' in their work. These are groups of consumers who are brought together by the interviewer to discuss and evaluate aspects of a product range, or an established or new brand. In a similar fashion, other recent forms of audience research have used family or household groups, groups of schoolchildren, women or other groupings. Group interviews can be especially valuable when, in reality, it is the group or subculture that the researcher wants to investigate rather than the subject they are discussing. However, if you do use group interviews, you will need to manage and to be aware of the group dynamics in the conduct of the interview.

Activity 10.11

a   Revisit the first chapter in this book. Plan and carry out an informal interview with a colleague, friend or family member about their everyday relationships with different types and forms of media. What conclusions might be drawn from this interview?

b   Conduct a series of interviews as part of a local oral history project on either memories of cinema before the Second World War, or memories of early television. What do these interviews provide which you could not get from other research sources?

c   Design and carry out a series of interviews with people to explore their attitudes to either satellite or digital television (at least two with those who do have domestic access and two with those who do not), or a recent widespread advertising campaign. You may define and negotiate any other approved topic if appropriate. Summarise your main findings and present them to a group on your course.

Concluding Notes

For many students, the Internet has become an important and exciting research tool and resource. The Internet makes available information on a huge number of topics and provides access to important databases, websites and reference materials. In general, therefore, online searches and Internet databases can provide an important compliment to more traditional systems and methods. However, it is vital that you use the Internet critically, evaluating the quality and the relevance of the information available for your own purposes. In many cases there is a lot of information that isn't available on the Internet and printed or other sources – books and journals, for instance, might be more effective. It is likely therefore that your research will refer to Internet sources but not exclusively rely upon them. You should make a point of clarifying these matters with your tutor as you develop your research plan and process (see Stein, 1999).

Researching the media is an exciting and generally rewarding part of your studies which offers you opportunities to test out or to develop your own particular interests and ideas. By working through some of the key ideas and issues we have outlined in this chapter – and the book as a whole – we hope that you will produce better, more informed and satisfying research projects. Good luck with your work!

Further Reading

Alasuutari, P. 1995: Researching Culture: Qualitative Method and Cultural Studies. SAGE.

Bell, J. 1987: Doing Your Research Project. OPEN UNIVERSITY PRESS.

Berger, A. 1991: Media Analysis Techniques. SAGE.

Berger, A. 2000: Media and Communication Research Methods. SAGE.

Bignall, J. 2002: Media Semiotics: An Introduction. MANCHESTER UNIVERSITY PRESS.

Bryman, A. 1988: Quantity and Quality in Social Research. UNWIN HYMAN.

Cottle, S. 2000: Ethnic Minorities and the Media. OPEN UNIVERSITY PRESS.

Cumberbatch, G. 1990: Television Advertising and Sex Role Stereotyping. BROADCASTING STANDARDS COUNCIL.

Curran, J. (ed). 2000: Media Organisations in Society. ARNOLD.

Deacon, D., Pickering, M., Golding, P., and Murdock, G. 1999: Researching Communications. ARNOLD.

Fairclough, N. 1995: Media Discourse. ARNOLD.

Ferguson, R. 1998: Representing Race: Ideology, Identity and the Media. ARNOLD.

Gunter, B. 2000: Media Research Methods. SAGE.

Hansen, A., Cottle, S., Negrine, R., and Newbold, C. 1998: Mass Communication Research Methods. PALGRAVE.

Hammersley, M. and Atkinson, P. 1983: Ethnography: Principles in Practice. TAVISTOCK.

Jensen, K.B. and Jankowski, N.W. (eds). 1991: A Handbook of Qualitative Methodologies for Mass Communication Research. ROUTLEDGE.

Jensen, K.B. (ed). 2002: A Handbook of Media and Communication Research: Qualitative and Quantitative Methodologies. ROUTLEDGE.

Jones, S. (ed). 1999: Doing Internet Research: Critical Issues and Methods for Examining the Net. SAGE.

Krueger, R.A. 1994: Focus Groups: A Practical Guide for Applied Research. SAGE.

Machin, D. 2002: Ethnographic Research for Media Studies. ARNOLD.

McNeill, P. 1990: Research Methods. ROUTLEDGE.

Morley, D. 1992: Television, Audiences and Cultural Studies. ROUTLEDGE.

Oppenheim, A.N. 1992: Questionnaire Design, Interviewing and Attitude Measurement. BLACKWELL.

O'Sullivan, T. 1996: 'Research interviews', in B. Allison, T. O'Sullivan, A. Owen, J. Rice, A. Rothwell and C. Saunders (eds), Research Skills for Students. KOGAN PAGE.

Ross, K. 1996: Black and White Media. POLITY.

Rothwell, A. 1996: 'Questionnaire design', in Allison, B., *et al.* Research Skills for Students. KOGAN PAGE.

Silverman, D. 2000: Doing Qualitative Research. SAGE.

Stein, S. 1999: Learning, Teaching and Researching on the Internet. LONGMAN.

Stokes, J. 2003: How to do Media and Cultural Studies. SAGE.

Tolson, A. 1996: Mediations: Text and Discourse in Media Studies. ARNOLD.

Trowler, P. 1996: Investigating Media. COLLINS.

Weber, R.P. 1990: Basic Content Analysis. SAGE.

Note: Terms in italics are defined within the glossary.

Aberrant decoding – an interpretation which, rather than recognise the *preferred meaning* of a media text, produces instead a deviant or unanticipated reading.

Anchorage – the fixing or limiting of a particular set of meanings to an image, often a photograph or advert, usually through the use of a caption or other written text.

Audience positioning – the process whereby *media texts* work to situate the reader, spectator, etc from a particular point of view or perspective.

Auteur – a film director who, it is claimed, is able to imbue his/her films with a recognisably distinctive personal vision or style.

Binary Opposites – a means of identifying the conflicting values or fundamental concepts inherent in all forms of texts, based on the structuralist work of Levi-Strauss.

Bricolage – the process of deliberately 'borrowing' or adapting signs or features from different styles or *genres* to create a new mixture of meanings; often associated with *postmodernism*.

Broadcasting flow – a reference to the continuous stream of television and radio output within which there is often a lack of distinctive programme boundaries.

Classical narrative structure – the dominant mode of storytelling found in Hollywood films, which involves three distinctive stages: a state of order or *equilibrium*, a disruption to that stability, and a climactic resolution which restores order and a new equilibrium and harmony.

Code – an organised cultural system of signs, language or symbols, and its rules, which govern and allow for the communication of meanings and interpretations.

Consensus – the set of ideas, beliefs and values that are shared and agreed by the majority of the population, the centre ground that by definition often excludes alternative positions.

Consumer society – modern complex *cultures* and societies which are defined by a dominant orientation towards the marketing and consumption of goods and services. These, it is argued, play central roles in the lifestyle cultures of modern times and in related processes which allow for the formation of identities. In consumer cultures, groups and individuals are increasingly defined in terms of their patterns of consumption, choice and expression, as related to leisure, clothing, music, food and many other goods and activities.

Content analysis – a research method used to systematically measure or compare the characteristics of selected samples of media output and content.

Convention – a widely accepted and recognised rule or device relating to aspects of *media texts* and their production and consumption.

Convergence – the ways in which different media and communication networks and technologies are coming together into new, digitally based, integrated systems. The PC, mobile phone, laptop and television are all merging the traditional boundaries and uses of communications and broadcasting. This is an increasing feature of the contemporary domestic, leisure and entertainment environment.

Cropping – the process of cutting down an image, usually a photograph, to focus on one particular aspect or meaning and to eliminate superfluous detail.

Cultural capital/competence – the particular knowledge, experience, taste and skills possessed by audiences which shape their choice and interpretation of *media texts*. Cultural capital is related to social class and other divisions, especially to educational experience and career.

Culture – often understood as the 'whole way of life' which distinguishes a society or social group. Culture refers especially to the systems of ideas, beliefs and values which characterise and make up the world of the group and the systems which allow for communication, representation and meaning, from languages to computers, music and digital images. (See also *Mediated culture, Popular culture, Situated cultures* and *Surveillance culture.*)

Demographics – demographic data refers to the social characteristics of the population being studied, e.g. social class, gender and age. For the purposes of media analysis, it is particularly helpful in identifying the social profile of the audience.

Denotation/Connotation – different 'levels' of meaning within a text: the first level, **denotation**, represents only what the text shows whereas the second level, **connotation**, includes the additional associations (or information) that the reader (or producer) brings to the image or text and 'adds' to the denotative meaning.

Deregulation – relaxing the commercial controls and limitations on the media imposed by the state, usually focusing in particular on ownership and range or requirements of services and their quality.

Discourse Analysis – a means of analysing texts based on linguistics and in recent times, the theories of Foucault. Discourse analysis identifies the culturally and socially produced sets of ideas and values that structure texts and representations. It helps to identify abstract and ideological assumptions about the world that may be implicitly contained in particular texts.

Encoding/Decoding – the linked processes of constructing and interpreting *media texts* as they are conceived, transmitted and received, involving producers (who **encode** meanings) and receivers (who **decode** the meanings).

Equilibrium/Disequilibrium – the tensions of *narrative*. A secure and harmonious state is often used to begin many media narratives. This equilibrium or balance is conventionally followed and disturbed by tension or events which cause unpredictability or disequilibrium to occur. The typical 'happy ending' requires the restoration of the balance or equilibrium depicted at the beginning.

Ethnography – a research method which aims to understand the social perspective and cultural values of a particular group, from the 'inside', by participating with or getting to know their activities in depth and in detail.

Femme fatale – a seductive and powerful female character who is able to entrap and exploit men for personal gain.

Film noir – a *genre* of films characterised by a distinctive visual style – low-key and high-contrast lighting emphasising light and shadows, and a *narrative* focusing on the dark side of human life.

Fly-on-the-wall documentary – a television documentary form which is characterised by unobtrusively filming subjects in their natural settings, and representing them with a minimum of on-screen presenter or voice-over narration, as if the camera was not there.

Gatekeeper – a journalist, especially an editor, who filters the flow of news stories in order to select which stories will be presented to the audience. The term is also applied to other decision-makers within media and cultural industries.

Genre – a way of categorising texts by identifying certain common characteristics in style, *narrative* and structure.

Global culture (Globalisation) – the results of greatly increased, worldwide, media and communication systems and the activities of international cultural markets. The local and the national are now linked in many ways to a wider world culture. **Globalisation** refers to the international economic, political and cultural processes which have accelerated this growth post-1950.

Global village – a phrase which is used to describe the ways in which modern electronic media have spread around, interconnected and 'shrunk' the world, making possible seemingly immediate forms of communication and cultural relationships associated in the past with small-scale communities.

Hegemony – the theory that those in power maintain domination through cultural influence rather than force. Cultural agencies such as the media privilege dominant ideologies (that serve to disguise the realities of social injustice) which prevail over competing or alternative ideas through becoming accepted as 'commonsense' wisdom.

Hypodermic needle model – a theory which asserts that the media are powerful agents of influence, capable of 'injecting' ideas and behaviours directly into relatively passive audiences of isolated individuals.

Iconography – the identification of particular visual signs strongly associated with particular genres. For example, guns, horses and stagecoaches in westerns or robots and spaceships in Science Fiction films.

Identification – the processes by which readers of a text negotiate a certain position with regard to its *narrative*, points of view and characters.

Ideology – a set of ideas, or a world view, which produces a partial and selective version of reality often to protect the interests of powerful social groups.

Independents – media producers who are free from control by larger media organisations and who are often more willing and able to engage in newer, less conservative forms of *media production*.

Integration – horizontal and vertical – **horizontal integration** occurs when a company takes over a competitor at the same level of production within the same market sector; **vertical integration** occurs when a company takes over another company which occupies a different stage of the manufacturing or distribution cycle.

International media flow – the patterns of import and export, *media production* and *media consumption* which result from the operation of worldwide media and cultural markets for films, television programmes, music, adverts, etc. Some countries and regions produce and export, others import and consume. Such patterns and relations of 'flow' have important consequences for identity and *globalisation*.

Internet – globally interconnected telecommunication and computer network systems which allow for diverse forms of interactivity and data interchange.

Intertextuality – the way in which *media texts* gain their meanings by referring to other media texts that the producers assume that the reader will be familiar with and recognise.

Male gaze – a term derived from feminist film theory which asserts that men are able to exercise control over women by representing them (through the camera lens) as passive sexual objects of male desire.

Manifest and latent meanings – different layers or levels of meaning within any one *media text* or item of media content. The distinction is associated with *content analysis*, which aims at the surface, unambiguous or manifest levels of meaning as opposed to the latent, deeper levels of interpretation.

Mass manipulation model – (see *Hypodermic needle model*)

Mass media (Mass communication) – organised and specialised modern *media institutions* such as the press, cinema and broadcasting, whose principal business involves the supply of the demand for forms of information and entertainment. *Mass communication* is used to describe what these agencies do, what they produce. Attached to both terms – and others, for example 'mass culture' or 'mass audience' – is the prefix 'mass'. This carries a series of one-dimensional assumptions about the homogeneity of the audience and the direct influence of the media.

Media concentration – a situation characterised by the domination of media markets by a small number (usually four or five) of large media corporations.

Media consumption – usually patterned activities of reading, watching, listening and buying which make up interaction with media texts and output. These are consumed in the sense of being used, involving our time, attention, money and so on. In the process, this use contributes to and takes place within wider symbolic and cultural settings and contexts.

Media and cultural imperialism – the use of media and communication systems to establish worldwide influence and dominance. International media and their markets are significant networks for political and cultural values and forms of identity, playing a key role in relations of dominance or dependence. Many 'developing nations' face problems maintaining cultural autonomy and independent identity in the face of Western and other forms of media export and output.

Media institutions – the historical organisations, routines and practices associated with the production and consumption of particular media forms such as television and cinema.

Media involvement – people's patterned and everyday involvement with the media. A distinction has been made between primary, secondary and tertiary forms of media involvement. These range from situations of high (**primary**) involvement, where listening, viewing or reading are the exclusive, focused activities, through those (**secondary**) where involvement accompanies other social or domestic activities, to the weakest, 'background' (**tertiary**) forms of interaction.

Media production – the organised processes and activities involved in making and distributing *media texts* and output. These usually require groups or teams of people working in a variety of commercial, technical and media settings and hierarchies.

Media reception – reading and making sense of *media texts* and output within particular locations and cultural contexts.

Media regulation – the laws, rules and guidelines which operate to define and restrict the parameters of what can be legitimately produced in the media. These may originate from state, government, commercial or other bodies and agencies.

Media saturation – a term used to describe the centrality and pervasiveness of the media and of mediated experience in modern, twenty-first century cultures. This implies the increasing involvement of the media in public, national and global life, the growth of time and expenditure spent in private, everyday *media involvement*, and the popularity of media-related or media-derived activities. As a result, media are held to 'saturate' society, culture and identity.

Mediated culture and **Mediation** – the ideas, images, knowledge, values, and so on, which are derived from modern media. **Mediated culture** comes from beyond our individual, daily or immediate experience. It results from media organisations which produce and *encode* versions of events and issues in their output. These are **mediated** into our individual contexts and situations.

Media texts – the output of the media in general and in particular: programmes, films, magazines, advertisements and so on. Media texts may be written, as in the case of newspapers and magazines, but also assume many other combinations of written, audio and visual media forms.

Mise en scène – whatever appears in a film frame – the setting, characters, lighting, props, etc.

Mode of address – how a *media text* speaks to its particular audience, and in so doing, helps to form the nature of the relationship between producer and audience.

Multimedia – the convergence of previously discrete media systems – the camera, the typewriter, the audio and video recorder – into new computer- and digitally based systems capable of managing diverse forms of data and format.

Multimodal – the increasing mixing and use of codes from one media form within another. For instance, the ways in which television news mixes sound, moving image and graphics, or how websites mix together sound, moving images and printed texts.

Multinational multimedia conglomerates – very large commercial organisations whose operations involve competition in worldwide markets across a range of television, film, press, music and other information and cultural sectors.

Myth – a social and historically determined idea which has gained the status of accepted truth or naturalness.

Narrative – the organisation, structure and dynamics of 'stories' derived from media and other sources.

Narrowcasting – the opposite of broadcasting, where programmes are aimed at quite specific, special-interest or minority audiences.

Naturalism – a commitment to representing the world in a manner which reproduces the surface detail as accurately as possible.

New media technologies – the large-scale technical developments in communication systems of the moment and their cultural consequences. A term which is used to refer to cable, satellite, digital and other computer-based media in the current phase.

News values – the criteria employed by journalists when deciding which stories are most newsworthy.

Open/Closed text – an **open text** is one which lacks a clear *preferred meaning* and is capable of several different readings. A **closed text** is one in which there is little scope for differential readings (because its preferred meaning is overtly *anchored*).

Oppositional decoding – an interpretation of a *media text* which involves a conscious rejection and subversion of its *preferred meaning*.

Participant observation – a method of research where the researcher attempts to become part of the *culture*, group or activity under investigation and records the 'inside stories' which take place.

Pluralism – the theory that power is dispersed among a range of interest groups in society, and that no one group is able to exercise consistent dominance. This plurality of power, it is argued, is reflected in the diversity of ideas and views found in the media.

Polysemic – reflecting the idea that all signs and texts are capable of many potential meanings and readings, and can be *decoded* in a variety of ways according to many factors, including the particularities of the *situated culture* of the reader.

Popular culture – the everyday activities, styles and way of life of 'ordinary people, including media forms such as pop music and television. It is often dismissed as trashy and throwaway in contrast to the perceived superiority and demands of 'high' culture such as classical music or literature. Popular culture may articulate tensions or challenges to the dominant status quo, as well as endorsing it or reinforcing it.

Postmodernism – the cultural and social conditions which are claimed to have replaced and superseded earlier forms of modern twentieth-century life. These involve, and result from, the rapid growth of media and communications systems, of global *culture* and widespread insecurities concerning identity, history, progress and truth. Some *media texts* and output are said to be postmodern in style, mixing irony, parody and pastiche across conventional *genres*.

Preferred meaning/reading – the ways in which texts are constructed to encourage the reader towards a dominant or consensual interpretation.

Primary and Secondary sources – in terms of research, **primary** data are those which you generate yourself, through your own direct investigation of a topic. **Secondary** data are those which you read about or consult at various stages in the research process.

Private sphere – the household, home or domestic space and the *situated culture* which characterises it. Often contrasted or counterposed with the *public sphere*.

Propaganda – media images and campaigns which are designed and managed to promote – or discredit – a particular point of view, ideology or party line. This is achieved through emphasis, manipulation, partial selection or suppression of information and imagery, with the aim of persuading audiences.

Public opinion – in the modern period this has come to be associated with the views and debates articulated in news coverage and other forms of media coverage of issues defined as significant to modern, democratic citizens. Media coverage often represents public opinion, in the form of opinion polls, etc.

Public service broadcasting – the policy enshrined within the BBC under John Reith and carried into all aspects of broadcasting in the UK until the 1990 Broadcasting Act. The policy guaranteed broadcasters a degree of autonomy from both commercial pressures and political interests in their mission to provide services for the national audience that 'informed, educated and entertained'.

Public sphere – the world of political and cultural affairs and events associated with modern, especially democratic, societies. The media, in large part, construct, relay and *mediate* this in their operations and coverage.

Qualitative methods – research practices which aim at understanding and interpreting social and cultural relations rather than measuring them.

Quantitative methods – research practices which aim to measure and statistically analyse social and cultural phenomena, usually on the basis of large-scale, representative samples of people, opinions or data.

Radical press – a label applied particularly to the various wings of the working-class and oppositional newspaper press in Britain beginning in the late eighteenth century. It refers more generally to newspapers or other publications – pamphlets, magazines, etc. – which have been produced and written to challenge or change aspects of the social and political order.

Realism – the degree to which media representations accurately reflect the way things really are, and not as we would wish them to be. There is no one criterion by which the realism of a *media text* may be judged.

Reality television – those television programmes specifically designed to represent 'ordinary' experience, people in real-life situations, utilising actual or sometimes reconstructed scenes of real events.

Representation – the cultural activity of making and communicating meanings. Events, people and issues are represented in media output, and may be represented in diverse and contrasting ways.

Ritual media interaction – patterned and regular contacts with the media which have special and social symbolic value. For instance, identifying with certain musical styles, or the images of particular film stars or media personalities, may have a ritualised social significance.

Scheduling – the process by which broadcast programmes are sequenced to ensure each programme maximises its potential audience.

Semiotics – the study of signs, sign systems and their meanings.

Situated cultures – those familiar and everyday settings and the particular patterns, relationships, ideas and beliefs which characterise them. Media consumption and reception take place in particular situations, which are defined not only in terms of location, but also in terms of the identities and points of view of the people involved. Best understood in contrast to *mediated culture*.

Stereotype – an oversimplified representation which is used to categorise and evaluate all members of a particular social group.

Structuralism – a range of theories which are characterised by an emphasis on the underlying system or set of rules which determine how *media texts* produce meaning.

Surveillance culture – the results of modern security systems and other data systems using CCTV (closed-circuit television) or computer-based networks to monitor social and public spaces and people.

Synergy – the process by which media companies acquire and harness the relations between two or more elements of a *media production* and distribution process. The aim is to increase efficiency and avoid duplication of resources and may, for example, involve using the same local news-gathering resources for both a local radio station and a local newspaper. Another example is the selling of two or more compatible products simultaneously, as in the multimedia merchandising surrounding the release of a 'blockbuster' movie.

Technological determinism – an overemphasis on the role of technology and machines as the principal, if not the sole cause of social, cultural and historical change and development.

Uses and gratifications – the range of needs and pleasures fulfilled through audience consumption of the media.

Virtual Reality (Virtual communities) – computer-simulated worlds, models and versions of life encountered online and in cyberspace. **Virtual communities** result from computer-mediated communication systems based around websites or bulletin boards on the Internet.

Voyeurism – the practice of gaining pleasure from looking at other people whilst remaining anonymous. It is most frequently associated with men deriving sexual pleasure from looking at women.

BIBLIOGRAPHY

Abercrombie, N. 1996: *Television and Society*. Polity Press.

Abrams, N., Bell, I. & Udris, J. 2001: *Studying Film*. Arnold.

Alasuutari, P. 1995: *Researching Culture: Qualitative Method and Cultural Studies*. Sage.

Allan, S. 2000: *News Culture*. Open University Press.

Allen, J. 1990: *Careers in TV and Radio*. Kogan Page.

Allen, R. 1987: *Channels of Discourse*. Methuen.

Alvarado, M. 1988: *Video Worldwide*. John Libbey.

Ang, I. 1985: *Watching Dallas – Soap Opera and the Melodramatic Imagination*. Methuen.

Ang, I. 1991: *Desperately Seeking the Audience*. Routledge.

Ang, I. 1996: *Living Room Wars: Rethinking Media Audiences for a Postmodern World*. Routledge.

Anwar, M. and Shang, A. 1982: *Television in a Multi-Racial Society: A Research Report*. Commission for Racial Equality.

Armes, R. 1978: *A Critical History of British Cinema*. Oxford University Press.

Armes, R. 1988: *On Video*. Routledge.

Bandura, A. and Walters, R. 1963: *Social Learning and Personality Development*. Holt Rinehart and Winston.

Barker, C. 1997: *Global Television: An Introduction*. Blackwell.

Barker, C. 1999: *Television, Globalization and Cultural Identities*. Open University Press.

Barker, M. 1989: *Comics, Ideology, Power and the Critics*. Manchester University Press.

Barker, M. and Petley, J. (eds). 2001: *Ill-Effects: The Media/Violence Debate*. Routledge.

Barnard, S. 1989: *On the Radio*. Open University Press.

Barnard, S. 2000: *Studying Radio*. Arnold.

Barnett, S. 2001: *Westminster Tales*. Continuum International.

Barnes, J. 1976: *The Beginnings of Cinema in Britain*. David & Charles.

Barr, C. 1986: *All Our Yesterdays*. BFI.

Barthes, R. 1973: *Mythologies*. Paladin.

Barthes, R. 1975: *S/Z*. Cape.

Barthes, R. 1977: *Image–Music–Text*. Fontana.

Barwise, P. and Ehrenberg, A. 1988: *Television and its Audience*. Sage.

Bauman, Z. 1998: *Globalization: The Human Consequences*. Polity.

Bazalgette, C. 1998: 'Still only 1898', Media Education Journal, Issue 24, Summer.

BBC International Broadcasting Audience Research. 1993: *World Radio and Television Receivers*. BBC.

Beharrell, M. 1993: *Protest, Press and Prejudice: RAF Greenham Common 1982–92*. Institute of Education, University of London.

Bennett, T. & Woollacott J. 1987: *Bond and Beyond: the Political Career of a Popular Hero*. Macmillan.

Bell, J. 1987: *Doing Your Research Project*. Open University Press.

Berger, A. 1991: *Media Analysis Techniques*. Sage.

Berger, A. 2001: *Media and Communication Research Methods*. Sage.

Berger, J. 1972: *Ways of Seeing*. Penguin.

Bignall, J. 1997, 2002: *Media Semiotics: An Introduction*. Manchester University Press.

Blanchard, S. and Morley, D. (eds). 1983: *What's This Channel Four? An Alternative Report*. Comedia.

Blandford, S., Grant B.K. & Hillier J., 2001: *The Film Studies Dictionary*. Arnold.

Blumler, J. and Katz, E. (eds). 1974: *The Uses of Mass Communication*. Sage.

Bordwell, D. & Thompson K. 1979: *Film Art: An Introduction*. McGraw-Hill.

Boyce, G. *et al.* (eds). 1978: *Newspaper History: From the 17th Century to the Present Day*. Constable.

Boyd, A. 1988, 1994, 1998: *Broadcast Journalism. Techniques of Radio and TV News*. Heinemann; Focal Press.

Branston, G. and Stafford, R. 1999: *The Media Student's Book*. Routledge.

Brierley, S. 1995, 2001: *The Advertising Handbook*. Routledge.

Briggs, A. 1995: *The History of Broadcasting in the UK*. Vols 1–5. Oxford University Press.

Briggs, A. & Burke, P. 2002: *A Social History of the Media*: From Gutenberg to the Internet. Polity.

Briggs, S. 1981: *Those Radio Times*. Weidenfeld & Nicolson.

British Rate and Data (*BRAD*). Maclean Hunter Ltd.

Bromley, M. & O'Malley, T. (eds.) 1997: *A Journalism Reader*. Routledge.

Brothers, C. 1997: *War and Photography: A Cultural History*. Routledge.

Brunt, R. 1992: 'A Divine Gift to Inspire' in D. Strinati and S. Wagg (eds), *Popular Media Culture*. Routledge.

Bryman, A. 1988: *Quantity and Quality in Social Research*. Unwin Hyman.

Buckingham, D. 1987: *Public Secrets*: EastEnders *and its Audience*. BFI.

Buckingham, D. 1996: Moving Images: Understanding Children's Emotional Response to Television. Manchester University Press.

Buckingham, D. 2000: *After the Death of Childhood*. Polity Press.

Buckingham, D. (ed.) 2002: *Small Screens: Television for Children*. Leicester University Press.

Bull, M. 2000: *Sounding Out the City: Personal Stereos and the Management of Everyday Life*. Berg.

Burke, D & Lotus, J. (1998) *Get a Life! : The Little Red Book of the White Dot Anti-television Campaign*. Bloomsbury.

Burnett, R. 1996: *The Global Jukebox: The International Music Industry*. Routledge.

Burns, T. 1977: *The BBC: Public Institution and Private World*. Macmillan.

Burton, G. 1990, 1997, 2002: *More Than Meets the Eye: An Introduction to Media Studies*. Arnold.

Cain, J. 1992: *The BBC: 70 Years of Broadcasting*. BBC.

Carr, E.H. 1961: *What is History?* Macmillan.

Casey, B., Casey, N., Calvert, B., French, L., and Lewis, J. (2002) *Television Studies: The Key Concepts*. Routledge.

Carter C., Branston G. & Allan S. (eds) 1998: *News, Gender and Power*. Routledge.

Carter, M. & McMillan, K. 1999: *Real Women: The Hidden Sex*. Women in Journalism.

Carter, M.D. 1971: *An Introduction to Mass Communications*. Macmillan.

Cater, N. 1985: *Ten 8*. no. 19.

Chambers, D. 2001: *Representing the Family*. Sage.

Chanan, M. 1980, 1995: *The Dream that Kicks: The Pre-History and Early Years of Cinema in Britain*. Routledge.

Channel 4. 1991: *This is Channel Four*. Channel 4.

Chater, K. 1989: *The Television Researcher's Guide*. BBC TV Training.

Chippendale, P. and Horrie, C. 1990: *Stick It Up Your Punter – The Rise and Fall of the Sun*. Heinemann.

Clarke, S. and Horrie, C. 1994: *Fuzzy Monsters: Fear and Loathing at the BBC*. Heinemann.

Clute, J. and Nicholls, P. (eds). 1993: *The Encyclopedia of Science Fiction*. Orbit.

Collett, P. 1986: 'The Viewers Viewed'. *The Listener*. 22 May.

Conroy, A. and Wilby, P. 1994: *The Radio Handbook*. Routledge.

Cook, J. (ed.). 1982: 'Television Sitcom'. BFI Dossier no. 17. BFI.

Cook, P. (ed.). 1985: *The Cinema Book*. BFI.

Cooke, L. 1984: *Media Studies Bibliography*. BFI.

Corner, J. (ed.). 1991: *Popular Television in Britain*. BFI

Corner, J. 1995: *Television Form and Public Address*. Arnold.

Corner, J. 1998: *Studying Media: Problems of Theory and Method*. Edinburgh University Press.

Corner, J. & Harvey, S. (eds.) 1996: *Television Times: A Reader*. Arnold.

Cottle, S. 2000: *Ethnic Minorities and the Media*. Open University Press.

Couldry, N. 2000: *The Place of Media Power: Pilgrims and Witnesses of the Media Age*. Routledge.

Cranfield, G.A. 1978: *The Press and Society*. Longman.

Creeber, G. (ed.) 2001: *The Television Genre Book*. BFI

Crisell, A. 1986, 1994: *Understanding Radio*. Methuen (1st edn); Routledge (2nd edn).

Crisell, A. 1997: *An Introductory History of British Broadcasting*. Routledge.

Cumberbatch, G., *et al*. 1990: *Television Advertising and Sex Role Stereotyping*. Broadcasting Standards Council.

Cumberbatch, G. 2001: *Representation of Minorities on TV*. Broadcasting Standards Council

Curran, J. and Porter, V. (eds). 1983: *British Cinema History*. Weidenfeld & Nicolson.

Curran, J. and Seaton, J. 1991, 1997 (5th edn): *Power without Responsibility: The Press and Broadcasting in Britain*. Routledge.

Curran, J. (ed.) 2000: *Media Organisations in Society*. Arnold.

Curran, J. 2002: *Media and Power*. Routledge.

Curran, J., Gurevitch, M. and Woollacott, J. (eds). 1977: *Mass Communication and Society*. Edward Arnold.

Curtis, L. 1984: *Ireland: The Propaganda War*. Pluto Press.

Danesi, M. 2002: *Understanding Media Semiotics*. Arnold.

Davis, A. 1988: *Magazine Journalism Today*. Heinemann.

Davis, D. 1969: *The Grammar of Television Production*. Revised by Elliot; further revised by Wooller. Published under the auspices of the Society of Film and Television Arts. Barrie and Jenkins.

Deacon, D. Pickering, M., Golding, P. and Murdock, G. 1999: *Researching Communications: A Practical Guide To Methods In Media And Cultural Analysis*. Arnold.

Denzin, N. 2002: *Reading Race*. Sage.

Department for Education and Skills, 2002: *An Assessment of Skill Needs in the Media and Creative Industries*. DfES.

Diawara, M. 1993: *Black American Cinema*. Routledge.

Donzelot, J. 1980: *The Policing of Families*. Hutchinson.

Dovey, J. 2000: *Freakshow: First Person Media And Factual Television*, Pluto.

Dowmunt, T. (ed.) 1993: *Channels of Resistance*. BFI/Channel 4.

Doyle, G. 2002: *Media Ownership*. Sage.

Doyle, G. 2002: *Understanding Media Economics*. Sage.

Du Gay, P., Hall, S., Janes, L., Mackay, H. and Negus, K. 1997: *Doing Cultural Studies: The Story of the Sony Walkman*. Open University/Stage.

Dimbleby, N., Dimbleby, R. and Whittington, K. 1994: *Practical Media*. Hodder & Stoughton.

Dutton, B. 1986, 1997: *The Media*. Longman.

Dutton, B. 1995, 2000 (3rd Ed.) *Media Studies an Introduction*. Longman

Dyer, G. 1982: *Advertising as Communication*. Methuen.

Dyer, R. 1977: 'Entertainment and Utopia'. *Movie*, vol. 24.

Dyer R 1986: *Heavenly Bodies: Film Stars and Society*. MacMillan.

Dyja E. (ed) 2000: *Film and Television Handbook 2001*. BFI.

Eco, U. 1981: *The Role of the Reader*. Hutchinson.

Eldridge, J., Kitzinger, J. and Williams, K. 1997: *The Mass Media and Power in Modern Britain*. Oxford University Press.

Ellis, J. 1982, 1992: *Visible Fictions: Cinema, Television, Video*. Routledge.

Evans, H. 1986: *Pictures on a Page*. Heinemann.

Fairclough, N. 1995: *Media Discourse*. Arnold.

Ferguson, M. 1983: *Forever Feminine: Women's Magazines and the Cult of Femininity*. Heinemann.

Ferguson, R. 1998: *Representing Race: Ideology, Identity and the Media*. Arnold.

Fiske, J. 1990: *Introduction to Communication Studies*. Methuen, Routledge.

Fiske, J. 1987: *Television Culture*. Routledge.

Fiske, J. 1989a: *Understanding Popular Culture*. Unwin Hyman.

Fiske, J. 1989b: *Reading the Popular*. Unwin Hyman.

Fiske, J. and Hartley, J. 1978: *Reading Television*. Methuen.

Fleming, D. (ed.) 2000: *Formations: A 21st Century Media Studies Textbook*. Manchester University Press.

Fountain, N. 1988: *Underground: The London Alternative Press 1966–1974*. Comedia.

Franklin, B. 1994: *Packaging Politics*. Edward Arnold.

Franklin, B. and Murphy, D. 1991: *What News? The Market, Politics and the Local Press*. Routledge.

Franklin, B. 1997: *Newszak and News Media*. Arnold.

Franklin, B. (ed.) 2001: *British Television Policy: A Reader*. Routledge

Fraser, P. 2002: '50 Ways to Improve Your Practical Work', *Media Magazine,* Issue 1. September 2002. English and Media Centre, London.

Frith, S. 1983: *Sound Effects*. Constable.

Frith, S. 1988: *Facing the Music*. Pantheon.

Frith, S. and Goodwin, A. (eds). 1990: *On Record*. Routledge.

Gallup Chart Services. 1993: *The UK Music Charts*.

Gamman, L. and Marshment, M. (eds). 1988: *The Female Gaze: Women as Viewers of Popular Culture*. The Women's Press.

Garfield, S. 1986: *Expensive Habits: The Dark Side of the Music Industry*. Faber and Faber.

Garnham, N. 1973, 1980: *Structures of Television*. BFI Television Monograph no. 1. BFI.

Garnham, N. 2000: *Emancipation, The Media and Modernity: Arguments about the Media and Social Theory*. Oxford University Press.

Gauntlett, D. (ed) 2000: *web.studies rewiring media studies for the digital age*. Arnold.

Gauntlett, D. & Hill, A. 1999: *TV Living: Television, Culture and Everyday Life*. Routledge.

Geraghty, C. 1991: *Women and Soap Opera*. Polity Press.

Geraghty, C. 2000: *British Cinema in the Fifties*. Routledge.

Geraghty, C. 2002: '*Doing Media Studies: Reflections on an Unruly Discipline', in Art, Design and Communication in Higher Education*, Volume 1, Number 1, pp. 25–36. Intellect Press.

Gerbner, G. and Gross, L. 1976: 'Living with Television: The Violence Profile'. *Journal of Communication*, vol.28, no. 3.

Gillett, C. 1983: *The Sound of the City*. Souvenir Press.

Glasgow University Media Group. 1976: *Bad News*. Routledge.

Glasgow University Media Group. 1985: *War and Peace News*. Open University Press.

Glasgow Media Group. 2000: *Viewing the World: News Content and Audience Studies*. DFID.

Goldie, G. 1977: *Facing the Nation: Television and Politics, 1936–76*. Bodley Head.

Golding, P. 1974: *The Mass Media*. Longman.

Golding, P. and Harris, P. (eds). 1997: *Beyond Cultural Imperialism: Globalization, Communication and the New International Order*. Sage.

Goodhart, D. and Wintour, C. 1986: *Eddy Shah and the Newspaper Revolution*. Coronet.

Goodman, S. and Graddol, D. 1996: *Redesigning English: New texts, New identities*. Routledge.

Goodwin, A. 1987: *TV Studies Bibliography*. BFI.

Goodwin, A. 1993: 'Riding with Ambulances: Television and its Uses', *Sight & Sound*, vol.3, no.1.

Goodwin, A. and Whannel, G. (eds). 1990: *Understanding Television*. Routledge.

Gordon, P. and Rosenberg, D. 1989: *Daily Racism*. Runnymede Trust.

Gough-Yates, A. 2003: *Understanding Women's Magazines*. Routledge.

Grahame, J., Jempson, M. and Simons, M. 1995: *The News Pack*. English & Media Centre, London.

Gray, A. 1992: *Video Playtime*. Routledge.

Griffiths, T. 1976: *Comedians*. Faber and Faber.

Gripsrud, J. 2002: *Understanding Media Culture*. Arnold.

Grossberg, L., Wartella, E. & Charles Whitney, D. 1998: *Media Making: Mass Media in a Popular Culture*. Sage.

Gunter, B. 2000: *Media Research Methods*. Sage.

Gunter, B., Sancho-Aldridge, J. and Winstone, P. 1994: *Television: The Public's View 1993*. Independent Television Commission Research Monographs series. John Libbey.

Gurevitch, M. 1991: 'The Globalisation of Electronic Journalism', in J. Curran and M. Gurevitch (eds), *Mass Media and Society*. Edward Arnold.

Hall, S. 1980: *Culture, Media, Language*. Hutchinson.

Hall, S.(ed) 1997: *Representation: Cultural Representations and Signifying Practices* Sage/OU.Halloran, J. 1970: *The Effects of Television*. Panther.

Hammersley, M. and Atkinson, P. 1983: *Ethnography: Principles in Practice*. Tavistock.

Hannerz, U. 1996: *Transnational Connections: Culture, People, Places*. Routledge.

Hansen, A., Cottle, S., Negrine, R. & Newbold, C. 1998: *Mass Communication Research Methods*. Palgrave.

Harcup, T. 1995: *A Northern Star – Leeds Other Paper and the Alternative Press 1974–1994*. Campaign for Press and Broadcasting Freedom.

Harris, R. 1983: *Gotcha: The Media, the Government and the Falklands Crisis*. Faber and Faber.

Harrison, S. 1974: *Poor Men's Guardians*. Lawrence & Wishart.

Hartley, I. (1983) *Goodnight children…Everywhere: An informal history of children's broadcasting*. Midas Books.

Hartley, J. 1982: *Understanding News*. Methuen.

Hartley, J., Goulden, H. and O'Sullivan, T. 1985: *Making Sense of the Media*. Comedia.

Hayward, P. and Wollen, T. (eds). 1993: *Future Visions: New Technologies of the Screen*. BFI.

Heap, N., Thomas, R., Einon, G., Mason, R. and Mackay, H. (eds). 1995: *Information Technology and Society*. Sage.

Hebdige, D. 1988: *Hiding in the Light*. Comedia/Routledge.

Hebdige, D. 1989: 'After the Masses'. *Marxism Today*, January.

Hedgecoe, J. 1991: *On Video*. Hamlyn.

Herman, A. & Swiss, T. (eds.) 2000: *The World Wide Web and Contemporary Cultural Theory*. Routledge.

Herman, E. and McChesney, R. 1997: *The Global Media: The New Missionaries of Corporate Capitalism*. Cassell.

Hesmondhalgh, D. 2002: *The Cultural Industries*. Sage.

Hetherington, A. 1985: *News, Newspapers and Television*. Macmillan.

Hill, J. 1986: *Sex, Class and Realism: British Cinema 1956-1963*. BFI

Hills, M. 2002: *Fan Cultures*. Taylor and Francis.

HMSO 1966: *Sound and Television Broadcasting in Britain*. HMSO.

HMSO 1992: *Social Trends 22*. HMSO.

Hobson, D. 1982: *Crossroads: The Drama of a Soap Opera*. Methuen.

Hobson, D. 1985: 'Ladies' Men'. *The Listener*. 25 April.

Hodgson, F. 1984: *Modern Newspaper Practice*. Heinemann.

Hodgson, F. 1987: *Modern Newspaper Editing and Production*. Heinemann.

Hoggart, R. 1957: *The Uses of Literacy*. Pelican.

Hood, S. 1980: *On Television*. Pluto Press.

Hood, S. (ed.). 1994: *Behind the Screens*. Lawrence & Wishart.

Howes, D. (ed.). 1996: *Cross-Cultural Consumption: Global Markets, Local Realities*. Routledge.

Hunter, I. Q. (ed.) 1999: *British Science Fiction Cinema*, Routledge.

ITC, 1998: *Violence and the Viewer*. ITC

Izod, J. 1989: *Reading the Screen*. Longman.

Jackson, P., Stevenson, N. & Brooks, K. 2001: *Making Sense of Men's Magazines*. Polity Press.

James, E. 1994: *Science Fiction in the 20th Century*. Oxford University Press.

James, L. 1976: *Print and the People 1819–1851*. Penguin.

Jenkins, K. 1991: *Re-thinking History*. Routledge.

Jensen, K.B. and Jankowski, N. (eds). 1991: *A Handbook of Qualitative Methodologies for Mass Communication Research*. Routledge.

Jensen, K.B. (ed.) 2002: *A Handbook of Media and Communication Research: Qualitative and Quantitative Methodologies*. Routledge.

Johnson, R. 1986: 'The Story So Far and Further Transformations?' in D. Punter (ed.), *Introduction to Contemporary Cultural Studies*. Longman.

Jones, S. (ed.) 1999: Doing Internet Research: *Critical Issues and Methods for Examining the Net*. Sage.

Jordan, T. 1999: *Cyberpower: The Culture and Politics of Cyberspace and the Internet*. Routledge.

Katz, E. and Liebes, T. 1986: 'Mutual Aid in the Decoding of *Dallas*' in P. Drummond and R. Paterson (eds), *Television in Transition*. BFI.

Katz, E. and Liebes, T. 1990: *The Export of Meaning*. Oxford University Press.

Kaye, M. and Popperwell, A. 1992: *Making Radio*. Broadside Books.

Kennedy, A.J. 1999: *The Internet: The Rough Guide*. Rough Guides Ltd.

Kennedy, H. 2001: *Introduction to The Matrix*. University of Gloucestershire (unpublished).

Keeble, R. 1994: *The Newspapers Handbook*. Routledge.

Keighron, P. 1993: 'Video Diaries: What's Up Doc?', *Sight & Sound*, October.

Kilborn, R. & Izod, J. 1997: *An Introduction to Television Documentary*. Manchester University Press.

Kingsley, H. and Tibballs, G. 1989: *Box of Delights*. Macmillan.

Knightley, P. 1978: *The First Casualty*. Quartet.

Knightly, P. 2000: First Casualty: *The War Correspondent as Hero and Myth: From the Crimea to Kosovo*. Prion Books.

Kress, G. and Van Leeuwen, T. 2001: *Multimodal discourse: The modes and media of contemporary communication*. Arnold.

Krueger, R.A. 1994: *Focus Groups: A Practical Guide for Applied Research*. Sage.

Kuhn, A. 1995: *Family Secrets: Acts of Memory and Information*. Verso.

Kumar, K. 1977: 'Holding the Middle Ground: The BBC, the Public and the Professional Broadcaster', in J. Curran, M. Gurevitch and J. Woollacott (eds), *Mass Communication and Society*. Arnold.

Langer, J. 1997: *Tabloid Television*. Routledge.

Langham, J. 1996: *Lights, Camera, Action*! BFI.

Lazarsfeld, P., Berelson, B. and Gaudet, H. 1944: *The People's Choice*. Duell, Sloan and Pearce.

Lealand, G. 1984: *American Television Programmes on British Screens*. Broadcasting Research Unit.

Lee, A.J. 1976: *The Origins of the Popular Press 1855–1914*. Croom Helm.

Levy, E. 1990: 'Social Attributes of American Movie Stars'. *Media Culture and Society*, vol. 12, no. 2.

Lewis, J. 1990: *Art, Culture and Enterprise*. Routledge.

Lewis, J. 1991: *The Ideological Octopus*. Routledge.

Lewis, P. and Booth, J. 1989: *The Invisible Medium: Public, Commercial and Community Radio*. Macmillan.

Livingstone, S. 1998: *Making sense of Television*. Routledge.

Livingstone, S. 2002: *Young People and New Media*. Sage.

Llewellyn, S. 2001: *A Career Handbook for TV, Radio, Film, Video and Interactive Media*. Skillset.

Local Radio Workshop. 1983: *Capital: Local Radio and Private Profit*. Comedia.

Longhurst, B. 1995: *Popular Music and Society*. Polity Press.

Lull, J. (ed.) 1988: *World Families Watch Television*. Sage.

Lull, J. 2000: *Media, Communication, Culture: A Global Approach*. Polity.

Lusted, D. (ed.), 1991: *The Media Studies Book*. Routledge.

Machin, D. 2002: *Ethnographic Research for Media Studies*. Arnold.

Mackay, H. & O'Sullivan, T. (eds.) 1999: *The Media Reader: Continuity and Transformation*. Open University/Sage.

Mackay, H. with Maples, W. & Reynolds, P. 2001: *Investigating the Information Society*. Open University Press.

Madge, J. 1989: *Beyond the BBC*. Macmillan.

Malm, K. and Wallis, R. 1984: *Big Sounds from Small Peoples*. Constable.

Masterman, L. 1984: *Television Mythologies: Stars, Shows and Signs*. Comedia.

Masterman, L. 1997: 'A Rationale for Media Education' in Kubey, R. (ed.) *Media Literacy in the Information Age: Current Perspectives*, pp. 15–69. Transaction Publishers.

Mattelart, A., Delcourt, X. and Mattelart, M. 1984: *International Image Markets*. Comedia.

May, J. 1996: 'This is the Big One', *20/20*, Winter.

Mayer, P. A. (ed.) 1999: *Computer Media and Communication: A Reader*. Oxford University Press.

McDonald, M. 1995: *Representing Women*. Arnold.

McGuigan, J. 1992: *Cultural Populism*. Routledge.

McGuigan, J. 1999: *Modern and Postmodern Culture*. Open University Press

McIntyre, I. 1993: *The Expense of Glory: A Life of John Reith*. HarperCollins.

McLaughlin, G. 2002: *The War Correspondent*. Pluto.

McLuhan, M. 1964: *Understanding Media*. Routledge and Kegan Paul.

McMahon, B. and Quinn, R. 1986: *Real Images*. Macmillan.

McMahon, B. and Quinn, R. 1988: *Exploring Images*. Macmillan.

McNair, B. 1993, 1996: *News and Journalism in the UK*. Routledge.

McNair, B. 1999: *An Introduction to Political Communication*. Routledge.

McNair, B. 1999: *News and Journalism in the UK*. Routledge.

McNair, B. 2000: *Journalism and Democracy*. Routledge.

McNeill, P. 1990: *Research Methods*. Routledge.

McQuail, D. 1975: *Communication*. Longman.

McQuail, D. 1983, 1987, 19942000991: *Feminism and Youth Culture: From 'Jackie' to 'Just Seventeen'*. MacMillan.

McRobbie, A. 1994: *Postmodernism and Popular Culture*. Routledge.

McRobbie, A. 1996: 'more! New Sexualities in Girls' and Women's Magazines' in J. Curran, D. Morley and V. Walkerdine (eds), *Cultural Studies and Communications*. Arnold.

McRoberts, R. 1987: *Media Workshops: Vol. 1, Words*. Macmillan.

Media Monitoring Unit. 1990: *Broadcasting and Political Bias*. Hampden Trust.

Medina, P. and Donald, V. 1992: *Careers in Journalism*. Kogan Page.

Messenger Davies, M. 1989: *Television is Good for Kids*. Hilary Shipman.

Metz, C. 1974: *Film Language*. Oxford University Press.

Miller, J. 1990: *Broadcasting: Getting In and Getting On*. Butterworth.

Miller, W. 1992: 'I Am What I Read'. *The Listener*, 24 April.

Millersen, G. 1989: *Video Production Handbook*. Focal Press.

Mitchell C. (ed) 2000: *Women and Radio: Airing Differences*. Routledge.

Monaco, J. 1977: *How to Read a Film: The Art, Technology, Language, History and Theory of Film and Media*. Oxford University Press.

Monk, C. 2000: 'Men in the 90s', in Murphy, R. (ed.) *British Cinema of the 90s*. BFI.

Monk, C. & Sargeant, A. eds. 2002: *British Historical Cinema*. Routledge.

Moores, S. 1993: *Interpreting Audiences*. Sage.

Moores S 2000: *Media and Everyday Life*. Edinburgh University Press.

Morgan, J. and Welton, P. 1986, 1992: *See What I Mean*. Edward Arnold.

Morley, D. 1980: *The Nationwide Audience*. BFI.

Morley, D. 1986: *Family Television*. Comedia.

Morley, D. 1991: 'Where the Global Meets the Local: Notes from the Sitting Room'. *Screen*, vol. 32, no. 1.

Morley, D. 1992: *Television, Audiences and Cultural Studies*. Routledge.

Morley, D. and Robins, K. 1995: *Spaces of Identity: Global Media, Electronic Landscapes and Cultural Boundaries*. Routledge.

Morley, D. 2000: *Home Territories: Media, Mobility and Identity*. Routledge.

Morrison, D. 1999: *Definitions of Violence: A Search for Understanding*. ITC.

Mulvey, L. 1975: 'Visual Pleasure and Narrative Cinema'. *Screen*, vol. 16, no. 3.

Murdock, G. 1974: 'The Politics of Culture' in D. Holly (ed.). *Education or Domination*. Arrow Books.

Murdock, G. and Golding, P. 1991: 'Culture, Communications and Political Economy' in J. Curran and M. Gurevitch (eds). *Mass Media and Society*. Edward Arnold.

Murphy, R. 1989: *Realism and Tinsel: Cinema and Society in Britain 1939-48*. Routledge.

Murphy, R. ed. 2000: *British Cinema of the 90s*. BFI.

Naylor, R., Driver, S. and Coruford, J. 2000: 'The BBC goes on line: Public service Broadcasting in yhe New Media Age in Gauntlett D. (ed). web studies. revising Media studies for the Digital Age. Arnold

Neale, S. 1999: *Genre and Hollywood*. Routledge.

Negrine, R. 1989, 1994: *Politics and the Mass Media in Britain*. Routledge.

Negus, K. 1992: *Producing Pop*. Edward Arnold.

Negus, K. 1996: *Popular Music in Theory*. Polity Press.

Nelmes, J. (ed.). 1999 (2nd Ed.) *An Introduction to Film Studies*. Routledge.

Newson, E. 1994: 'Video Violence and the Protection of Children', *Psychology Review*, November, vol. 1., no. 2. pp. 2-5.

Niblock, S. 1996: *Inside Journalism*. Blueprint.

Nightingale, V. 1996: *Studying Audiences: The Shock of the Real*. Routledge.

Norman, B. 1984: *Here's Looking at You*. BBC.

O'Malley, T. 1994: *Closedown? The BBC and Government Broadcasting Policy, 1979–92*. Pluto.

Oppenheim, A.N. 1992: *Questionnaire Design, Interviewing and Attitude Measurement*. Blackwell.

Orlebar, J. 2002: *Digital Television Production: A Handbook*. Arnold

Orwell, G. 1949: *1984*. Secker & Warburg.

Orton, L. 2001: *Media Courses UK 2001*. BFI.

Ostergaard, B. (ed.). 1997: *The Media in Western Europe: The Euromedia Handbook*. Sage.

O'Sullivan, T., Hartley, J., Saunders, D., Montgomery, M. and Fiske, J. 1994: *Key Concepts in Communication and Cultural Studies*. Routledge.

O'Sullivan, T. 1996: 'Research Interviews', in B. Allison, T. O'Sullivan, A. Owen, J. Rice, A. Rothwell and C. Saunders (eds), *Research Skills for Students*. Kogan Page.

O'Sullivan, T. 1997: 'What Lies Between Mechatronics and Medicine? The Critical Mass of Media Studies.' *Soundings*, issue 5, pp. 211–21.

O'Sullivan, T. and Jewkes, Y. (eds). 1997: *The Media Studies Reader*. Arnold.

O'Sullivan, T. 2000 'Media History' and 'Public Service Broadcasting' in Fleming, D. (ed): *Formations: A 21st Century Media Studies Textbook*. Manchester University Press.

Oswell, D. 1998: 'Early children's broadcasting in Britain: Programming for a liberal democracy' in *Historical Journal of Film, Radio and Television*, Vol.18, No.3. Carfax.

Oswell, D. 2002: Television, Childhood and The Home. Oxford

Packard, V.I. 1957: *The Hidden Persuaders*. Longman.

Partridge, S. 1982: *Not the BBC/IBA – The Case for Community Radio*. Comedia/Minorities Press Group.

Paulu, B. 1981: *Television and Radio in the UK*. Macmillan.

Peacock, A. 1986: *Report of the Committee on Financing the BBC*. Cmnd 9824. HMSO.

Peak, S. and Fisher, P. (eds). (Annual:) *Guardian Media Guide*. Fourth Estate.

Pennachioni, I. 1984: 'The Reception of Television in North East Brazil.' *Media Culture and Society*, vol. 6, no. 4.

Perkins, T. 1979: 'Rethinking Stereotypes', in M. Barrett, P. Corrigan, A. Kuhn and V. Wolff (eds), *Ideology and Cultural Production*. Croom Helm.

Peterson, R.A. and Berger, D.G. 1975: 'Cycles in Symbolic Presentation: The Case of Popular Music'. *American Sociological Review*, vol.40.

Peterson, R.C. and Thurstone, L. 1933: *Motion Pictures and Social Attitudes*. Macmillan.

Philo, G. (ed.) 1999: *Message Received*. Longman.

Pickering, M. 2001: *Stereotyping: The Politics of Representation*. Palgrave.

Pines, J. (ed.). 1992: *Black and White in Colour*. BFI.

Posener, J. 1982: *Spray it Loud*. Pandora.

Poster, M. 1995: *The Second Media Age*. Polity.

Power, M. and Sheridan, G. (eds). 1984: 'Labour Daily? – Ins and Outs of a New Labour Daily and Other Media Alternatives'. Campaign for Press and Broadcasting Freedom.

Price, S. 1998: *Media Studies*. Longman.

Propp, V. 1968: *Morphology of the Folk Tale*. University of Texas Press.

Pullen, K. 2000: 'I Love Xena.com: Creating Online Fan Communities' in Gauntlett, D. (ed.) *web.studies: rewiring media studies for the digital age*. Arnold.

Quilliam, S. and Grove-Stephansan, I. 1990: *Into Print*. BBC.

Rayner, P., Wall, P. & Kruger, S. 2001: *Media Studies: The Essential Introduction*. Routledge.

Richards, J. 1984: *The Age of the Dream Palace: Cinema and Society in Britain 1930-1939*. Routledge.

Real, M.R. 1996: *Exploring Media Culture: A Guide*. Sage.

Reeves, G. 1993: *Communications and the 'Third World'*. Routledge.

Reith, J. 1949: *Into the Wind*. Hodder & Stoughton.

Rheingold, H. 1994: *The Virtual Community: Finding Connection in a Computerised World*. Minerva.

Robertson, J.C. 1989: *The Hidden Cinema: British Film Censorship 1913–1972*. Routledge.

Rojek, C. 2001: *Celebrity*. Reaktion Books.

Rosen, M. and Widgery, D. 1991: *The Chatto Book of Dissent*. Chatto & Windus.

Ross, K. 1996: *Black and White Media*. Polity Press.

Rothwell, A. 1996: 'Questionnaire Design', in B. Allison, T. O'Sullivan, A. Owen, J. Rice, A. Rothwell and C. Saunders (eds), *Research Skills for Students*. Kogan Page.

Said, E. (1991) *Orientalism*. Peregrin Books.

Sales, R. 1986: 'An Introduction to Broadcasting History' in D. Punter (ed.), *An Introduction to Contemporary Cultural Studies*. Longman.

Scannell, P. 1987a: 'The State and Society: Broadcasting Rituals'. Open University D209.

Scannell, P. 1996: *Radio, Television and Modern Life*. Blackwell.

Scannell, P. and Cardiff, D. 1991: *A Social History of British Broadcasting. Vol.1*. Blackwell.

Scannell, P. and Cardiff, D. 1981: 'Popular Culture: Radio in WW2'. Open University U203.

Schiller, H. 1969: *Mass Communication and American Empire*. Kelley.

Schiller, H. 1976: *Communication and Cultural Domination*. International Arts & Science Press.

Schiller, H. 1991: 'Not Yet the Post-Imperialist Era?' *Critical Studies in Mass Communication*, vol.8.

Schlesinger, P. 1987: *Putting 'Reality' Together – BBC News*. Methuen.

Schlesinger, P. 1991: *Media State and Nation*. Sage.

Schlesinger, P., Dobash, R.E., Dobash, R.P. and Weaver, C. 1992: *Women Viewing Violence*. BFI.

Schlesinger, P., Murdock, G. and Elliott, P. 1983/9: *Televising Terrorism: Political Violence in Popular Culture*. Comedia.

Seymour-Ure, C. 1996: *The British Press and Broadcasting Since 1945*. Blackwell.

Shaw, P. 1992: 'Fanzines' in Hamilton, I. (ed.) *The Faber Book of Soccer*. Faber.

Shippey, T. (ed.). 1991: *Fictional Space: Essays on Contemporary Science Fiction*. Oxford University Press.

Shuker, R. 2001: *Understanding Popular Music*. Routledge.

Silj, A. (ed.). 1988: *East of Dallas*. BFI.

Silverman, D. 2000: *Doing Qualitative Research*. Sage.

Silverstone, R. 1999: *Why Study the Media?* Sage.

Skillset/DCMS, 2001: *The Report of the Skillset/DCMS Audio Visual Industries Training Group: Skills for Tomorrow's Media*. Skillset/DCMS.

Slevin, J. 2000: *The Internet and Society*. Polity.

Smith, A. 1993: *Books to Bytes: Knowledge and Information in the Postmodern Era*. BFI.

Smith, J. 1990: *Misogynies*. Faber and Faber.

Snagge, J. and Barsley, M. 1972: *Those Vintage Years of Radio*. Pitman.

Sontag, S. 1977: *On Photography*. Penguin.

Sreberny-Mohammadi, A. 1991: 'The Global and the Local in International Communications', in J. Curran and M. Gurevitch (eds), *Mass Media and Society*. Edward Arnold.

Stafford, R. 1993: *Hands On*. BFI.

Stead, P. 1989: *Film and the Working Class*. Routledge.

Stein, S. 1999: *Learning, Teaching and Researching on the Internet*. Longman.

Stevenson, N. 2002: *Understanding Media Cultures: Social Theory and Mass Communication*. Sage.

Stokes, P. 1992: *No Apology Needed: The Story of the N.W.N..* Blacket Turner.

Stokes, J. 2003: *How to do Media and Cultural Studies*. Sage.

Stokes, J. & Reading, A. (eds) 1999: *The Media in Britain: Current Debates and Developments*. MacMillan.

Storey, J. 1999: *Cultural Consumption and Everyday Life*. Arnold.

Street, S. 1999: 'Radio for Sale: Sponsored Programming in British Radio during the 1930s' in *Sound Journal* www.speke.ukc.ac.uk/sais/sound-journal

Street, S. 2002: A concise history of British Radio 1922-2002. Kelly Publications.

Street, J. 2001: *Mass Media, Politics and Democracy*. Palgrave.

Strinati, D. and Wagg, S. (eds). 1992: *Come On Down: Popular Media Culture in Post War Britain*. Routledge.

Svennevig, M. 1998: *Television Across the Years: The British Public's View*. ITC/University of Luton Press.

Swanson, G. 1991: 'Representations', Chapter 6 in D. Lusted (ed.), *The Media Studies Book*. Routledge.

Tasker, Y. 1993: *Spectacular Bodies: Gender, Genre and the Action Cinema*. Routledge.

Tasker, Y. 1998: *Working Girls: Gender and Sexuality in Popular Cinema*. Routledge.

Taylor, A.J.P. 1965: *English History 1914–45*. Clarendon Press.

Taylor, J. 1991: *War Photography*. Comedia.

Taylor, P. 1992: *Propaganda and Persuasion in the Gulf War*. Manchester University Press.

Thompson, E.P. 1968: *The Making of the English Working Class*. Penguin.

Thompson, J.B. 1988: 'Mass Communication and Modern Culture: Contribution to a Critical Theory of Ideology'. *Sociology*, vol. 22, no. 3.

Thompson, J.B. 1995: *The Media and Modernity*. Polity Press.

Thussu, D.K. (ed.) 1998: *Electronic Empires: Global Media and Local Resistance*. Arnold.

Tilley, A. 1991: 'Narrative', Chapter 3 in D. Lusted (ed.), *The Media Studies Book*. Routledge.

Todorov, T. 1973: *The Fantastic: Towards a Structural Approach*. Case Western Reserve University Press.

Tolson, A. 1996: *Mediations: Text and Discourse in Media Studies* Arnold.

Tomlinson, J. 1991: *Cultural Imperialism*. Pinter.

Tomlinson, J. 1999: Globalization and Culture. Polity.

Tracey, M. 1985: 'The Poisoned Chalice? International Television and the Idea of Dominance'. *Daedalus*, vol. 114, no. 4.

Tracey, M. 1998: *The Decline and Fall of Public Service Broadcasting*. Oxford University Press.

Trowler, P. 1989, 1996: *Investigating the Media*. Tavistock (1st edn); HarperCollins (2nd edn).

Tufte, T. 2000: *Living with the Rubbish Queen: Telenovelas, Culture and Modernity in Brazil*. University of Luton Press.

Tunstall, J. 1983: *The Media in Britain*. Constable.

Tunstall, J. 1996: *Newspaper Power: The New National Press in Britain*. Clarendon Press.

Tunstall, J. (ed.) 2001: *Media Occupations and Professions: A Reader*. Oxford University Press.

Turkle, S. 1984: *The Second Self: Computers and the Human Spirit*. Granada.

Turner, G. 1996: *British Cultural Studies: An Introduction*. Routledge.

Turnock, R. 2000: *Interpreting Diana: The Death of a Princess*. BFI.

Van Dijk, J. 1999: *The Network Society*. Sage.

Van Zoonen, L. 1994: *Feminist Media Studies*. Sage.

Varis, T. 1974: 'Global Traffic in Television'. *Journal of Communication*, vol. 24.

Varis, T. 1984: 'The International Flow of Television Programmes'. *Journal of Communication*, vol. 34, no. 1.

Walker, A. 1986: *Hollywood England*. Harrap.

Ward, K. 1989: *Mass Communications and the Modern World*. Macmillan.

Watson, J. and Hill, A. 1999: *A Dictionary of Communication and Media Studies*. Arnold.

Watts, H. 1984: *On Camera*. BBC.

Watts, H. 1992: *Directing on Camera*. Aavo.

Weber, R.P. 1990: *Basic Content Analysis*. Sage.

Webster, F. 1995: *Theories of the Information Society*. Routledge.

Wells, L. (ed.) 2000: *Photography: A Critical Introduction*. Routledge.

Wenden, D.J. 1974: *The Birth of the Movies*. Dutton.

Whitaker, B. (ed.). 1984: *News Ltd: Why You Can't Read All About It*. Comedia.

Williams, K. 1998: *'Get Me a Murder a Day': A History of Mass Communications in Britain*. Arnold.

Williams, R. 1965: *The Long Revolution*. Pelican.

Williams, R. 1966: *Communications*. Chatto & Windus.

Williams, R. 1974, 1990: *Television, Technology and Cultural Form*. Fontana (1st edn); Routledge (2nd edn).

Williams, R. 1976: *Keywords: A Vocabulary of Culture and Society*. Fontana.

Williamson, J. 1978: *Decoding Advertisements: Ideology and Meaning in Advertising*. Marion Boyars.

Willings Press Guide. Vol. I. Reed Information Services.

Winn, M. 1977: *The Plug-in Drug*. Penguin.

Winship, I. and McNab, A. 1996: *The Student's Guide to the Internet*. Library Association.

Winship, J. 1987: *Inside Women's Magazines*. Pandora.

Winston, B. 1998: *Media Technology and Society: A History from the Telegraph to the Internet*. Routledge.

Winston, B. 2000: *Lies, Damn Lies and Democracy*. BFI.

Wolffsohn, A. 1996: 'Shaping the Future', *Spectrum*, 23, Autumn. Independent Television Commission.

Woolf, M. and Holly, S. 1994: *Employment Patterns and Training Needs 1993/4: Radio Survey*. Skillset.

Zelizer, B. & Allan, S. eds. 2002: *Journalism after September 11*. Routledge.

Zenith Media. 1995: *UK Media Handbook*. Zenith.

Please note that any references to Activities are in italics while references to Figures are in bold

A & R (artists and repertoire)   169
A & M   164
aberrant decoding   124–125, 285
The Accused   86
action codes   47
action films   59
Adams, Bryan   142
Adams, Gerry   76
Address to Journeymen and Labourers   197
Adult Contemporary (AC)   174
Advertiser   184
advertising   155–156
    aberrant coding   124–125, 285
    enigma codes   48
    lingerie   36–37
    masculinity, images of   91–93
    mobile phones   37–38
    Newbury Weekly News   186
    sex role stereotyping   83–84
advertising revenue   146–150
Advertising Standards Authority (ASA)   48, 86, 125, 154
Afghanistan, war in   40, 77, 97
AI   57
Al Capone   73
Al Pacino   60
Al-Qaida   42
Album Oriented Rock (AOR)   174
Ali G   125
Aliens film   47, 50, 89, 90
The Ali G Show   56
Allen, Robert   121
Ally McBeal   90

alternative media   10, 157
American Dream   74, 103
American Motion Picture Poll   83
American Pie   55
anchorage   33–41
Anderson, Gillian   90
Anderson, Pamela   92
Ang, Ien   126, 130, 265
Annan Report on Broadcasting (1977)   211
anti-monopoly controls   153
AOL   141, 152
Apocalypse Now   45
apocalyptic films   59
appearance, gender   82–85
Are you Being Served?   93
Arena magazine   87
Armageddon   59
Armes, R.   200
Artisan Entertainment   159
artists and repertoire (A & R)   169
As Time Goes By   50
ASA (Advertising Standards Authority)   48, 86, 125, 154
Associated Newspapers   182
Astley, Rick   164
audience positioning   120, 285
audiences   112–139
    cinema   120–121
    community   157
    encoding/decoding model   123–125
    investigating   275–276
    mass manipulation model   112–114
    media violence   114–116
    minority   157
    mode of address   120–125
    newspapers and magazines   122–125
    political persuasion   116–118

pre-production 245–246
racism among 98
radio 119, 122
reception theory 125–131
television 118–119, 121–122
uses/gratification 118–125
audiovisual space 235
Austin Powers 166
auteur 285

Back to the Future 50
Bad Girls 128
Bad Timing 45
Baker, Martin 120
Baker, Norma Jean 60, 81
Bandura, A. 115, 116
BARB (Broadcasters Audience Research Board) 214, 276
Barbarella 57
Barker, Martin 78–79
Barthes, Roland 27, 71
Barwise, P. 5
Basic Instinct 62, 91
Battle of Britain 97
BBC (British Broadcasting Corporation)
BBC 2 211
BBC 3 217
BBC 4 217
case study 203–208, 210
media saturation 5
World Service 77
BBC English 122
BBC News 24 156
BBFC (British Board of Film Classification) 112, 113, 153
BeachMate 55
The Beast from 20,000 Fathoms 57
Beatles 162, 177
Beatty, Warren 145
Beckham, David 64, 66
Beckham, Victoria (Posh) 35, 66
bedroom culture 133, 134
Beharrell, M. 182–183, 187–188
Behind Enemy Lines 73

Benetton 154
Bennett, T. 63
Benny, Jack 207
Berger, D.G. 162
Beverley Hills Cop 102
Bicentennial Man 57
Big Breakfast Show 106, 250
Big Brother (George Orwell) 30
Big Brother (TV programme) 18, 59, 64, 65, 93, 110
Big Issue 182
Big Sleep 49
The Bill 47
binary oppositions 41–42, 97, 285
bioscope 200
Black Dwarf 197
Black Hawk Down 73
Blackboard Jungle 177
Blackburn, Tony 66
The Black and White Minstrel Show 98
Blade Runner 17, 57, 58
Blair, Tony 144
Blair Witch Project 55, 145, 159
Blake 7 214
Blanchett, Kate 63
'blaxploitation' films 102
Bleak House 46
Blind Date 150
Blue Planet 216
Blue Velvet 17, 50
Blumler 118, 119
BMG company 164
'Bobo Doll' 116
The Bodyguard 120, 142, 177
Bogart, Humphrey 82
Bond, James 44, 45, 62, 63
Bonnie and Clyde 74
Born on the Fourth of July 45
Boy George 87
Boyz n the Hood 102
Boyzone 179
Brazil 58
bricolage 18, 37, 285

Britain
    cinema, history   200
    general elections (1987, 1992 and 2001)
        74, 117
    music retailers   171
    propaganda   74–75
    radio formatting   175–176
British Board of Film Classification
        (BBFC)   112, 113, 153
British Broadcasting Company   204
British Broadcasting Corporation *see* BBC
        (British Broadcasting Corporation)
British Film Institute   95, 118
British nation, ideology   94–96
Broadcast   141
broadcasting   133, 154, 155, 224
    case studies   203–208
    see also Public Service Broadcasting
Broadcasting Act (1981)   211
Broadcasting Act (1990)   212
Broadcasting over Britain (John Reith)   204
Broadcasting Standards Commission   154,
        155
Bronson, Charles   83
Brookside   46, 93, 105, 211
Brosnan, Pierce   63
Brunt, Rosalind   94
BSE (mad cow disease)   97
BSkyB   143, 144, 145, 158, 213
Buckingham, David   114, 115, 125
Bulger, James   30, 113, 114
Bulletin Board Systems (BBSs)   227
Burton, Tim   53, 148

Cable News Network   236
    CNN news   156
cable systems   223
Caddick, Andy   35
Cagney and Lacey   90
calligraphy   34–35
camaraderie   158
Campaign   141
Campbell, Duncan   152
Carlton Communications   157
Carr   190

Carrey, Jim   60
Carter, Meg   85
Cartoon Network   179
case studies
    British cinema   200–203
    broadcasting   203–218
    Internet   178–180
    music industry   162–180
    newspapers and magazines   181–188,
        196–199
    science fiction   89–90
    video games   137–138
Cast Away   8
Casualty   47
Cathy Come Home   109, 209, 210
CBeebies   217
CBS records   145, 162, 165
CCTV (closed circuit television)   30–31,
        109
CD recorders   168
celebrities, television   64–67
Celebrity Big Brother   65
Celebrity Ready, Steady, Cook   65, 66
Celebrity Squares   65
Centre for Contemporary Cultural Studies,
        Birmingham   123
Chanan, M.   191, 200
Chandler, Raymond   49
Changing Rooms   65
Channel 4   160, 211
Channel 4 News   156
Chaplin, Charlie   59, 238
character functions   44–45
Charlie's Angels   90
chat shows   55, 64, 106
children, media violence   114–116
children's books   31–32
Children's Hour   206
Child's Play 3   113, 114
Chippendale, Peter   123, 150
Choice (urban black music)   176
Chris Tarrant Breakfast Show   250
Chrysalis   162
Churchill, Sir Winston   151
cinema

audiences 120–121
  case study 200–203
  independent production 177–178
  libel 153
  postmodernism 17
  reception theory 131
  representations 71–73, 102
  see also films; Hollywood cinema
Cinema Commission 202
'cinema truth' 107
Citizen Kane 45, 47
Classic FM 17, 145, 245
Classical (US radio) 174
Close Encounters 50
closed circuit television (CCTV) 30–31,
  109
closed texts 27
Clooney, George 59, 62
Coalface 107
Cobbett, William 197
codes 28–32
  aberrant decoding 124–125, 285
  action 47
  enigma 47–48, 49
  genre 30
  narrative 30, 44–50
  polysemic 27, 31, 124, 131, 269, 290
  symbolic 28, 36, 39, 43
  technical 28, 35, 38, 43
  written 28, 35–36, 38, 43
Cohen, Sacha Baron 125
Cold War 97
Collett, Peter 132, 135
Collins, Joan 128
colour, use of 43
Comedians 79
Commando 62
commodification 228
commodities 6–8, 11–12
communications revolution 221
community audiences 157
compilation albums 165
computer games 42
computer literacy 194
computerisation 223–224

Conan the Barbarian 62
Conan the Destroyer 62
Connery, Sean 60, 63
connotations 27
consensus 285
Conservative Party 74, 143, 144
consumer choice 224, 225
consumer society 13, 285
Contemporary Christian Radio 174
Contemporary Hit Radio (CHR) 174
content analysis 267, 269–275, 285
  stages 274–275
conventions 50, 285
convergence 223, 233, 286
Cool Edit Pro 247
Copeland, David 30
Coprock 106
copyright 165
Coronation Street 81, 91, 103, 119, 128, 210
Corrs, the 173
Cosby, Bill 129
The Cosby Show 103, 129–130, 131
Cosmopolitan magazine 88
Country (US radio) 175
courses, media 260
covers, book 31–32
Cranfield, G.A. 193
Crimewatch 47
Crisell, Andrew 46, 131
Croft, Lara 36–37
cropping 32, 286
Cruise, Tom 59, 61, 62
cultivation analysis 276
cultural capital/competence 126, 286
cultural circulation map **15**
cultural factors, demand 193
cultural intermediaries 169
cultural pessimists 226
culture
  gay 86, 93, 128
  'high' and 'low' 16–17
  and mass communication 14–18
  mass-produced 16
  meaning 14, 286
  of mediation 8

national 230–232
popular 16–17, 19
situated 8, 27, 105, 292
Curran, J. 143, 150, 198, 226, 267

Dad's Army 214
Dahl, Sophie 86, 154
Daily Courant 196
Daily Mail 74, 97, 99, 147
Daily Record 183
Daily Star 65, 143
Daily Telegraph 32, 74, 85, 147, 198
Daily Universal Register 196
Daily Worker 151
Dallas 126, 130, 233, 236, 237–238, 250
Dalton, Timothy 63
Dame Edna Everage 106
The Dam Busters 97
dance music 180
Dances with Wolves 53
Dando, Jill 30
The Darling Buds of May 145
Day, Robin 209
de Niro, Robert 60
de Saussure, Ferdinand 27
Death on the Rock 76
decoding
    defined 26
    media forms 28
    process 29
    see also encoding/decoding
The Defiant Ones 102
Defoe, Daniel 2
demand 192, 193–194
demographics 146, 286
denotation/connotation 286
deregulation 286
design 34–35
Desmond, Richard 65
Destructive 198
determinism 195, 223, 292
developing nations 234
dialogue 120
Diana, Princess of Wales, death of 95, 153, 210

diary research 3, 4
DiCaprio, Leonardo 63
Die Hard 44, 60
A Different World 103
differential styles, demand 193
Dillinger, John 73
Dimbleby, Richard 208, 209
Disclosure 62
discourse analysis 40–41, 267, 286
disequilibrium analysis 44, 50–51
disintermediation 178
Disney Corporation 142
distribution, music industry 170–171
diversity 225, 233
Dixon of Dock Green 210
Do the Right Thing 102
D.O.A 45
docu-soaps 54–55
documentaries 106–110
documentary realism 106–109
dominant hegemonic position 124
Donaher, Noele 109
Double Indemnity 91
Double Your Money 209
Douglas, Michael 61, 62, 66
Dovey, J. 55
Dr No 62
Dressed to Kill 86
Driving School 66
Duchovny, David 90
dumb blonde 79–81
'dumbing down' 14, 17, 18, 155
Duracell 124–125
DVDs
    classification of films 153
    libel 153
    media saturation 4
    popularity 6
    time periods, coverage of 46
    see also videos
Dyer, Richard 60, 62, 119, 126
Dyke, Greg 218
Dynasty 128

East End News   182
East is East   96
EastEnders   26, 91, 103, 104, 125, 214
Eastwood, Clint   53
easy listening   174
Easy Listening Radio   175
ECHR (European Convention on Human
    Rights)   153
Eco, U.   125
economics
    advertising revenue   146–150
    institutional determinants   141–151
    ownership   141–146
    and regulation   155–156
Edison, Thomas   200
editing   256–257
Edward Scissorhands   53
'effect' concept   118
Ehrenberg, A.   5
Eldorado   150
Elizabeth II, Queen   94–95, 121, 208
Ellis, John   52, 60, 132
EMI   152, 164, 171
Emmerdale   105
encoding/decoding   28–41, 286
    anchorage   33–41
    audiences   124–125
    codes   28–32, 47–48, 49
    definitions   26
    Hall model   123–124, 125, 126
English, Sir David   143
enigma code   47–48, 49
equilibrium/disequilibrium analysis   49–50,
    286
ER   109, 211
Erin Brockovich   60, 62
Esther   55
E.T.   50
Ethiopia, famine in   100
ethnic preferences, reception theory
    130–131
ethnography   279–280, 286
European Commission   152
European Convention on Human Rights
    (ECHR)   153

Evans, Harold   144
events, media coverage   11, 13, 30
Ewing, J.R.   238
Executive Decision   97
The Express   65

face-to-face interaction   10, 11
The Face   17, 36
Fairbanks, Douglas   59
Falklands War (1982)   75, 77–78, 97, 151,
    152
Falling Down   62
Family Fortunes   54
family viewing   133–135
The Family   107
fanbases   118
fanzines   158–159
Farewell My Lovely   49
Fatal Attraction   62, 91, 141
Fawlty Towers   98
femininity   81
feminism   82
femme fatale   287
Ferguson, Marjorie   88, 273
FHM magazine   7, 53, 92
Fight Club   121
film noir   52, 287
film stars   59–64
    age   83
    appearance   82
    marriage/relationships   61
films
    audiences   112–113
    British   96
    character functions   45
    equilibrium/disequilibrium analysis   50
    genre   52–53, 55–56
    intertextuality   36
    male images   92–93
    mass communication   17
    science fiction   57–59
    silent   106
    stereotyping   81
    westerns   52, 53, 56

see also cinema; DVDs; film stars;
    Hollywood cinema; television;
    videos
Financial Times   117, 146, 168
First Cinematographic Act   202
First World   235
First World War (1914-18)   151, 202
Fiske, J.   129
Fleming, Ian   63
flow   131, 132
    one-way   237
    two-step   116
fly-on-the-wall documentary   107, 251, 287
football fanzines   158–159
Forbidden Planet   89
Forces Programme   207, 208
Ford, John   53
The Fosters   103
Foucault, Michel   40
Four Weddings and a Funeral   96, 159, 166
France, broadcasting in   207
Frankenstein   59
Franklin, B.   181, 183, 185, 187
free time   4
freedom, limits of   145, 150–151
freesheets   182
Freeview   213
Friends   81, 211
Frith, Simon   169
From Russia with Love   62
Fuller, Simon   179
The Full Monty   159
fundamentalism   40, 41

Gagging Bills   197
game shows   54
gangsters   73
Gannon, Lucy   91
Garland, Judy   60
Garnett, Alf   99
gatekeeper   169, 287
Gates, Gareth   176
Gauntlett, David   222
gay, meaning   30
gay culture   86, 93, 128

gender
    appearance   82–85
    ideology   81–97
    media technology   136–139
    reception theory   126–130
    sexuality   93–94
    television   135–136
gender roles   87–91
General Strike (1926)   206
genre   52–59, 287
    codes   30
    films   52–53, 55–56
    iconography   32, 52, 57
    ideology   73–74
    investigations   263, 267–275
    science fiction   57–59
    television   54–56, 210
George, Barry   67
Geraghty, Christine   54, 103, 128
Gerbner, G.   276
Ghost   105
Ghostwatch   114
Gimme, Gimme, Gimme   56
Glasgow University Media Group   75
Gledhill, Christine   60
global culture   216, 230–234, 287
    modernisation   234
    and national culture   230–231
    points of view   233–234
    'shrinking' of world   8
global language   231
Global Media Atlas   226
global village   231–232
globalisation *see* global culture
The Godfather   45, 74
Godzilla   59
Gold   175
Goldblum, Jeff   72
Golding, P.   192, 195
Gone with the Wind   98
Goodfellas   53
Goodness Gracious Me   104
Goodwin, Andrew   110
Gordon, P.   99
Gordy, Berry   104

The Gorgon 197
Gospel 175
GQ magazine 7, 53, 87
Graef, Roger 107
Graf, Steffi 64
Granada 157
Gray, Ann 126–127, 136
Greene, Sir Hugh 209
Gremlins 50
grey power 194
Grierson, John 107
Griffiths, Trevor 79
Gross, L. 276
The Guardian 34, 35
Gulf War (1991) 75, 97, 151, 152, 237
The Gulf Between Us 77
Gunter, B. 181

Hackers 136
Haley, Bill 98, 177
Hall, Stuart 123–124, 125, 126
Halliwell, Geri 53
Halloran, James 118
Halloween 86
Hamilton, Neil and Christine 67
The Hand that Rocks the Cradle 91
A Hard Day's Night 177
Hard News 85
hardware 6–8
Hardy, Oliver 121
Harry Potter and the Philosopher's Stone 31–32, 217
Hartley, J. 41
Haskell, Gordon 176
Hawn, Goldie 60, 81
Hear'Say 176, 180
Heartbeat 105
Heat magazine 65
Hebdige, D. 233
hegemony 69–74, 124, 130, 145, 287
Hello! magazine 65
Herbert, Chris and Bob 179
heritage films 96
Herman, E. 233
The Herald 183

Hetherington, A. 75
The Hidden Persuaders 112
High Fidelity 49
Hip Hop Connection 172
Hispanic stations (US) 175
historical permanence 11
histories 190–220
    conditions of media development 192–203
    demand 192, 193–194
    encoding/decoding 28
    independent production 157
    mediation 14
    music industry 162–164
    sense of history 191–192
    supply 192, 194–196
    timeline 190
Hitchcock, Alfred 148
HMV 171
Hobson, Dorothy 86
Hoffman, Dustin 82, 145
Hoggart, Richard 210
Holby City 47
holiday programmes 101
Hollywood cinema 71–73, 97, 102, 121, 141
    see also cinema
Home and Away 81
Home Service 208
homogeneity 233
Hope, Bob 207
horizontal integration 141, 164, 287
Horrie, Chris 123, 150
House Party 102
Hussein, Saddam 75
Huxtable, Cliff 130
hyperculture 232
hypodermic needle model 112–114, 287

iconography
    celebrities 64
    genre 30, 52, 57
    intertextuality 36
    meaning 287
    multimodal texts 43

websites   43
identification   49, 120, 125, 287
ideology
    binary oppositions   41
    British nation   94–96
    definitions   70, 287
    examples   70–71
    gender   81–97
    genre   73–74
    Hollywood cinema   71–73
    myth   71–73
    race   98–104
    representations   70
    science fiction   57
Illustrated London News   198
I'm a Celebrity - Get me out of Here!   66, 67
images
    denoted   27
    dominant   69
    of masculinity   91–92
    mass media   10
    Third World   100–101
    see also stereotyping
Imbruglia, Natalie   53
iMovie   247
impartiality   75
imperialism see media imperialism
imports and exports   236–237
In the Heat of the Night   102
In Sickness and In Health   99
Independence Day   58, 72, 73, 90
independent critical research   267–268
Independent Magazine   33
Independent Media Centre   78
independent production   157–188
    case study   178–180
    defined   157–160
    film   159–160
    football fanzines   158–159
    life-cycle   160
    principles   157
    video   159–160
Independent Television Commission (ITC)
        114, 154, 155, 215
Independent Television News (ITN)   209

independents, meaning   287
The Independent   37, 143, 157
information society   13
information super-highway   222
institutional break   10
institutions see media institutions
integration see horizontal integration;
        vertical integration
Intelligencers   196
International Broadcasting Company   207
international media flow   288
Internet
    case study   178–180
    film stars, promotion of   61
    media institutions   155
    music press   172
    new technologies   226–229
    piracy   168
intertextuality   18, 36–41
interviews   253–256
    body language   255
    'crossing the line'   256
    guidelines   254
    informal   281–283
    research   280
    vox pops   256
inventions   195, 196
inverted pyramid structure   251, **252**
investigations
    audiences   275–276
    genres   267–275
    media production   266–267
    media texts   267–275
    types   264–266
    see also research
The Invasion of the Body Snatchers   57
IRA (Irish Republican Party)   76, 152
ISDN (Integrated Services Digital
        Network)   227
Ishtar   145
Island Records   163, 164
It Ain't Half Hot Mum   98
It Came from Beneath the Sea   57
ITC (Independent Television Commission)
        114, 154, 155, 215

ITN (Independent Television News)   209
ITV Digital   145, 213
ITV television company   5, 154

Jackie Brown   53
Jackie magazine   88
Jackson, Michael   87, 129, 177
James Bond   44, 45, 62, 63
Jaws   105
Jazz   175
The Jazz Singer   98
The Jeffersons   103
Jerry Springer   55
Johnny Mnemonic   57
Jolie, Angelina   36, 53
Jonathan Creek   46
Jordan   53
journalists   75–76, 182–183
Jowell, Tessa   215
Junior   62
Jurassic Park   50, 105
Just Seventeen   88

Kane, Andy   65
Katz, E.   118, 119, 130
Kennedy, H.   57
Kennedy, President John F.   210
Kerrang!   172, 177
Kevin and Perry Go Large   55
KICK FM   186
Kidman, Nicole   61, 62
Kindergarten Cop   62
kinetoscope   200
King, Rodney   100
Kiss FM   176
KLF record company   169
Knightley, Philip   77
Knight's Tale   178
Kosovo crisis (1999)   77
Kournikova, Anna   53
Kramer vs Kramer   92
Kuffs   121
Kuhn, A.   29
Labour Party   26–27, 117, 144
Lakesiders   66

Lamb, Sir Larry   143
Lang, Fritz   57
Lang, Jack   237
Laurel, Stan   121
Lazenby, George   63
Le Voyage dans La Lune   57
Lealand, G.   237
lean forward/lean back   229
The League of Gentlemen   50
Lee, Spike   100
Leeds Other Paper   182
lesbians   93, 128
A Letter to Brezhnev   159
Levi 501 jeans   142
Levi-Strauss (French anthropologist)   41
Levy, E.   83
Lewis, Jerry   82
Lewis, Justin   130, 131
libel   153–155
Liebes, T.   130, 237
Light Programme   208
Listen Without Prejudice   171
Listener Research Unit   207
Little Big Man   53
Livingstone, S   2, 5
Lloyd's Weekly News   198
Loach, Ken   109
Loaded magazine   53, 92
Lock Stock and Two Smoking Barrels   92, 93
Looking Good   55
Lopez, Jennifer   53
Lord of the Rings trilogy   160
Los Angeles riots (1992)   100
Love Story   105, 126
Lull, James   133, 135, 238
Lumière brothers   200, 201
Lynch, David   17, 50, 148

McCall, Davina   59
McChesney, R.   233
McDonald, Trevor   103
McGuinness, Martin   76
MacKenzie, Kelvin   148–149, 150
McLuhan, Marshall   8, 232
McMahon, B.   28, 35, 38, 43

McRobbie, Angela 88
Mad Max 59
Madonna 86, 129, 165, 176, 178
magazines *see* newspapers and magazines
Magic Lanterns 201
major record companies
    growing power 164–166
    versus independents 162–164
Making Sense of Men's Magazines 92
Malcolm X 100
male gaze 85
Manchester Free Press 182
Marion and Geoff 54
marketing, music industry 170
markets 194
Marx, Karl/Marxism 70, 143
masculinity 81
    changing roles 91–93
mass communication 4, 7, 8, 9, 10–12, 224
    and culture 14–18
    signs 26
Mass Communication and American Empire
    235
mass manipulation model 112–114, 287
mass media 4, 7
    identifying 10–12
    see also mass communication
mass-produced culture 16
masthead television 177
Match of the Day 214
The Matrix 57, 90
Maxim 92
Maxwell, Robert 144, 147, 150, 153
media concentration 288
media consumption 288
media forms 7
media imperialism 234–238, 288
    assessing 235–237
    imports/exports 235–237
    perspectives/problems 237–238
media institutions
    advertising revenue 146–150
    anti-monopoly controls 153
    broadcasting 155
    economic determinants 141–151

external regulations 151–155
independent production 157–185
as institutions 140–148
Internet 156, 168
libel 153–155
meaning 288
moral standards 152–153
ownership 141–146
political controls 151–152
professional autonomy 148–151
public interest 154
statutory/legal controls 194
see also media production
media involvement 2, 3, 131, 288–289
media messages 10–11, 73
media news, management 76–78
media practice
    interviews 253–256
    post-production 256–258
    pre-production 242–246
    production 249–253
    professionalism 259
    resources 247–249
    technology 247–249
media production 249–253
    content 250–253
    independent 157
    investigating 266–267
    mass communication 15
    style 249–250
    see also media institutions
media reception *see* reception theory
media saturation 2, 4–13, 25
    index of 12
media spending power 193
Media Studies University courses 260
media technology
    case study 137–138
    gender 136–139
media texts 25–51
    anchorage 33–41
    audience positioning 120, 285
    binary oppositions 41–42
    covers 32
    cropping 32

design 34–35
discourse analysis 40–41
investigating 267–275
mass communication 15
multimodal 42–44
open/closed 27, 290
photographs 27, 29–30, 32, 35
pleasure of 49
polysemic 27, 31, 124, 131, 269, 290
realism 105
media violence 114–116
media-mix 5
mediation
and situation 8–9, 27
and social concern 13–14
'mega' events 11, 13, 30
Meldrew, Victor 56
Méliès, Georges 57
men, appearance 86–87
Men in Black 58
Menace II Society 102
Men's Health 87
Mercuries 196
messages 10–11, 73
text messaging 26
Messenger Davies, Máire 116
Metro series 182
Metz, C. 201
MI5 152
Michael, George 170, 171
Miller, W. 117
Mind Your Language 98
mind-bending 13
Miners Campaign Tapes 160
Ministry of Defence (MoD) 77, 151, 152
Minogue, Kylie 53, 164, 170
minority audiences 157
Minority Report 59
Miramax 160
Mirren, Helen 90
The Mirror 35, 41, 65, 77, 110, 123, 144, 146
Mission Impossible 178
Mixmag 172

mobile phones 26
advertising 37–38
MoD (Ministry of Defence) 77, 151, 152
modality judgements 106
mode of address, audiences 120–125
modernisation, global culture 234
Mojo magazine 172
Memento 45
Monopolies and Mergers Commission 152
Monroe, Marilyn 60, 81
monster films 59
Monument Valley 53
Moore, Roger 63
moral panic 14, 99
moral standards 152–153
more magazine 88
Morley, David 4, 126, 135, 280
Moroder, Georgio 169
Morrison, Marion 60
Moss, Carrie Ann 57
motion, scientific study of 201
Motown 164
Mrs Merton 106
MS magazine 88
Mugabe, Robert 75
multi-skilling 260
multimedia PC packages 247
multimodal texts 42–44
multinational conglomerates 142, 212, 232–233
Mulvey, Laura 85, 120
Murdoch, Rupert 123, 143, 144, 152, 232
Murdock, G. 14
Murphy, D. 181, 183, 185, 187
Murphy, Eddie 102, 129
music industry 162–180
A & R (artists and repertoire) 169
distribution 170–171
majors 162–166
market, mediating 169
marketing 170
music press 171–173
piracy 168
radio airplay 173–174

radio formatting   174–175
revenue flow   **167**
success   179–180
music press   171–173
music retailers   171
Music Week   163
MusicNet   168
Muslim groups   41, 42
My Beautiful Laundrette   45, 159
My Best Friend's Wedding   59
myth   71–73

Napster case   155, 168
narration   46–47
narrative   30, 250, 290
narrative codes   44–50
narrators   48–49
narrowcasting   133, 134, 147, 290
National Council for the Training of
        Journalists   182
national culture   230–232
National Lottery   67
National Readership Survey   88
nationalism, British   94–97
Nationwide   126
NATO (North Atlantic Treaty
        Organisation)   77
Natural Born Killers   113, 114
naturalism   290
Nazi Germany, political propaganda in   112
negotiated position   124
Negus, Keith   163, 169
Neighbours   170
Neil, Andrew   143
neophiliacs   226
New Age music   175
New Line   160
'new man'   92
New Manchester Review   182
new media technologies   221–229, 290
New Musical Express (NME)   172, 178
Newbury Weekly News
    competition   185–186
    news values   186–188
    origins   184

readership   184–185
revenue   186
News 24   217
news
    discourse analysis   40
    realism   106–109, **108**
    regulation   155–156
    representations   76–78
News at Ten   155, 214, 216
News Chronicle   147
News International Corporation   157, 212,
        232
news values   186–188, 290
News of the World   85
Newsnight   78
Newspaper Society   181
newspapers and magazines
    audiences   122–125
    broadsheets   147
    case studies   181–188
        Newbury Weekly News   184–188
        radical and popular press
        (nineteenth century)   196–199
    celebrities   65
    design   34–36
    intertextuality   36
    'lads' magazines   53
    libel   153
    local   181, 182
    male singers   87
    mastheads   34
    media saturation   7
    men's   91–93
    political support   117
    tabloids   147
    trade   141
    women's magazines   88
    see also journalists; *Music Press*
Newsquest Media Group   181
Newsweek   36
niche targeting   133, 134, 147
Niggaz with Attitude (NWA)   180
Night Mail   107
999   47
Nine O' Clock News   156

Nineteen Eighty-Four (George Orwell)   13
Noland, Chuck   8
Northern Star   182
Notting Hill   96, 120
Now   65
NYPD   109

Oakenfold, Paul   169
Observer   144, 150
OFCOM (Office for Communications)
        155, 260
Official Secrets Act   152
The Office   54
OK! magazine   65
Olympic Games   11, 121
One Foot in the Grave   56
Only Fools and Horses   214
open texts   27, 290
Opportunity Knocks   209
oppositional position   124, 290
Oprah Winfrey Show   55
Orbit, William   169
orientalism   41–42
Orwell, George   13, 30
O'Sullivan, T.   140, 205
ownership
        case study   181–183
        concentration of   141–143
        and power   143–144
                limits   144–146

Packard, Vance   112
Pagemaker   247
Paine, Tom   197
Panorama   78, 155
Parkinson   64
participant observation   290
Payne studies (media violence)   114
PCC (Press Complaints Commission)
        153, 154
Peacock Committee   211
Peak Practice   91
Peeping Tom   86
Pennachioni, I.   238
'penny gaffs'   202

Penny Politician   197
The People's Choice   116
perception, science of   200
Perfect Partners   55
Perkins, Tessa   78
personal stereo   7, 131
Peterloo Massacre (1819)   197
Peterson, R.A.   162
PG (Parental Guidance)   153
photographs   27, 29–30, 32, 35, 200
Photoshop   247
Pickford, Mary   59
'picture gaffs'   202
Pierce, C.S.   27
Pilger, John   144
Pilkington Committee   211
piracy, Internet   168
Pitt, Brad   62
PJ Harvey   163, 164
plausibility   105
Plugge, Captain Leonard   207
The Plug-in Drug   113
The Plums   208
pluralism   74, 130, 145–146, 290
Poitier, Sidney   102
Police   107
Police, Camera, Action   30
police series   56
political controls   151–152
Political Handkerchief   198
political persuasion   116–118
political representations   74–76
Political Touchwood   198
Polygram   164
polysemic codes/media texts   27, 31, 124,
        131, 269, 290
Poor Man's Guardian   198
Pop Idol   64, 65, 176, 224
Pop Stars   55, 110, 176, 180
popular culture   16–17, 19, 290
Porcupine   198
pornography   85
Portsmouth and Sunderland Newspaper
        group   182
'Posh Spice'   35

post-production 256–258
    editing 256–257
    review/evaluation 257–258
Poster, Mark 222
Postmaster General 203
postmodernism 17–18, 79, 290
power
    major record companies 164–166
    of media 12–13
    and ownership 143–144
pre-production 242–246
    audience 245–246
    medium 246
    purpose 242–244
Predator 62
preferred meaning 124–125, 285, 290
Presley, Elvis 98
press barons 194
Press Complaints Commission (PCC)
       153, 154
Pressplay 168
Pretty Woman 62
Prevention of Terrorism Act 152
primary media involvement 3, 131
Prime Suspect 90
Prisoner: Cell Block H 128
The Prisoner 50
Private Eye 153, 160
private sphere 19, 290
production *see* media production
Production Log (portfolio) 243, 257, 258
professional autonomy 148–151
professionalism 259
propaganda 74–76, 112, 291
Propp, Vladimir 44
Pryor, Richard 102
Psycho 86
public communication 18
public interest 153, 154
Public Service Broadcasting
    case studies
        BBC (1920-1945) 203–208
        digital age (1990-present) 212–215
        expansion/competition (1945-1990)
        208–212

    future 215–218
    meaning 291
public sphere 18
Pullen, Kirsten 128
Pullman, Bill 72
Pulp Fiction 17, 45, 56, 160
PWL company 164

Q magazine 172
qualitative approaches 264, 279–283, 291
quantitative research 264, 291
Quantum Leap 47
QuarkExpress 247
Queen Mother 35
Queen (pop group) 176
Queer as Folk 93
questionnaires, research 276–279
    developing 277–279
Quiet Storm 175
Quigley Poll 83
Quinn, R. 28, 35, 38, 43
quiz shows 54, 209

race
    changing representations 102
    entertainment 98–99
    ideology 98–104
    reception theory 130–131
    social problems 99–100
    stereotyping 78
    television 103–104
    see also ethnic preferences
racism 98, 99, 100
Radcliffe, Mark 176
radical press 196–199, 291
Radio 1 173
radio
    airplay 173–174
    audiences 119, 122
    discourse analysis 40
    formatting 174–176
    public service broadcasting 205
    reception theory 131
    time periods, coverage of 46
Radio Authority 154, 155, 176, 260

Radio Luxembourg   207
Radio Normandy   207
Radio Times   7
RAJAR   119
Rambo films   61
rapists   85–86
Ray of Light album (Madonna)   169
Readers Digest   7
Real Lives   76, 154
Real, Michael   4, 17
realism   104–106, 291
    news   106–109, 108
reality television   109–110, 291
Rebel Without a Cause   45
reception theory   125–131
    active readers   125–126
    context of reception   131–137
    cultural competence   126
    ethnic preferences   130–131
    extrication   125
    gender preferences   126–129
    implication   125
    mass communication   15
    radio   119
Red Flannel   160
Reith, John   203, 204–207, 208, 217
Relentless Records   176
remote controls   26
representations   69–104
    alternative   69
    hegemony   69–74
    Hollywood cinema   71–73, 102
    ideology   70
    meaning   291
    media power   12–13
    myth   71
    news   76–78
    political   74–76
    science fiction   57
    stereotypes   10, 78–81
    see also realism
research
    content analysis   269–275
    independent critical research   267–268
    reasons for study   1–4

    social production of   263–264
    types   264–266
    see also investigations
research questionnaires   276–279
Reservoir Dogs   53, 160
resources   247–249
retailers, music   171
Rheingold, Howard   227–228
Ricci Lake   55
Richard and Judy   211
Right to Reply   211
Rights of Man   197
Rising Damp   99
Ritchie, Guy   92, 93
ritual interaction   4
ritual media interaction   291
Road Trip   55
Roberts, Julia   60, 62
Robin Hood, Prince of Thieves   142
Robinson Crusoe   2, 8
Rocketship Xm   90
Rocky   145
Rocky Horror Picture Show   56
Rojek, C.   67
role models   115
Rolling Stone magazine   36
Rolling Stones   162
A Room With a View   96
Rosenberg, D.   99
Rothwell, A.   277–279
Rough Guide series   101
Rough Trade   162
Rowland, Tiny   144
Rowling, J.K.   31–32
royal family   94–95
The Royle Family   48, 54
Run, Lola, Run   45

S Club 7   179
Said, Edward   41–42
Samsung   38
sans serif   34
satellite television   224
Saturday Night Fever   177
Saving Private Ryan   45

Scary Movie 1 and *2*   56
scheduling   291
Schiller, H.   235
Schlesinger, Philip   267
Schwarzenegger, Arnold   59, 62, 97
science fiction   57–59
   case study   89–90
Scorsese, Martin   53
The Scotsman   183
Scream films   55, 56, 113, 141
Screen Digest   141
The Searchers   45, 53
Seaton, J.   143, 150, 198, 226
Second World   235
Second World War (1939-45)   13, 95, 97,
      151, 207–208
secondary media involvement   3, 131
Secret Society   152
segments   132
semiotics   27–28, 120, 267, 291
Sense and Sensibility   96
September 11 2001 atrocities   **1**, 11, 30, 41,
      76, 147, 210
The Seven Year Itch   81
sexuality, gender   93–94
Shaft   102
Shawshank Redemption   120
shooting scripts   251
'shop shows'   202
The Siege   97
signs   26, 43
silent films   106
The Simpsons   47, 70–71, 106, 130, 145, 211
simulated illusion   228
singles, music industry   174
Sinn Fein   32, 76
situated culture   8, 27, 105, 292
situation, and mediation   8–9, 27
Sky News   156
Sky TV Guide   7
Sleeping with the Enemy   62
Sleepy Hollow   53
Smith, Will   72
SMS (short message service)   26
Snatch   92

Sniffin Glue   158
So Graham Norton   64, 66
So Solid Crew   176
soap operas
   axing of   150, 211
   cultural differences   54
   docu-soaps   54–55
   female characters   91, 128
   gender issues   135
   and narration   46
   and photographs   29
   realism   105
   stereotyping   81
   theme tunes   26
Soapstars   55
social class   146, 187
social concern, and mediation   13–14
social problems, race   99–100
Soldier, Soldier   91
Sontag, S.   29
Sony   164, 165, 171
Sony Walkman   7, 131
South East Arts Association   160
Soviet Russia, political propaganda in   112
Spears, Britney   92, 164
specialised technologies   10
Spector, Phil   169
Spice Girls   66, 177, 179
Spielberg, Steven   50
'spin-doctors'   12
Stallone, Sylvester   60, 61, 62, 145
Stanwyck, Barbara   91
Star Crash   59
Star Pets   179
Star Trek   59, 118
Star Wars   58, 59, 141, 142
Stargate   59
Starman   59
Statue of Liberty   72
Steptoe and Son   210
stereotypes   10, 78–81, 292
   dumb blonde   79–81
   see also gender
Stone, Oliver   113
Stone, Sharon   91

A Stranger Among Us 91
Street Crime UK 47
StreetMate 42, 55, 59
Streisand, Barbra 83
structuralism 120, 292
'subsidiary forms of circulation' 60
success
    alternative route to 180–181
    manufacture of 179–180
Sugar magazine 172
Sunday Times 37
The Sun
    and celebrities 65
    and ideology 75, 85, 97, 99
    and mass communication 14
    and media institutions 143, 144, 145,
      146, 147, 148, 173
    and media saturation 7
    and mode of address 123
    and political persuasion 117
    and race 110
    readership 275
supply 192, 194–196
surveillance culture 292
Sutherland, John 34
Swanson, G. 80
Sylvania Waters 109
symbolic codes 28, 36, 39, 43
synergy 142, 166, 177, 292

Take a Break 7
Take That 179
Take Your Pick 209
Taliban, war against 40, 77, 97
Tamla Motown record label 104
Tarantino, Quentin 17, 53
target groups 10
Taxi Driver 53
Taylor, Damilola 30
team working 244
technical codes 28, 35, 38, 43
technological determinism 195, 223, 292
technologies 195
    new 221–229, 290
teen comedies 55

Telecommunications Act (2002) 215
telenovelas see soap operas
telescreens 13
Teletubbies 142, 214
television
    audiences 118–119, 121–122
    celebrities 64–67
    closed circuit 30–31, 109
    discourse analysis 40
    ethnic representations 103–104
    gender 135–136
    genre 54–56, 210
    'Golden Age' 209
    independent production 176–177
    media saturation 4–5
    multi-set homes 6, 133
    and race issues 101
    reception theory 132
    satellite 224
    time periods, coverage of 46
    uses and gratifications 118–119, 292
    viewing patterns 133, **134**
    see also cinema; films; radio; reality
      television; soap operas; videos
Television Act (1954) 209
Television is Good for Kids (Máire Messenger
    Davies) 116
'Tell Sid' Campaign 48
Tennant, Neil 171
Terminator films 58, 90
terrorism 1, 42, 76
    Prevention of Terrorism Act 152
tertiary media involvement 3, 131
Texas Chain Saw Massacre 86
text messaging 26
texts *see* media texts
That Was The Week That Was 210
Thatcher, Margaret 144
Thaw, John 59
The Celebrity Weakest Link 65
The Good, the Bad and the Ugly 53
The Last Starfighter 59
theme tunes 26
There's a Poison Going on 178
Theroux, Louis 67

The Outlaw Josey Wales 50
Third Programme 208
Third World 235
Third World images 100–101
This Life 109
Thriller 129
Tilley, A. 47, 50
Time magazine 245
Time Warner 141, 152
The Times 34, 143, 157, 196, 274, 275
Titanic 105, 141, 142
title sequences 250
Today newspaper 143, 145
Tolson, A. 40, 60
Tomb Raider 36, 37, 90
Tomlinson, J. 238
Too Pure 164
Top of the Pops 171, 176
Total Recall 59
Total Rock 176
Trafalgar, Battle of (1805) 191–192
Trainspotting 96, 159
Trelford, Donald 144
triangulation 264
Trinity Mirror 181
Trisha 55
Triumph, advertising by 36–37
True Lies 97
The Tube 176
Tufte, T. 238
Tunstall, J. 3, 131, 267
Turkle, Sherry 136
Turnock, Rob 95
Twin Peaks 17, 56, 106
Twin Towers atrocities 1, 11, 30, 41, 76, 147, 210
Twins 62
2.4 Children 56
2001: A Space Odyssey 58
typefaces 34–35
Tyson, Mike 64

U2 rock group 165, 173
U (Universal) 153
Ulysses 46

UNESCO (United Nations Educational, Scientific and Cultural Organisation) 235–236
The Unforgiven 53
United States
 imports/exports 236–237
 Payne studies, media violence 114
 radio formatting 174–175
Urban Contemporary 175
uses and gratifications 118–120, 292

Van Zoonen, Lisbet 269, 270
The Vanessa Show 55
VCTV (viewer-controlled television) 224
vertical integration 141, 165, 287
video cassette recorders (VCRs) 136
Video Diaries 55
Video Nation 55
Video Recordings Act (1983) 112
videos
 independent production 159–160, 176–177
 libel 153
 media saturation 4
 software 136
 time periods, coverage of 46
 see also DVDs
Vietnam War (1954-75) 77, 151
violence *see* terrorism
Virgin Records 164
virtual communities (virtual reality) 118, 227, 292
virtual time 232
Viz 160
Vodafone, advertising by 37
voice of the nation 203–208
The Voice 104
vox pops 256
voyeurism 85, 110, 292
Walking with Dinosaurs 214, 216
Walkman 7, 131
Wall Street 62
Walt Disney Corporation 160
Walters, R. 115, 116
The Waltons 70, 71

War of the Worlds 115
Warner 164
The War Game 59
Waters, Eddie 79
Watson, Paul 107, 109
Wayne, John 53, 60, 62, 83
Wayne's World 121
We Speak for Ourselves 208
Weaver, Sigourney 89
webcasting 225
Webster, F. 227
The Wedding Singer 178
Welles, Orson 114–115, 148
Welsh Arts Council 160
western films 52, 53, 56
Westworld 59
When Saturday Comes 158
'Where's Lucky?' (advertising campaign)
    48
White Dot Society 5
Who Wants to be a Millionaire? 54
wicked, meaning 30
Will and Grace 93
William Shakespeare's Romeo and Juliet 250
Williams, Raymond 16, 131, 132, 195, 210
Williams, Robbie 170
Williamson, J. 71
Willis, Bruce 59, 60, 97
Willis, John 95
Winfrey, Oprah 103
Winn, Marie 113

Winship, Janice 88, 123
Woman's Own 7
women, appearance 85–86
Women in Journalism 85
women's fiction 128
Woollacott, J. 63
The Word 176
Working Man's Friend 198
Workshop Movement 160
World in Action 155
World Cup 121
World Trade Centre atrocities **1**, 11, 30, 41,
    76, 147, 210
World Trade Organisation 78
World Wide Web 227
The World is not Enough 45
Would Like to Meet 55
written codes 28, 35–36, 38, 43

X-Files 90
X-Men 57
Xena: Warrior Princess 128–129

Yates, Paula 67
You Only Live Twice 62
Young People, New Media 133
Young, Will 176

Z Cars 210
Zeta Jones, Catherine 61, 66